Have you got questions?

- ✦ Is a cash or accrual accounting system right for you? pg. 311
- ✦ Is there a way to disable QuickFill? pg. 486
- ✦ How do I deal with reconciliation problems like differences in the opening balance? pg. 94-96
- ✦ How can I backup my Quicken files? pg. 141-142, 315-316
- ✦ Where can I get free tax advice? pg. 422
- ✦ How can I print a Quicken graph? pg. 8-9
- ✦ What can I do with Quicken's Financial Planners? pg. 259-265
- ✦ Can I produce a loan amortization schedule with Quicken? pg. 214-216
- ✦ Is there any way to get Quicken to enter transactions for me? pg. 157-164, 344-351
- ✦ What are "Other" reports? pg. 273
- ✦ Can I update my stock prices from an online service such as Prodigy? pg. 242-243
- ✦ Can I use a mouse with Quicken? pg. 13-16
- ✦ How can I correct a printer problem? pg. 74
- ✦ How can I import or export Quicken data? pg. 496-497
- ✦ Is there any way to pay bills electronically with Quicken, as opposed to writing checks? pg. 117-121
- ✦ What is a Quick Report? pg. 8
- ✦ What do I need to know about starting a new year and saving last year's data? pg. 436-437
- ✦ When do I have to file Federal Payroll Tax Returns? pg. 382
- ✦ What are postdated checks and transactions? pg. 106-107
- ✦ What strategies should be used for over-budget situations? pg. 196
- ✦ Should I void or delete unneeded transactions? pg. 25-26

Get Answers — Get Osborne

ANY QUESTIONS?

QUICKEN 7 MADE EASY

Mary Campbell

Osborne **McGraw-Hill**

Berkeley New York St. Louis San Francisco
Auckland Bogotá Hamburg London Madrid
Mexico City Milan Montreal New Delhi Panama City
Paris São Paulo Singapore Sydney
Tokyo Toronto

Osborne **McGraw-Hill**
2600 Tenth Street
Berkeley, California 94710
U.S.A.

For information on translations or book distributors outside of the U.S.A., please write to Osborne **McGraw-Hill** at the above address.

Quicken 7 Made Easy

1234567890 DOC 99876543

ISBN 0-07-881971-7

Acquisitions Editor
Scott Rogers

Associate Editor
Bob Myren

Technical Editor
Robert Kermish

Project Editor
Mark Karmendy

Copy Editor
Paul Medoff

Proofreader
Mick Arellano

Indexer
Elizabeth Reinhardt

Computer Designer
Peter F. Hancik

Illustrator
Marla J. Shelasky

Cover Designer
Compass Marketing

Quality Control Specialist
Joe Scuderi

CONTENTS

ACKNOWLEDGMENTS

We wish to thank the many individuals at Osborne/McGraw-Hill and Intuit for their help with this project. Special thanks are due to Acquisitions Editor Scott Rogers who did everything possible to help us meet impossible deadlines, Project Editor Mark Karmendy, who focused all of his waking moments on the book for weeks, Associate Editor Bob Myren, who prepared all the chapters as quickly as possible, and Bob Kermish, who gave us a 24-hour turnaround on his technical edits. The other editorial and production staff members also did an excellent job. Copy Editor Paul Medoff and Proofreader Mick Arellano did everything they could to help us meet an impossible time schedule. Special thanks also go to Elizabeth Reinhardt for an excellent index and for all of her help in getting the chapters done. Thanks are due as well to Gabrielle Lawrence for handling all the others tasks that needed to be done in this time frame so we could focus on this project.

INTRODUCTION

Whether you are trying to manage your personal finances or those of your business, Quicken can end your financial hassles. The package contains all the features necessary to organize your finances, yet because they're jargon-free you can focus on your financial needs without becoming an accountant or a financial planner.

If you use the package for your personal finances, you will find that you can easily determine your financial worth or create a report with the information you need for your tax forms. You can also create budget reports or a list of all your cash, check, or credit card transactions. Everything you do will be with the benefit of menus and easy-to-use quick-key combinations. You will soon wonder how you managed your finances without Quicken.

If you are trying to manage a small business *and* deal with all the financial issues, Quicken can make the task seem manageable. Whether your business is a part-time venture or employs several people, Quicken provides all the capabilities you need to look at your profit and loss picture, analyze your cash flows, or put together a budget. Quicken's ability to handle the recording of payroll information makes it easy to monitor what you owe for federal and state income tax withholding, FICA, and other payroll-related costs such as workers' compensation and federal and state unemployment taxes. Although it is not quite the same as having an accountant on your payroll, Quicken can make an otherwise unmanageable task possible.

About This Book

Quicken 7 Made Easy is designed to help you master Quicken's features so you can apply them to your financial situation. Even if you are a complete novice with the computer, you will find that you can learn from the step-by-step exercises in each chapter. As you work through the exercises, you will feel as though you have a seasoned computer pro guiding you each step of the way.

This book offers more than just instruction for using Quicken's features. The exercises throughout the book are based on the authors' personal and business transactions. Although names of the banks, suppliers, and employees, as well as dollar amounts have all been changed, all of what you read is based on factual illustrations, much like the ones you will need to record your own transactions.

Throughout the book we have included financial tips. When we started our business 12 years ago, we had to invest a considerable amount of time in finding answers to even the simplest questions such as federal and state agency filing requirements. We have tried to include some of this information to simplify what you are facing if your business is new.

Conventions Used

There are step-by-step examples for you to follow throughout the book. Every entry that you need to type is shown in boldface to make these exercises easy to follow. In addition, the names of menus, windows, and reports are shown with the same capitalization followed by Quicken.

The names of keys such as F2, Enter, and Tab are shown in keycaps. In situations where two keys must be pressed at the same time, the keycaps are joined with a hyphen, as in Ctrl-Enter. If you use the keyboard rather than the mouse to make menu selections, you will find it convenient that this book boldfaces the letter needed to make each selection. (Quicken 7 will highlight the letter.) In the Main Menu and pull-down menus, this highlighted letter alone is sufficient to make your selection. In the menu at the top of the Register Report and Write Checks screens, you will need to use the Alt key in combination with the highlighted letter to activate the menu and define your selection.

In cases where there are two ways to perform the same task, we have shown you the most efficient approach. As you learn more about the package, you can feel free to use whichever approach you prefer.

Quicken can provide the help you need to organize your personal finances. The package will enable you to establish accounts for monitoring checking and savings accounts, credit cards, and investments. In this section you will learn how to record and organize your financial information with Quicken's easy-to-use features. You will also learn how to prepare reports for taxes, budgeting, and computing your net worth.

PART 1

QUICK START

CHAPTER

investments banking FILE register expenses DEDUCTIONS
tips finances INCOME equity net pay
checks revenue bank statements
statements
dividends assets business tips
INCOME
banking business tips cash flow
budget FILE FILE reports
DEDUCTIONS business tips checks
statements cash flow tips mortgage
net pay taxes bank revenue
mortgage cash business tips
business tips dividends tips
investments
register statements
reports business tips taxes
expenses tips
equity investments INCOME
checks statements bank cash
assets checks budget tips finances net pay

1 AN OVERVIEW OF QUICKEN AND YOUR COMPUTER COMPONENTS

Quicken is a powerful single-entry accounting system that allows both individuals and small businesses to track their financial resources. It is an integrated system in that it accumulates the information you enter and then provides a variety of methods to group and present that information.

Quicken is as easy to use as your current manual recording methods—but it is much faster. You will be surprised at how automatic using the package can become. It can memorize and record your regular transactions or write a check for your signature. It also organizes your information for you. This chapter's overview shows you the components of the package and examples of screens used to enter data and the output that is produced. You do not need to sit at your computer to read and understand this chapter. Later chapters, however, give step-by-step directions for using Quicken's features, and you will want to follow along.

This chapter also introduces the various components of your computer system and their relationship to Quicken. You learn how Quicken uses your computer system, disk space, memory, and the keyboard. Some of the important keys are introduced through a series of visual examples. In later chapters you use these keys to enter and review Quicken data.

Quicken Overview

Quicken can handle all aspects of your financial management. Everything from initial recording and maintenance of information through organizing and reporting is handled by the package. Quicken provides features for recording your financial transactions easily. You can have a direct entry made to a register that is an accounts journal or have Quicken write a check and record the information automatically. Once your information has been recorded, you can have it presented in a variety of standard and customized reports.

Recording Financial Transactions

If you are tired of entering financial transactions in a handwritten journal, you will appreciate the recording abilities of Quicken. Entries are always neat—even if you have corrected several errors in the recording process—and there is no need to worry about math errors, since the package does arithmetic for you.

Accounts are the major organizational units in Quicken. Each piece of information you record affects the balance in a Quicken account. You can establish checking and savings accounts for both personal and business purposes. In addition, you can establish credit card accounts, asset accounts (stocks and real estate), and liability accounts (mortgage and other payable loans). You can also transfer funds among these accounts with the Transfer feature—for example, moving funds from savings to checking account. You can store all of your account in a single file on your computer. Later, as your experience grows, you might want to create additional accounts in your Quicken file.

Quicken supports specialized investment accounts to allow you to track a collection of investments. You can enter information for stocks, bonds, mutual funds, and other investments. You can use features like the one shown in Figure 1-1 for updating the market price of your investments and determining your gain or loss. Quicken 7's new forms for entering transaction entries make keeping track of your investments easier than ever. The new portfolio views make it easier to track your progress toward investments goals.

Quicken can record the details of your financial transactions, both money you earn (income) and what you spend it on (expenses). Quicken can differentiate income from a number of sources, such as salary and dividend income. It also supports entry of all types of expenses, from mortgage payments to clothing purchases. If you use Quicken to record business finances, you can keep track of freight charges, payroll costs, and so on. You can also customize the package to handle additional sources of income or expenses.

The information recorded on a financial event is called a *transaction.* Purchasing an asset such as a car, or making payment for services or goods such as groceries, is considered a transaction. In Quicken, you must record your transactions in order to have the correct balance in your accounts. This is accomplished by using a *register,* which is similar to a notebook or journal for record keeping. This serves the same purpose as your checkbook register, but with the power of the Quicken system you can generate powerful reports that help you manage your finances. Thus, one of the major components of the system is the register that you establish for each of your accounts (checking, savings, and other assets and liabilities). Figure 1-2 provides an example of entries in the Quicken register using Quicken's compressed format.

Print/Acct View Shortcuts Reports Activities F1-Help

Portfolio Update for Investments

Security Name	Type	Market Price	Shares	Market Value	Last Price	Chg Mkt Val
Ganges Mutual Fund	Mut	13.210 ↑	1,000.00	13,210.00	11.950	1,260.00
Glenn Packing	Sto	30 ↓	100.00	3,000.00	30 1/2	-50.00
Haven Publishing	Sto	22 ↑	500.00	11,000.00	20	1,000.00
-Cash-						
Total Market Value				25,000		

Investments F8-Show Detail F9-All Accounts
Esc-Main Menu Ctrl-B Buy Ctrl-S Sell Ctrl-N Reinvest Ctrl-L Other Action

Updating the market price for your investments
Figure 1-1.

Print/Acct Edit Shortcuts Reports Activities F1-Help

Date	Num	Payee · Memo · Category	Payment	C	Deposit	Balance
1/01		Opening Balance		X	4,000 00	4,000 00
1/02		Arlo, Inc.			12,500 00	16,500 00
1/02	101	Office All	65 00			16,435 00
1/08	102	Computer Outlet	300 00			16,135 00
1/15	103	Quick Delivery	215 00			15,920 00
1/15	104	Safety Airlines	905 00			15,015 00
1/20	105	Alltel	305 00			14,710 00
1/20	106	Postmaster	28 25			14,681 75
1/22	107	Fix-It-All	1,100 00			13,581 75
1994	Memo:	Equipment Contract				
	Cat:	Equip Mnt/B				
1/25	108	Laser 1	1,500 00			12,081 75
1/30	109	Quick Delivery	55 00			12,026 75
1/31	110	John Smith	1,560 13			10,466 62
1/31	111	Mary McFaul	2,284 22			8,182 40
2/01	112	Internal Revenue Service	1,379 00			6,803 40
2/28	_Pymt	John Smith	1,560 13			5,243 27
2/28	_Pymt	Mary McFaul	2,284 22			2,959 05

ANB Business (Alt+letter accesses menu) Current Balance: $ 0.00
Esc-Main Menu Ctrl◄┘ Record Ending Balance: $30,732.70

The Quicken register window
Figure 1-2.

With any checking account, reconciling the balance is tedious. Quicken reduces the time needed to reconcile the difference between the bank's balance and yours. Through the reconciliation process, you can accurately maintain the balance in your checking account and avoid the embarrassment of overdrawing your account. Quicken adjusts your register for service charges and interest earned on your checking account balance.

The ability to write and print checks is another interesting Quicken feature. Quicken is capable of automating all your check writing activities. Figure 1-3 shows a check entry form on the screen. You can acquire checking supplies from Intuit (the company that developed and markets Quicken) that allow you to write checks directly from the register and print them on your printer. While this option is particularly attractive for business activities, it can be useful for your personal checking account as well. Quicken supports the use of the CheckFree service which allows you to create a check in Quicken, then electronically transmit the payment request without ever printing a check. But even if you write your checks by hand, you can still benefit from maintaining your transactions in Quicken.

Reports Provided by Quicken

The value of any accounting system lies in its ability to generate useful and informative reports that assist you in making financial decisions. With Quicken, you can prepare home, business, and investment reports and preview them on the screen before printing. You can access the detail behind a summary report while viewing the report. You can also customize a

1

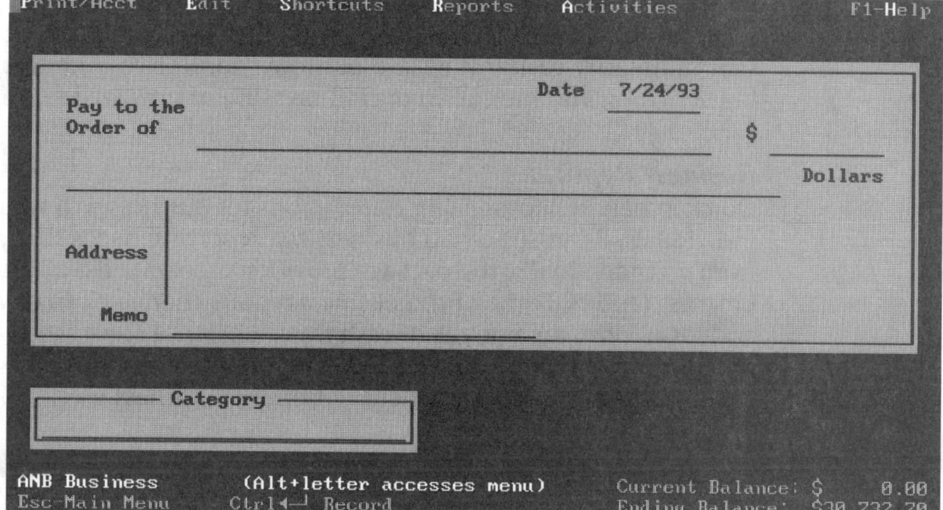

Check Writing window
Figure 1-3.

report displayed on your screen. Figure 1-4 shows an onscreen personal Cash Flow report.

Home Reports

Besides providing you with a printout of your check register, Quicken generates other reports tailored for personal financial management. They

File/Print Edit Layout Reports Activities F1-Help

CASH FLOW REPORT

1/ 1/94 Through 9/30/94
PERSONAL-Bank, Cash, CC Accoun
7/24/93

Category Description		1/ 1/94- 9/30/94
INFLOWS		
Salary Income		3,585.99
TOTAL INFLOWS		3,585.99
OUTFLOWS		
Automobile Expenses:		
Auto Fuel	46.00	
Total Automobile Expenses		46.00
Clothing		100.00
Dining Out		120.00

Cardinal Bank
Esc-Leave report

Cash Flow Report screen display
Figure 1-4.

will become valuable as the year progresses, showing how you have spent your money, as well as how much you have. You can create personal reports that summarize cash inflow and outflow, monitor your budget, summarize tax activities, and look at an overall measure of how well you are doing.

Business Reports

Quicken handles accounting transactions for businesses as well as for individuals. Because a small business has reporting needs that are different from an individual's, the package provides a separate list of standard business reports. Some of the business reports that you can create are a profit and loss report, an analysis of cash flow, a balance sheet, accounts payable and receivable reports, and a payroll report. Quicken also allows you to create customized reports for either home or business use.

Investment Reports

With Quicken's investment accounts, you can record and track all of your investments. The five standard investment reports provide information on portfolio value, investment performance, capital gains, investment income, and investment transactions.

Quick Reports

Quicken 7 provides a QuickReport feature that you can invoke from an account register. Depending on the field that is active when you press Alt-Z or choose **Q**uick Report from the **R**eports menu in the register, the report will provide information on other transactions with the same value in the current field. If you are on a category field for Medical:Doctor expense in the current transaction, the QuickReport that Quicken displays when you press Alt-Z will show all transactions with this value in the category field. If you are on the payee field and the current transaction has Consumers Power for the payee, all transactions with Consumers Power for the payee will display on the Quick Report.

Creating Graphs

Reports provide a summary or detailed record of transactions. They can be shared with others wanting to look at your financial status but they do not provide a quick overview look at a financial situation. Graphs have always done a much better job at giving a picture of a situation with a quick look. You can use graphs to look at trends and other comparison information on your screen as shown in Figure 1-5, where you can see a comparison between budget and actual figures for categories over budget. Quicken provides graphs to look at income and expenses, net worth, budget and actual figures,

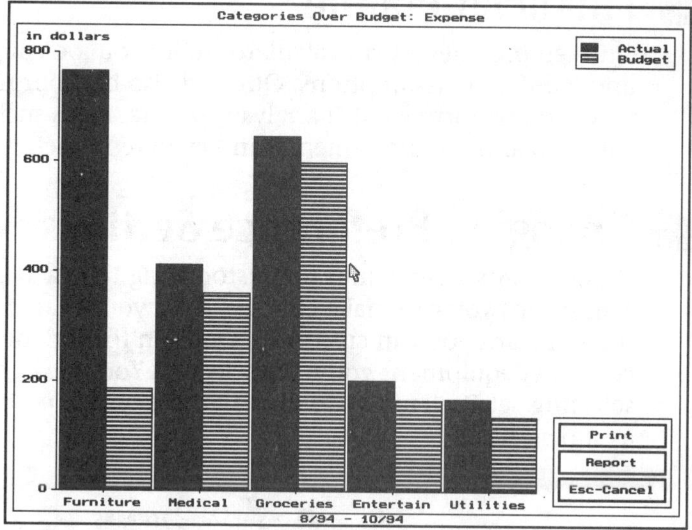

Expense Categories Over Budget graph
Figure 1-5.

and investments, with numerous graph options in each category. Figure 1-6 provides another example with a Portfolio Value Trend by Security.

Quicken 7's new QuickZoom feature for graphs lets you take a closer look at the details that comprise the graph on the screen. As you move around with your mouse or the keyboard, a magnifying glass will mark the current selection. When you press Enter, Quicken zooms in for a closer look at a graph or a report.

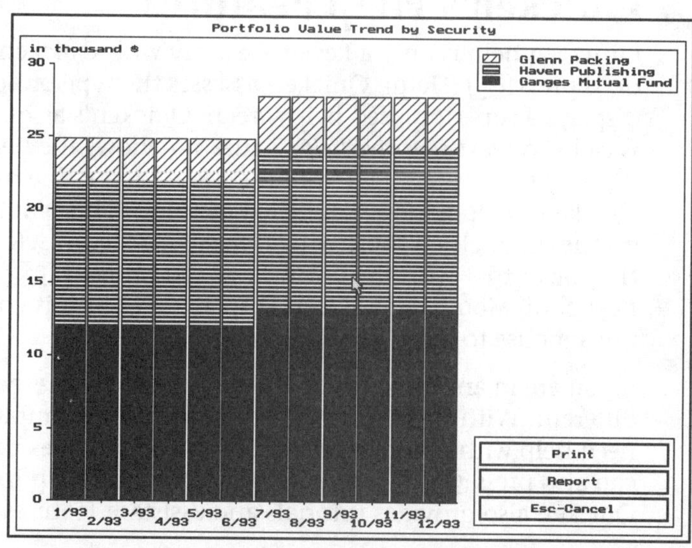

Portfolio Value Trend by Security
Figure 1-6.

Financial Planners

Quicken provides a loan calculator to let you look at monthly payments under different assumptions. Quicken also has four more financial planners to let you perform what-if analysis in other areas such as retirement or college planning, investments, and even refinancing a loan.

Changing Preference Settings

Quicken provides features for customizing the package to meet your needs. This means you can make changes to fit your exact reporting requirements. It also means you can customize Quicken to work properly with the computer equipment you have selected. You make these changes by selecting Set **P**references to display the menu of custom settings for Quicken, as shown here:

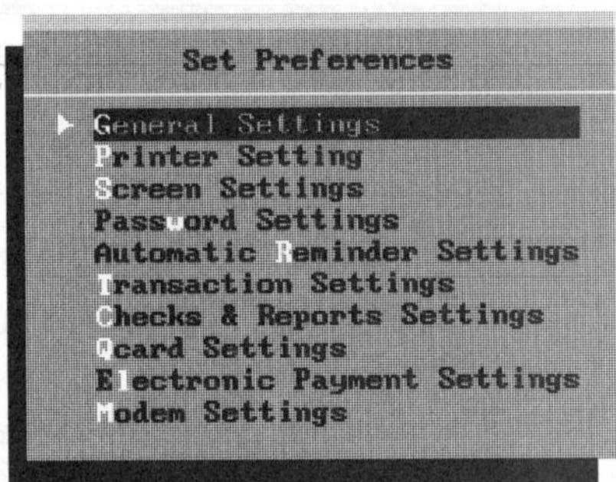

Quicken's Help Features

Onscreen help is only a keystroke away with Quicken. All you ever need to do is press F1 (Help). Quicken assesses the type of help you need and displays a superimposed help screen. Quicken's assessment of your situation is called *context-sensitive help*. Figure 1-7 shows the help screen that Quicken displays if you press F1 from the Main Menu. The highlighted text in Quicken's help windows is called *hypertext*. This text provides access to help on the highlighted topic when selected. You can select this text by moving the cursor to it with the arrow keys and pressing Enter. In the section "The Keyboard, Mouse, and Screen Display" later in this chapter, you learn how to use a mouse to make selections.

If you are in another area of Quicken, the help presented might be very different. With the register on the screen, for example, Quicken assumes you need help with completing entries and so provides that information. You can also press Ctrl-F1 for direct access to the Help Index at any time. Quicken also provides tutorials and assistant features to help you get started.

1

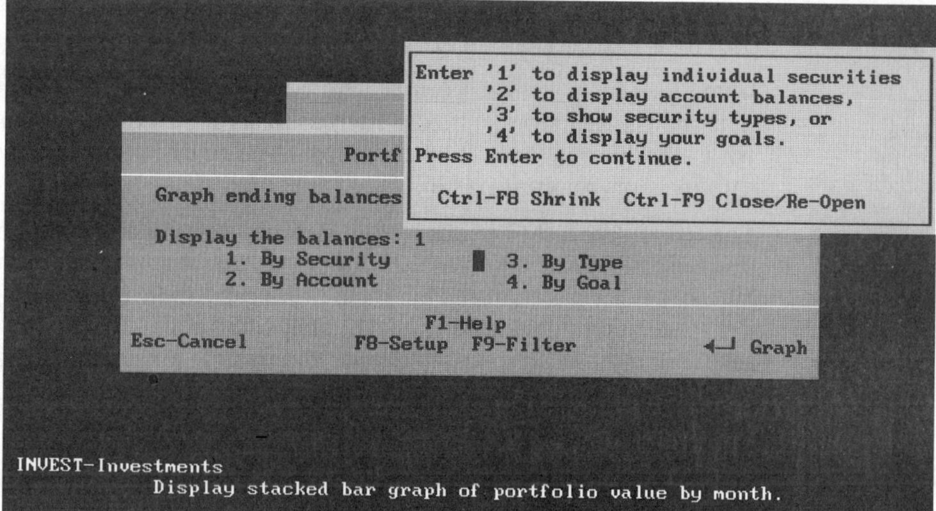

Help screen for Main Menu
Figure 1-7.

Quicken 7 provides a Qcard feature in several different areas of the program. *Qcards* are small boxes that contain prompting information to guide you through entries. Figure 1-7 shows a Qcard used with an investment account. Qcards can be toggled on and off by pressing Ctrl-F9. The Qcard feature has been turned off throughout this book in order not to obscure any information on the screen. If you want to turn them off in any area of the program, press Ctrl-F9 when they appear.

Quicken and Your Computer System

You may have had your computer long enough to feel like a pro operating it, but if Quicken is your first computer package, read the rest of this chapter carefully. It will eliminate much of the confusion experienced by new users in attempting to figure out what is in memory, what is on disk, and exactly how their computer makes it possible for a package like Quicken to do so much work so quickly. If you are already knowledgeable about your system, you may want to skim the rest of the chapter just to see how Quicken works with the computer. It is assumed you are using an IBM PC or compatible running the DOS operating system.

Memory

There are two kinds of memory in your computer: RAM and ROM. *ROM* is read-only memory—you cannot affect its contents so it's of little concern. *RAM* is random-access memory—temporary storage inside your computer.

RAM contains the program you are running (for example Quicken, 1-2-3, or dBASE) and the data you are currently working with in the program.

If you lose the power to your machine, you lose the contents of RAM. This is why permanent storage media such as disks are an essential component of your computer system. If your data is saved to disk, you can always load it into memory again if it is lost in a power failure.

The amount of RAM in your system is determined by the computer you have purchased and any additional memory you may have added to the system. Memory is measured in kilobytes (K) or megabytes (MB), with 1K representing the space required to store approximately a thousand characters of information and 1MB representing the space required to store approximately one million characters. Some systems have as little as 256K of memory, while others may have 1MB or even 16MB of memory capacity. Quicken requires a system with at least 512K in order to run the program, and 640K if you want to use IntelliCharge with a modem. The amount of memory you have determines the number of transactions you can have in a Quicken account and the complexity of the reports you can generate, since Quicken uses memory for these activities.

Disk Storage

Disk storage on your system may consist of one or more hard disks and floppy disks in either 3 1/2-inch or 5 1/4-inch sizes. Quicken requires a hard disk, with at least 2.6MB of available space. Like RAM, disk space is measured in either K or MB.

Most hard disks provide from 60 to 209MB of storage capacity. This means you will have room for Quicken as well as other software packages such as dBASE, WordPerfect, or 1-2-3.

A letter is used to represent each drive. Typically, hard disks are called drives C and D, while floppy disk drives are designated drives A and B.

All the program files you need for Quicken are stored on your hard disk. The following illustration shows a possible configuration of the directories on a hard disk.

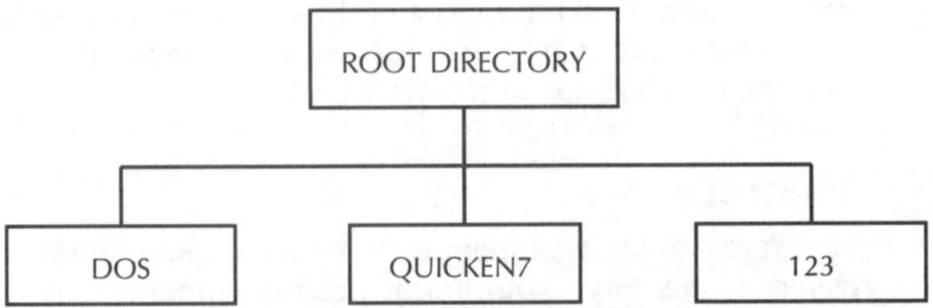

In this illustration, the root directory (main directory) would be used to contain batch files (files containing DOS instructions) on the hard disk. Separate directories are maintained for DOS and any other program. When you install Quicken on your hard disk, it creates its own directory, QUICKEN, and a batch file called Q.BAT.

The Keyboard, Mouse, and Screen Display

The screen and the keyboard or mouse serve as the central communication points between you and Quicken. Everything you want to tell the package must be entered through the keyboard or selected with a mouse. If you are using a keyboard, you are already familiar with many of the keys; they are used to enter data regardless of the type of program you are using. Function keys and key combinations have special meanings in Quicken; they are used to issue the commands. Even if you have used these keys in other programs, you will find that they provide different options in each program and thus are assigned to different tasks in Quicken.

The mouse allows you to make selections and perform tasks without using the keyboard. You will have new terms and new ways of doing things to learn as you click, double-click, and drag with a mouse to accomplish activities. You will learn about each of these new options in this section.

Quicken uses the screen to communicate information to you. Quicken supports both monochrome monitors (one color) and monitors that can display many colors. Your screen must have a graphics card to view graphs. Explanation of the screen is also covered here, since it often provides information about which keys to use for various features and commands.

Keyboard Styles

Not all keyboards are alike, although virtually all of them provide every key you need to use Quicken. However, you may have to look around to find the keys you need, especially if you are getting used to a new keyboard. On all the older model PCs and compatibles, the arrow keys move the cursor (or highlight) around on your screen. These keys are located on the *numeric keypad,* at the far right side of the keyboard. They are also used to enter numbers when the Num Lock key is depressed to activate them. With Num Lock off, the arrow keys move the cursor in the direction indicated on the key top. If these keys are not set properly for your use, just press Num Lock and they assume their other function.

On newer model keyboards, called the IBM *enhanced keyboards,* there are separate arrow keys to the left of the numeric keypad that move the cursor. This allows you to leave the number lock feature on for numeric data entry and use these arrow keys to move around on the screen.

Mouse Devices

Quicken 7 supports all Microsoft-compatible mouse devices. Quicken automatically recognizes a compatible mouse and displays a mouse pointer that looks like a small rectangle on the screen. As you roll the mouse over your desktop, the mouse pointer moves to different locations on your screen.

Your mouse device may have one, two, or three buttons on top. Button one is the leftmost button, and you will perform most tasks using it. Buttons two and three are optional and allow you to perform additional Quicken tasks.

Mouse Actions A mouse button can be used to perform a variety of actions. You can click the button by pressing it and quickly releasing it. You can double-click a button by completing two clicks in rapid succession. You can Shift-click the mouse by pressing the Shift key while you click the button. You can hold the button down by pressing it without releasing the button. You can drag with the mouse by continuing to hold down the mouse button while rolling the mouse across the desktop. Mouse actions require you to position the mouse pointer on the desired screen element before proceeding.

Left Mouse Button Tasks As mentioned, the left mouse button is used for most Quicken tasks. With this button, you can accomplish the following actions:

- Select a command from the Main Menu or pull-down menus.
- Accomplish the action of a function key with a click of the key representation.
- Finalize a record by clicking on Ctrl↵.
- Select a register transaction.
- Return to the Main Menu by clicking Esc-Main Menu.
- Display a Split Transaction window by clicking Split in the selected transaction.
- Display the Category and Transfer List window by clicking the Cat: in the selected transaction.
- Scroll through transactions by clicking the vertical scroll bar.
- Page up or page down with a click on the side of the scroll box.

Double-clicking is not used as often as the click action. You can use a double-click to select any item in a list. You can double-click a field in an account register to activate the QuickReport window, then make a selection for the type of QuickReport that you want. Dragging moves you to a different location in a list as you drag the scroll box vertically. Holding down the mouse button with the mouse pointer in a list or register scrolls up or down the list or register.

Optional Right or Center Mouse Button Tasks The right button on a two-button mouse performs the same two tasks as the center button on a three-button mouse. You can click the button instead of pressing Esc to leave the current task. You may need to click repeatedly to return to the Main Menu if you have already made several selections.

Third Mouse Button Tasks If you have a three-button mouse you can press its third or right button to access help. This help will be context sensitive.

Menu Selections

Quicken provides menus to simplify your feature and command selections. Quicken's Main Menu, shown here, leads to all the major tasks or activities the program performs.

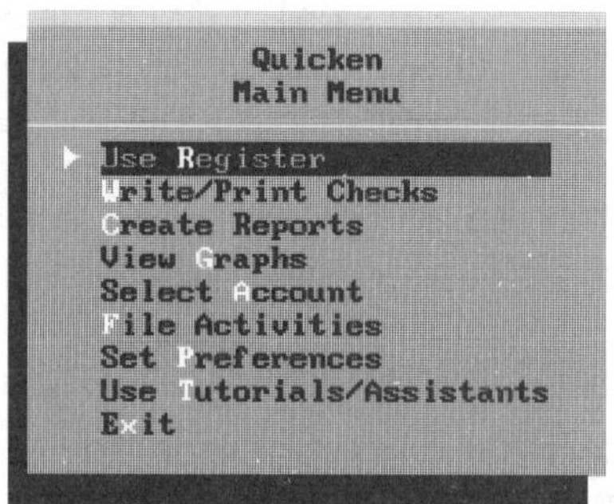

Quicken supports two menu styles. If you are a new Quicken user, when you install Quicken 7, it automatically selects menus which provide highlighted letters for each Main Menu option, as shown in the preceding illustration. The menu options that appear at the top of subsequent screens and activate pull-down menus also have highlighted letters.

The older style Main Menu has a number in front of each Main Menu selection. If you would like to change your current menu style, you can select Set **P**references, **S**creen Settings, Menu **A**ccess and then choose either Function keys or the Alt key. The techniques learned in the following sections for the use of the mouse and keyboard allow you to use either type menu.

Since there are two different menu styles as well as the ability to use either the mouse or the keyboard, there is a variety of correct options for making menu selections. Rather than listing each option in the exercises in later chapters, instructions are provided to select the required menu option. You can choose whichever method you prefer for making the selection.

Making Menu Selections with a Mouse

To select an activity from any menu, you first need to move the mouse pointer to the desired activity. Next, you must click the left mouse button. Subsequent menus that may be displayed support the same selection method.

You can activate pull-down menus at the top of the screen by clicking the desired option, depending on which style menus you use.

Making Menu Selections with the Keyboard

If you are using the keyboard to make menu selections, you can select any activity from the Main Menu by using the ↑ and ↓ keys, on the right side of your keyboard, to move your cursor to the desired activity and then pressing the Enter key. (The keys on your keyboard will display arrow symbols rather than words.) If you are using the Alt-key style menu, you can type the highlighted letter to select an option. With the older style menus, you can type the number or letter to the left of the desired menu activity. Remember that if you have the older style keyboard, the arrows are on the numeric keypad, so Num Lock has to be off in order to move the cursor.

Effects of Menu Selections

When you make a selection from the Main Menu, Quicken sometimes superimposes another menu on top of it. You make a selection from this submenu to refine the task you want to complete. Again, you can use the arrow keys, type a character, or type a number to make your selection, depending on which style menu you have. You can also use the mouse to select any menu option by clicking the desired choice.

In addition to the Main Menu selections, Quicken also provides *pull-down menus* on many of the screens. These menus are called pull-down menus since they come down from the top of the screen, as shown in Figure 1-8. The name of each menu is shown at the top of the screen. With the Alt-key style menus, a letter in each of the options is highlighted. You can press the Alt key in combination with this letter to pull down the menu. On the older style menus, you can activate the pull-down menus by pressing one of the keys labeled F1 through F10—the *function keys*. These keys are located either at the top or at the left side of your keyboard, depending on the model. You can also make selections with the Quick keys, described in the next section, without pulling down the menus. To close a menu without

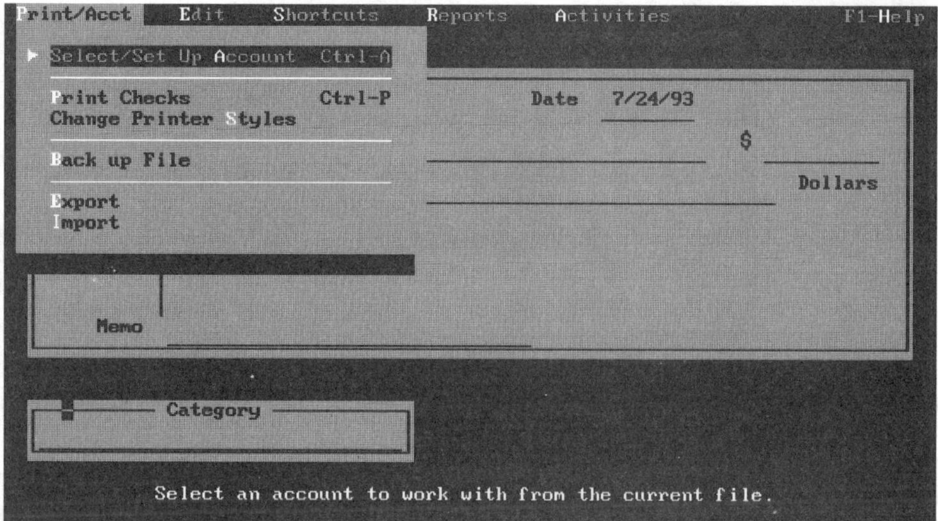

Pull-down menu
Figure 1-8.

making a selection, press the Esc key, or if you are using a mouse, click the right mouse button (two button) or middle mouse button (three button).

Some selections result in the appearance of a *window* on the screen. Windows differ from menus in that there are a number of pieces of information for you to complete. If you want to use the option already chosen (the *default*), there is no need to make a change. You can simply press Enter to accept that choice and move to the next *field,* where you will supply information. If you do not understand what is expected in a field, you can press F1 (Help) for an explanation. Figure 1-9 shows one of the Quicken windows. This one is for entering a printer style when you are customizing printer support.

QuickFill Saves Entry Time

No matter how proficient you are with the keyboard, the quickest way to enter data is to have Quicken do it for you. Quicken's feature is designed to do just that. Quicken maintains a list of options for many fields. As you type a transaction, QuickFill will attempt to match what you type to entries in lists for fields such as payee, category, security, goal, action, and type. Quicken checks its list as soon as you type a character and displays the first match it finds. As you type additional letters Quicken is able to refine the match. You can press Enter to accept the entry or use Ctrl-+ to advance through other options on the list that also match the beginning letter. For the payee field, Quicken checks payees in memorized transactions and the last three months of transactions. When you accept the payee, Quicken copies the entire transaction which you can edit if you choose. In addition,

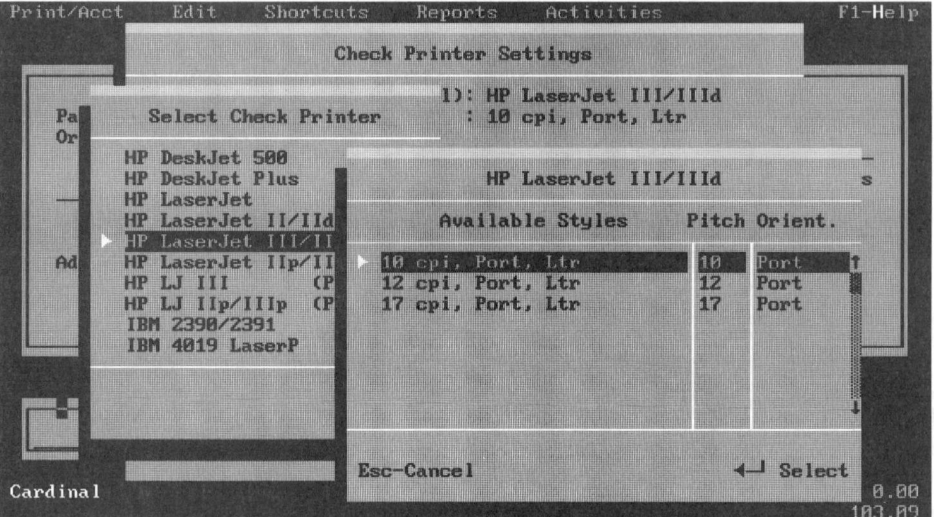

The Quicken window
Figure 1-9.

any field in a Quicken window with a diamond next to it will automatically display a list if diamond fields are activated in the Set P**r**eferences **G**eneral Setting option. Typing a letter will take you to the correct location in the list for further review and selection. If the diamond field option is off, you can press Ctrl-L to display the list.

Quick Keys

Quick keys provide access to commands. You can use them throughout Quicken to speed up transaction entry in the register, check writing, and report printing. All Quick key commands are initiated by pressing the Ctrl key in combination with another key. When you pull down a menu, you see "Ctrl-" and a letter next to menu items that can be activated with a Quick key combination. The Quick key combinations work while the menu is pulled down, but they also work without your pulling the menu down. The more you use the Quick keys, the easier it will be to remember the combination needed for each activity.

As you work with them, you will find that a few of the combinations are assigned different tasks depending on the activity you are performing. For example, Ctrl-B searches backward when you are using Find in the register, but it creates a backup of your files when you are at the Main Menu.

As you become familiar with Quicken, you will find these keys help you reduce time spent on financial record keeping. The Quick keys are listed on the inside cover of this book.

Special Keys

If you have used your computer with other programs, you will find that many of the special keys work the same in Quicken as in other programs. For example, the Esc key is used to cancel your most recent selection. It can be used to close any menu except the Main Menu, and it also closes most windows, returning you to the previous screen. The Spacebar, at the bottom of the keyboard, is used when making entries to add blank spaces. The Backspace key deletes the last character you typed, the character to the left of the cursor. Del deletes the character above the cursor.

The Shift key is used to enter capital letters and the special symbols at the top of non-letter keys. It also provides access to the numbers on the numeric keypad when Num Lock is off. Caps Lock enters all letters in capitals if you press it once, but it does not affect the entry of special symbols, which always require the Shift key. To enter lowercase letters with Caps Lock on, hold down the Shift key. To turn Caps Lock off, just press it a second time.

The Tab key usually moves you from field to field. Pressing Shift and Tab together moves the cursor backward through the fields on the screen. Ctrl-End moves the cursor to the bottom of the display; Ctrl-Home moves you to the top of the display.

The Pg Up and Pg Dn keys move you up and down screens and menus.

Quicken uses the + and - keys on the numeric keypad to quickly increase and decrease numbers such as date and check number. When these keys are pressed once, the number increases or decreases by one. However, since the keys all repeat when held down, holding down either of these keys can rapidly effect a major change. The + and - keys perform their functions in appropriate fields whether Num Lock is on or off. You can Shift-click the right mouse button (two-button) or center mouse button (three-button) for the same effect.

The inside cover of this book provides a concise reference to each of these keys.

Memorized and Scheduled Transactions are Time Savers

You can memorize transactions and record them again at a later time. A quick check of the date and transaction amount is often all that is needed when you record them again later. This capability has been extended with Quicken 7's new scheduled transaction feature. With scheduled transactions you can have Quicken automatically enter one or more transactions for you. You can choose to be prompted about these entries or let Quicken automatically handle the complete task of recording monthly payments to the orthodontist, the newspaper, or the bank for your home mortgage payment.

Help With Calculations

One of the problems paying bills and writing checks is that it is easy to make a math mistake. A simple mistake can result in a bank statement that does not reconcile or a misapplied discount for a bill. You are likely to experience lot of frustration when you make these mistakes as well. When you are making entries with Quicken, it never makes a mistake with its calculations. It even provides a few features to help you with intermediate calculations you might want to perform before recording a transaction amount.

Quicken has a calculator that will pop-up on your screen at your request. Quicken 7 also has a new QuickMath feature that does quick math checks without a calculator.

The Calculator

Quicken has its own calculator, which allows you to perform basic computations on the screen. You can perform computations using the mathematical operators such as + for addition, – for subtraction, * for multiplication, and / for division. Simple calculation involving two numbers or more complex formulas is possible. The calculator displays its results on screen. However, once the numbers leave the screen, you cannot bring them back into view. As a caution, this could make error detection difficult for lengthy calculations.

A significant feature of Quicken's calculator is its ability to compute a payment amount or other figure needed in the *current transaction entry* (the one in use) and then place, or *paste,* the result onto the screen. Figure 1-10 shows the calculator. You could use the calculator to compute a total of nine invoices for $77.00 each, for example. In this manner, one check could be written to cover all nine invoices. You can also compute discounts or interest on a loan. Once Quicken computes the amount, you can use the Paste feature to place the amount in the payment field.

You activate the calculator through the menu bar at the top of the Check Register, Write Checks, or Reconciliation screen by selecting **A**ctivities, **C**alculator. You can also activate it by using the Quick key Ctrl-O. When the calculator is activated, Quicken automatically turns on the numeric keypad so you can use it in making your calculations.

QuickMath

The QuickMath feature activates a formula bar in any field that accepts a numeric entry. All you need to do is type an equal sign (=) in the field. Next, type the numbers and operators needed to perform your calculation. When you are finished, type another equal sign (=) or press Enter for the result.

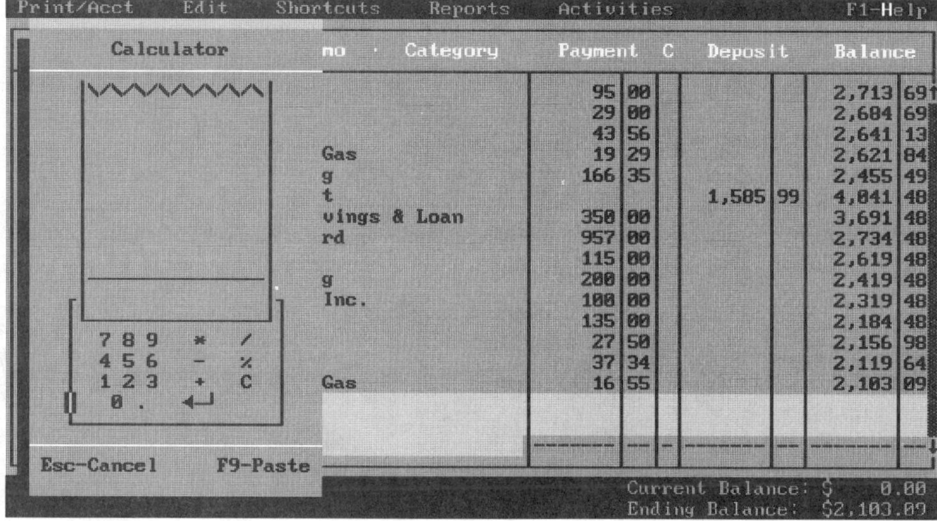

The Quicken calculator
Figure 1-10.

The Calendar

Quicken 7 has a new calendar feature that will display a calendar month on the screen when you press Ctrl-K. You can add notes to the dates. Dates with notes will display an N in the date box as shown in Figure 1-11.

Calendar window added to Quicken 7
Figure 1-11.

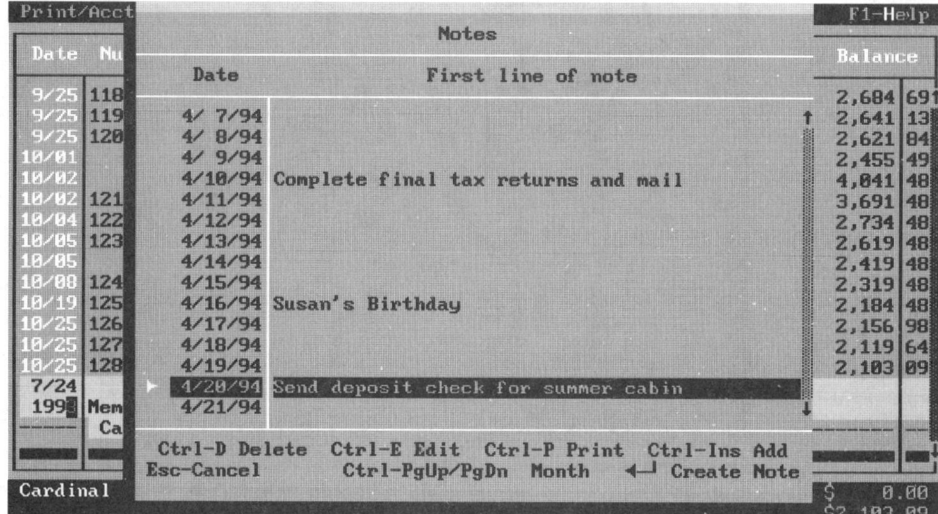

Figure 1-12. You can add notes to any calendar date

You can press Ctrl-N to see the note attached to the date or use the same option to add a note to another date. The list of notes displayed in Figure 1-12 shows how they can be used as reminders for both financial and non-financial activities. You can have Quicken remind you about your to-do list of items if you like. Once a note is entered, you can highlight the first line of the note and press Ctrl-E to edit when the list of first lines is displayed.

You can also use the calendar for other activities such as keeping track of scheduled transactions. They will display a T in the box for any date where a transaction is scheduled. You can press Ctrl-T to see the list of scheduled transaction groups.

You can change the month displayed by pressing Pg Up or Pg Dn. With a month you can use the arrow keys to highlight a specific date. To move to that date in the register, press Ctrl-G.

C H A P T E R

investments banking FILE register expenses DEDUCTIONS
tips finances equity net pay
checks revenue bank statements
statements business tips
dividends assets
INCOME cash flow
banking business tips FILE reports
budget FILE business tips checks
DEDUCTIONS
statements cash flow tips mortgage
net pay taxes bank revenue
business tips
mortgage cash dividends tips
business tips investments
register statements
taxes
business tips
expenses tips
equity investments INCOME
checks statements bank cash
assets checks budget tips finances net pay

2

MAKING REGISTER ENTRIES

If you maintain a checking account or monitor a savings account, you are already familiar with the concept of the Quicken register. The register is the backbone of the Quicken system. It allows you to maintain information on checking accounts, cash accounts, and other assets and expenses. With the register, you maintain current status information for an account so you know the precise balance. You also keep a history of all the transactions affecting the balance. The capabilities of the Quicken register extend beyond the entries normally made in a checkbook register since they allow you to easily categorize entries as you make them. This extra capability extends the usefulness of the recorded information and facilitates report creation.

In this chapter you will learn to create and maintain a single account. This account will represent a checking account balance, and the transactions will simulate those you might have in a personal account. The techniques you learn will be used repeatedly as you work with the Quicken package.

Maintaining a Register

Quicken's register works much like the manual checking account register shown in Figure 2-1. Starting with the account balance at the beginning of the period, each check written is recorded as a separate entry, including the date, amount, payee, and check number. Additional information can be added to document the reason for the check. This information can be useful in the preparation of taxes or to verify that an invoice has been paid. As each check is entered, a new balance is computed. Other bank charges such as check printing, overdraft charges, and service fees must also be subtracted from the account balance. Deposits are recorded in a similar fashion. Since interest earned is often automatically credited to the account, it should be entered as it appears on the monthly bank statement. (Quicken cannot compute the interest earned on your account since there is no way for the package to know the dates that checks clear at your bank; this information is needed to compute the interest earned.)

Although it is easy to record entries in a manual check register, most individuals at least occasionally make a mistake in computing the new balance. Recording transactions in Quicken's register eliminates this problem. It also provides many other advantages such as categories for classifying each entry, automatic totaling of similar transactions within a category, easily created reports, and a Search feature for quickly locating specific entries.

Before entering any transactions in Quicken's register, you need to create a file and set up an account. This means assigning a name to the account and establishing a balance. You will also want to learn a little about Quicken's built-in categories, which allow you to categorize every transaction. You may already do this with some transactions in your check register, marking those you will need to refer back to, for instance. This activity is optional in Quicken, but using the categories will increase the usefulness of the reports you can create.

RECORD ALL CHANGES OR CREDITS THAT AFFECT YOUR ACCOUNT

NUMBER	DATE	DESCRIPTION OF TRANSACTION	PAYMENT/DEBIT		T	FEE IF ANY (-)	DEPOSIT/CREDIT (+)		BALANCE $	
	1/1 1994	Opening Balance 1st U.S. Bank					1,200	00	1,200 1,200	00 00
100	1/4 1994	Small City Gas & Light Gas & Electric	67	50					67 1,132	50 50
101	1/5 1994	Small City Times Paper Bill	16	50					16 1,116	50 00
	1/7 1994	Deposit - Salary monthly pay					700	00	700 1,816	00 00
102	1/7 1994	Small City Market Food	22	32					22 1,793	32 68
103	1/7 1994	Small City Apartments Rent	150	00					150 1,643	00 00
104	1/19 1994	Small City Market Food	43	00					43 1,600	00 00
105	1/25 1994	Small City Phone Company Phone Bill	19	75					19 1,580	75 93
	2/10 1994	Dividend Check Dividend from ABC Co.					25	00	25 1,605	00 93

Manual entries in a checking account register
Figure 2-1.

Establishing Your File and an Account

Establishing a file and an account is easy once you install Quicken and start it with the instructions in Appendix A, "Special Quicken Tasks."

You can choose menu selections to help you set up a new file or, if you want even more help, you can access a Quicken Assistant to help you get started with the setup. If you have data from Quicken 6, you can use the data in Quicken 7 without conversion. Quicken will locate your old files during installation and allow you to use them without change. If you have an earlier release of the product you will want to consult the information in the box "Upgrading from an Earlier Release" for the exact procedure you need to follow.

Regardless of which approach you choose, you need to have a file for storing any data entered with Quicken. When you provide a name, Quicken adds several filename extensions since one Quicken file actually consists of several different files on your disk. You also need to provide an account name. Quicken can store data for various account types, with as many as 255 accounts in one Quicken file. You will find all the steps you need in the sections that follow, regardless of your situation.

Upgrading from an Earlier Release

Intuit provides an upward compatibility path for all Quicken users whether they are working with Quicken 1, Quicken 6, or some release in between. The procedure for converting your data to use with Quicken 7 is automatic with some of the later releases and requires just a bit more effort with earlier versions. Look for your release in the list that follows to see if you need to do anything to convert your data.

- Quicken 6 Conversion is automatic during installation.
- Quicken 5 Conversion is automatic during installation.
- Quicken 4 Install Quicken, then choose **F**ile Activities from the Main Menu. Choose **S**elect Setup/File, then select the Quicken 4 data file that you want to update and let Quicken know whether you want to back it up first. After conversion, check your category list and delete any categories marked with an asterisk as they have not been used with any transactions.
- Quicken 3 Same procedure as Quicken 4.
- Quicken 2 You must use a special utility to convert your files to the Quicken 7 format. Contact Intuit at the number in the product manual for Quicken 7 to obtain a copy.
- Quicken 1 Your files require a two-step conversion process. They must be updated to Quicken 2 before they can be updated to Quicken 7. You can contact Intuit for information on the required utility.

Once you convert the files from any release to Quicken 7 you will not be able to use the files again with the earlier release. If you need to work with the earlier release again, you should maintain a backup copy of your data for that purpose.

Creating a New File

The steps in this section enable you to create a new Quicken 7 file if you want new files later. You also learn how to change the location of the file. Follow these steps:

1. Choose **F**ile Activities from the Main Menu.
2. Select Set File **L**ocation and change the pathname if necessary.

The pathname is the drive and directory where the file will be stored.

3. Press Enter to finalize the entry.
4. Choose **S**elect/Set Up File.
5. If you have already created other Quicken files you will need to select <Set Up New File>. (If there are no other Quicken files, Quicken assumes you want to set up a new file rather than select an existing one; you can skip this step.)
6. Type **QDATA** as a name for the file, which can consist of one to eight characters, and then press F10 (Continue).
7. Select Both Home and Business for the categories as shown in Figure 2-2.

   You can type a **3** or click the Home and Business option with your mouse.
8. Press Enter or click the ↵ Continue option with your mouse.
9. Highlight the file and press Enter.

   Quicken takes you to the screen for creating an account.
10. Press Esc until you are back at the Main Menu.

    Now follow the separate instructions in the next section for creating a new account. The stand-alone procedure described here can be used if you ever need to create a new account without a file.

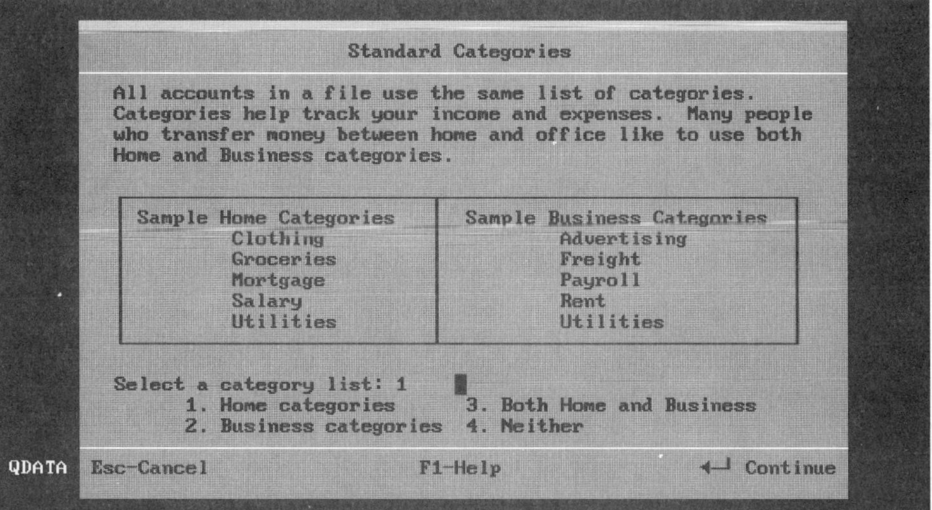

Sample Quicken categories
Figure 2-2.

Creating a New Account

The account used for the examples in the next few chapters is called 1st U.S. Bank. In the unlikely event that this name happens to be the same as one of your existing accounts, you need to use another name to maintain the integrity of your existing data. Follow these steps:

1. Choose Select **A**ccount from the Main Menu.
2. If you have already established an account in the current file you will need to select New Account and press Enter. You will see the screen shown in Figure 2-3.

   If this is the first account for the file this step will not be necessary.
3. Type **1** for the account type and press Enter.

   If you prefer working with the mouse you can click the ↵ Continue option at the bottom of the screen at any time instead of pressing Enter.
4. Type **1st U.S. Bank** and press Enter.

   Account names can contain from 1 to 15 characters.
5. Type **1200** and press Enter.
6. Type **1/1/94** and press F10.
7. Type **1**, press Enter to specify Bank Statement as the source of the 1,200 entry and press Enter again.
8. Press Esc to display the Main Menu.

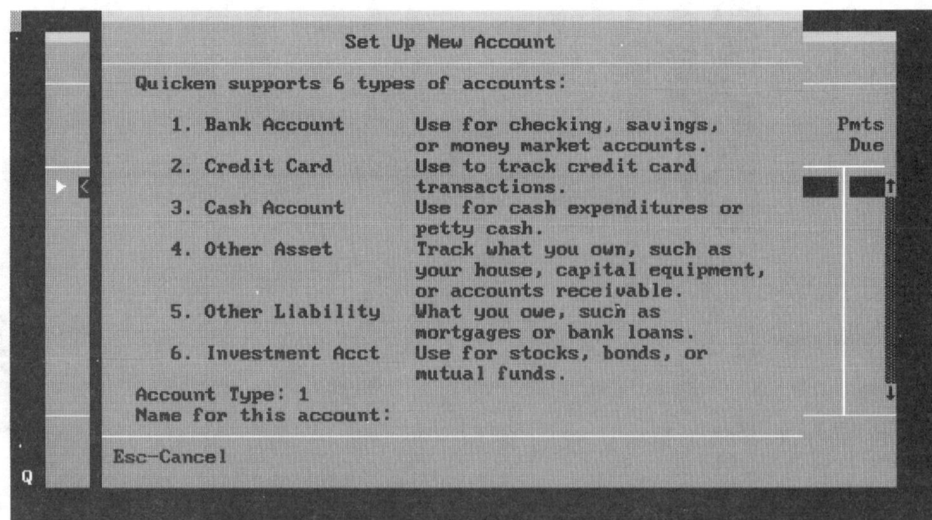

Setting up a Quicken account
Figure 2-3.

Performing the Task if You Are Already Using Quicken 7

Even though you already have a file and one or more accounts set up from your earlier Quicken sessions, you will want to create a file and an account that match the ones used in the examples. You should follow the steps in the two preceding sections to insure that your practice sessions do not affect the integrity of your existing data.

Using the Assistant to Create a Quicken File

The Quicken Assistant screen can lead you through the process of setting up a file. You will get extra help as you move through the process. One of the additional information screens that is displayed when you use the Quicken Assistant is shown in Figure 2-4. The Assistant leads you through the process of naming a file for use, selecting a set of categories to use with your entries, and defining an account to use. Follow these steps to use the Assistant:

1. Choose **T**utorials/Assistants from the Main Menu.
2. Select Create New **F**ile.
3. Read the information screens that describe Quicken files and press Enter or click ↵ Continue after each.
4. Respond to Quicken's questions and review the information before finalizing.

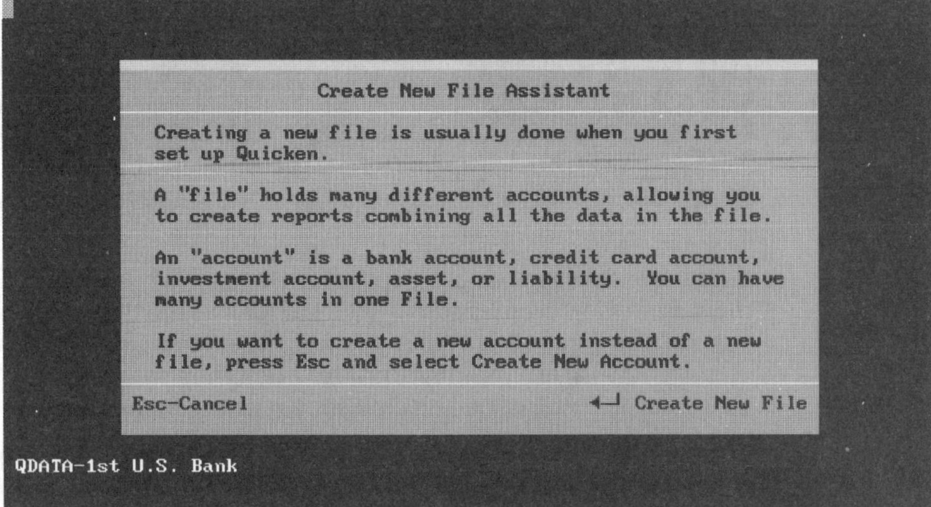

The Assistant screen
Figure 2-4.

5. When you complete the procedure for creating a new file you can choose Create New **A**ccount from the Tutorials/Assistants menu and complete the second procedure.
6. Press Esc until the Main Menu is displayed.

Converting Quicken 5 or Quicken 6 Data to Use with Quicken 7

If you have followed the directions in Appendix A, Quicken has searched your hard disk and located your Quicken 5 or Quicken 6 files. Since they can be read directly by Quicken 7, there is no need to convert them.

If you change the name of the install directory Quicken suggests, your existing Quicken data will not be available until you choose **F**ile Activities from the Main Menu and Set File **L**ocation to the Quicken 5 or Quicken 6 directory.

If you are using a release of Quicken prior to Quicken 5, your files must be converted before using them with Quicken 7. Check the instructions in the box, "Upgrading from an Earlier Release."

The Quicken Register

You can choose Use **R**egister from the Main Menu to display the register for 1st U.S. Bank. Initially, the top of the Register window looks like this:

```
Print/Acct   Edit   Shortcuts   Reports   Activities                    F1-Help
                                            Payment  C   Deposit    Balance
Enter the date of the transaction here.
Press Tab to continue.

Ctrl-F7 for More
Ctrl-F8 to Shrink Qcards                             X   1,200 00   1,200 00
Ctrl-F9 to Close/Re-Open Qcards
7/13
1993 Memo:
      Cat:
```

Qcards are displayed to provide help with the entry of data. You can remove them from view by pressing Ctrl-F9 to look at the first entry in the register as shown in Figure 2-5. When you want the Qcards to display again, just press Ctrl-F9 again. Throughout this book they will be closed in order to give you the best look at the data shown in the figures and illustrations.

Although you have not yet recorded any transactions, Quicken has already entered the account name, the opening balance, and the opening date.

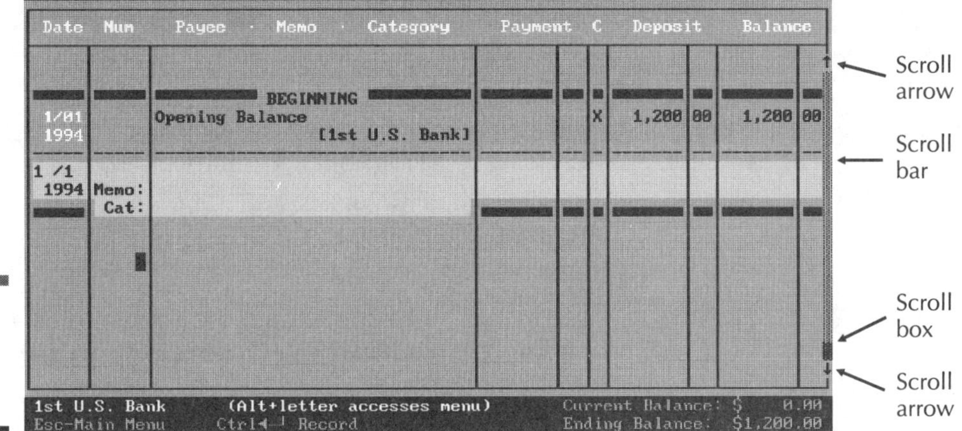

New Account Register window
Figure 2-5.

Quicken has also automatically entered X in the C (cleared) field of the register, indicating that the balance has been reconciled and is correct. This field will be used in Chapter 4, "Reconciling Your Quicken Register," when you reconcile your entire account. The account balance is also shown at the bottom of the screen. This will be discussed in more detail later as it is affected by the current date and its relationship to the dates used in the transactions entered.

The area at the far right of the register window is the *scroll bar*. It has an arrow at the top and bottom and a scroll box inside it. As you enter more transactions, you can use a mouse with these screen elements to scroll through the register.

The highlighted area below the opening balance entry is where the first transaction will be entered. Remember, a transaction is just a record of a financial activity such as a deposit or withdrawal (credit or debit). The fields used are the same for all transactions (see Figure 2-5). Table 2-1 provides a detailed description of each of these fields.

As you make the entries for the first transaction, notice that Quicken moves through the fields in a specific order. After entering data in a field, you press Enter and the cursor automatically moves to the next field in which you can enter data. Some fields, such as Date and Payee, must have an entry in all transactions, and either the Payment or Deposit field requires an entry. Other fields are optional and are used when needed. If you do not need an entry in an optional field, you just press Enter and the cursor moves to the next field. For example, since the check number (Num) field is used only when writing checks, making an entry is optional.

Fields in Register Window
Table 2-1.

Field	Contents
Date	Transaction date. You can accept the current date entry or type a new date.
Num (number)	Check number for check transactions. Leave field blank by pressing Enter for noncheck transactions.
Payee	Payee's name for check transactions. For ATM transactions, deposits, service fees, and so on, a description is entered in this field.
Payment	Payment or withdrawal amount. For deposit transactions, this field is left blank. Quicken supports entries as large as $9,999,999.99.
C (cleared)	Press Enter to skip this field when entering transactions. You will use it in Chapter 4 for reconciling accounts and noting checks that have cleared the bank.
Deposit	Deposit amounts. For a payment transaction, this field is left blank. The same rules as for Payment apply.
Balance	A running total or the sum of all prior transactions. It is computed by Quicken after you complete each transaction.
Memo	Optional descriptive information documenting the transaction.
Category	Optional entry used to assign a transaction to one of Quicken's categories. Categories are used to organize similar transactions and can facilitate reporting.

Recording Your Transactions in the Register

The highlighting is already positioned for your first transaction entry when you open the Register window. If you have used the ↑ key to move to the opening balance entry, you need to press Ctrl-End to reposition the highlight properly. In the next sections you enter eight sample transactions representing typical personal expenses and deposits. Don't worry if you make a mistake in recording your first transaction. Just leave the mistake in the entry and focus on the steps involved. In the second transaction you will correct your errors. Follow these steps to complete the entries for the first transaction (use the ← key, if necessary, to move the cursor to the month in the date field):

1. Type **1/4/94** and press Enter.

Notice that "1/04" is displayed on the first line of the Date field and that the cursor automatically moves to the second line of the column the second time you press the / key. Also note that even though you only entered 94, Quicken displays the full year, 1994.

At this point you can see how Quicken dates are changed. Move the cursor to the Date field using ←, and press + or - to increase or decrease the current date. A light touch to the key alters the date by one day. Holding down these keys causes a rapid date change. If you use the + or - option to change the date, Enter or Tab is still required to move to the next field. If you use + and - to change the transaction date and want to return to the current system date for the next transaction, press T with the cursor in the Date field. (If you test this feature now, be sure to reenter the 1/4/94 date before proceeding.)

2. Type **100** and press Enter to place the check number in the Num field. With your mouse, you can click the next field where you want to make an entry instead of pressing Enter.
3. Type **Small City Gas & Light** and press Enter to complete the entry for Payee for this check.

   There is a limit of 31 characters on the Payee line for each transaction. Notice that the cursor moves to the Payment field, where Quicken expects the next entry.
4. Type **67.50** and press Enter.

   Since this is a check transaction, the amount should be placed in the Payment field. Notice that when you type the decimal, Quicken automatically moves to the cents column of the Payment field.
5. Type **Gas and Electric** and press Enter.

   You are limited to 31 characters on the Memo line. Since this is your first category entry, a message displays. Press F10 to acknowledge it.
6. Type **U** in the Cat (category) field.

   The Quicken QuickFill feature attempts to guess the category that you want to use and supplies UIC. You can accept the entry by pressing Enter, keep typing to refine the selection, or press Ctrl-+ or Ctrl-- to scroll through the list of options one at a time.
7. Type **t** to refine the selection.

   Your screen should look like the one in Figure 2-6.
8. If you are going to use a category, you must enter a valid Quicken option to stay within the standard category structure. To see Quicken's Standard Categories, press Ctrl-C and use the arrow keys to review your options. Press Esc to return to the register.

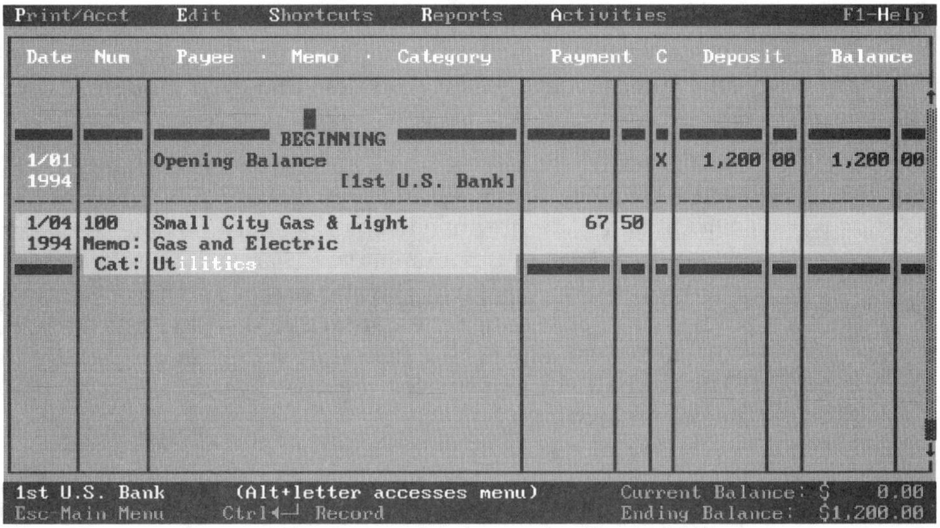

Screen before completing first sample transaction entry
Figure 2-6.

9. Press Enter to complete the transaction data entry.

   Quicken displays the OK to Record Transaction? window to see if you are ready to record the transaction.

10. Select Record Transaction to confirm the recording of the transaction.

    Your screen displays a balance of 1,132.50.

You have now completed your first transaction successfully. Since everyone makes mistakes in entries, you will want to learn how to correct those errors. This is easily done with Quicken.

Making Revisions to the Current Transaction

One of the advantages Quicken has over manual entries is that changes can be made easily and neatly. An incorrect amount or other error can be altered as soon as you notice the mistake or later on. The procedure you use depends on whether you have already recorded the transaction. Quicken's QuickFill feature can save you time, whether you are correcting an existing transaction or entering a new transaction.

Correcting Your Example

In this section you learn how to correct mistakes in the current transaction, practicing the techniques covered briefly in Chapter 1, "An Overview of

2

Quicken and Your Computer Components." First, make the following transaction entries:

1. Type **1/5/94** and press Enter.

   Notice that before you type the new date, Quicken automatically entered the 1/4/94 date for you. It always records the date from the previous transaction unless there was none, in which case it records the current date. Here, you must enter the date since you are entering several days' transactions in one session. If you enter transactions daily, you do not need to change the date between transactions since each of your entries will be for the current day.
2. Type **110** and press Enter.

   Notice that the previous check number was 100. This check number should have been recorded as 101.
3. Press ← five times to move the cursor to the second 1 in the entry.
4. Type **01** to change 110 to 101 and then press Enter to finalize.

   This correction method employs Quicken's character replacement feature; new characters type over the old entries.
5. Type **S** and notice that Quicken may automatically fill in the same payee from the previous transaction.

   This illustrates Quickens QuickFill feature. If you press Enter, Quicken completes the current transaction with the entries from the previous transaction. Quicken uses QuickFill for Payee and Category fields as you record in the account register. Quicken checks the Memorized Transaction List and looks at the payees in the last three months of transactions as it searches for an entry that matches what you type.

CAUTION: If the 1/5/94 transaction date is after your current system date, QuickFill will not be operational for the payee but will still work for categories.

Quicken uses the first match it finds and shows <Mem> for a memorized transaction or the date of the transaction in angle brackets as in <1/4> for a transaction recorded in the register 1/4/94. You can press Ctrl-+ to look through the list for additional matches. Ctrl-- moves backward through the list. You can also continue typing to refine Quicken's selection.

If QuickFill is not operating for you, choose Set **P**references from the Main Menu and select **G**eneral Settings. Change the Activate QuickFill to Y.

6. Continue typing **Smalll City Times**, since Quicken has not provided the match that you need.

   This entry contains an extra *l*. Use Ctrl-← twice to move to the *C* in "City." Then press the ← key twice to move your cursor to the third *l* and press Del to delete the character at the cursor.

7. Press Enter to finalize the Payee entry.
8. Type **6.50** for the payment amount.

NOTE: If you had intended to enter 16.50, moving to the 6 and typing a 1 would change the entry to 1.50, not the 16.50 you need. Even if you have insert mode on (a flashing cursor), you still cannot insert the 1 without pushing the 6 to the right.

9. Move the cursor one position to the left of the 6 by pressing ← five times. With insert mode off (small underscore cursor), type **1**; Quicken places the 1 in front of the 6.
10. Press Enter to move to the Memo field.
11. Type **Magazine subscription** and press Enter.

    If you had intended this entry to be the newspaper bill, you would need to make a change. Use ↑ to reactivate the Memo field.

12. Press Ctrl-Backspace, which deletes the entire entry. Then, type **Paper bill** and press Enter.
13. Type **M** for the category.

    Quicken uses the QuickFill feature and presents the Meals & Entertn category. You want to use the Miscellaneous category.

14. Press Ctrl-+ and Quicken displays the Med. category designation. Press Ctrl-+ and Quicken displays the Misc. category designation. Press Ctrl-+ again and Quicken displays the Mort Int category. Press Ctrl-- to return to the Misc category.

    If you had continued to type Mi in the category field, Quicken would have presented Misc as the category, and you would have stopped typing and accepted it by pressing Enter.

15. Press Ctrl-Enter to record your second transaction.

    Your register should look like the one in Figure 2-7.

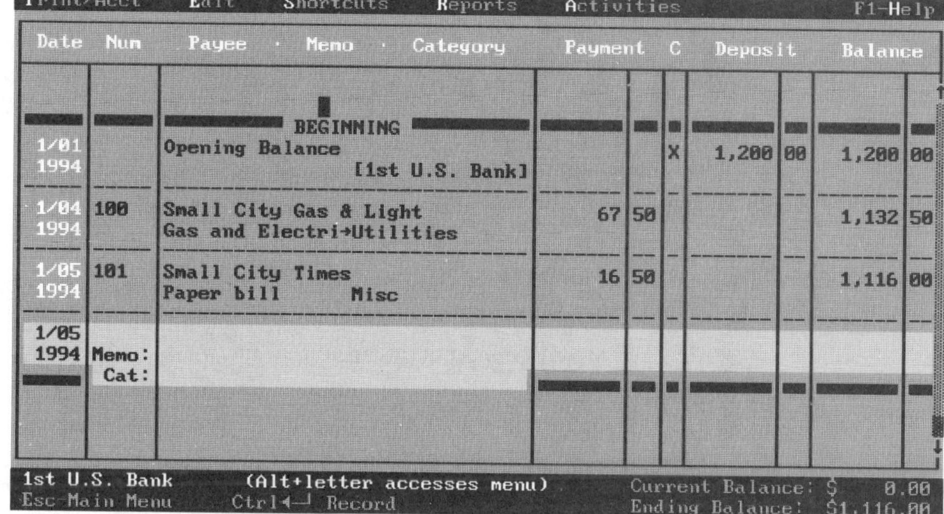

Register screen after second sample transaction

Figure 2-7.

A number of mistakes were included in this transaction, but you can see how easy it is to make corrections with Quicken.

NOTE: You can also click Ctrl ↵ Record or press Enter twice to record your transaction.

Additional Transaction Entries

You are now somewhat familiar with recording transactions in the Quicken register. In order to test your knowledge and expand your transaction base for later, enter the following additional transactions in your register, using the same procedure as in the previous transaction entries. Remember to leave a blank space in the Num field of deposits when a check number is not provided. You can use the QuickFill when entering Payee or Category fields.

Date: 1/7/94
Payee: Deposit-Salary
Deposit: 700.00
Memo: Monthly pay
Category: Salary

Date: 1/7/94
Num: 102
Payee: Small City Market
Payment: 22.32
Memo: Food
Category: Groceries

Date: 1/7/94
Num: 103
Payee: Small City Apartments
Payment: 150.00
Memo: Rent
Category: Housing

Date: 1/19/94
Num: 104
Payee: Small City Market
Payment: 43.00
Memo: Food
Category: Groceries

When entering this transaction, Quicken 7 copies the information contained in the Payment, Memo, and Cat fields when you press Enter after completing the Payee field. Press Ctrl-Backspace to clear the 22.32 payment amount. Type the correct payment amount and press Ctrl-Enter.

Date: 1/25/94
Num: 105
Payee: Small City Phone Company
Payment: 19.75
Memo: Phone bill
Category: Telephone

Date: 2/10/94
Payee: Dividend check
Deposit: 25.00
Memo: Dividends check from ABC Co.
Category: Div Income

After typing the entries for the last transaction, your screen should resemble the one in Figure 2-8. Press Ctrl-Enter to record the last transaction.

Viewing a Compressed Register

You can switch back and forth between the standard register and a *compressed register,* which lets you see three times as many transactions on your screen. For a view that shows one line for each transaction, like Figure 2-9, press Ctrl-Q or choose **R**egister View from the **A**ctivities menu. Pressing Ctrl-Q or making the menu selection again toggles back to the original view. To change the default Quicken setting to the compressed view, choose **S**creen Setting from the Set **P**references menu, and then choose **R**egister View and option 2 Compressed to save two lines for every transaction displayed.

Ending a Quicken Session and Beginning a New One

You do not need to finish all your work with Quicken in one session. You can end a Quicken session after entering one transaction or continue and enter transactions representing up to several months of financial activity, but you should always use the orderly approach provided here and never turn your system off without first exiting from Quicken.

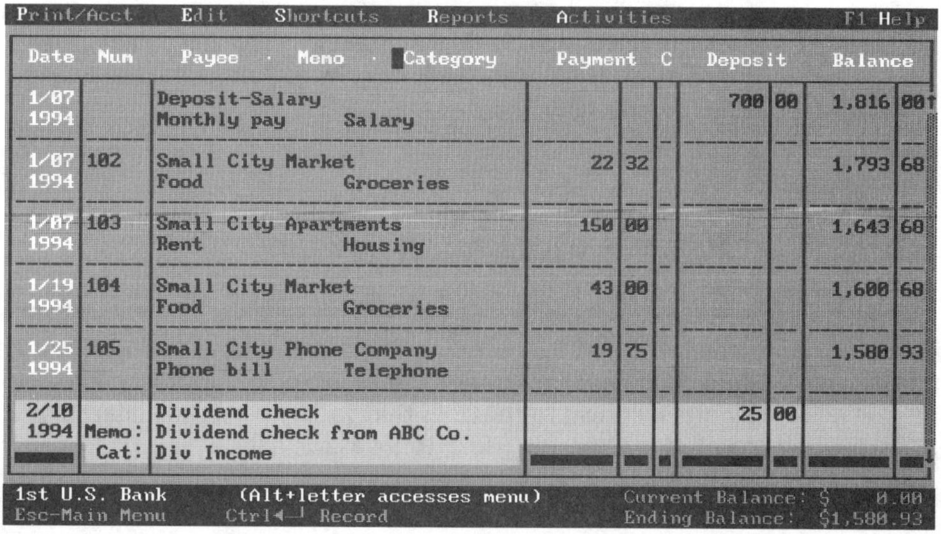

```
Print/Acct   Edit   Shortcuts   Reports   Activities              F1-Help
Date  Num    Payee  · Memo  · Category     Payment  C  Deposit    Balance
1/07         Deposit-Salary                             700 00   1,816 00
1994         Monthly pay      Salary
1/07  102    Small City Market                22 32              1,793 68
1994         Food             Groceries
1/07  103    Small City Apartments           150 00              1,643 68
1994         Rent             Housing
1/19  104    Small City Market                43 00              1,600 68
1994         Food             Groceries
1/25  105    Small City Phone Company         19 75              1,580 93
1994         Phone bill       Telephone
2/10         Dividend check                              25 00
1994  Memo:  Dividend check from ABC Co.
       Cat:  Div Income
1st U.S. Bank      (Alt+letter accesses menu)      Current Balance: $     0.00
Esc-Main Menu      Ctrl◄┘ Record                   Ending Balance:  $1,580.93
```

Register screen after typing and finalizing entries in last transaction
Figure 2-8.

```
Print/Acct   Edit   Shortcuts   Reports   Activities                F1-Help
 Date  Num    Payee  · Memo  · Category    Payment  C   Deposit    Balance
                      BEGINNING
 1/01      Opening Balance                          X  1,200 00   1,200 00
 1/04 100  Small City Gas & Light            67 50                1,132 50
 1/05 101  Small City Times                  16 50                1,116 00
 1/07      Deposit-Salary                                700 00   1,816 00
 1/07 102  Small City Market                 22 32                1,793 68
 1/07 103  Small City Apartments            150 00                1,643 68
 1/19 104  Small City Market                 43 00                1,600 68
 1/25 105  Small City Phone Company          19 75                1,580 93
 2/10      Dividend check                                 25 00   1,605 93
 2/10
 1994 Memo:
      Cat:
                         END
1st U.S. Bank      (Alt+letter accesses menu)     Current Balance: $     0.00
Esc-Main Menu      Ctrl←┘ Record                  Ending Balance:  $1,605.93
```

Compressed register shows one line for each transaction

Figure 2-9.

Ending a Quicken session requires that you go to the Main Menu. You can click the right mouse button or press Esc when the register is active to return to the Main Menu. You may need to perform the action several times if menus are active. Choose E**x**it from the Main Menu to end your session. All of the data in your Quicken files will be saved for subsequent sessions.

To reenter Quicken, use the instructions provided earlier in this chapter to boot your system (if necessary); then, type **Q** and press Enter to access the Quicken package. You always enter the Main Menu when you first load the package. Selecting Use **R**egister takes you back to the register to record additional transactions. Quicken always brings the last account you worked with to the screen.

NOTE: Quicken automatically enters the current date in the Date field for the first transaction in a session.

Remember that for purposes of the examples, you will specify dates that are unlikely to agree with the current date. This approach allows you to create reports identical to the ones that will be presented later. If you are now reentering Quicken, use 2/10/94 as the date.

Reviewing Register Entries

Reviewing transaction entries in the Quicken register is as easy as, and more versatile than, flipping through the pages of a manual register. You can scroll through the register to see all the recorded transactions or use the Find feature to search for a specific transaction. You can also focus on transactions for a specific time period with the Go to Date feature.

Scrolling Through the Register

Once you enter a number of transactions in the register you may not be able to see all of them on your screen at the same time. You can use either the mouse or the keyboard to scroll through your entries.

If you want to work with the mouse you will use the scroll bar and the scroll box or arrows labeled in Figure 2-5. You can drag the scroll box up or down to change the transactions displayed on the screen. Dragging requires you to move the mouse pointer to the box and move it up or down while pressing the left mouse button. You can move it to any location within the scroll bar. The scroll bar length represents the length of all your transactions in the register. This means that moving the box to the top will put you at the top of the register and moving it to the middle of the bar will place you about at the mid-point of your register entries. You can also click the scroll arrows at the top and bottom of the register to move at a slower pace through the register.

If you prefer the keyboard to the mouse, you can put some of the keys introduced in Chapter 1 to work in the Quicken register. You can probably guess the effects that some of the keys will have from their names. The ↑ and ↓ keys move the highlighting up or down a transaction. Quicken scrolls information off the screen to show additional transactions not formerly in view. Once a transaction is highlighted, the → and ← keys move across the current transaction. The Pg Up and Pg Dn keys move up and down one screen at a time.

The functions of some keys vary between releases of Quicken; some key functions are not as obvious as those just discussed. The following examples show how the keys work in Quicken 7.

The Home key moves the cursor to the beginning of the current field in a transaction. When Home is pressed twice, the cursor moves to the beginning of the current transaction. If you press Home three times or press Ctrl-Home, Quicken moves the cursor to the top of the register.

The End key moves the cursor to the end of the current field. If you press End twice, Quicken moves the cursor to the last field in the current transaction. If you press End a third time or press Ctrl-End, Quicken moves the cursor to the bottom of the register.

Pressing Ctrl-Pg Up moves the highlight to the beginning of the current month. Pressing it a second time moves the highlight to the beginning of the previous month. Pressing Ctrl-Pg Dn moves the highlight to the first transaction in the next month. You can use the mouse rather than the keyboard to scroll in the register. The following mouse actions will help you locate the place you want to be quickly:

- Click the vertical scroll bar arrows to scroll to the next or previous transaction.
- Hold the mouse button down on the scroll bar to move quickly through the transactions.
- Click above or below the scroll box to move up or down one page of transactions.
- Drag the scroll box up or down in the scroll bar to move to a different location.

As you enter more transactions, the value of knowing quick ways to move between transactions will become more apparent.

Using the Find Feature

Quicken's Find feature allows you to locate a specific transaction easily. You can find a transaction by entering a minimal amount of information from the transaction on a special Find window. Activate the Find window with the Quick key Ctrl-F or press Alt-E to activate the Edit menu and then select **F**ind. The Edit menu displays all the Quick key sequences such as Ctrl-F for Find.

Quicken can look for an exact match entry in any field with a forward or backward search. You can also use Quicken's wildcard feature to locate a transaction with only part of the information from a field. After looking at the examples in the next two sections, you can refer to the rules for finding entries in Table 2-2.

Finding Matching Entries

To look for a transaction that exactly matches data, all you need to do is fill in some data in the window. Quicken will search for entries in the Num, Payee, Memo, Category, Payment, C, or Deposit field. You do not need to worry about capitalization of your data entry since Quicken is not case sensitive. When you enter the data for your first Find operation, the fields will be blank. For subsequent Find operations you can edit the data in the

2

Locating transactions
Table 2-2.

Entry	Quicken Finds
electric	electric, Electric, ELECTRIC, electric power, Electric Company, Consumer Power Electric, new electric
=Electric	Electric, ELECTRIC, electric
~electric	groceries, gas—anything but electric
e..c	electric, eccentric
s?n	sun, sin, son—any single letter between an *s* and an *n*
..	ice, fire, and anything else except blanks
~..	all transactions with a blank in that field

window, type over what's there, or clear the entire window by pressing Ctrl-D and beginning again with blank fields. For example, to locate a specific check number in the 1st U.S. Bank register developed earlier, complete the following steps:

1. Press Ctrl-Home or drag the scroll box to the top of the scroll bar.

This ensures that you start at the beginning of the register so you can conduct a complete forward search through the data. (Quicken also supports a backward search to allow you to locate entries above the currently highlighted transaction.)

2. Choose **F**ind from the **E**dit menu.

   You can press Alt-E to open the Edit menu to make your selection or you can click it with your mouse.
3. Move the cursor to the Num field by pressing the ← key five times and type **103**.
4. Press Ctrl-N or click Ctrl-N at the bottom of the screen to find the next matching transaction. Quicken closes the Find window and highlights the transaction.

Quicken started the search with the current transaction and proceeded toward the bottom of the register attempting to find matching transactions, in this case the one with 103 in the Num field. You could have entered data in other fields in the Find window if you wanted to specify multiple criteria for locating transactions. You might make entries for the Date, Payee, and Memo fields all in one Find window. Quicken finds only the transactions that match all of your entries.

The more transactions in the register, the more useful Quicken's Find capability becomes. For instance, you might want to find all the transactions involving a specific payee or all the transactions on a certain date. Visually scanning through hundreds of transactions could take a long time and you could still miss a matching transaction. Quicken makes no mistakes and finds the matching transactions quickly.

You can also speed up the search process by bypassing the Edit menu and using the Quick keys for your Find selections. Let's perform a second Find operation, one that begins the search with the current transaction and searches back toward the first entry in the register. To use the Quick keys to do this, follow these steps:

1. Press Ctrl-F to open the Find window. (This approach replaces opening the Edit menu and selecting Find.)
2. Type **100**.

   You can also press Ctrl-D or click the Ctrl-D option with your mouse when you first open the Find window to clear it of all entries.
3. Press Ctrl-B to search backward through the entries and highlight the transaction for check number 100.

If you were performing a search in which several transactions might match your entry, you could continue to search with repeated presses of Ctrl-N (forward) or Ctrl-B (backward) after completing the entries in the Find window.

Key Word Search

You can enter a less than exact match and still locate the desired transactions if you search the Payee, Category, or Memo field. Quicken will locate any entry that contains the text you type. To look for an exact match, you must precede your entry with an = (equal sign), or change Set **P**references, **T**ransaction Settings, and Exact matches on finds and filters to Y. Try this for a quick look at the Key Word Search feature:

1. Press Ctrl-F to open the Find window.
2. Press Ctrl-D to clear all the entries from this window.
3. Type **Small** in the Payee field.
4. Press Ctrl-N to search from the current location toward the end of the document. Quicken highlights the next entry for "Small City Times."

If you continue to press Ctrl-N, Quicken moves through the transaction list, highlighting each entry containing "Small." After you have found all matching transactions, pressing Ctrl-N again causes Quicken to display a message indicating there are no more matching transactions. You can press Enter to search from the beginning of the register or Esc to end the search.

Searching for Multiple Entries

You can use multiple key word search entries in a Find window or combine the Key Word Search feature with exact match entries. As an example, follow these steps to look for transactions with "Market" in the Payee field, a payment of 22.32, and "Groceries" for the category entry:

1. Press Ctrl-Home to move to the beginning of the register.
2. Press Ctrl-F to open the Find window.
3. Press Ctrl-Backspace to clear the Payee field.
4. Type **Market** in the Payee field and press Enter.
5. Type **22.32** in the Payment field and press Enter two times.
6. Type **Groceries** in the Category field. Your Find entries should look like this:

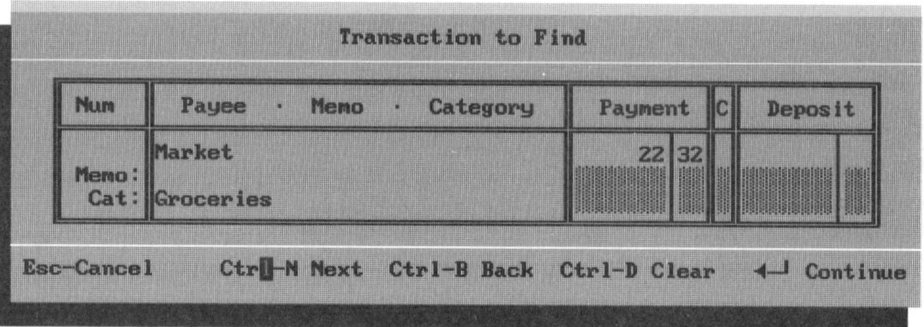

7. Press Ctrl-N.

Your transaction for Small City Market should be highlighted. Press Ctrl-N again to repeat the forward search. Quicken displays the message indicating that there are no further matches.

8. Press Esc to end the search.

Using the Go to Date Feature

You may sometimes want to find one or more transactions for a given date. The Go to Date feature allows you to locate the first transaction entry for a specified date. You can use either the Choose **G**o to Date option from the **E**dit menu or press Ctrl-G to begin a date search.

When the window opens, fill in the date that you are searching for. A date search works a little differently than Find since you do not have to be concerned with whether the date is before or after the current transaction. The following steps illustrate a date search:

1. Press Ctrl-Home. Then select Ctrl-G to open the Go to Date window.
2. Type **1/7/94**, as shown here:

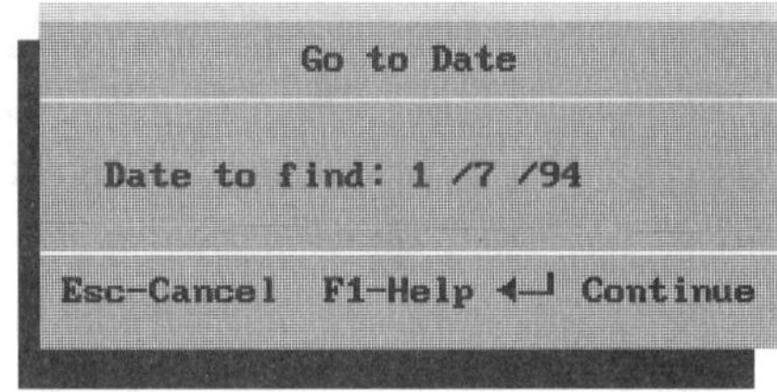

and press Enter. Quicken goes to the first transaction for the date you entered.

You could now examine all the remaining transactions for the date by pressing ↓.

Revising Transactions

You have already learned how to make revisions to transactions in the check register as you are recording a transaction, but sometimes you may need to make changes to previously recorded transactions. It is important to note that although Quicken allows you to modify previously recorded transactions, you cannot change the balance amount without entering another transaction. This protects you from unauthorized changes in the register account balances. By forcing you to enter another transaction, Quicken is able to maintain a log of any change to an account balance.

You may also find it necessary to void a previously written check, deposit, or any other adjustment to an account. Voiding removes the effect of the original transaction from the account balance, although it maintains the history of the original transaction and shows it as voided. To remove all traces of the original transaction, you must use Quicken's Delete Transaction command. You can use either Quick keys or selections from Quicken's Edit menu to void and delete transactions. To reinstate voided transactions, you delete the word "VOID" and the X in the C column (which was entered automatically), reenter the transaction amount, and press Ctrl-Enter to finalize the change.

Changing a Previous Transaction

The following steps must be used when changing a previously recorded transaction:

1. Move to the desired transaction.
2. Then use the same techniques discussed in the "Making Revisions to the Current Transaction" section of this chapter.

Quicken does not allow you to change the balance amount directly. You need to enter another transaction to make an adjustment. Another option is to void the original transaction and enter a new transaction.

Voiding a Transaction

When you void a transaction, you undo the financial effect of the transaction. Using the Void operation creates an automatic audit trail (or record) of all transactions against an account, including those that have already been voided. Let's try the Void option with check number 100; follow these steps:

1. Move the highlighting to check number 100.
2. Press Ctrl-V and select Void Transaction to void the current transaction or choose **V**oid Transaction from the **E**dit menu.

Another option is pressing Alt-E and selecting **V**oid Transaction from the Edit menu. With either approach, the word "VOID" is now entered in front of the payee name, as shown in Figure 2-10.

3. Press Esc to return to the Main Menu. Quicken displays the Leaving Transaction window.
4. Press Enter to select item 1, record changes, and leave.

If after voiding a transaction you want to continue to work in the check register, you can move to the category field by using Tab, Enter, or the arrow keys. Press Enter one more time to select item 1, Record transaction, from the OK to Record Transaction? window. If you change your mind and do not want to void the transaction, you can highlight item 2, Do not record, before pressing Enter.

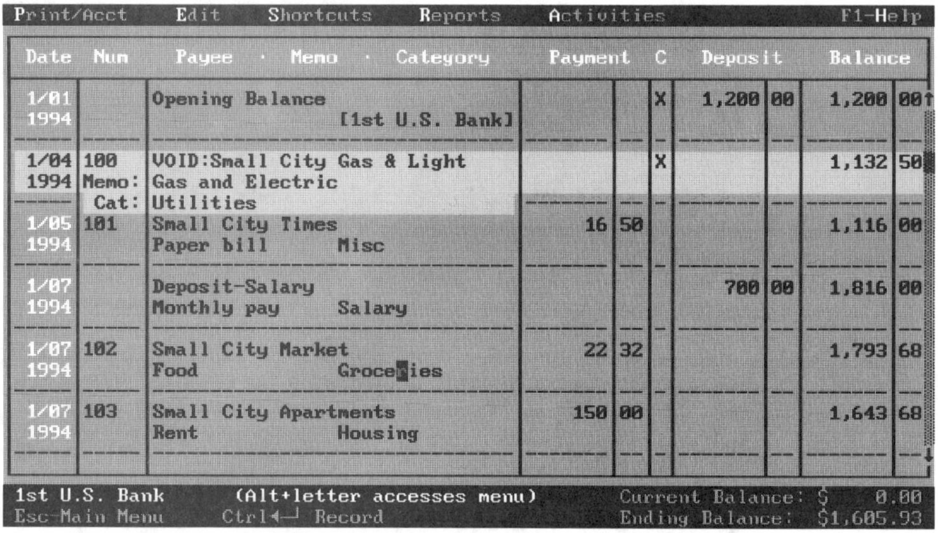

Print/Acct   Edit   Shortcuts   Reports   Activities   F1-Help

Date	Num	Payee · Memo · Category	Payment		C	Deposit		Balance	
1/01 1994		Opening Balance [1st U.S. Bank]			X	1,200	00	1,200	00
1/04 1994	100 Memo: Cat:	VOID:Small City Gas & Light Gas and Electric Utilities			X			1,132	50
1/05 1994	101	Small City Times Paper bill Misc	16	50				1,116	00
1/07 1994		Deposit-Salary Monthly pay Salary				700	00	1,816	00
1/07 1994	102	Small City Market Food Groceries	22	32				1,793	68
1/07 1994	103	Small City Apartments Rent Housing	150	00				1,643	68

1st U.S. Bank   (Alt+letter accesses menu)   Current Balance: $ 0.00
Esc-Main Menu   Ctrl◄┘ Record   Ending Balance: $1,605.93

Voided transaction
Figure 2-10.

Deleting a Transaction

You can delete a transaction with Ctrl-D or by opening the Edit menu with Alt-E and selecting **D**elete transaction. Try this now by deleting the voided transaction for check number 100.

1. If you are at the Main Menu, open the Register window again by selecting Use **R**egister and pressing Enter.
2. Move the highlighting to the voided transaction for check number 100.
3. Press Ctrl-D to delete the transaction. Quicken displays the Caution Modifying A Reconciled Transaction window.

This displays because a voided transaction has an X in the C column just like a transaction marked as cleared when you reconcile you account.

4. Press Enter to confirm the deletion.

Reinstating a Transaction

There is no "undo" key to eliminate the effect of a delete; you must reenter the transaction. For practice, reinstate the transaction for check number 100 with these steps:

1. Press Ctrl-End or drag the scroll box to the bottom of the scroll bar to move to the end of the register.

2. Type **1/4/94** and press Enter to set the date to 1/4/1994.
3. Type **100** and press Enter to supply the check number in the Num field.
4. Type **Small City Gas & Light** and press Enter to complete the entry for the payee for this check.
5. Type **67.50** and press Enter.
6. Type **Gas and Electric** and press Enter.
7. Type **Utilities** and press Enter to complete the transaction.
8. Press Enter when the OK to Record Transaction? window displays. The transaction is reentered into the register.

You can see from this example that you expended a considerable amount of effort to rerecord this transaction. Avoid unnecessary work by confirming the void or deletion before you complete it.

CHAPTER

investments banking FILE register expenses DEDUCTIONS
tips finances equity net pay
checks statements bank statements
dividends assets business tips
INCOME cash flow
banking business tips FILE reports
budget FILE business tips checks
DEDUCTIONS tips mortgage
statements cash flow
net pay taxes bank revenue
business tips
mortgage cash dividends tips
business investments
register statements
business tips taxes
expenses tips
equity investments INCOME
statements bank cash
checks assets checks budget tips finances net pay

3 QUICKEN REPORTS

In Chapter 2, "Making Register Entries," you discovered how easy it is to enter transactions in the Quicken system. In this chapter you find out about another major benefit—the ability to generate reports. These reports present your data in an organized format that allows you to analyze the data. With Quicken 7, a Report menu allows you to customize a report while viewing it and to zoom in for a closeup look at details. You can use Quicken to produce a quick printout of the register or create reports that analyze and summarize data. Some of these reports, such as the Cash Flow report and the Itemized Categories report, would require a significant amount of work if they were compiled manually. This chapter focuses on these basic types of reports and some customizing options. More complex report types are covered in later chapters.

Before looking at the various reports, let's look first at how Quicken works with printers. Although Quicken supports most popular printers without any special effort on your part, you should know a few of the essentials of printers. This chapter teaches you how to change the basic print settings if Quicken does not create acceptable output with the current configuration. You can define three different printers or predefine three different options for one printer.

Default Printer Settings

Quicken is preset to interface with most of the popular printers, including IBM compatibles; Hewlett-Packard LaserJets, DeskJet, and ThinkJet; IBM ProPrinter and 4216; Epson; NEC 3530 and 8023A; and Okidata 83, 92, 182, 192, 292, and 320. Default parameters set the number of characters per inch, the paper type, and the standard port on your machine for connecting the first printer. If you have one of the printers listed here or a model that mimics one of them, you will be able to print your Quicken reports without making any changes. If your printer is producing less than acceptable results or you want to use settings different than the default, consult "Changing the Printer Settings" at the end of this chapter. If not, Quicken will probably interface with your printer, and you will not need to make any changes to the Quicken printer settings after you complete the installation for Quicken described in Appendix A.

Printing the Check Register

Although it is convenient to enter transactions on the screen, a printout of your entries is often easier to review and much more portable than a computer screen. Try printing the register first without changing the print settings. If your output is very different from the sample shown in this chapter, try customizing your print settings and then print the register again. You will find instructions for making these changes at the end of this chapter. To print your register, follow these steps:

1. Choose Use **R**egister from Quicken's Main Menu.

   Your latest register transactions should appear on the screen.
2. Select **P**rint/Acct from the menu at the top of the screen.

Whether you click the pull-down menu option, type the highlighted letter, or highlight the menu option and press Enter, the menu shown in Figure 3-1 is displayed.

3. Select **P**rint Register.

   Alternatively, pressing Ctrl-P opens the Print Register window directly, without first going through the Print/Acct menu. Figure 3-2 shows the Print Register window. Depending on your installation selections, your screen might show different printer options.

4. Type **1/1/94** and press Enter.

   This entry selects the first transaction to be printed by date.

5. Type **1/31/94** and press Enter.

   This entry establishes the last transaction to be printed. The dates supplied in steps 4 and 5 are inclusive; that is, Quicken will print all register transactions with dates from 1/1/94 through 1/31/94.

6. Select 1, for Report Printer, and press Enter to tell Quicken where to print the output from the print operation.

   This is the default option—the selection Quicken makes unless you designate another option. You can print to four different print options: (1) a report printer, (2) an alternative report printer (a second printer or a different print option for the first printer, such as landscape or compressed), (3) a check printer, or (4) an ASCII file on disk. Quicken allows you to select different print options for different types of output. Thus, for a quick draft of a report you might select the alternative

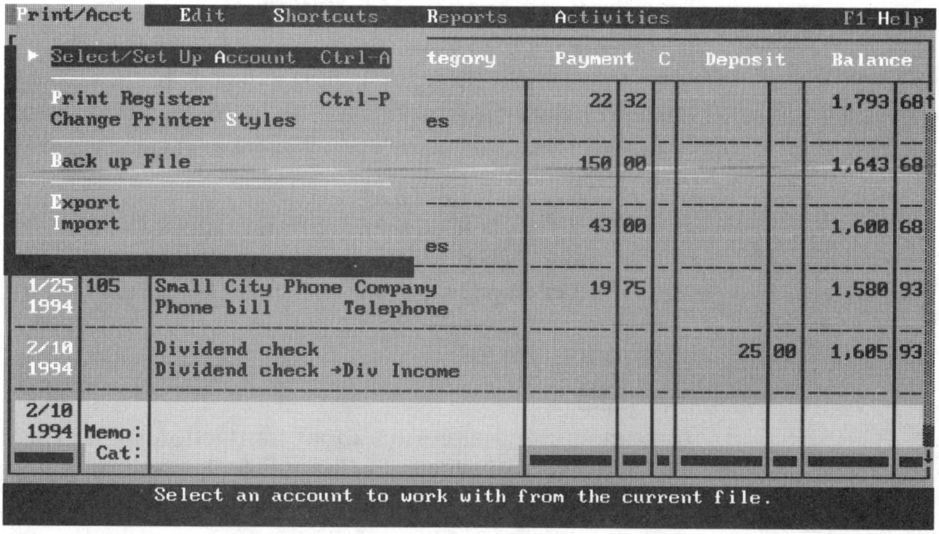

```
Print/Acct   Edit   Shortcuts   Reports   Activities                F1-Help
 ▸ Select/Set Up Account  Ctrl-A   tegory    Payment  C  Deposit    Balance
   Print Register         Ctrl-P              22 32               1,793 68
   Change Printer Styles            es
   Back up File                              150 00               1,643 68
   Export
   Import                                     43 00               1,600 68
                                    es
 1/25  105  Small City Phone Company          19 75               1,580 93
 1994       Phone bill       Telephone
 2/10       Dividend check                             25 00     1,605 93
 1994       Dividend check →Div Income
 2/10
 1994 Memo:
       Cat:
          Select an account to work with from the current file.
```

Print/Acct menu
Figure 3-1.

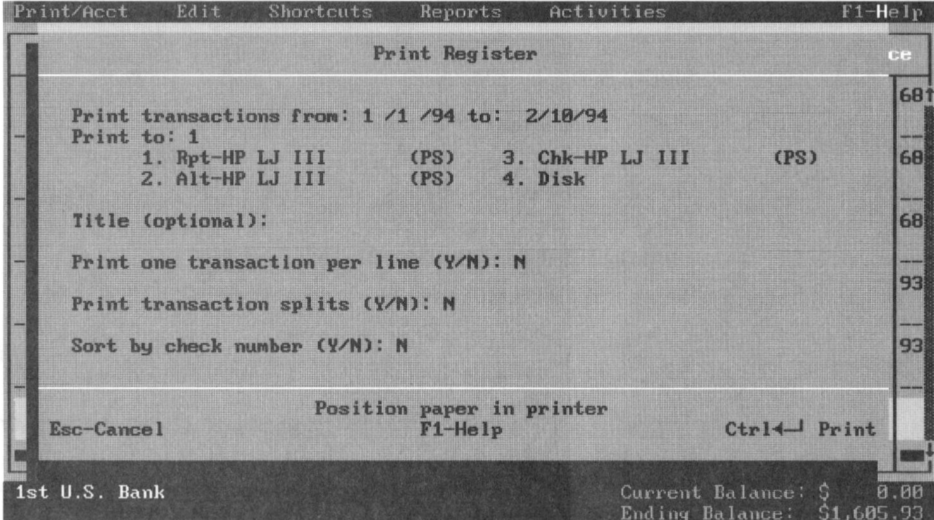

Print Register window items and options
Figure 3-2.

printer, a high-speed device of marginal quality, and later choose a report printer to print the final copy on a laser printer. You will learn how to select these printing options in the "Changing the Printer Settings" section later in the chapter.

Selecting option 4, Disk, creates an ASCII text file for exporting Quicken data to other computer programs. You would use the Disk option if you wanted to use the data from the register in your word processor or some other program that can read ASCII text files.

7. Type **January Transactions** and press Enter.

   This customizes the title of the check register. If you do not make an entry in this field, Quicken uses the default option Check Register for the report heading. You can use up to 36 characters to customize your heading.

8. Press Enter.

   This selects Quicken's default option to allow three lines for each transaction Quicken prints. If you want to have more transactions printed on each page, type **Y** and press Enter. This option prints the document using only one line per transaction by abbreviating the information printed.

9. Press Enter.

   You can ignore the prompt about transaction splits. This type of transaction is introduced in Chapter 6, "Expanding the Scope of Financial Entries." For now, leave the default setting as N.

10. Press Enter again to accept the default option for Sort by check number.

    With a setting of N, Quicken prints the register in order by date and then by check number. If you want to sort by check number first and then by date, type **Y** and press Enter. If you are writing checks from two different checkbooks, changing this option can affect the order in which transactions are listed.

11. Press Ctrl-Enter.

    Once you complete the Print Register window, Quicken is ready to print the check register for the period you defined. Make sure your printer is turned on and ready to print before completing this entry.

Your printed register should look like the sample transactions shown in Figure 3-3. Notice that the date at the top-left corner of your report is the current date, regardless of the month for which you are printing transactions.

NOTE: For an even quicker look at selected register transactions, move to a field in a register transaction and press Alt-Z. This Quick Reports feature will display all transactions matching the current field.

```
                                   January Transactions
1st U.S. Bank                                                                  Page 1
2/14/94

 Date   Num          Transaction              Payment  C   Deposit    Balance
-----  ----- ---------------------------- ---------- - ---------- ----------
 1/01        Opening Balance                           X   1,200.00   1,200.00
 1994  memo:
        cat: [1st U.S. Bank]

 1/04  100   Small City Gas & Light            67.50                  1,132.50
 1994  memo: Gas and Electric
        cat: Utilities

 1/05  101   Small City Times                  16.50                  1,116.00
 1994  memo: Paper bill
        cat: Misc

 1/07        Deposit-Salary                                 700.00  1,816.00
 1994  memo: Monthly pay
        cat: Salary

 1/07  102   Small City Market                 22.32                  1,793.68
 1994  memo: Food
        cat: Groceries

 1/07  103   Small City Apartments            150.00                  1,643.68
 1994  memo: Rent
        cat: Housing
```

1st U.S. Bank checking account register printout
Figure 3-3.

Printing the Cash Flow Report

The Cash Flow report generated by Quicken compares the money you have received during a specified time period with the money you have spent. Quicken provides this information for each category used in the register. In addition, the Cash Flow report will combine transactions from your Bank, Cash, and Credit Card accounts. (Cash and Credit Card accounts are discussed in Chapter 6.) Preparing the Cash Flow report for the transactions you recorded in the 1st U.S. Bank account in Chapter 2, "Making Register Entries," involves the following steps from the Main Menu:

1. Select **C**reate Reports.

   You can also access the Reports menu directly from the register by selecting the menu title **R**eports. You will see a pull-down menu offering options for standard personal, business, and investments reports, as well as custom reports.

2. Select **H**ome Reports from the Reports menu.

   Quicken then allows you to define the type of report you want from the pull-down menu added to the screen.

3. Select **C**ash Flow.

   You will see the Cash Flow Report window, as shown here:

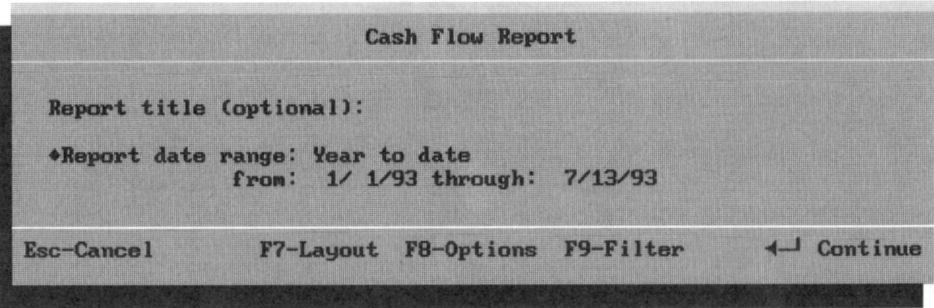

4. Type **Cash Flow Report** -, press Spacebar, then type your name and press Enter.

   If you press Enter without making an entry, Quicken uses the default title for the report. With this report, the default title is "Cash Flow Report." If you choose to personalize the report, you can use up to 39 characters for a report title.

When you finalize the report name entry, Quicken displays a list of reporting period options. With your own data you will probably select something like Last Month, This Month, or Year To Date, but with this sample data the only way to ensure that you see the same reports shown on the disk is to select Custom Date as the reporting period.

5. Select Custom Date from the list of reporting period options and press Enter.

   You can double-click Custom Date or highlight it and press Enter.

6. Press Enter, then change your beginning report date to 1/1/94 and press Enter.

   Quicken automatically places the beginning of the current year's date in this space. You need to decide whether to type a new date or press + or -, depending on the current date in your system.
7. Change your report ending date to 1/31/94.
8. Press Enter, and the Cash Flow report appears on your screen. (The entire report does not appear on your screen.)
9. Press ↓ to bring the rest of the report to the screen.

NOTE: The Cash Flow report has inflows and outflows listed by category.

10. Move the highlight to the outflow for groceries.
11. Press Ctrl-Z to use Quicken 7's Zoom feature, which lets you look at the transactions that make up the 65.32 shown for groceries. The screen in Figure 3-4 shows the grocery transactions displayed with the Zoom feature.
12. Press Esc to return to the report.

    You can continue to examine the details for any of the entries and print the report when you have finished.
13. Select the **F**ile/Print menu and then select **P**rint Report.

    This brings the Print Report window to your screen. You need to select the type of printer you are using. The default option is the standard report printer.

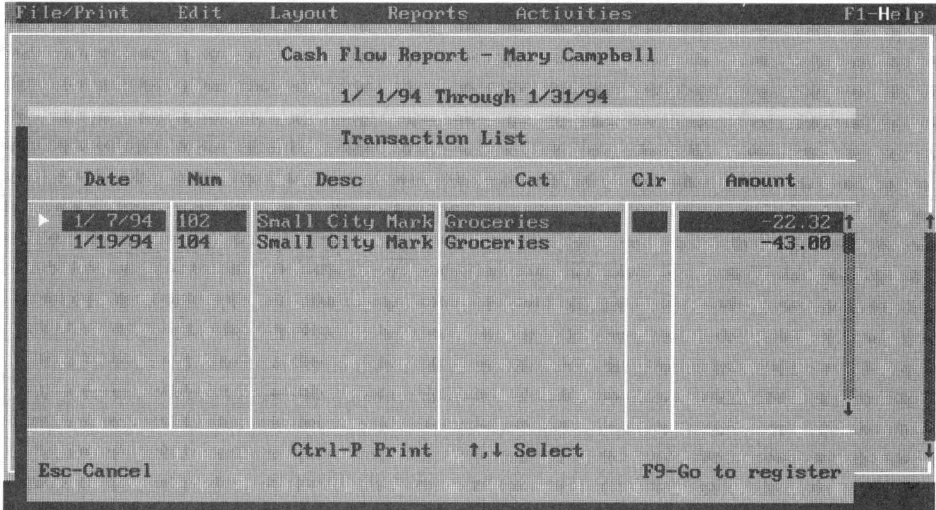

Using Quicken's Zoom feature
Figure 3-4.

NOTE: Ctrl-P is the quick key for printing without menu selections.

14. Press Ctrl-Enter to select the Report Printer default option, as well as other defaults. The report shown in Figure 3-5 is printed.

    You can choose to have Quicken send the Cash Flow report to (1) the report printer, (2) an alternative report printer, (3) a check printer, (4) a disk, as an ASCII file, or (5) a disk, as a 1-2-3 file. If you need to customize any of the printer settings, press F9 (Set Up Printer) before accepting any of the options. This lets you specify a custom report printer or alternative report printer and then select this new option from the menu. Use ← or → to select the printer options listed.
15. To leave the report, press Esc until you get to the Main Menu.

Redoing the Last Report

Quicken remembers the last report that you defined and lets you redo it easily, whether you have zoomed in to focus on detail or added transactions. The following steps demonstrate how you can view the Cash Flow report from the Main Menu with Quicken 7's Redo Last Report feature:

1. Select **C**reate Reports.

```
                    Cash Flow Report - Mary Campbell
                       1/ 1/94 Through 1/31/94
QDATA-1st U.S. Bank                                                  Page 1
2/14/94
                                                1/ 1/94-
                    Category Description        1/31/94
                  ----------------------- -----------
                  INFLOWS
                    Salary Income                 700.00
                                          -----------
                  TOTAL INFLOWS                   700.00

                  OUTFLOWS
                    Groceries                      65.32
                    Housing                       150.00
                    Miscellaneous                  16.50
                    Telephone Expense              19.75
                    Water, Gas, Electric           67.50
                                          -----------
                  TOTAL OUTFLOWS                  319.07

                                          -----------
                  OVERALL TOTAL                   380.93
```

Standard Cash Flow report
Figure 3-5.

2. Select **R**edo Last Report.

Presto!—the Cash Flow report reappears on your screen.

Printing the Itemized Categories Report

The Itemized Categories report lists and summarizes all the transactions for each category used in the register during a specific time period. Although here you will be using this report to work only with the information in the 1st U.S. Bank checking account, the report is much more sophisticated than it might appear. It summarizes information from your Bank, Cash, and Credit Card accounts and, unlike the Cash Flow report, also incorporates category information from Other Asset and Other Liability accounts, which you will establish in Chapter 6, "Expanding the Scope of Financial Entries."

You can print your Itemized Categories report by following these steps (starting from the Main Menu):

1. Select **C**reate Reports.
2. Select **H**ome Reports.
3. Select **I**temized Categories.
4. If the title field of the Itemized Categories Report window is blank, press Enter. If not, press Ctrl-Backspace to erase it and then press Enter.

This action selects the Quicken default title of "Itemized Category Report." You could also personalize the report title by typing **Itemized Category Report**—and your name and pressing Enter.

5. Select Custom Date from the list of report period options. You can undo this quickly by pressing End followed by Enter.
6. Type **1/1/94** and press Enter.

   Quicken automatically places in this window either the current year's beginning date or the date of the last report you created. You could also change the date with the special date change keys, + and -.
7. Type **1/31/94**.

   This tells Quicken to create a report of itemized categories through the end of January.
8. Press Enter.

   This brings the Itemized Categories report to the screen. You can scroll down the report by using ↓.
9. Press Ctrl-P.

   This opens the Print Report window on your screen.
10. Press Enter to print the Itemized Categories report.

    You have the same options here that you had with the Cash Flow report. By pressing Enter, you select the Report printer option. Once again, you could have selected printing to an alternative report printer or a check printer or created an ASCII file or a 1-2-3 file. Pressing Enter prints the Itemized Categories report. Note that the report is two pages long. If your printer has the compressed print capacity, you may want to print your reports in that mode to capture more of the report on each page. The top of page 1 of the Itemized Categories report is shown in Figure 3-6.
11. To leave the report, press Esc until you are in the Main Menu.

Format Options with the Cash Flow and Itemized Categories Reports

When printing both the Cash Flow and Itemized Categories reports, you have several customization options. These are not like the custom reports discussed in later chapters, since you can make only limited modifications. In most situations these options will meet your needs, but remember that you can access help on each of the options once you open the Customizing window. Just as in other areas of Quicken, you get help by pressing F1.

Although the customizing options for the reports require a little time to learn, the end result can be a dramatic difference in the appearance and

```
                           ITEMIZED CATEGORY REPORT
                            1/ 1/94 Through 1/31/94
QDATA-All Accounts                                                       Page 1
2/14/94

 Date   Acct     Num     Description       Memo       Category     Clr Amount
 ----- -------- ------ ---------------- ----------- --------------- - ---------

       INCOME/EXPENSE
         INCOME
           Salary Income
           -------------
 1/ 7 1st U.S.        Deposit-Salary   Monthly pay Salary                700.00
                                                                      ---------
           Total Salary Income                                           700.00
                                                                      ---------
         TOTAL INCOME                                                    700.00


         EXPENSES
           Groceries
           ---------
 1/ 7 1st U.S. 102    Small City Marke Food        Groceries             -22.32
 1/19 1st U.S. 104    Small City Marke Food        Groceries             -43.00
                                                                      ---------
           Total Groceries                                               -65.32
```

Itemized Categories report
Figure 3-6.

content of the reports. Since the customization options for the Cash Flow and Itemized Categories reports are similar, the important options are covered together. You can use them to change the labeling information on the report, as well as the basic organization of the entries.

Changing the Column Headings

Quicken allows you to change the column headings on both the Itemized Categories and Cash Flow reports. You can print a report for the standard monthly time period or change it to one week, two weeks, half a month, a quarter, half a year, or one year. You make this change from the Create Summary Report window, shown in Figure 3-7. Figure 3-8 shows a report created with time periods used as the column headings.

Follow these steps to create a Cash Flow report showing weekly time periods (starting from the Main Menu):

1. Select **C**reate Report.
2. Select **H**ome Reports.
3. Select **C**ash Flow.
4. Type **Cash Flow**—and your name and press Enter.

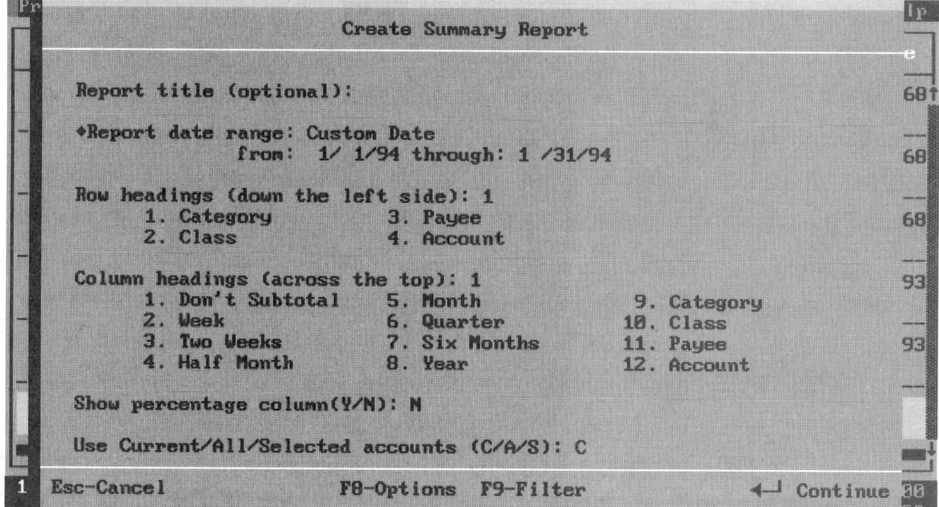

Create Summary Report window to customize a Cash Flow report
Figure 3-7.

5. Select Custom Date from the list of reporting period options and press Enter or click in the next field.
6. Type **1/1/94** and press Enter.

   You can just press Enter if you used this same time period for your last report.

Cash Flow - Mary Campbell
1/ 1/94 Through 1/31/94

QDATA-All Accounts Page 1
2/14/94

Category Description	1/01- 1/15	1/16- 1/31	OVERALL TOTAL
INFLOWS			
Salary Income	700.00	0.00	700.00
TOTAL INFLOWS	700.00	0.00	700.00
OUTFLOWS			
Groceries	22.32	43.00	65.32
Housing	150.00	0.00	150.00
Miscellaneous	16.50	0.00	16.50
Telephone Expense	0.00	19.75	19.75
Water, Gas, Electric	67.50	0.00	67.50
TOTAL OUTFLOWS	256.32	62.75	319.07
OVERALL TOTAL	443.68	-62.75	380.93

Cash flow with half-month column option
Figure 3-8.

7. Type **1/31/94** again, but do not press Enter.

   Pressing Enter creates the report without customizing.

8. Press F7 (Layout) to open the Create Summary Report window.

   Quicken responds to your request by displaying the Create Summary Report window, shown in Figure 3-7. Notice that the heading and the dates from the previous screen are still displayed. You can make further changes if needed or press Enter five times to move to the Column Headings field.

9. Select Half Month and press Enter.

   Your selection of Half Month for the column heading will cause the data to be split into two columns plus a total. You can also change the row headings. Your options for row headings are payee, account, category, or class.

10. Press Enter to accept the current N setting for show % column.

    If you change this setting to Y, Quicken will add another column to the report to show the percent of the total for each entry.

11. Type **A** to select **A**ll accounts for the last option in the window.

    If you want to make this change with a mouse, you can click this field with the mouse to cycle through the each option.

12. Press Enter to continue.

    Quicken displays the completed report on the screen. Figure 3-8 shows the result of the preceding steps.

Changing the Row Headings

The Create Summary Report window shown in Figure 3-7 also allows you to change the row headings shown in a Cash Flow or Itemized Categories report. Instead of categories as row headings, as in Figure 3-8, one of your options is to change the screen to show the payee in this location. Figure 3-9 shows the report created after changing the Row Headings field to option 3, Payee, and the column heading back to the default, 1.

You can make your changes from the menu at the top of the report. To change the row headings, select **L**ayout, **R**ow Heading, and **P**ayee. Changing the column headings requires you to select **L**ayout, Column **H**eadings, and **O**ne Column. This causes the report to display without any extra columns that subtotal your data.

```
                         Cash Flow - Mary Campbell
                          1/ 1/94 Through 1/31/94
QDATA-All Accounts                                                        Page 1
2/14/94
                                                        1/ 1/94-
                                    Payee                1/31/94
                        ------------------------    -----------
                        Deposit-Salary                   700.00
                        Small City Apartments           -150.00
                        Small City Gas & Light           -67.50
                        Small City Market                -65.32
                        Small City Phone Company         -19.75
                        Small City Times                 -16.50
                                                    -----------
                        OVERALL TOTAL                    380.93
```

Using payee names as row headings
Figure 3-9.

Changing the Report Options

You can also access a second set of options from the Create Summary Report window by pressing F8 (Options) to display the Report Options window for the Cash Flow report. The options allow you to select report organization and determine how transfers are handled. The Report Options window for the Itemized Categories report has a few more items at the bottom than the Cash Flow report, as shown in Figure 3-10.

The Report Organization field allows you to change from the default organization of separate totals for income and expenses to one that shows the cash flow basis.

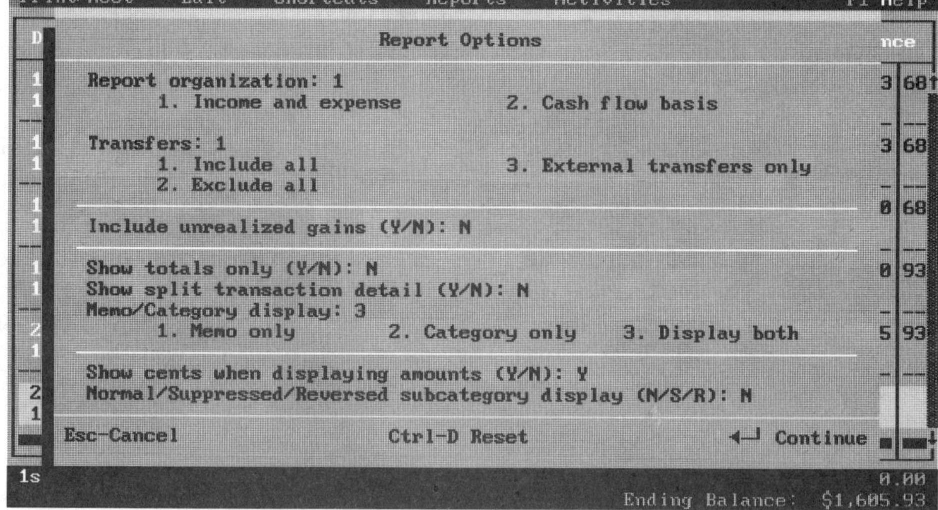

Report Options window for Itemized Categories report
Figure 3-10.

The Transfers field allows you to define how you want your reports to handle transfers between accounts. For example, when Quicken transfers cash from your check register to your savings register, do you want these transfers included or excluded from the individual reports? Transfers will be covered in more detail in Chapter 10, "Creating Custom Reports."

The extra items at the bottom of the Report Options window for the Itemized Categories report allow you to specify that any combination of totals, memos, and categories, or any one of these alone, is shown on the report. Notice that you have the option of showing cents and subcategories in the report form. The default setting for cents is Y. For subcategories, the default setting is N for Normal, which causes subcategories to display.

Filtering Reports

Filters allow you to select the data to be shown on a report. You will want to read the overview that follows and then do the exercise at the end for practice with filters. You can choose to show a specific payee, memo field matches, or category matches. This allows you to create a report for all entries relating to utilities or groceries, for example. You can use a standard report form to display a report for a specific payee, such as Small City Times, or you can enter **Small** to locate records that contain "Small." You open the Filter Report menus from the report menus by pressing the F9 key.

If you want to customize Quicken to find only records that exactly match your entries, you can select Set **P**references and then select **T**ransaction Settings. You need to set option 7, Exact matches on finds and filters, to Y.

The Filter Report option (on the Create Summary Report menu) for the Itemized Categories Report window is shown in Figure 3-11. You might enter **Small** in the Payee field in this window. Processing this request would create a report of all the records with a Payee entry beginning with "Small." This item allows you to modify the printed report further by limiting the report to transactions meeting the following criteria: payee, memo, category, and class.

The Filter Transactions window provides many additional options. You can designate whether to include transactions below, equal to, or above a certain amount. To do this, move to the item Below/Equal/Above by pressing Enter or Tab; typing **B**, **E**, or **A**; and pressing Enter again. Next, enter the amount to be used in the comparison and press Enter.

The next field on the Filter Transactions window allows you to limit printing to payments, deposits, unprinted checks, or all if you enter **P**, **D**, **U**, or **A** in this field.

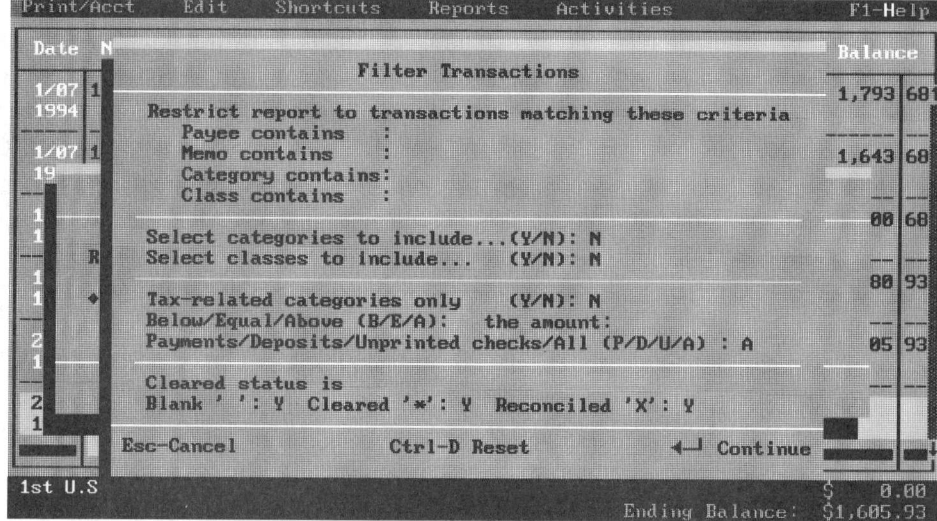

Filter Transactions window for Itemized Categories report
Figure 3-11.

Try Quicken's Filter feature now to create a Cash Flow report for all the transactions that begin with "Small" in the Payee field. From the Main Menu, complete the following steps:

1. Select **C**reate Reports.
2. Select **H**ome Reports.
3. Select **C**ash Flow.
4. Type a new title and press Enter or press Enter without an entry to accept the current title.
5. Select Custom Date for the reporting period and press Enter.
6. Check the From and Through dates and type **1/1/94** and **1/31/94** if the dates do not contain these entries.
7. Press F9 to activate the Filter window.
8. Type **Small** and press Ctrl-Enter to return to the Cash Flow Report window.
9. Press Enter until the report is created.

Since the report shows categories for the row headings, you cannot tell if the correct information is displayed, but you can make a customization to have Quicken list the payee names. With Quicken 7 you can use the menu at the top of the report to make your changes.

1. Select the **L**ayout menu option and then select **R**ow Headings.

2. Select Payee and press Enter.
3. Press Esc until you are back at the Main Menu.

Working with Category Totals

You can create an Itemized Categories report that only shows the totals. To create a total report for January transactions, follow these steps (starting from the Main Menu):

1. Select **C**reate Reports.
2. Select **H**ome Reports.
3. Select **I**temized Categories.
4. Press Enter to accept the default title.
5. Select Custom Date from the list of report period options and press Enter.
6. Type **1/1/94** and press Enter for the From date if the field does not already contain 1/1/94. Type **1/31/94** for the Through date, if it contains a different entry.
7. Press F7 to open the Create Transaction Report window.
8. Press F8 to open the Report Options window.
9. Press Enter or Tab to move to Show totals only and type **Y**.
10. Press Ctrl-Enter to return to the Create Transaction Report window.
11. Press Ctrl-Enter again to create the report.

Wide Reports

Some of the Quicken reports contain too much information to fit across one screen. You encountered a wide-screen report in this chapter when you prepared the Itemized Categories report. Although you cannot see the entire report on the screen at once, you can use the arrow keys to navigate around the screen and change the portion of the report that you are viewing.

Quicken automatically prints wide reports on multiple pages. You can tape the sheets together, or if your printer permits, you can use special features such as landscape printing (with the paper turned sideways) on a laser printer or compressed characters on laser or dot-matrix printers. You will learn how to make these changes to the print settings momentarily. For now, all you need to know is how Quicken handles a report that is too wide for the screen and how you navigate to look at the different parts of the screen.

You can tell when you are viewing a wide report by the border framing that Quicken uses. When a complete report is shown, all the edges are framed.

When only a partial report is displayed, the edges where there is additional information do not have a frame. When you initially view a wide report, there is no frame on the right edge. You will notice the arrows displayed in the lower-right corner of the screen, indicating the report extension.

Moving Around the Screen

You can move around the report by using the arrow keys. In addition, you might want to move quickly around the report by using several other Quicken keystrokes.

- Press Tab to move one field to the right.
- Press Shift-Tab to move one field to the left.
- Press Pg Up to move up one screen.
- Press Pg Dn to move down one screen.
- Press Home twice to move to the upper-left corner of the report.
- Press End twice to move to the lower-right corner of the report.

Remember that you can also use the scroll bars at the side and bottom of a report if you are using a mouse.

Full- and Half-Column Options

The Itemized Categories report allows you to view the Payee, Memo, and Category fields at full or half width. Figure 3-12 shows the report at the default half-column width setting. This allows the report to print across 80 columns and to display on the screen. To expand the columns to full width select **L**ayout and Full Column **W**idth. Once the columns are shown at full width, selecting **L**ayout followed by Half Column **W**idth returns the columns to half width. This kind of key is called a *toggle.*

Printing Wide Reports

Quicken normally prints wide reports by printing in vertical strips, which you can then tape together. You do not have to modify your printing instructions in order to print wide reports.

If your printer supports compressed or landscape printing, you can capture more of a report on a page by using one of these features. Landscape mode prints 104 characters across an 8 1/2 × 11-inch page and compressed print prints 132 characters on an 8 1/2 × 11-inch page (at 10 characters per inch). You can use the Set **P**references option in the Main Menu, or, when the report is displayed on the screen, go to the Print Report window by selecting

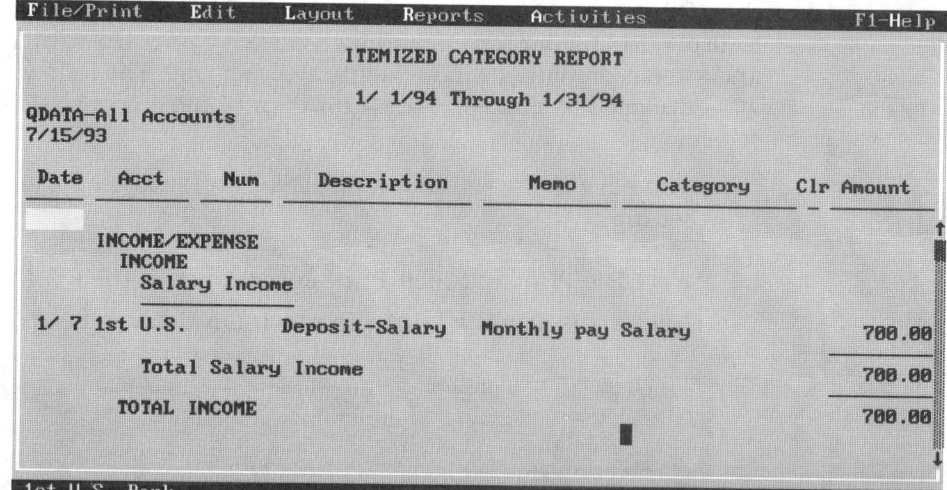

Using the default half-column width display for the Itemized Category report
Figure 3-12.

File/Print, selecting **P**rint Report, pressing F9 (Set Up Printer), selecting Settings for Printing Reports, and choosing a style with more characters per inch (cpi) or Landscape printing.

Changing the Printer Settings

Unless you want to use a special feature or the current settings are not working properly, you can skip this section. If you choose to go through this section, be sure to have your printer manual handy to check the specific features offered by your printer.

Quicken allows you to define four different sets of print settings. These settings are for the report printer, an alternative report printer, a check-writing printer, and a printer for graphs. For most users these settings will refer to the same printer. For other users with several printers accessible from their machine different tasks may be more appropriately performed with different printers. The procedure is identical for modifying any of these options once you choose the one you want to change.

During installation you can select from many popular printers. The preset parameters for a printer are for pitch, paper size, and the parallel printer port 1.

You can change the printer settings by selecting Set **P**references from Quicken's Main Menu and then selecting **P**rinter Settings to alter the print settings. Another way to accomplish the same task is to select **F**ile/Print and then **P**rint Report to open the Print Report window when a Quicken report is displayed on your screen, and then press F9 (Set Up Printer). The menus and screens presented will be identical either way. The following example was developed by changing the settings once the report was displayed on the screen.

Once you have a Quicken report displayed, follow these steps to change the print settings:

1. Select **F**ile/Print and then **P**rint Report to open the Print Report window.

   Quicken displays the Print Report window, shown here:

```
                         Print Report

Print to: 1
      1. Rpt-HP LJ III        (PS)     4. Disk (ASCII file)
      2. Alt-HP LJ III        (PS)     5. Disk (1-2-3 file)
      3. Chk-HP LJ III        (PS)

Print row labels on all pages (Y/N): N
Pages to Print [1-2]:    All

                    Position paper in printer
Esc-Cancel              F9-Set Up Printer                  ↵ Print
```

   If you want to print with one of the default settings, choose option 1 or 2.

2. Press F9 (Set Up Printer).

   From this step on, you will not be able to make the same entries shown in the example. Since each printer is different, you will want to configure Quicken to work with your printer rather than the printer used here. Quicken displays a list of the four printer settings that can be changed: Printing Checks, Printing Reports, Alternate Printing Reports, and Printing Graphs.

3. Select settings for Printing Reports.

   Quicken displays a list of printers and their available styles. You can move in this list with the arrow keys to locate the style you want or press Esc and select another printer from the list, as shown in Figure 3-13. If you select a style with more characters per inch or landscape mode (or both), Quicken alters the report display to correspond to your selection.

4. If you want to change the style, move the cursor to the desired option and press Enter. Quicken displays a screen like the one in Figure 3-14.

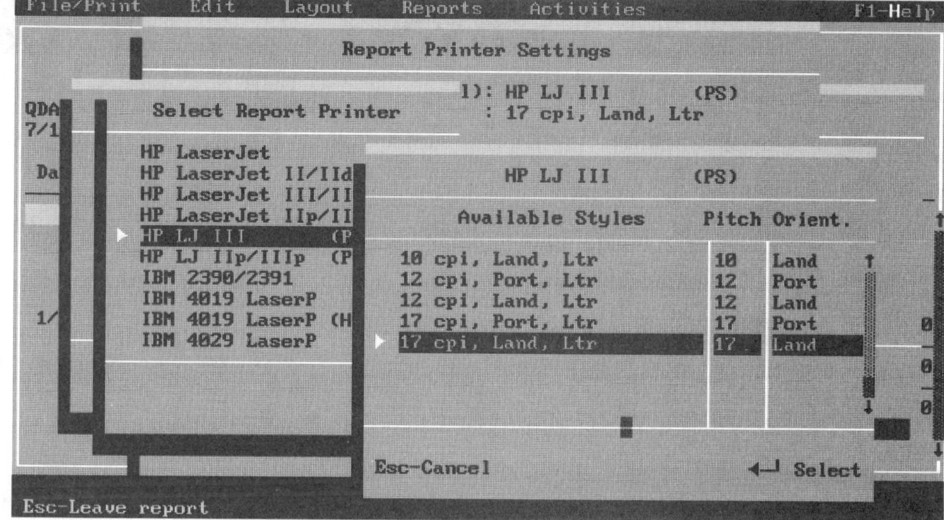

Selecting a printer and style
Figure 3-13.

The default is to print to LPT1, which is the standard port on your machine for connecting the first printer. If you are setting up a second printer, you need to know whether it is attached to LPT2 or some other port. Other settings on the Report Printer Settings window let you set the lines per page, characters per line, print pitch, and a pause between pages. Table 3-1 lists some hints for altering these settings, although your printer manual will be your specific reference source.

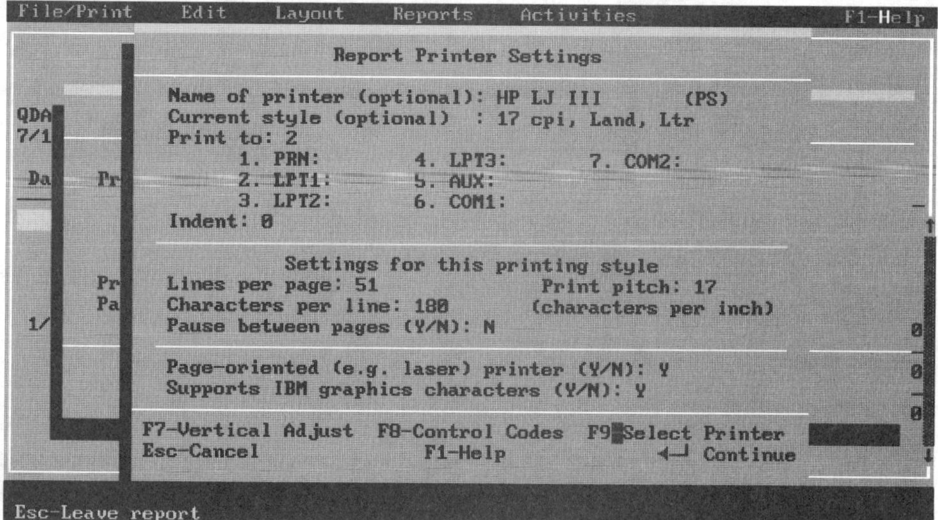

HP Laser Jet II control codes generated by Quicken
Figure 3-14.

Problem	Solution
Output too wide for a page	Use compressed or landscape mode
No form feed at the end of the report	Change the print control codes
Partial blank page left in printer	Check the page length
Unreadable output	Wrong printer is selected
Strange characters print	Printer cable is loose or incorrect printer type selected
Unable to access font cartridges	Set control codes for desired print options

Printing Problems and Possible Solutions
Table 3-2.

NOTE: If you want to change the printer rather than the style, press Esc, select a new printer, select a style, and press Enter.

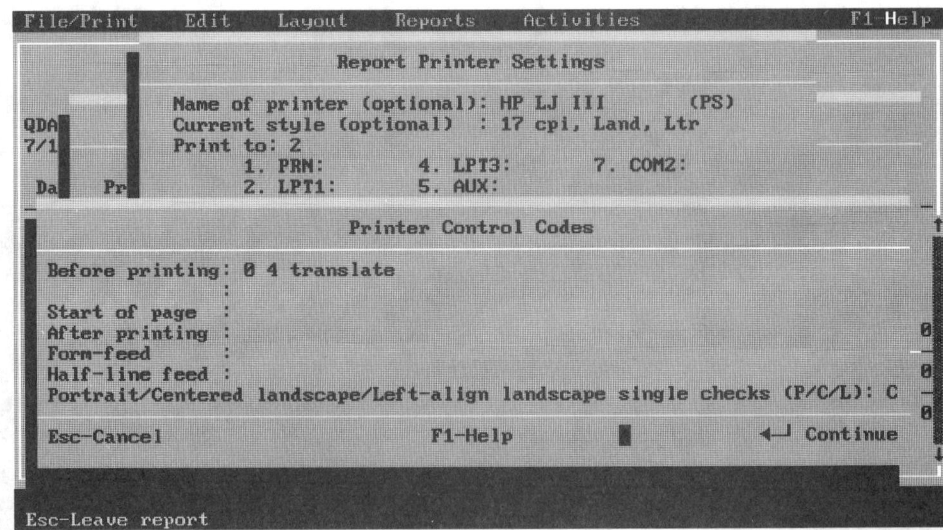

Choosing specific print settings
Figure 3-15.

5. Press F8 (Control Codes) to display the control codes that are transmitted to your printer every time you print.

   Figure 3-15 provides an example of printer control codes generated by Quicken for the HP LaserJet III. You can change these codes to use different fonts, line widths, and so on. Knowing which codes to use is a bit tricky unless you are familiar with your printer manual. Each manufacturer uses different codes to represent the various print features. For now, press Enter to move through them without making changes or press Esc. Quicken takes you back to the Report Printer Settings window.

6. Press Ctrl-Enter to view the Print Report window.
7. Type the number of the printer you wish to use and press Enter.

CHAPTER

investments
banking
FILE
register
expenses
DEDUCTIONS
tips
finances
INCOME
equity
net pay
checks
statements
dividends
assets
INCOME
business tips
cash flow
banking
FILE
budget
FILE
business tips
checks
DEDUCTIONS
tips
mortgage
statements
cash flow
revenue
net pay
taxes
bank
business tips
mortgage
cash
dividends
tips
business tips
investments
register
statements
taxes
business tips
expenses
tips
equity
investments
INCOME
checks
statements
bank
cash
assets
checks
budget
tips
finances
net pay

4 RECONCILING YOUR QUICKEN REGISTER

Reconciling your account is the process of comparing your entries with those of the bank. This allows you to determine whether differences between the bank's record of your balance and your record are due to errors or timing differences. Timing differences occur because your balance is accurate up to the present date but the bank records were compiled at an earlier date before transactions you have recorded cleared the bank. These timing differences must be reconciled to ensure there is no discrepancy caused by an error. If you are serious about monitoring your financial activities, a monthly reconciliation of your checking accounts, both personal and business, should be considered a necessary step in your financial record keeping.

In addition to timing differences, there may be transactions not recorded in your register or errors in the amount entries. With manual check registers, there can also be addition and subtraction errors when checks and deposits are recorded. This is one type of error you do not need to worry about with Quicken since its calculations are always perfect if you record the amount correctly.

Another cause of differences is transactions which the bank has recorded on your bank statement but which you haven't entered in your register yet. For example, you may have automatic monthly withdrawals for house or automobile payments or savings transfers to another bank account or mutual fund. In addition, you may have a bank service charge for maintaining your checking account or printing checks, or you may have earned interest. These differences are addressed in more detail throughout this chapter.

In this chapter you will look at how reconciliation works and walk through a reconciliation exercise. The last part of the chapter deals with problems that can occur and the methods for getting your account to agree with your bank's records. This part of the chapter does not require entries, since it is designed to show potential problems rather than additional corrections to your entries.

Quicken's Reconciliation Process

Quicken reduces the frustration of the monthly reconciliation process by providing a systematic approach to reconciling your checking accounts. Since there are more steps in this process than in the exercises you have completed so far, looking at some overview information first will help you place each of the steps in perspective to the overall objective of the process.

A Few Key Points

There are three points to remember when using the Quicken reconciliation system. First, Quicken reconciles only one checking account at a time, so you have to reconcile each of your personal and business accounts separately.

Second, you should make it a habit to reconcile your checking accounts on a monthly basis. You can easily monitor your checking balances once you begin a monthly routine of reconciling your accounts, but attempting to reconcile six months of statements at one sitting is a frustrating experience, even with Quicken.

Third, before beginning the formal Quicken reconciliation process, visually examine your bank statement and look for any unusual entries, such as check numbers that are out of the range of numbers you expected to find on the statement. (If you find checks 501 and 502 clearing, while all the rest of the checks are numbered in the 900s, you might find the bank has charged another customer's checks against your account.) This examination provides an indication of what to look for during the reconciliation process.

An Overview of the Process

When you begin reconciliation, Quicken asks for information from your current bank statement, such as the opening and ending dollar balances, service charges, and any interest earned on your account. (Quicken also records these transactions in the check register and marks them as cleared since the bank has already processed these items.)

Once you have entered this preparatory information, Quicken presents a summary screen for marking cleared items. All the transactions you recorded in the 1st U.S. Bank account, as well as the service charge and interest-earned transactions, are shown on this screen.

Quicken maintains a running total of your balance as you proceed through the reconciliation process. Each debit or credit is applied to the opening balance total as it is marked cleared. You can determine the difference between the cleared balance amount and the bank statement balance at any time. Your end objective is a difference of zero.

The first step is to check the amounts of your Quicken entries against the bank statement. Where there are discrepancies, you can switch to your Quicken register and check the entries. You may find incorrect amounts recorded in the Quicken register or by your bank. You may also find that you forgot to record a check or a deposit. You can create or change register entries from the Register window.

Once you have finished with the entry, you put an asterisk (*) in the C column to mark the transaction as cleared. After resolving any differences between your balance and the bank's, you can print the reconciliation reports. The asterisks are used in the cleared column until Quicken confirms an entry. Then Quicken automatically replaces them with an X, which you will see as this lesson proceeds.

Preparing the Printer for Reconciliation

Before you begin reconciliation, you should check your printer settings. This is important because at the end of the reconciliation process, you are given an opportunity to print reconciliation reports. You can't change printer settings after Quicken presents you with the Print Reconciliation Report window; it's too late. If you attempt to make a change by pressing Esc, you are returned to the Main Menu and have to start over. However, you will not need to complete the detailed reconciliation procedure again.

Use Set **P**references in the Main Menu to check your printer settings now. When you return to the Main Menu, you will be ready to start the reconciliation example.

A Sample Reconciliation

From reading about the objectives of the reconciliation process, you should understand its concept. Actually doing a reconciliation will fit the pieces together. The following exercise uses a sample bank statement and the entries you made to your register in Chapter 2, "Making Register Entries." These steps assume you are starting from the Main Menu:

1. Select Use **R**egister.

   You should be in the 1st U.S. Bank register with the entries created in Chapter 2.

2. Select **A**ctivities.

   Quicken displays the pull-down Activities menu shown here:

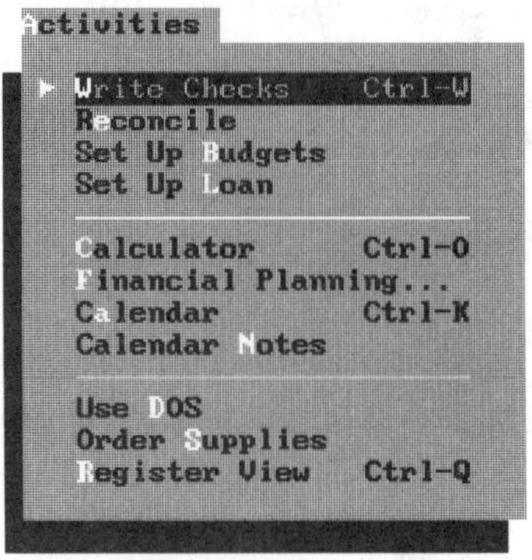

3. Select R**e**concile to enter Quicken's reconciliation system.

You see the Reconcile Register with Bank Statement window, shown in Figure 4-1. Figure 4-2 is a copy of your first bank statement from 1st U.S. Bank; you will use it to respond to Quicken's prompts for information.

The first time you reconcile an account, Quicken automatically enters the opening balance shown in the register. Since you are reconciling your account with the first monthly bank statement, this should be the balance on your screen.

4. Press Enter to move to the Bank Statement Opening Balance field and type **1398.21**, then press Enter.
5. Type **1/1/94** and press Enter.
6. Type **2/1/94** and press Enter.
7. Type **11.50** and press Enter to complete the Service Charge field.

You must enter all the service and similar charges in a lump sum. In this case, the bank has a monthly service charge and a check printing charge that total 11.50 (3.50 + 8.00). Although it is easy enough to add these two simple numbers in your head, if you need to compute a more complex addition, you can always call up the Calculator with Ctrl-O, or QuickMath with an equal sign (=). You would type the first number you want to add, press +, then type the next number, and so on. You can transfer the total from the calculator into a numeric field on the screen with F9 (Paste). The QuickMath feature is even quicker since you use it in the field where you want the number.

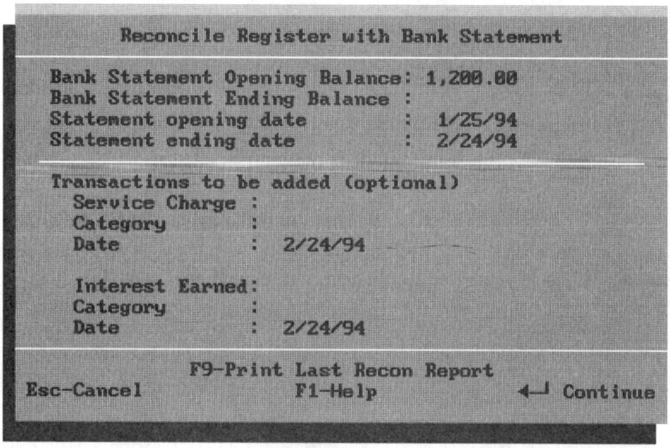

```
             Reconcile Register with Bank Statement

   Bank Statement Opening Balance: 1,200.00
   Bank Statement Ending Balance :
   Statement opening date        :  1/25/94
   Statement ending date         :  2/24/94

   Transactions to be added (optional)
     Service Charge :
     Category       :
     Date           :  2/24/94

     Interest Earned:
     Category       :
     Date           :  2/24/94

                  F9-Print Last Recon Report
 Esc-Cancel                F1-Help               ←┘ Continue
```

Reconcile Register with Bank Statement
Figure 4-1.

1st U.S. Bank
P.O. Box 123
Small City, USA

DATE 2/5/94

PAGE 1 **OF** 1

John D. Quick
P.O. Box ABC
Small City, USA

DATE	DESCRIPTION	AMOUNT	BALANCE
1-1	Deposit	1,200.00	1,200.00
1-6	100 check	77.50-	1,122.50
1-7	Deposit	700.00	1,822.50
1-11	101 check	16.50-	1,806.00
1-12	103 check	150.00-	1,656.00
1-20	102 check	22.32-	1,633.68
2-1	Loan payment deduction	225.00-	1,408.68
2-1	Service charge	11.50-	1,397.18
2-1	Interest	1.03	1,398.21

Date	Check	No.	Amount
1-6	#	100	77.50-
1-11	#	101	16.50-
1-20	#	102	22.32-
1-12	#	103	150.00-

STATEMENT

Bank statement for 1st U.S. Bank account
Figure 4-2.

8. Type **Ba.**

   QuickFill suggest Bank Chrg for the Category.
9. Press Enter or click the next field to accept this entry.

Entering a category is optional; however, to take full advantage of Quicken's reporting features, you should use a category for all transactions. You can type the entire category name or use Ctrl-C to pick one yourself if QuickFill's suggestion does not work for you.

10. Type **2/1/94** as a date for the bank charge and press Enter.
11. Type **1.03** and press Enter to complete the Interest Earned field.
12. Type **I** to see QuickFill's suggestion of Int Inc and press Enter to accept the suggestion.
13. Type **2/1/94** and press Enter.

4

The screen in Figure 4-3 appears. This is a summary screen where you will mark cleared items. It also shows totals at the bottom. You will find all your register entries and the new service charge and interest transactions in this window. If you press the ↓, you will see that the new transactions are marked as cleared with an asterisk in the C column. Also note that the cleared balance shown is your opening balance of 1200.00 modified by the two new transactions. Quicken also monitors the difference between this cleared total and the bank statement balance.

14. The cursor in the left margin points to the 1/7/94 deposit. Press Enter after verifying that this is the amount shown on your bank statement.

Print/Acct   Edit   Shortcuts   Reports   Activities   F1-Help

NUM	C	AMOUNT	DATE	PAYEE	MEMO
		700.00	1/ 7/94	Deposit-Salary	Monthly pay
100		-67.50	1/ 4/94	Small City Gas & Light	Gas and Electric
101		-16.50	1/ 5/94	Small City Times	Paper bill
102		-22.32	1/ 7/94	Small City Market	Food
103		150.00	1/ 7/94	Small City Apartments	Rent
104		-43.00	1/19/94	Small City Market	Food
105		-19.75	1/25/94	Small City Phone Compa	Phone bill
======	=	============	========	====================	====================
	*	-11.50	2/ 1/94	Service Charge	
	*	1.03	2/ 1/94	Interest Earned	

To Mark or Unmark Items, press SPACE or ↵
To Add or Change Items, press F9

RECONCILIATION SUMMARY

```
Items You Have Marked Cleared (*)
--------------------------------------  Cleared (X,*) Balance      1,189.53
1   Checks, Debits            -11.50    Bank Statement Balance     1,398.21
1   Deposits, Credits           1.03      Difference                -208.68
```

F1-Help   F8-Mark Range   F9-View Register   Ctrl-F Find   Ctrl F10-Done

Screen for marking cleared items
Figure 4-3.

Note that Quicken enters an * in the C column on this screen and also in the C field of your check register.

15. The arrow cursor points to the entry for check number 100. Since the bank statement entry and the summary entry do not agree, press F9 (View Register).

You see the screen shown in Figure 4-4. The transaction for check number 100 is highlighted in the 1st U.S. Bank register. If you looked at your canceled check for this transaction, you would see that it was for 77.50 and that it cleared the bank for that amount. Since the register entry is wrong, you must make a correction.

16. Press Shift-Tab, type **77.50**, and press Enter.

Because you pressed F9 in the previous step, your cursor was in the C column. Pressing Shift-Tab lines your cursor up with the beginning of the payment field and allows you to enter the new figure.

17. The cursor is now in the blank C column; type * and press Enter.
18. Press F9 (View as List) and select option 1 when you see the Leaving Transaction window.

Quicken enters the changes and returns to the Uncleared Transaction List window. Notice that you have corrected the amount to 77.50 and

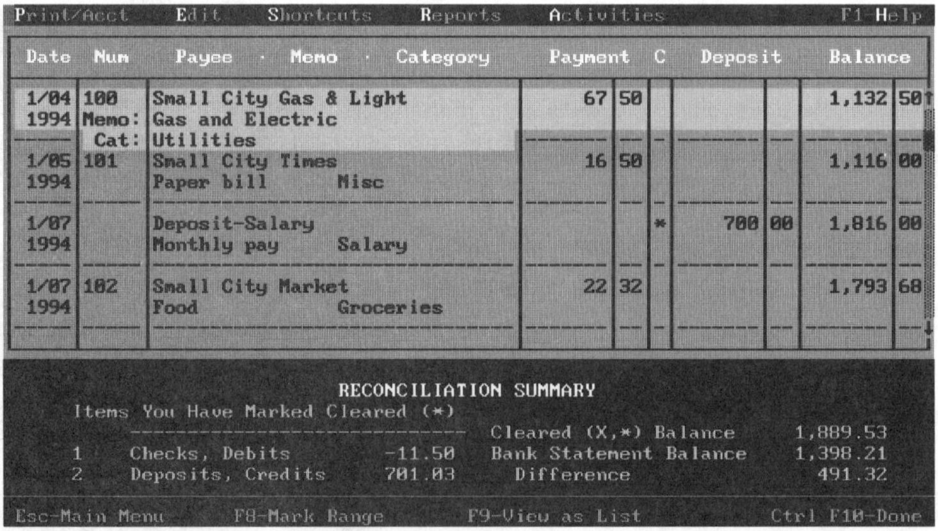

Print/Acct Edit Shortcuts Reports Activities F1-Help

Date	Num	Payee · Memo · Category	Payment	C	Deposit	Balance
1/04 1994	100	Small City Gas & Light Memo: Gas and Electric Cat: Utilities	67 50			1,132 50
1/05 1994	101	Small City Times Paper bill Misc	16 50			1,116 00
1/07 1994		Deposit-Salary Monthly pay Salary		*	700 00	1,816 00
1/07 1994	102	Small City Market Food Groceries	22 32			1,793 68

RECONCILIATION SUMMARY

Items You Have Marked Cleared (*)

			Cleared (X,*) Balance	1,889.53
1	Checks, Debits	-11.50	Bank Statement Balance	1,398.21
2	Deposits, Credits	701.03	Difference	491.32

Esc-Main Menu F8-Mark Range F9-View as List Ctrl F10-Done

Check Register window
Figure 4-4.

that Quicken indicates that the account has been reconciled by the * in the C column.

19. Press F8 (Mark Range), and the Mark Range of Check Numbers as Cleared window appears as shown here:

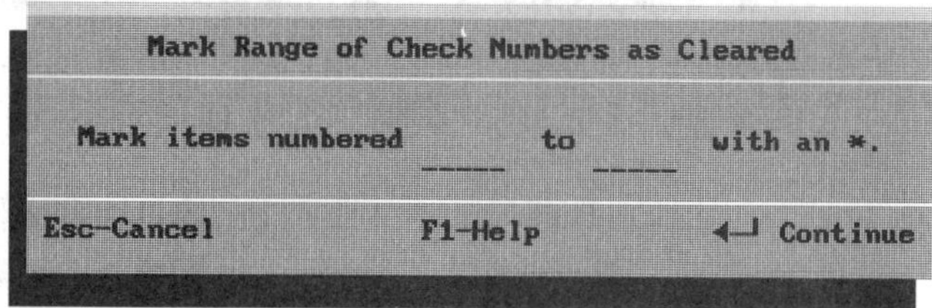

4

This Quicken feature allows you to simultaneously mark a series of checks as having cleared the bank during the reconciling period, provided that the checks are consecutive. Before typing the range of checks to be cleared, remember to compare the amounts shown in the uncleared transaction list with the bank statement amounts. Marking a range of check numbers only works when the amounts are the same.

20. Type **101** and press Enter.
21. Type **103** and press Enter.

Your screen shows that 101 through 103 have had an asterisk added to the cleared column. Notice that your Difference amount is 225.00. When you check the bank statement, you might remember that this difference corresponds to the amount of the automatic deduction for an automobile loan you have with 1st U.S. Bank. Since this amount is not shown on your list of uncleared items, the transaction is not yet recorded in your register.

22. Press F9 (View Register).
23. Press Ctrl-End to move to the end of the register.
24. Type **2/1/94** in the date column and press Enter twice.

You enter the date 2/1/94 in the date column so the transaction will be recorded on the same date that the bank deducted the amount from your account. You can record the date as the current date if you wish. Press Enter twice to move to the Payee field; since this is an automatic deduction, you don't use a check number.

25. Type **Automatic Loan Payment** in the Payee field and press Enter.
26. Type **225** in the Payment field and press Enter.

27. Type * in the C field and press Enter.
28. Press Enter again to move the cursor to the Memo field.
29. Type **Auto payment** and press Enter.
30. Press Ctrl-C. Press ↓ until the subcategory for Auto Loan is highlighted as shown in Figure 4-5 and press Enter. This step demonstrates how you can enter a category from Quicken's category list without typing a category name.
31. Press Ctrl-Enter to record the transaction.

The transaction is inserted in the correct date location in the register and the Difference field indicates that you have balanced your checking account for this month by showing an amount of 0.00. Figure 4-6 shows the transaction for the automatic loan payment and a difference of 0.00; you can complete the reconciliation from this screen or press F9 (View as List) and return to the List of Uncleared Items screen and end the reconciliation process.

32. Press Ctrl-F10, and the Congratulations! Your Account Balances window appears as shown here:

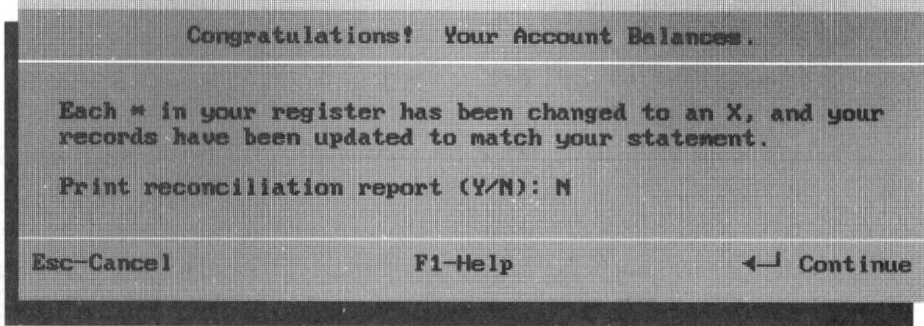

33. Type **Y** and press Enter; the Print Reconciliation Report window, shown in Figure 4-7, appears. If you have not turned your printer on, you should do so now.

You must complete this window to print the reconciliation reports. As explained in the section preceding step 1, it is too late to change your printer settings at this point.

34. Select the desired printer and press Enter.
35. Type **2/24/94** and press Enter.

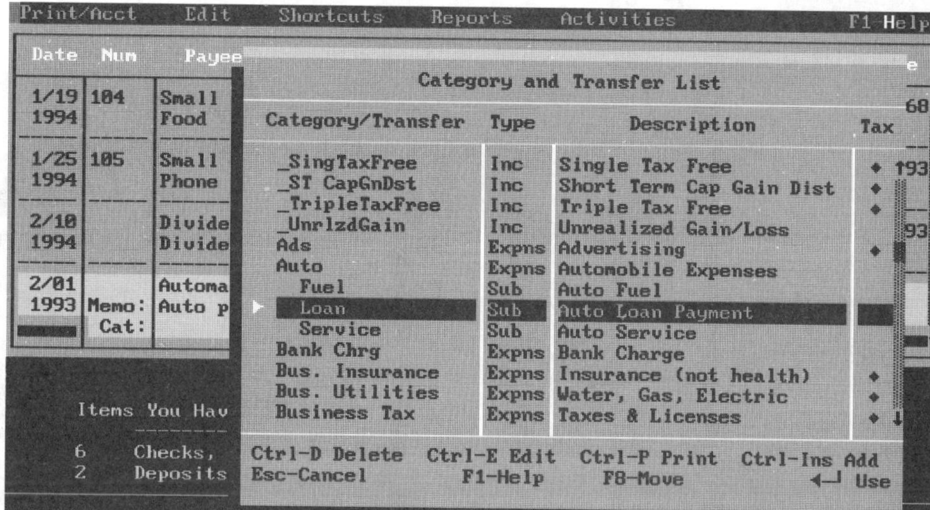

Selecting Auto:Loan for a category
Figure 4-5.

This changes the reconciliation date to conform to the example date.

36. Press Enter to accept the default heading for the report.
37. Type **F** and press Enter to select Full Report.

```
Print/Acct   Edit   Shortcuts   Reports   Activities                F1-Help
Date  Num   Payee · Memo · Category         Payment  C  Deposit    Balance
1/25  105   Small City Phone Company          19 75                 1,570 93
1994        Phone bill      Telephone
2/01        Automatic Loan Payment           225 00  *              1,345 93
1994        Auto payment    Auto:Loan
2/10        Dividend check                                25 00     1,370 93
1994        Dividend check →Div Income
2/01
1994  Memo:
      Cat:
                       RECONCILIATION SUMMARY
  Items You Have Marked Cleared (*)
                                        Cleared (X,*) Balance      1,398.21
  6   Checks, Debits      -502.82       Bank Statement Balance     1,398.21
  2   Deposits, Credits    701.03         Difference                   0.00
Esc-Main Menu      F8-Mark Range      F9-View as List       Ctrl F10-Done
```

Additional entries in the Check Register window
Figure 4-6.

```
                    Print Reconciliation Report

  Print to: 1
       1. Rpt-HP LaserJet III/IIId    3. Chk-HP LJ III        (PS)
       2. Alt-HP LJ III        (PS)   4. Disk

  Reconcile date:  2/24/94

  Report title (optional):

  Full report/Summary and uncleared only (F/S): S

                     Position paper in printer
Esc-Cancel                   F1-Help                   Ctrl◄┘ Print
```

Print Reconciliation Report window
Figure 4-7.

You have now completed your reconciliation process, and Quicken is printing your reconciliation reports.

38. When printing stops, press Esc to close the Print Reconciliation Report window.

NOTE: If the automobile referred to in the reports is used for business, the interest on loan payments for it is tax deductible (with certain limitations).

Quicken's Reconciliation Reports

Since you selected Quicken's Full Report option, you have received four reconciliation reports entitled "RECONCILIATION SUMMARY," "CLEARED TRANSACTION DETAIL," "UNCLEARED TRANSACTION DETAIL UP TO 2/24/94," and "UNCLEARED TRANSACTION DETAIL AFTER 2/24/94." Three of these reports are shown in Figures 4-8 through 4-10. (Note that spacing in these figures may differ from what appears on your screen because adjustments were made to fit all of the onscreen material onto these pages.)

The first page of the Reconciliation Summary report, shown in Figure 4-8, shows the beginning balance of 1,200.00 and summarizes the activity the bank reported for your account during the reconciliation period in the section labeled "BANK STATEMENT — CLEARED TRANSACTIONS:". The first part of the section headed "YOUR RECORDS — UNCLEARED

```
                         Reconciliation Report
1st U.S. Bank                                                      Page 1
2/24/94
                         RECONCILIATION SUMMARY


    BANK STATEMENT -- CLEARED TRANSACTIONS:

        Previous Balance:                                        1,200.00
                                                           --------------
             Checks and Payments:           6 Items               -502.82
             Deposits and Other Credits:    2 Items                701.03
                                                           --------------
        Ending Balance of Bank Statement:                        1,398.21

    YOUR RECORDS -- UNCLEARED TRANSACTIONS:


        Cleared Balance:                                         1,398.21
                                                           --------------
             Checks and Payments:           2 Items                -62.75
             Deposits and Other Credits:    1 Item                  25.00
                                                           --------------

        Register Balance as of  2/24/94:                         1,360.46
                                                           --------------
             Checks and Payments:           0 Items                  0.00
             Deposits and Other Credits:    0 Items                  0.00
                                                           --------------

        Register Ending Balance:                                 1,360.46
```

Reconciliation Summary Report
Figure 4-8.

TRANSACTIONS:" summarizes the difference between your register balance at the date of the reconciliation, 2/24/94, and the bank's balance. In this case, there are two checks that have been written and one deposit made to your account that were not shown on the bank statement. The report shows any checks and deposits recorded since the reconciliation date. In your sample reconciliation, no transactions were entered after 2/24/94, so the register balance at that date is also the register ending balance.

The CLEARED TRANSACTION DETAIL report, shown in Figure 4-9, provides a detailed list with sections called "Cleared Checks and Payments" and "Cleared Deposits and Other Credits"—the items they contain were part of the reconciliation process. Notice that this report provides detail for the CLEARED TRANSACTIONS section of the RECONCILIATION SUMMARY report.

The UNCLEARED TRANSACTION DETAIL UP TO 2/24/94 report, shown in Figure 4-10, in sections headed "Uncleared Checks and Payments" and

```
                     Reconciliation Report
1st U.S. Bank                                                    Page 2
2/24/94
                   CLEARED TRANSACTION DETAIL


  Date     Num        Payee            Memo           Category     Clr   Amount
-------- ----- ---------------- -------------- --------------- --- -----------

Cleared Checks and Payments

 1/ 4/94 100   Small City Gas & Gas and Electri Utilities        X       -77.50
 1/ 5/94 101   Small City Times Paper bill      Misc             X       -16.50
 1/ 7/94 102   Small City Marke Food            Groceries        X       -22.32
 1/ 7/94 103   Small City Apart Rent            Housing          X      -150.00
 2/ 1/94       Automatic Loan P Auto payment    Auto:Loan        X      -225.00
 2/ 1/94       Service Charge                   Bank Chrg        X       -11.50
                                                                    -----------
Total Cleared Checks and Payments                  6 Items              -502.82


Cleared Deposits and Other Credits

 2/ 1/94       Interest Earned                  Int Inc          X         1.03
 1/ 7/94       Deposit-Salary   Monthly pay     Salary           X       700.00
                                                                    -----------
Total Cleared Deposits and Other Credits           2 Items               701.03

                                                                    ===========
Total Cleared Transactions                         8 Items               198.21
```

Cleared Transaction Detail report
Figure 4-9.

```
                     Reconciliation Report
1st U.S. Bank                                                    Page 3
2/24/94
            UNCLEARED TRANSACTION DETAIL UP TO  2/24/94


  Date     Num        Payee            Memo           Category     Clr    Amount
-------- ----- ---------------- -------------- --------------- --- -----------

Uncleared Checks and Payments

 1/19/94 104   Small City Marke Food            Groceries                -43.00
 1/25/94 105   Small City Phone Phone bill      Telephone                -19.75
                                                                    -----------
Total Uncleared Checks and Payments                2 Items               -62.75


Uncleared Deposits and Other Credits

 2/10/94       Dividend check   Dividend check  Div Income                25.00
                                                                    -----------
Total Uncleared Deposits and Other Credits         1 Item                 25.00

                                                                    ===========
Total Uncleared Transactions                       3 Items               -37.75
```

Uncleared Transaction Detail Up to 2/24/94 report
Figure 4-10.

"Uncleared Deposits and Other Credits," provides the details of uncleared transactions included in your register up to the date of the reconciliation. This report provides detail for the UNCLEARED TRANSACTIONS section of the RECONCILIATION SUMMARY report.

The UNCLEARED TRANSACTION DETAIL AFTER 2/24/94 report (not shown) provides detail for those transactions that are recorded in the check register after the date of the reconciliation report. In this illustration there were no transactions recorded; this is shown in the final section of the RECONCILIATION SUMMARY report.

These four reports are all printed automatically when you select Quicken's Full Report option. If you had selected Quicken's Summary option, which is the default option, you would have received only the RECONCILIATION SUMMARY report and the UNCLEARED TRANSACTION DETAIL UP TO 2/24/94 report.

Additional Reconciliation Issues and Features

The reconciliation procedures shown earlier provide a foundation for using Quicken to reconcile your accounts. However, there are some additional issues covered in this section that may prove useful in balancing your accounts in the future.

Updating Your Opening Balance

The importance of maintaining a regular reconciliation schedule has already been noted, and you should balance your checking account before you begin to use Quicken to record your transactions. However, there may be times when the opening balance Quicken enters in the Reconcile Register with Bank Statement window differs from the opening balance shown in the check register.

This can happen in three different situations. First, when you reconcile in Quicken the first time, there may be a discrepancy due to timing differences. Second, there may be a difference if you start Quicken at a point other than the beginning of the year and then try to add transactions from earlier in the year. Third, balances may differ if you use the reconciliation feature *after* recording Quicken transactions for several periods.

First-Time Reconciliations

If you open a new account and begin to use Quicken immediately, there will not be a discrepancy, but a discrepancy will occur if you do not enter the first transaction or two in Quicken. For example, suppose you opened an account on 12/31/93 for 1300.00 and immediately wrote a check for a 1993 expenditure of 100.00. Then you decided to start your Quicken register on 1/1/94, when the balance in your manual register was 1200.00. The bank statement would show the opening balance at 1300.00. In order to reconcile the difference between the bank statement and the Quicken Register balance on 1/1/94, you can do one of two things.

The first option is to open the check register by using F9 (View Register) while in the reconciliation procedures. Enter the 100.00 check, correct the opening balance to reflect the beginning bank balance of 1300.00, and proceed with the reconciliation process.

An alternative to the option above is to have Quicken enter an adjustment in the reconciliation to correct for the difference between the check register's and the bank statement's beginning balances. When Quicken enters the opening balance as 1200.00 and you change it to agree with the bank statement's 1300.00, then proceed with the reconciliation and end with a Difference entry other than zero, Quicken displays a Create Opening Balance Adjustment window, shown in Figure 4-11, which provides a written description of the nature of the problem and offers to make an adjustment.

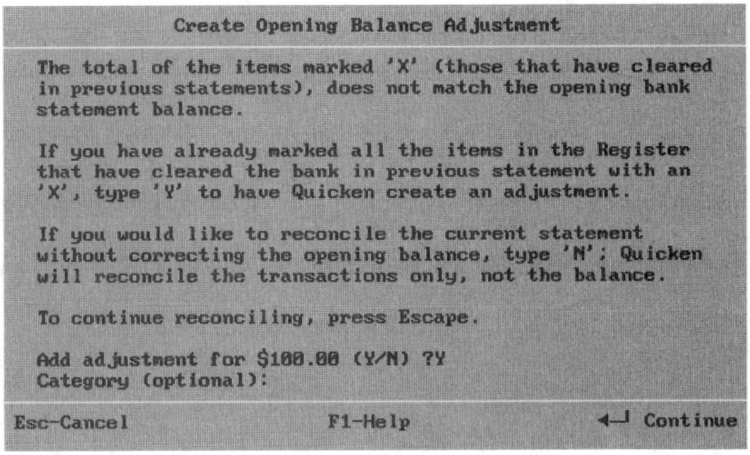

Create Opening Balance Adjustment

The total of the items marked 'X' (those that have cleared in previous statements), does not match the opening bank statement balance.

If you have already marked all the items in the Register that have cleared the bank in previous statement with an 'X', type 'Y' to have Quicken create an adjustment.

If you would like to reconcile the current statement without correcting the opening balance, type 'N'; Quicken will reconcile the transactions only, not the balance.

To continue reconciling, press Escape.

Add adjustment for $100.00 (Y/N) ?Y
Category (optional):

Esc-Cancel F1-Help ↵ Continue

Create Opening Balance Adjustment window
Figure 4-11.

At this point, you will have a –100.00 balance in the Opening Bal Difference field. You can have Quicken make a correction by following these steps:

1. Type **Y** and press Enter. Type a category for the difference and press Enter.

   Quicken then reconciles the balances by making an adjustment to the check register for the 100.00 transaction. The Problem: Check Register Does Not Balance with Bank Statement window appears to let you know if there is still a difference.

2. If you want to search for the problem on your own, press Esc followed by F9 (View as List) to return to the list of transactions and the Reconciliation Summary.

   If you want Quicken to make an adjustment for you, press Enter instead, and the Adding Balance Adjustment Entry window appears.

   Then type **Y** and press Enter twice. The Register Adjusted to Agree with Statement window appears after Quicken makes an adjustment for the difference. Type **Y** and press Enter. Quicken brings the Print Reconciliation Report window to the screen. You can now complete the reconciliation report printing process. Note that if you select N in any of these windows, you will be returned to the reconciliation process.

Adding Previous Transactions to Quicken

You most likely purchased Quicken at a point other than the beginning of your personal or business financial reporting year. In this case, you probably started recording your transactions when you purchased Quicken and entered your checking account balance at that time as your opening balance. This discussion assumes that you have been preparing reconciliations using Quicken and now want to go back and record all your previous transactions for the current year in Quicken. Obviously, your bank balance and Quicken balance will not agree after the transactions have been added.

Follow these steps:

1. Since you are going to be adding to your Quicken register, be sure to have the latest printout of your Quicken register. If not, print your check register now, before you enter any additional transactions. This gives you a record of your transactions to date, which is important should you later need to reconstruct them.

2. Go to your Quicken Register window and change the date and balance columns to correspond to the bank statement that you used at the beginning of the year.

NOTE: The importance of saving your earlier bank statements is apparent. Old statements are not only important for the reconstruction of your Quicken system, but also in the event you are audited by the Internal Revenue Service. It only takes one IRS audit to realize the importance of maintaining a complete and accurate history of your financial transactions.

3. Using your manual records and the past bank statements, enter the previous transactions in your Quicken register. Remember to enter bank service charges and automatic payment deductions if you have not been doing so prior to using Quicken.
4. When you have completed the updating process, compare your ending check register balance with the printed copy you made in step 1. This is important because if they do not balance, you have made an error in entering your transactions. If this is the case, determine whether the difference is an opening account balance difference or an error. (Your options for fixing any discrepancies between opening balances were described earlier in this chapter in the section "First-Time Reconciliations.")
5. The next time you reconcile your Quicken account (assuming you have reconciled the account before), type the opening balance on the latest bank statement over that provided by Quicken in the Reconcile Register with Bank Statement window.
6. Before completing the new reconciliation, go to the check register and type **X** to indicate the cleared transactions in the C column for all transactions that have cleared in previous months.
7. Reconcile the current month's transaction. (Go to the section "A Sample Reconciliation" if you need help.)

First-Time Reconciliation for Existing Users

Although you may have been using Quicken for some time, you may not have used the Reconciliation feature before. The recommended process is as follows:

1. Begin with the first bank statement, and start reconciling each of the past bank statements as if you were reconciling your account upon receipt of each of the statements.
2. Follow this process for each subsequent statement until you have caught up to the current bank statement.

Correcting Errors

Hopefully, there will not be many times when you need Quicken to correct errors during the reconciliation process. However, there may be times when you can't find the amount displayed in the Difference field on your reconciliation screen, and rather than searching further for your error, you want to have Quicken make an adjustment to balance your register with your bank statement.

This situation could have occurred in the 1st U.S. Bank reconciling process described in the section "Quicken's Reconciliation Process." Recall that you made an adjustment of $10.00 to check number 100 in order to correct for your recording error, but if you had been careless in the reconciliation process you might have missed the error when comparing your bank statement with your check register. In this case, your Uncleared Transaction List window would show a $10.00 difference after clearing all items. If you search for the difference and still can't find the amount, you can follow these steps to have Quicken make the adjustment.

CAUTION: This process could have a serious impact on your future reports and check register; don't take this approach to the reconciliation difference lightly.

1. Press Ctrl-F10 and the Problem: Check Register Does Not Balance with Bank Statement window will appear. This time Quicken informs you that there's a $10.00 difference.

At this point you can still return to the register and check for the difference by pressing the Esc key.

2. Press Enter, and the Adding Balance Adjustment Entry window appears.
3. Type **Y** and press Enter.

You have told Quicken that you do not want to search any longer for the difference and you want an adjustment to be made. The adjustment will be dated the current date and will be recorded as "Balance Adjustment." If you had typed **N**, Quicken would have returned you to the reconciliation screen and you would have continued to search for the difference.

4. Press Enter again and the Register Adjusted to Agree with Statement window appears telling you that *'s have been changed to X's.

This indicates that Quicken has made a check register entry for the difference and that you are going to accept the Balance Adjustment description in the Payee row of the register. (You can always make a correction later if you find the error.) Otherwise, you could have used another description such as misc. or expense/income.

5. Type **Y** and press Enter; a Print Reconciliation Report window, like the one displayed in Figure 4-7, appears. Now you can complete the window as described in the "A Sample Reconciliation" section of this chapter.

C H A P T E R

investments banking FILE register expenses DEDUCTIONS
tips finances INCOME equity net pay
checks revenue bank statements
statements business tips
dividends assets
INCOME cash flow
banking business tips FILE reports
budget FILE business tips checks
DEDUCTIONS
statements cash flow tips mortgage
net pay taxes bank revenue
business tips
mortgage cash dividends tips
business tips investments
register statements taxes
business tips
reports expenses tips
equity investments INCOME
checks statements bank cash
assets checks budget tips finances net pay

WRITING AND PRINTING CHECKS

In addition to recording the checks you write in Quicken's register, you can also enter check-writing information on your screen and have Quicken print the check. Although this requires you to order special preprinted checks that conform to Quicken's check layout, it means that you can enter a transaction once—on the check-writing screen—and Quicken will print your check and record the register entry.

You can order Quicken checks in five different styles (both tractor-feed and laser options are available) to meet varying needs. Regardless of the style, there is no problem with acceptance by banks, credit unions, or savings and loans because they have the required account numbers and check numbers preprinted on the checks.

You can create standard 8 1/2 × 3 1/2-inch checks, a voucher-style check that has a 3 1/2-inch tear-off stub, and wallet-style checks in the 2 5/6 × 6-inch size with a tear-off stub added. You can order all these for traditional printers or order the regular or voucher checks for laser printers directly from Intuit.

You can generate an order form from Quicken's check-writing screen. If you want to print out the order form, you can choose **W**rite/Print Checks from the Main Menu. Then select **A**ctivities, and Order **S**upplies. If you select a printer number and press Enter, the order form prints, and you can return to the Main Menu by pressing Esc when the printing completes. You will see from the form that Quicken also sells window envelopes to fit the checks and can add a company logo to your checks.

Even if you are not certain whether you want to order check stock, you can still try the exercises in this chapter. You may be so pleased with the ease of entry and the professional appearance of the checks that you will decide to order checks to start entering your own transactions. You definitely will not want to print your own checks without the special check stock, since banks will not cancel payments on checks without a preprinted account number.

You can also enter transactions in Quicken for transmission to the CheckFree payment processing service via modem. Your Quicken register entries will be updated after transmission, and the CheckFree Processing Center will handle the payment for you. This chapter provides some information on this service, since you might want to consider it as a next step in the total automation of your financial transactions.

Writing Checks

Writing a check in Quicken is as easy as writing a check in your regular checkbook. Although there are a few more fields on a Quicken check, most of these are optional and are designed to provide better record keeping for your expense transactions. All you really need to do is fill in the blanks on a Quicken check form.

Entering the Basic Information

To activate the check-writing features, you can select **W**rite/Print Checks from the Main Menu. The exercise presented here is designed to be entered after the reconciliation example in Chapter 4, "Reconciling Your Quicken Register," but it can actually be entered at any time. If you are already in the register, there is no need to return to the Main Menu first; all you need to do is select **A**ctivities and select **W**rite Checks from the pull-down menu.

Figure 5-1 shows a blank Quicken check form on the screen. The only field that has been completed is the Date field; by default, the current date is placed on the first check. On checks after the first, the date matches the last check written. For this exercise, change the dates on all the checks written to match the dates on the sample transactions.

You should already be familiar with most of the fields on the check-writing form from the entries you made in Quicken's register. However, the Address field was not part of the register entries. It is added to the check for use with window envelopes; when the checks are printed, all you have to do is insert them in envelopes and mail them.

As many as three monetary amounts can appear in the bottom-right corner of the screen. The Checks to Print field holds the total dollar amount of all the checks written but not yet printed. This will not show until you fill in the first check and record the transaction.

Current Balance is a field that changes from 0.00 only if you write checks with dates after the current date, called *postdated checks.* Postdated checks do not affect the current balance but alter the ending balance. They are written to record future payments. If you are reading this chapter before February 1994, all of your transactions will be postdated, since the dates on the checks are in that month. Ending Balance is the balance in the account after all of the checks written have been deducted.

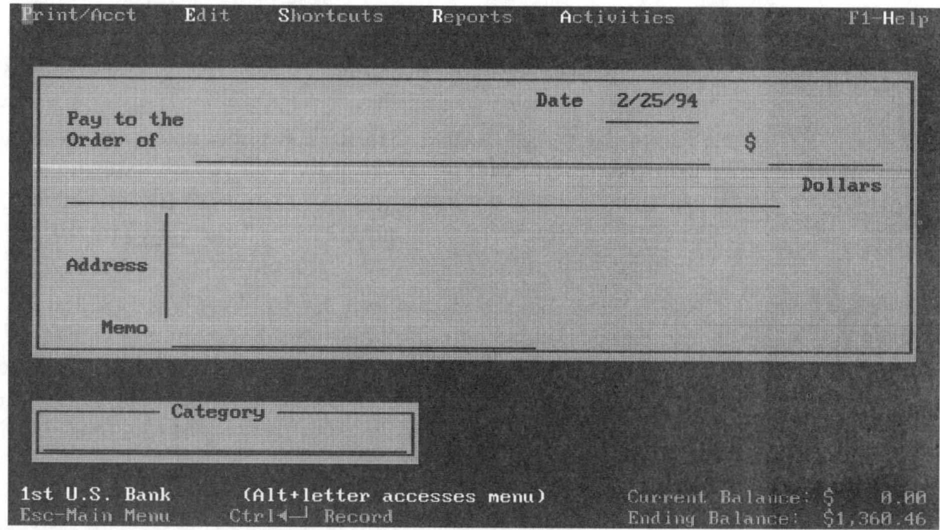

Blank check-writing window
Figure 5-1.

You can use Tab or Enter to move from field to field on the check form. If you want to move back to a previous field, you can use Shift-Tab. When you have finished entering the check information and are ready to record it, you can press Ctrl-Enter to record the transaction automatically. Another possibility is to press Enter with the cursor at the end of the last field category. With the latter approach, Quicken prompts you to confirm that you want to record the transaction. If you use this approach, type **1** and press Enter; the check is recorded for later printing.

Follow these instructions to enter the information for your first check:

1. Type **2/13/94** and press Enter.

   You can also use + or - to change the date.
2. Type **South Haven Print Supply** and press Enter.
3. Type **58.75** and press Enter.

   Amounts as large as $9,999,999.99 are supported by the program. Notice that when you complete the amount entry, Quicken spells out the amount on the next line and positions you in the Address field. Although this entire field is optional, if you are mailing the check, entering the address here allows you to use a window envelope.
4. Type a quotation mark (") to automatically copy the payee name down to this line.
5. Type **919 Superior Avenue** and press Enter.
6. Type **South Haven, MI 49090** and press Enter until the cursor is in the Memo field.
7. Type **Printing Brochure - PTA Dinner** and press Tab or Enter.
8. Press Ctrl-C and type **c** to jump to the Cs in the category list.

   This is a quick way to bring up the category list to select an appropriate category.
9. Move the cursor to the Charity field because you are donating the cost of this printing job by paying the bill for the Parent Teacher Association. Move down to the Cash entry under charity because you are donating cash, not your services. Press Enter to add the entry to the Category field.

   Cash is a subcategory below Charity. You will learn more about subcategories later in the book, but for now it is sufficient to know that they help to organize your data better. If you were to assign some charitable contributions directly to the main category, Charity, and assign other transactions to the subcategories, Charity:Other would be included on your reports.

Remember, you can also use Quicken 7's QuickFill feature by typing **C** and pressing Ctrl-+ until the Charity:Cash category appears on your screen. With either approach, your screen looks like the one in Figure 5-2.

10. Press Ctrl-Enter to complete and record the transaction.

You can enter as many checks as you want in one session. Use the preceding procedure to enter another transaction. Check each field before you press Tab or Enter, but don't worry if you make a mistake or two; you learn how to make corrections in the next section. Enter this check now:

Date:	2/13/94
Payee:	Holland Lumber
Payment:	120.00
Address:	Holland Lumber 2314 E. 8th Street Holland, MI 49094
Memo:	Deck repair
Category:	Home Rpair

Remember, you can use Ctrl-C to select Home Rpair from the category list.

Press Ctrl-Enter to record the transaction when you have finished. Although Quicken moves you to the next check, you can press Pg Up to see the check, as shown in Figure 5-3.

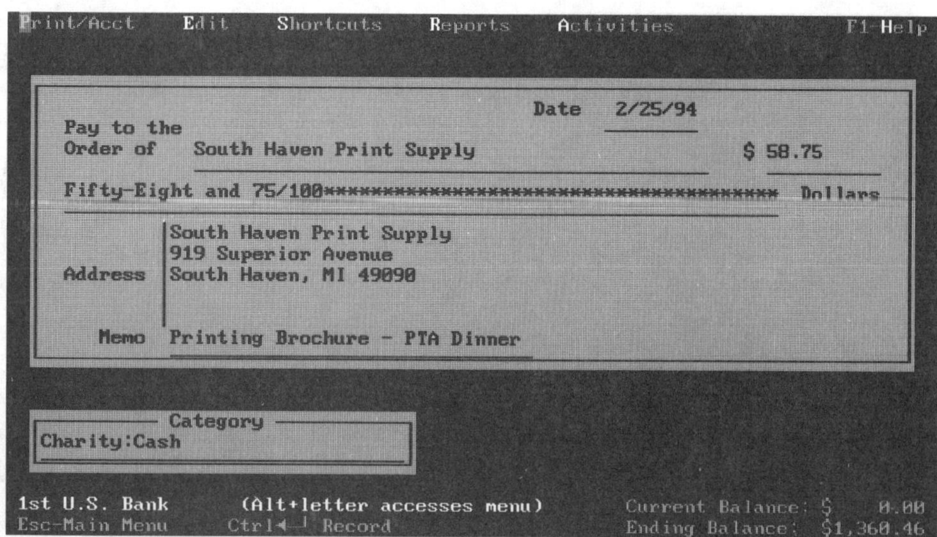

Entering the first check transaction
Figure 5-2.

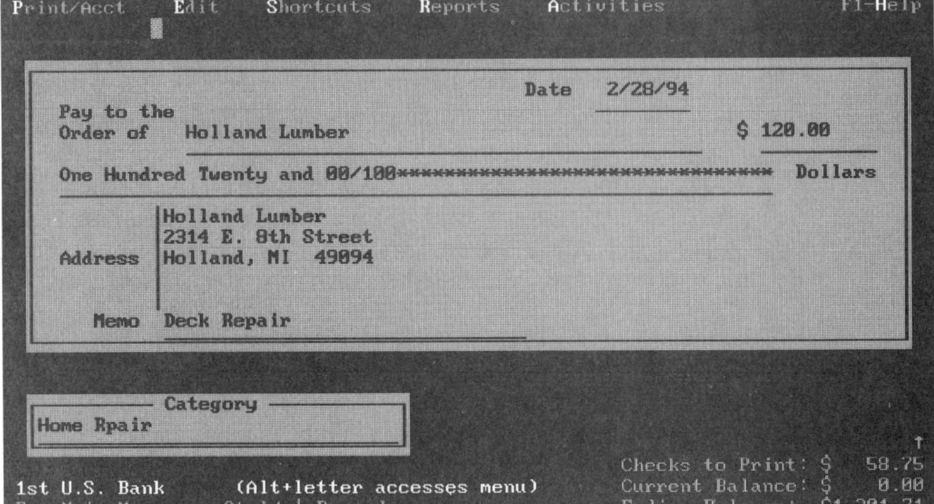

Entering a check for Holland Lumber
Figure 5-3.

Reviewing and Making Corrections

Corrections can be made to a check before or after completing the transaction. Although it is easiest to make them before completion, the most important thing is catching the error before printing the check. To prevent problems, you will always want to review your transactions before printing.

Now let's enter one more transaction exactly as shown in Figure 5-4, including the spelling error in the Memo field. Then you will take a look at making the

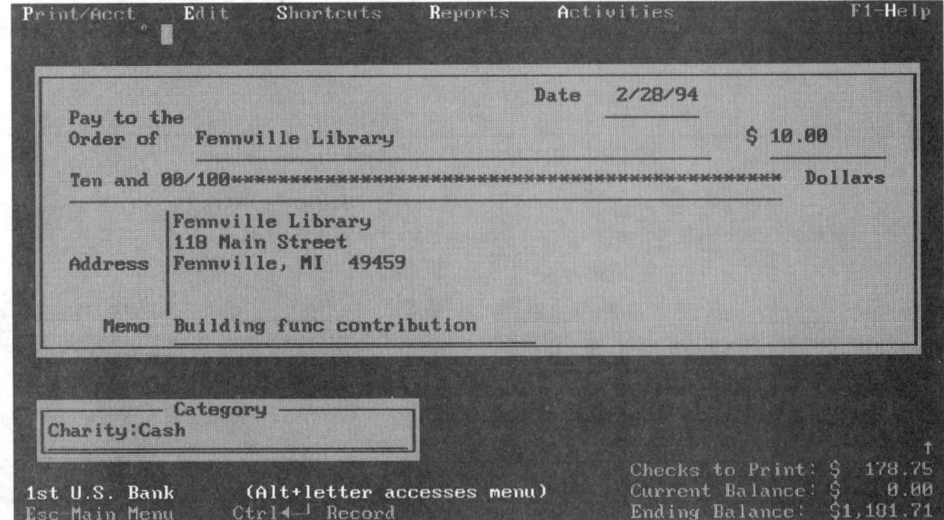

Entering a check with errors
Figure 5-4.

required corrections. Press Pg Dn to move to a new check form if you are still looking at the check for Holland Lumber, and make the following entries without recording the transaction. (Do not correct the misspelling.)

Date:	2/13/94
Payee:	Fennville Library
Payment:	10.00
Address:	Fennville Library 110 Main Street Fennville, MI 49459
Memo:	Building func contribution
Category:	Charity

One mistake in the entries in Figure 5-4 is obvious. The word "fund" in the Memo field is spelled wrong. Suppose you were planning to be a little more generous with the contribution; the amount you intended to enter was 100.00. Quicken has already generated the words for the amount entry, but it changes the words if you change the amount. All you need to do is move back to the fields and make corrections, since the transaction has not been recorded yet. Follow these instructions:

1. Press Tab three times to move to the Amount field.

   Although Tab normally takes you to the next field, pressing it at the last field takes you to the first field on the screen. Another approach is to press Shift-Tab. Each time you press it, the cursor moves back one field. This works, but it needs to be pressed a few more times than Tab because of the cursor location and the destination field.
2. Use → to position the cursor immediately after the 1 in the Amount field.
3. Press Ins to turn on insert mode, and type another **0**.

   The amount now reads "100.00."
4. Press Ins to turn insert mode off.

   Your cursor will display as a large rectangle when insert mode is on.
5. Press Tab six times to move to the Memo field.
6. Press Ctrl-→ twice to move to the c in "contribution." Press ← twice. Type **d** to replace the c in "func." The correct check will be for $100.00 with a Memo field entry of "Building fund contribution."
7. Press Ctrl-Enter to record the transaction.

You can browse through the other transactions by using Pg Up and Pg Dn to move from check to check. Pressing Home repeatedly takes you to the first check and pressing End repeatedly takes you to the last check, which is a blank check form for the next transaction. Make any changes you want, but record them with Ctrl-Enter before using Pg Up or Pg Dn to move to a new check. Quicken updates the balances if you change an Amount field.

To delete an entire transaction, you can use Ctrl-D and confirm the delete. Since the checks have not been printed, there is no problem in deleting an incorrect transaction. After printing, you must void the entry in the register, rather than deleting the check, since you will need a record of the disposition of each check number.

If you are curious about how these entries look in the register, you can select Activities. Press Enter to select the register. Ctrl-R is the shortcut for these actions. You see the checks you have written in the register with ***** in the Num field. Figure 5-5 shows several entries made from the check-writing screen.

Postdating Checks

Postdated checks are written for future payments. The date on a postdated check is after the current one; if you enter a check on September 10 for a December 24 payment, the check is postdated. Postdated entries are allowed to permit you to schedule future expenses and write the check entry while you are thinking of it. It is not necessary to print postdated checks when you print checks. Quicken displays both a current and an ending balance for your account.

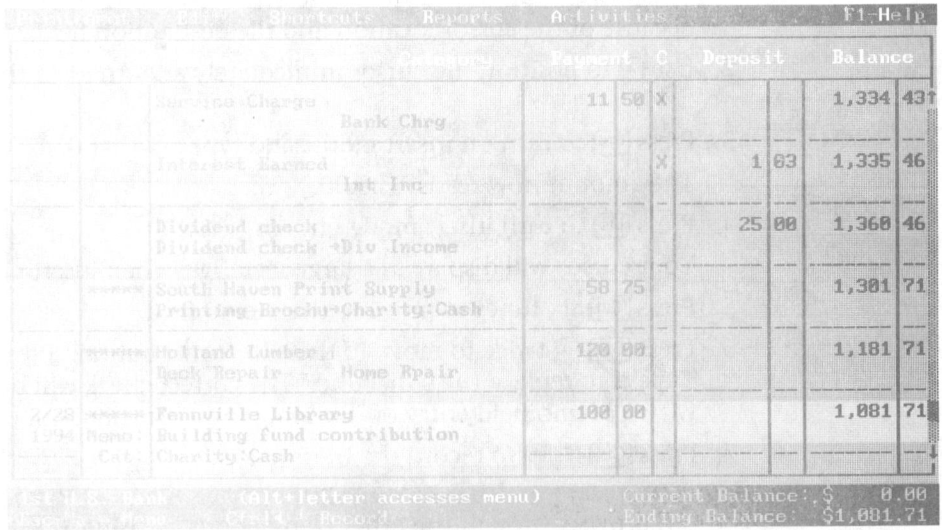

```
                   Shortcuts    Reports    Activities                F1-Help
                              Category     Payment  C   Deposit    Balance
         Service Charge                     11 50   X              1,334 43
                         Bank Chrg
         Interest Earned                            X       1 03   1,335 46
                         Int Inc
         Dividend check                                    25 00   1,360 46
         Dividend check →Div Income
   ***** South Haven Print Supply           58 75                  1,301 71
         Printing Brochu→Charity:Cash
   ***** Holland Lumber                    120 00                  1,181 71
         Deck Repair       Home Rpair
2/28 ***** Fennville Library               100 00                  1,081 71
1994 Memo: Building fund contribution
      Cat: Charity:Cash
                    (Alt+letter accesses menu)     Current Balance:  $    0.00
              Ctrl←┘ Record                        Ending Balance:   $1,081.71
```

Figure 5-5. Check transactions in the register with asterisks for check numbers

Depending on when you are entering the February 1994 checks in these examples, Quicken may be classifying the entries as postdated. The only difference is that you have the option to print only checks before a certain date when postdated checks are recorded.

Complete these entries to write a check for an upcoming birthday by entering the following after returning to the check writing window by selecting **W**rite Checks from the **A**ctivities menu:

Date:	3/8/94
Payee:	Keith Campbell
Payment:	25.00
Memo:	Birthday gift
Category:	Gifts

Note that the Address field was deliberately left blank, as shown in Figure 5-6, since this is a personal check that will not be mailed. What makes this check different than all the others is that while the current date is supposedly 2/13/94, the check is written for 3/8/94 (later than the current date). Press Ctrl-Enter to finalize.

Now that you have written a few checks, you should try printing a few. You can use plain paper even if you have check stock, since these are just practice examples.

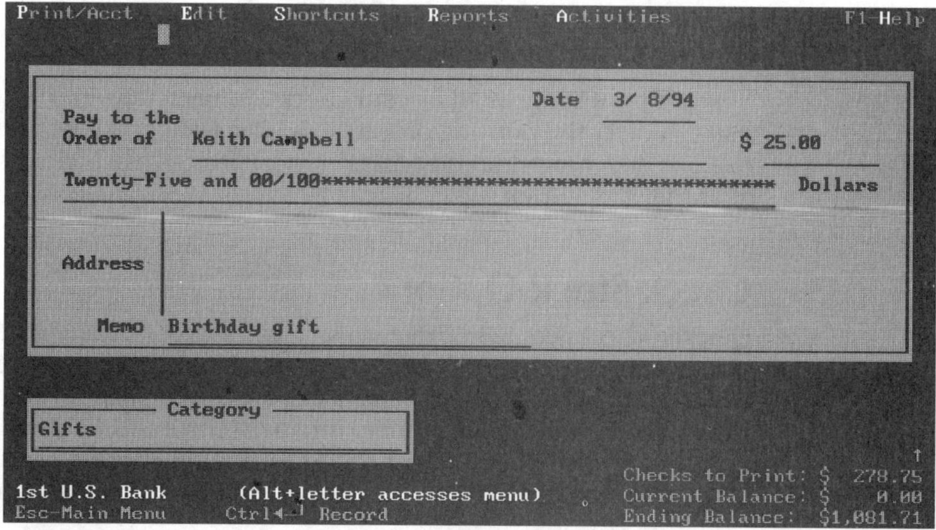

Check to Keith Campbell as birthday gift
Figure 5-6.

Putting Earlier Tactics to Work

Even though you are working with the check-writing screen, many of Quicken's special features that you learned to use in earlier chapters still work. You can use the Calculator if you need to total a few invoices or perform another computation for the check amount. All you have to do is move to the Amount field and press Ctrl-O to activate the Calculator. Once you have completed your computations, use F9 (Paste) to place the result in the Amount field.

NOTE: You can also use Quicken 7's new QuickMath feature to total. Just type = (an equal sign), then type numbers and operators. When you press Enter, the result is put in the amount field.

The Find command will let you locate checks based on an entry value in a specific field. You can use shortcut key to invoke these feature or the pull-down Edit menu (see Chapter 2, "Making Register Entries"). The Calendar features mentioned in Chapter 1 and discussed more fully in Chapter 6 provide another option for locating entries by date.

Printing Checks

Printing checks is easy. The only difficult part of the process is lining the paper up in your printer, but after the first few times even this will seem easy, as Quicken has built some helps into the system for you.

You can print some or all of your checks immediately after writing them, or you can defer the printing process to a later session. Some users wait until a check is due to print it and others elect to print all their checks immediately after they are written.

Check Stock Options

Quicken checks come in three sizes—regular checks, wallet checks, and voucher checks. Figure 5-7 provides a sample wallet check. The voucher design is shown in Figure 5-8. All styles are personalized and can be printed with a logo. The account number, financial institution number, and check number are printed on each check. Special numbers have been added to the edges of the checks for tractor-feed printers to assist in the alignment process.

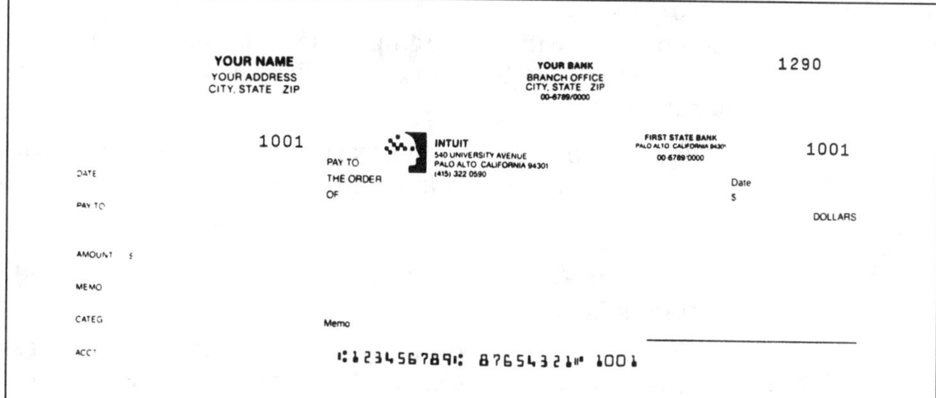

A sample wallet check
Figure 5-7.

Printing a Sample to Line Up Checks

Although you are ready to print the checks you created in the last exercise, if you have never lined up checks in the printer before, you will want to walk through the steps required. This will ensure perfect alignment of the preprinted check forms with the information you plan to print. The procedure is different for tractor-feed printers and laser printers. The laser printer is actually the easier of the two, since all you really need to do is insert the checks into the paper tray.

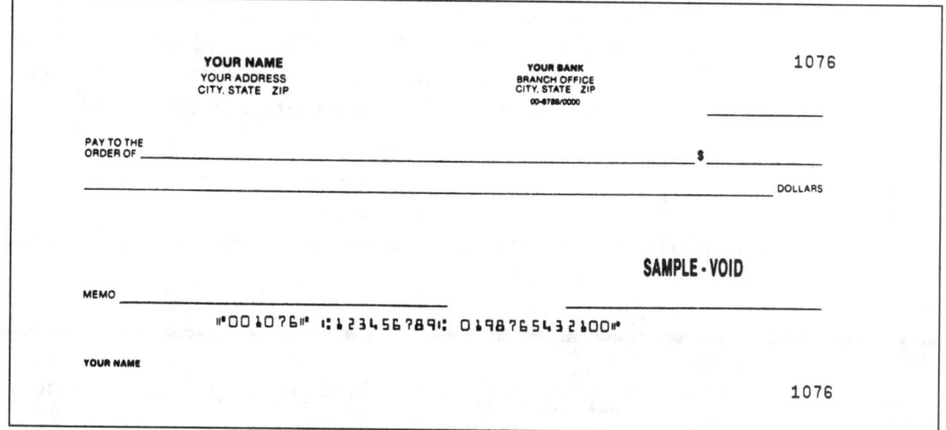

A sample voucher check
Figure 5-8.

Tractor-Feed Printers

Quicken comes with some sample checks for practicing check printing on a tractor-feed printer. Naturally, you will only be interested in this option if you have a tractor-feed printer.

To print a sample check with a tractor-feed printer, follow these instructions from the Write/Print Checks menu:

1. Insert the sample checks in the tractor feed as you do with any printer paper.

   You can purchase Forms Leader pages from Intuit that assure proper alignment of the checks in the printer. This way you won't waste a check at the beginning of each check writing session.
2. Turn on your printer and make sure that it is on line and ready to begin printing.
3. Select **P**rint/Acct and select **P**rint Checks.

   Another option is to press Ctrl-P, rather than opening the Acct/Print menu. The Print Checks window appears.
4. Type the number of the printer you will be using and press Enter.

   This is likely to be **3** for the check printer. The next two selections let you control how many checks will be printed.
5. Press Enter to accept the defaults of ALL and checks dated through the current date.
6. Press F9 (Print Sample); then, after reading Quicken's sample check note, press Enter.

   Quicken prints your sample check. Check the vertical alignment by observing whether the "XXX" for date and amount, the word "Payee" for "Pay to the Order of," and the phrase "This is a void check" for the memo are printed just above the lines on the sample check.

NOTE: Do not move the check up or down after printing; Quicken does this automatically.

7. Press Ctrl-Enter if the sample check has aligned properly. If not, continue with the remaining steps.

8. (You will use this step only if your sample check did not align properly.) Look at the pointer line printed on your sample check. The arrow at each end points to a number on your tractor-feed sheet; this is your printer *position number*.

NOTE: If your pointer line is not on one continuous line, you must check your printer settings to see that the pitch is 10 and that the indent value is 0. You cannot at this time continue with the following steps to achieve the correct results. Note the correct alignment position and consult Table 5-1, "Correcting Printer Errors."

Press Esc to leave the print process for now.

Print Problem	Correct Solution
Print lines are too close	Printer is probably set for eight lines to the inch—change to six
Print lines wrap—the date and amount are too far to the right	Too large a pitch is selected—change to 10 pitch
Print does not extend across the check—the date and amount print too far to the left	Too small a pitch size is selected (perhaps compressed print)—change to 10 pitch and turn off compressed print if necessary
Print does not align with lines on check	Checks not aligned properly in printer— reposition following instructions in this chapter
Print seems to be the correct size but is too far to the right or left	Reposition checks from right to left
Printout shows the printer control codes	Printer control codes must be preceded with a backslash (\)
Printer is spewing paper or producing illegible print	The wrong printer has probably been selected—check selection in the printer list
Printer does not print	Printer is probably not turned on, not on line, or not chosen in the printer list; or the cable may be loose
Print looks correct but is indented	Change indent setting to 0 in Print Settings window

Correcting Printer Errors
Table 5-1.

9. Type the position line number and press Enter.

   Quicken automatically causes a form feed and prints another sample check. This time your check should be properly aligned; if you need to fine-tune the alignment, use the knob on your printer to manually adjust the alignment.
10. Make any horizontal adjustments that may be necessary by moving the paper clamps.

    Once you have aligned your checks properly, you should examine the location of the checks in your printer; notice where your position numbers line up with a part of your printer, such as the edge of the sprocket cover.
11. Press Enter in the Position Number field when your sample check is properly aligned.

You are now ready to print your checks.

Laser Printers

Quicken's laser-printer checks come either one or three to a page and, as mentioned, are the easiest of the checks to print. When using these forms, all you need to do is insert the forms into your printer the same way you insert regular paper (face up, with the top of the paper positioned toward the printer, and so on). If you tear the tractor-feed strips off the sample checks that come with Quicken, you can use them with your laser printer. You can also use regular printer paper. You can purchase Laser Form Leaders from Intuit to allow you to use check stock that is less than a full sheet in length.

The key point to remember with laser printers is to check the printer settings before printing your checks. This can be accomplished from Quicken's Write/Print Checks menu:

1. Select **P**rint/Acct.
2. Select Change Printer **S**tyles.
3. Select Settings for Printing **C**hecks.
4. Press Esc to access the Select Check Printer window, use ↑ or ↓ to place the arrow next to your type of printer, and press Enter.
5. Select a style and press Enter.
6. Press Enter or Tab eight times to arrive at "Page-oriented," type **Y**, and press Enter (if the setting is already set for Y, you can just press Enter).
7. Press Ctrl-Enter to close the Check Printer Settings window.

8. Press Ctrl-P to open the Print Checks window.
9. Make any needed changes to the printer selected or the type of checks and place a sheet of plain paper in your printer.
10. Press F9 (Print Sample).

    Hold the sample up to the light with a sheet of check stock to check alignment.
11. If the sample did not print correctly make changes as needed and try another sample. You will be able to change the vertical alignment before printing the final checks.
10. Press Ctrl-Enter.

    The Enter Check Number window is displayed.
11. If you are working with a partial page of check stock, press F9 and indicate how many checks are left on the page before pressing Enter.

12. If you are not pleased with the alignment, press F7 (Vertical Adjust) and type the number of 1/12th inch adjustments needed in the Vertical Check Adjustment window shown here:

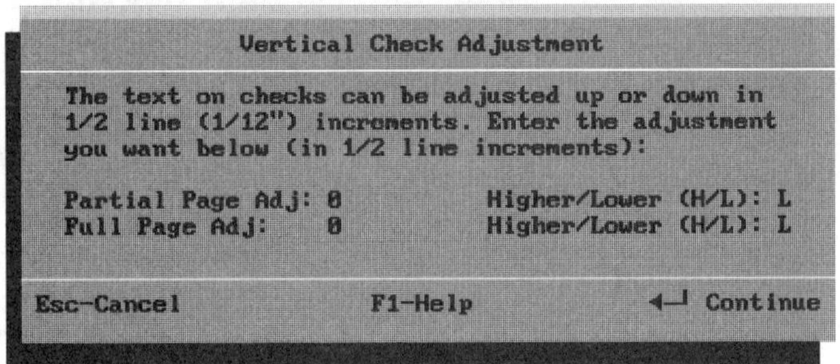

    You will need to specify **H** or **L**, for higher or lower, next to the type of page adjustment that you want.
13. Enter the first check number and press Enter to print the checks.

    Quicken prompts you to see if the checks have printed OK. If you respond with No, the Print Checks window appears again for reprinting. Review Table 5-1 if you are still having problems.

Selecting Checks to Print

When you are ready to print checks, you need to tell Quicken the printer you want to use, the check style you have selected, the checks to print, and the first check number. The instructions that follow assume that you have already checked the alignment for your check stock and that you are beginning from the Main Menu.

1. Select **W**rite/Print Checks.
2. Select **P**rint/Acct and select **P**rint Checks.

   Another option is to press Ctrl-P, rather than opening the Acct/Print menu. The Print Checks window appears.
3. Type the number of the printer you will be using and press Enter.

   This will probably be **3** for the check printer.
4. Type **S** to print selected checks. Typing **A** causes Quicken to print all the checks.
5. Press Enter or Tab, type the number that corresponds to the check style you wish to use, and press Enter.

   Since you have already printed samples, there is no need to print additional ones now. In subsequent sessions you might want to use F9 (Print Sample) to print a sample before proceeding.
6. Press Ctrl-Enter and the Select Checks to Print window appears, as in Figure 5-9. Checks that will be printed show "Print" in the far-right column. You can mark additional checks for printing by highlighting the entry and pressing Spacebar. This allows you to select specific checks.

   If any checks are marked for printing that you do not want to print, you can press Spacebar with the cursor pointing at the check to turn off the print command for that check. Spacebar toggles the print designation on and off.
7. Press Enter and type **1001** to enter the beginning check number in the Enter Check Number window.

   Your entry should match the one shown here:

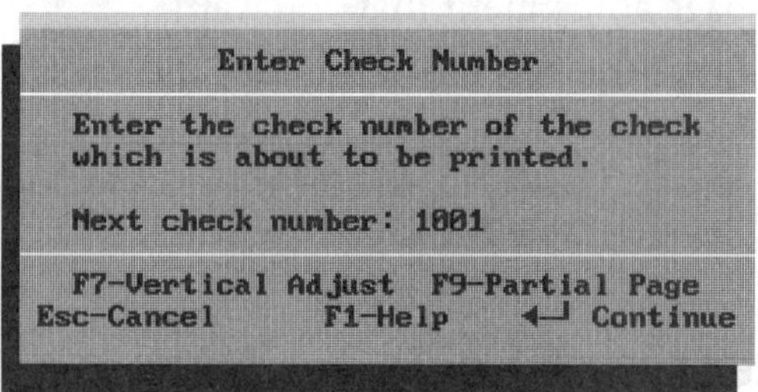

Enter Check Number
Enter the check number of the check
which is about to be printed.
Next check number: 1001
F7-Vertical Adjust F9-Partial Page
Esc-Cancel F1-Help ↵ Continue

You must always make this check number agree with the number of the first check you place in the printer. You should double-check this entry because Quicken will use it to complete the register entry for the check transaction. As it prints a check, it replaces the asterisks in the register with the actual check number. You can use + and - to change the check number. You can also select F9 (Partial Page) or F7 (Vertical Adjust) to tell Quicken where to start printing laser checks and if you want to adjust the printing alignment.

8. Press Enter to print your checks.
9. Quicken 7 responds with a Did checks print OK? window, shown here:

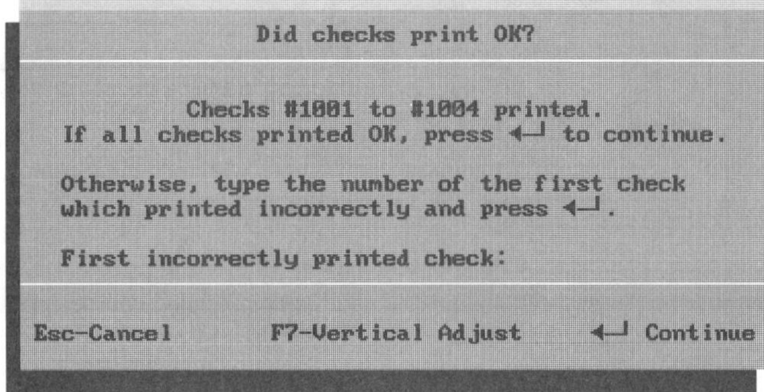

Did checks print OK?
Checks #1001 to #1004 printed.
If all checks printed OK, press ←┘ to continue.
Otherwise, type the number of the first check
which printed incorrectly and press ←┘.
First incorrectly printed check:
Esc-Cancel
F7-Vertical Adjust
←┘ Continue

Review the checks printed and check for errors in printing. If you used preprinted check forms, your checks might look something like the ones in Figure 5-10.

10. If there are no errors, press Enter to close the check printing windows and to return to the Write Checks screen. Press Ctrl-R to look at the register entries with the check numbers inserted. If there are problems with the checks, follow the directions in the next section.

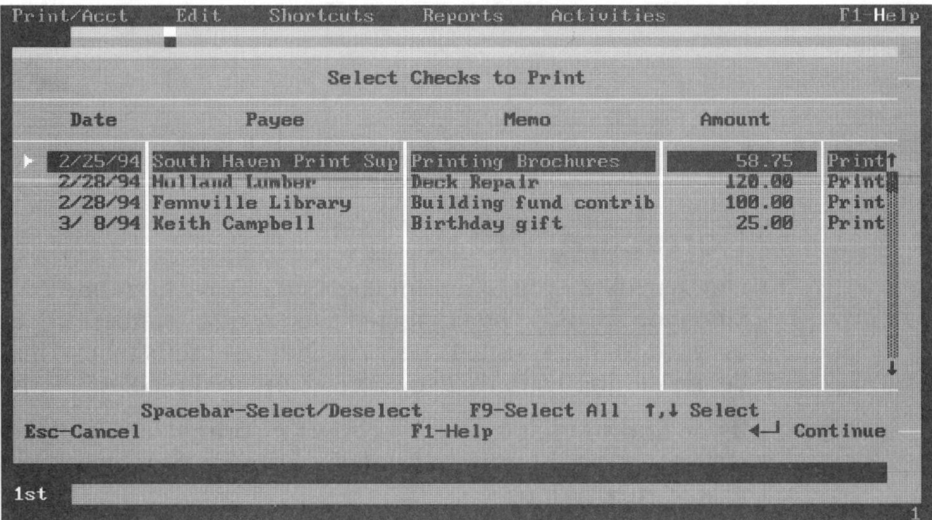

Selecting the checks to print
Figure 5-9.

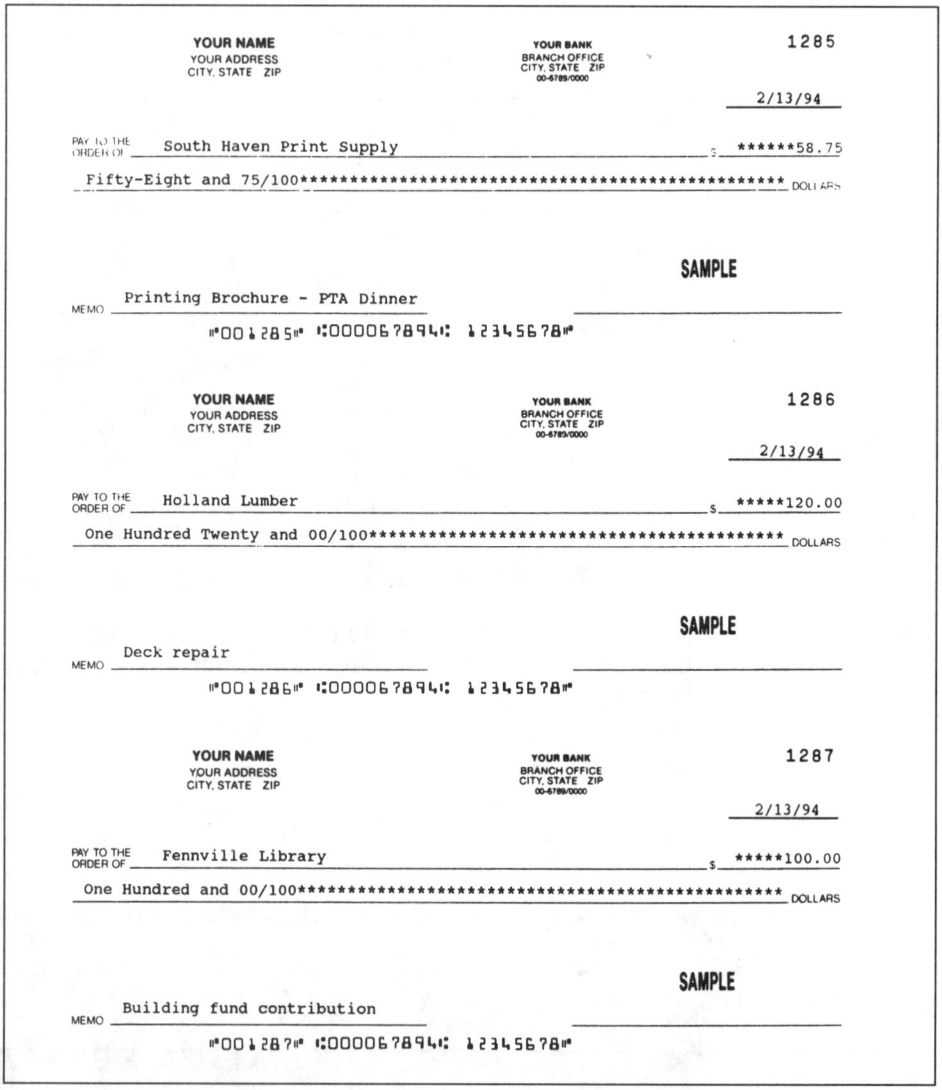

YOUR NAME
YOUR ADDRESS
CITY, STATE ZIP

YOUR BANK
BRANCH OFFICE
CITY, STATE ZIP
00-6789/0000

1285

2/13/94

PAY TO THE ORDER OF South Haven Print Supply $ ******58.75

Fifty-Eight and 75/100** DOLLARS

SAMPLE

MEMO Printing Brochure - PTA Dinner

⑈001285⑈ ⑆000067894⑆ 12345678⑈

YOUR NAME
YOUR ADDRESS
CITY, STATE ZIP

YOUR BANK
BRANCH OFFICE
CITY, STATE ZIP
00-6789/0000

1286

2/13/94

PAY TO THE ORDER OF Holland Lumber $ *****120.00

One Hundred Twenty and 00/100** DOLLARS

SAMPLE

MEMO Deck repair

⑈001286⑈ ⑆000067894⑆ 12345678⑈

YOUR NAME
YOUR ADDRESS
CITY, STATE ZIP

YOUR BANK
BRANCH OFFICE
CITY, STATE ZIP
00-6789/0000

1287

2/13/94

PAY TO THE ORDER OF Fennville Library $ *****100.00

One Hundred and 00/100** DOLLARS

SAMPLE

MEMO Building fund contribution

⑈001287⑈ ⑆000067894⑆ 12345678⑈

Standard check sample printout
Figure 5-10.

Correcting Mistakes

Quicken allows you to reprint checks that have been printed incorrectly. Since you are using prenumbered checks, new numbers will have to be assigned to the reprinted checks as Quicken prints them. First, make sure before starting again that you correct any feed problems with the printer.

If you find yourself frequently correcting printer jams and having to reprint checks, you might want to print checks in smaller batches or set your printer to wait after each page.

Complete the following steps to restart and finish your printing batch:

1. If you did not press Enter when you finished printing checks, Quicken is still waiting for you to identify the first incorrectly printed check and reprint the desired checks (for checks that did not print or that printed incorrectly). Type the check number of the first check you want to reprint and press Enter.
2. The Print Checks window appears. Press Ctrl-Enter to open the Select Checks to Print window. The highlighted transaction will be on the check you designed.
3. Select the checks to be reprinted by using Spacebar and press Enter.
4. Check the next Check Number field against the number of the next check in your printer. Type a change if appropriate. Press Enter to confirm the beginning check number for this batch and begin printing.
5. Press Enter to indicate that all the checks have printed correctly when they stop printing; otherwise repeat the steps described in this section.

Using CheckFree

CheckFree eliminates the need for printing checks. After entering data into Quicken 7, you can electronically transmit the information to CheckFree. The CheckFree service handles the payments for you by printing and mailing a paper check or by initiating a direct electronic transfer.

Although the ability to interface with CheckFree is part of Quicken 7, you must subscribe to the service before using it the first time. To subscribe, complete the CheckFree Service Form included in the Quicken package or contact CheckFree at (800) 882-5280. Currently, CheckFree's monthly charge of $9.95 entitles you to 20 transactions without an additional charge. Additional transactions are billed in increments of 10 with an additional $3.50 charge for each increment.

Setting Up Quicken to Interface with CheckFree

To use CheckFree with Quicken, you must change your settings and set up the bank account specified on the CheckFree Service Form. You must set up your modem so that you can use Quicken's electronic payment capability. You must also compile an electronic payee list and write electronic checks.

Completing Modem Settings

To set up your modem to establish a link between your computer and your bank via the telephone line, select Set **P**references from the Main Menu. Next, choose **M**odem Settings. The Modem Settings window shown in Figure 5-11 is displayed. You can accept the defaults for the modem speed

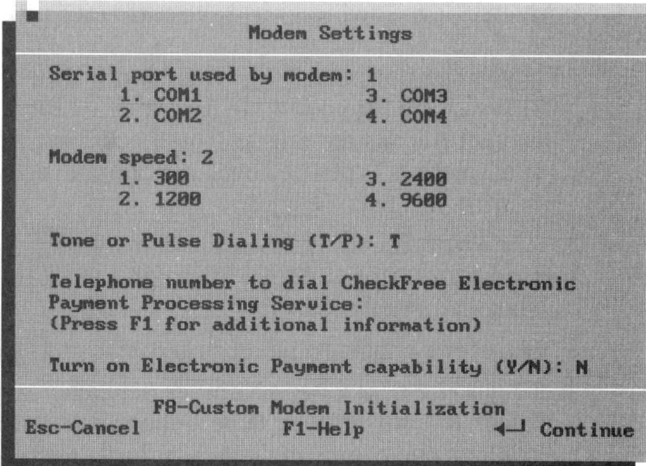

Modem Settings form
Figure 5-11.

and the computer port to which the modem is attached or change them to conform to your needs.

You must enter the phone number supplied by CheckFree for transmission. Next, turn on the electronic payment feature by typing **Y** in the last field on the screen. When entering the phone number, type a comma if your phone system requires a pause. You can return to the Main Menu by pressing Esc and enter electronic payment settings.

Completing Account Settings

You can specify any bank account for use with CheckFree provided you supply the bank information to CheckFree on their service form. To change an account for use with CheckFree, choose Set P**r**eferences from the Main Menu and select E**l**ectronic Payment Settings. Quicken presents a window with your current account listed, like the one shown here:

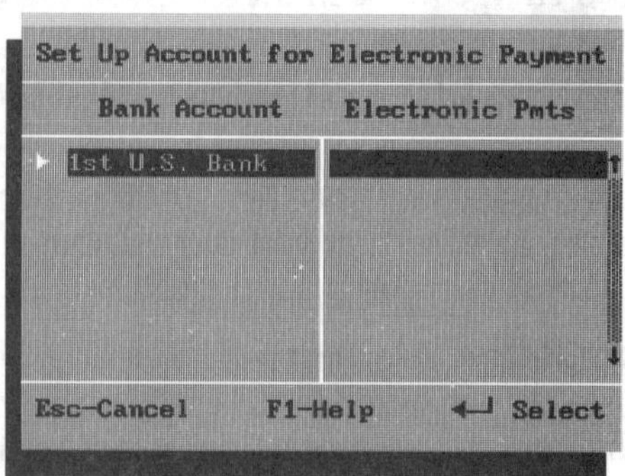

Highlight the name of the account you wish to enable electronic transmissions for and press Enter. Respond with **Y** and press Enter on the next screen to enable payments, and complete the form shown in Figure 5-12 for your account. CheckFree supplies you with the number for the last field on this form. You are now ready to enter electronic payees or either check or register transactions and transmit them.

Compiling an Electronic Payee List

You can begin writing checks and gradually compile a payee list as you enter each check or you can take a few minutes and make the needed entries to those you send checks to on a regular basis. If you want to enter payees before writing checks, you can press Ctrl-Y or select Electronic Pa**y**ee List from the **S**hortcuts menu. As you select <Setup Electronic Payee> for each new entry, Quicken will display a window like this allowing you to enter the name, address, and account for each payee:

Edit Electronic Payee

Name: Cleveland Property Management

Street Address

City : State: Zip :

Phone:

Account Number:

Esc-Cancel ↵ Continue

There is also an option that lets you enable fixed payments to a payee.

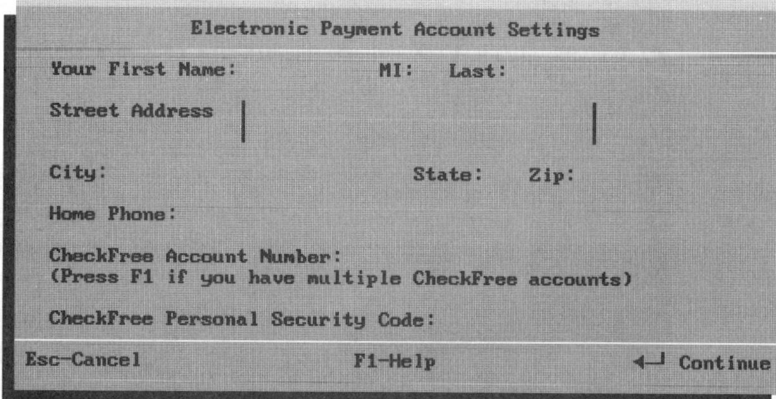

Electronic Payment Account Settings

Your First Name: MI: Last:

Street Address

City: State: Zip:

Home Phone:

CheckFree Account Number:
(Press F1 if you have multiple CheckFree accounts)

CheckFree Personal Security Code:

Esc-Cancel F1-Help ↵ Continue

Electronic Payment Settings window
Figure 5-12.

NOTE: The Electronic Payee List option on the **S**hortcuts menu is only available after activating electronic payments.

Writing Electronic Checks

The procedure for writing electronic checks is almost identical to the format for creating checks that you print, covered earlier in this chapter. Your check displays Electronic Payment if you have electronic payments set for the current account, although you can toggle to a paper check with F9 any time you need to. Quicken automatically postdates the payment date by five working days to allow for transmission of the payment to the payee. The Pay To field must contain the name of an electronic payee. If your entry does not match an existing payee, Quicken allows you to add it, as shown in Figure 5-13. Once you have finished with your entries, press Ctrl-Enter.

NOTE: Just as you must notify you bank if you want to stop payment on a check, you must notify CheckFree. Voiding the transaction on your screen is not the solution; you must select Trans**m**it Stop Payment Request option from the **E**dit menu when you need to do this.

Quicken lists your electronic checks in the register. The check numbers will consist of a number of > symbols before transmission and E_PMT after

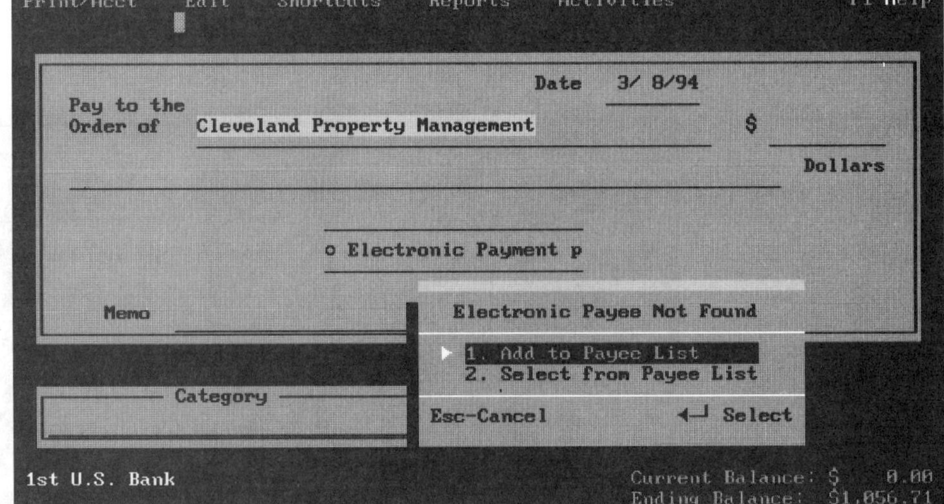

Electronic check with new electronic payee being added
Figure 5-13.

transmission. You can enter these electronic payments directly in the register, rather than through the Write Checks screen if you prefer.

Transmitting Electronic Payments

Electronic payments are transmitted through the **W**rite/Print Checks screen or the register. Select **P**rint/Acct and Transmit Payments to display the Transmit Payments window. You can preview your transmission with F9 (Print Sample) or press Enter to start the transmission process.

Sending and Receiving Other E-Mail Messages

Once you have installed CheckFree, three new menu options appear at the bottom of the **A**ctivities menu, as shown in Figure 5-14. These options allow you to send, check, and view E-mail with CheckFree. The menu options you will use for these activities are Send Electronic **M**ail, Chec**k** Electronic Mail, and **V**iew Electronic Mail. These options will not appear in the **A**ctivities menu if CheckFree is not installed.

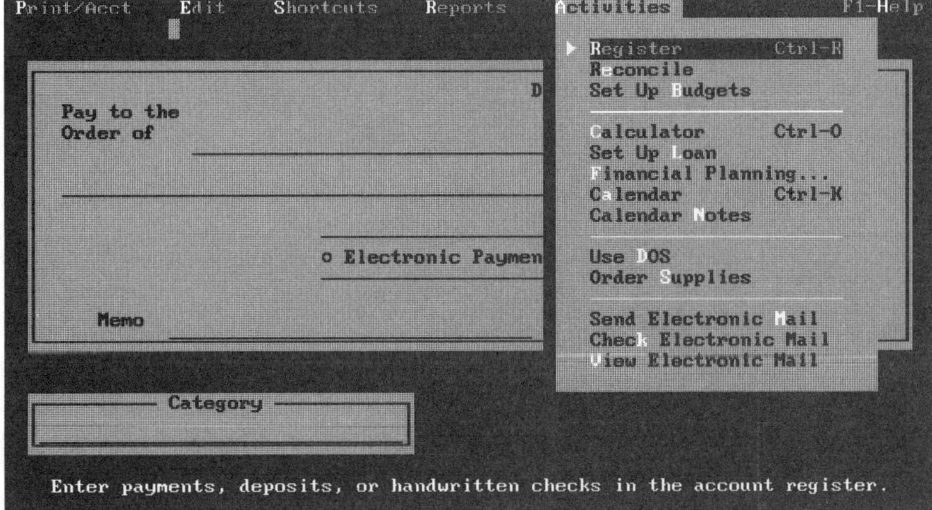

Activities menu after Electronic Payment feature is activated
Figure 5-14.

T I P S

investments banking FILE register expenses DEDUCTIONS
tips finances equity net pay
checks revenue bank statements
statements
dividends assets business tips
INCOME
cash flow
banking business tips
FILE reports
budget FILE
business tips checks
DEDUCTIONS
statements cash flow
tips mortgage
net pay taxes bank
revenue
business tips
mortgage cash
dividends tips
business tips
investments
register statements
taxes
business tips
expenses tips
equity investments
INCOME
checks statements bank cash
assets checks budget tips finances net pay

101 PC AND DOS TIPS

Whether Quicken is the first program you have used on your system or is one of many, you will want to look through the PC and DOS tips in this section. Even if your primary interest is in Quicken, you may be able to learn a little bit more about your computer and DOS (Disk Operating System) if you read a few of these each day.

1. Buy unformatted disks and format them yourself to save money.
2. Always create a label for your disks before you store data on them.
3. Write protect disks containing backup copies of data.
4. Wrist pads may help avoid carpal tunnel syndrome especially if you regularly use notebook computers.
5. Consider buying a keyboard membrane to protect the keyboard from food and beverages if you insist on eating at the computer.
6. Always keep disks in boxes to protect them from dust and spills.
7. If you spill something into your keyboard, save your current files immediately, then turn your keyboard upside down and shake it gently. Contact your computer store for additional options, which will depend on the type of keyboard and the liquid spilled.
8. Use static spray on carpets or install an anti-static carpet near the computer, especially in cold, low-humidity climates, to avoid static electric shock.
9. Avoid obvious magnetic fields for disks as well as the not-so-obvious ones such as television sets, vacuum cleaners, and conveyor belts at airports.
10. Consider propping your monitor up on a monitor stand or even a small box if the height is better for reading screen information.
11. If your printer tells you that your toner cartridge is low, pull it out and shake the cartridge gently from side to side before reinserting it. You will get several hundred pages more. We usually do this a time or two before recycling the cartridge.
12. Look for a reliable supplier who can refill toner cartridges or reink ribbons.
13. Don't put disks in a hot car or car trunk. Your data is likely to be unreadable.
14. Establish a directory structure for your PC that models your manual filing system.
15. Keep the environment around your PC dust free. If it is not, you should consider having your PC cleaned at your computer store. Simply cleaning a PC can fix apparent malfunctions which may have you considering getting a new one.
16. Keep your PC away from windows; heat, sunlight, and moisture can damage it. Also, a system at the window is more likely to attract the attention of a burglar.
17. Position the PC monitor then check the glare on the screen before setting up the entire system. Reflected light from outside, or hallway lights, can make it difficult to read the screen.

18. If you cannot avoid glare, by an anti-glare screen or screen cover. The best way of reducing glare is to use indirect lighting. The best way to produce it is a strong, direct, overhead light source.
19. Secure your system with wire cables to the floor or wall if you cannot restrict access to the system after hours.
20. Make sure you are using a comfortable chair if you sit at the computer for hours. Some users prefer backless computer chairs over other options.
21. Create a regularly scheduled backup plan and assign responsibility for meeting it.
22. Backup important files that are being updated regularly after each major update even if this is twice a day.
23. Consider joining a computer users group to learn more about PCs.
24. Put a blank disk in disk drives when traveling with a computer as a replacement for the cardboard in the drive when you first received it.
25. Use surge protectors to keep your PC from being damaged by a sudden surge in your power line. Universal power sources can be used to give you time to save data if your power goes out.
26. Consider buying a power strip which you can plug all of your computer's elements into. You can use the power switch to turn your entire system on at once. Many such power strips are also surge suppressors.
27. If you find you need more memory or disk space, see if you can add it to your existing unit instead of upgrading to a new computer. You can greatly enhance your computer's performance by adding on memory, a second or larger hard disk, or features such as internal modems; usually at less cost than buying a new system. On the other hand, if you have a model that is more than a couple of years old, its clock speed may be so slow that upgrading it would not be a good idea.
28. If your desk tends to be cluttered, use a trackball instead of a mouse. Unlike a mouse, trackballs are not actually moved around on the desk; instead, you move the ball itself.
29. Use a screen saver program to provide security for your work. A screen saver takes control of your screen and hides it by displaying an image whenever you haven't touched the keyboard or mouse for awhile. Some screen savers let you assign a password that must be entered before the screen will clear.
30. If you have more than one computer but only one printer, use a printer switch box, which lets you switch which computer has access to the printer at any one time. This makes it easier to share one printer.

31. You can create very professional looking documents by using special paper. Paper that is preprinted with a design can make even the simplest document look professionally prepared, enhancing your image when presenting business or financial papers.
32. Avoid keeping vital files only on your computer. A very important backup is to have hard-copies or printouts filed appropriately, especially for personal files that you may not have off-site backups for. Circumstances which can destroy your computer files may not destroy your printouts. For example, keep a printout of financial data in a fireproof safe box so that it can't get destroyed as easily.
33. If you find you are frequently short of hard disk space, try these solutions. You may simply need to delete old files regularly. You can start saving data files on floppy disks instead of on your hard drive. Consider getting a disk compression utility which squeezes files into smaller spaces on your disk, or zipping old files with a file compression program and expanding them only when they are needed.
34. If you find yourself frequently receiving out of memory messages, you may be trying to do too much with your computer. If you use Terminate and Stay Resident programs (TSRs) such as screen capture programs or other utilities, try to avoid their use. Consider upgrading your version of DOS to DOS 5 or 6 or buying a memory management program which can better allocate your memory resources. You can also install new memory chips to add memory to your system.
35. Remember to check the kind of memory you have against the kind of memory your programs need. Some programs can only use conventional memory, others can use expanded but not extended or vice versa. If you have the wrong kind of memory for the program you want to use, see if you can find a memory manager that can fool the computer into thinking it has a different type of memory.
36. Invest in a high resolution monitor when you first get your system. Even programs that use lower resolutions will look better on the high resolution systems. More recent programs which require higher resolutions may be unreadable on a low resolution monitor.
37. Computer-based fax boards are a great solution for faxing documents. You can use these boards to fax a document directly from your computer, without printing it out. When the fax is printed by the recipient, your document is much more readable, since there will be no scanning errors.
38. Make sure your computer is 100% DOS and IBM compatible. Some aren't. Programs written to run under DOS may not run correctly if the system is not completely compatible.

39. Make sure your cables are securely attached to their connectors. If you simply attach them, but don't secure them, they may fall out, or you may experience errors because information is getting lost when the connections are loose.
40. If you usually use programs that do lots of computations, consider a math co-processor. Math co-processors help your computer do calculations faster so math intensive programs run quicker. These include graphics packages and many spreadsheets.
41. Make sure you know your disk drive capacities and buy disks to match. Disk drives cannot read disks formatted to greater capacity. Attempting to format a disk to a higher capacity than it is designed for means that any information you try to save on that disk is going to be gibberish.
42. Remember to clean your mouse ball and keyboard occasionally, using compressed air or a special vacuum. Many mice can be opened so that you can remove the ball from the bottom to clean it separately.
43. Never spray cleaners directly on your computer or computer screen. You can spray a cloth then wipe the monitor screen or keyboard to insure that moisture does not damage your computer.
44. Write protect disks that contain important data so they cannot be formatted accidentally. To do this cover the notch on a 5 1/4 inch disk or slide the tab on a 3 1/2 inch disk toward the outside edge to expose the hole beneath it.
45. Use the DOS ATTRIB command to make read-only those important files that you will not need to update. An entry of ATTRIB MYFILE +R at the DOS prompt will make MYFILE read-only.
46. Establish a naming standard for all of your files. Although you will probably not be creating new Quicken files, when you create data for other programs, these naming standards are essential in keeping data organized and in DOS file management. For example, if you write a monthly budget report with your word processing program, you might want to use a name such as BGT94JAN and follow this pattern throughout the year rather than entering the next months as FEB94BGT, 94MARBGT, and BUDG0494. Although any of these other entries would have been fine if used as the pattern for the entire year, mixing them will cause problems.
47. Regardless of the current directory, you can activate the root directory by typing **CD** at the DOS prompt.
48. If you are working from the DOS prompt, type **CD..** to move up one level in your directory structure.

49. If you have DOS 4 or higher you can use the DOSSHELL which provides menus and a visual of your disk structure. Type **DOSSHELL** at the DOS prompt to activate it.
50. Type **VER** at the DOS prompt to find out which version of DOS is installed on your system.
51. You can create a bootable disk with the FORMAT /S command.
52. Always make a copy of your AUTOEXEC.BAT and CONFIG.SYS files before modifying them. You can copy them to a bootable disk that you can place in drive A to start your system.
53. Add the command DOSSHELL to your AUTOEXEC.BAT file if you want the DOS Shell to display when you boot your computer.
54. Add a path statement to your AUTOEXEC.BAT file if you want to be able to start programs from any directory. You will need to list all of the program directories that you want to work like this in the PATH statement.
55. If you have DOS 5 or DOS 6 you can search for a file across directories if you add the /S switch to your DIR command. For example, if you cannot find the file MYDATA, start from the root directory on your disk, enter **DIR MYDATA /S**. DOS will search not only the root directory but all directories beneath it.
56. You can add REM commands to your AUTOEXEC.BAT and CONFIG.SYS files to document changes.
57. Don't use the same names for programs and batch files in the same directory. There is no way for you to control which one DOS will find first and execute.
58. Use the |MORE addition with DIR and TYPE to control when more information is displayed on your screen. For example, to display an ASCII file onscreen such as a file you might use to store a Quicken report needed in another program, you would type **TYPE BUDGET.ASC |MORE**. DOS would display the first screen, wait for you to press a key, then display the next screen.
59. You can change your DOS prompt to any message with the PROMPT Command. For example, typing **PROMPT UNAUTHORIZED USERS BEWARE$G** will display this at the DOS prompt:

    ```
    UNAUTHORIZED USERS BEWARE>
    ```

60. If full pages of graphics do not print on your laser printer, you may need to add memory to it.
61. Using Shift-Prt Sc may not give the results you want if your screen contains graphic characters in addition to text. Type **GRAPHICS** at the

DOS prompt and press Enter before trying to print using the print screen option again.

62. Create a batch file to backup your data to make the task easier.
63. You may not be able to use every byte on a disk for data storage when you have multiple files on the disk since space is allocated by allocation units. These vary in size by disk, but the smallest allocation unit in common use today is 1,024. A file that contains one character will require this minimum space allocation on the disk.
64. You can undelete accidentally deleted files with DOS 5 and above as long as UNDELETE is your next action. If you continue to work, the space currently occupied by the deleted files may be used for the new files that you create. You will need to use a utility such as Norton's Utilities to undelete files if you have a version of DOS prior to DOS 5.
65. Press Ctrl-C to interrupt a DOS command.
66. Press F3 to copy the previous DOS command to the DOS prompt.
67. Press F2 followed by the character that you want to stop at in the previous DOS command. The characters which precede this character will be copied to the DOS prompt line. For example, if your previous DOS command was COPY BUDGET94 A: and you wanted your next command to be COPY BUDGET95 A:, you could press F2, type **4**, type **5**, then press F3 rather than typing the entire command.
68. Some programs allow you to temporarily exit to the DOS prompt and return to the program when you type **EXIT**. This is also good to remember if you accidentally make the switch to DOS and want to return to your program.
69. When naming files, avoid the use of special characters other than the underscore (_). Also, do not use spaces in filenames.
70. If a file is larger than the capacity of your disk, use BACKUP to make a copy of the file.
71. Use the * wildcard to accept any filename or filename extension ending. For example, COPY BUDG*.W* A: will copy all files that have BUDG as the first four characters in their filename and W as the first character in the filename extension.
72. Use the ? wildcard each time to you want to accept any character for a specific position in a filename or filename extension. For example, ??BUDG will accept files names such as 93BUDG or 94BUDG.
73. Never use wildcards to delete files unless you check first what will be deleted by using the same pattern with the DIR command and reviewing the list of filenames that displays.

74. If you have DOS version 3.2 or higher you can use the XCOPY command instead of COPY. If you use the /P option with XCOPY, it will prompt you before copying each file.
75. XCOPY with the /D:date option will copy files changed on or after a specific date. It is a good way to make a copy of changed data between backups.
76. Another handy option with XCOPY that is not available through the COPY command is the /S switch. Using this switch will copy all non-empty subdirectories below the directory you are copying.
77. You can use FORMAT with the /F switch to format a disk as low density in a high density drive. For example, FORMAT A: /F:720 will format a 3 1/2 inch disk as low density even though the drive may be high density. Check the switch options available for your version of DOS for the FORMAT command, as there are different switches to create a low density format in earlier releases.
78. Knowing some commonly used filename extensions will make it easier to determine what a file contains. Check this list:

.ASC	ASCII file
.BAK	Backup file
.BAT	Batch file
.COM	Program file
.EXE	Program file
.SYS	System file
.TXT	Text file

79. DOS refers to disk drives as the letter of the drive followed by a colon. Drive A is A: to DOS.
80. Don't use filenames like CON, PRN, and LPT1. They are reserved for DOS use and refer to devices or parts of your hardware.
81. You can add volume labels to disks when they are formatted or later with the LABEL command. A volume label can be as long as 11 characters and is used as an internal label for the disk that displays when you look at the disk directory.
82. You can print a directory listing with the entry DIR >PRN if you have a printer attached to your system.
83. If you want to look at just the filenames in a directory, try DIR /W to list more than one filename on a line.

84. Use the TREE command if you are working from the DOS prompt and want to look at the directory structure of your disk.
85. Use the CLS command to clear your screen display of incorrect DOS command entries if you are getting frustrated and want to start fresh.
86. If you have Windows, you can use File New in the Program Manager to create a program item for Quicken, enabling it to run under Windows. You can also use the File Run command to run Quicken under Windows without adding an icon for it.
87. You can use the /A switch to append a new file created with BACKUP to a disk that already contains backup data. This is especially useful if you are creating backups of selected files in different directories.
88. The BACKUP /D:date option allows you to backup only those files changed on or after a specified date.
89. Using the /S option with BACKUP backs up data in subdirectories.
90. You cannot restore backup data with COPY. Only the RESTORE command can read data written with BACKUP.
91. If you have DOS 5 or higher, you can install DOSKEYS and access your entire history of DOS prompt entries with the ↑ key.
92. If you get the DOS message: Not ready reading drive X, Abort, Retry, Fail?, check to be sure that you have referenced the correct drive. If the drive is correct, you may have forgotten to put a disk in or close the drive door.
93. Check your entry for spelling mistakes if DOS tells you that it can't find a file or that you have entered a bad command or filename.
94. Use COMP or DISKCOMP to compare a file or disk before mailing off a copy to someone else to insure that the copy is good.
95. Access help for DOS 5 or 6 commands with entries such as HELP XCOPY or XCOPY /?.
96. Run a defragmentation program if you begin to get sluggish performance from your hard disk. Norton's Utilities Speed Disk is one option.
97. You can delete commands like FDISK and FORMAT from computers accessible by many people to prevent accidental or planned deletion through these commands of data on a hard disk.
98. You can use COPY CON FILENAME.BAT to create a short batch file. Although there is no option for corrections other than starting over, everything you type will be saved.
99. If you have DOS 5 or higher, use the new DOS Editor rather than EDLIN.

100. You can change the order of directory listing entries with the /O switch in DOS 5 or 6. DIR /O-D sorts from the newest file date to the oldest.
101. If you use DOS Shell, you don't have to wait for it to finish reading all the disk information. You can press Esc and change drives or perform another task.

PART 2

HOME APPLICATIONS

C H A P T E R

investments banking FILE register expenses DEDUCTIONS
tips finances INCOME equity net pay
checks revenue bank statements
statements
dividends assets business tips
INCOME cash flow
banking business tips
budget FILE FILE reports
DEDUCTIONS business tips checks
statements cash flow tips mortgage
net pay taxes bank revenue
business tips
mortgage cash dividends tips
business tips investments
register statements
business tips taxes
reports expenses tips
equity investments INCOME
checks statements bank cash
assets checks budget tips finances net pay

EXPANDING THE SCOPE OF FINANCIAL ENTRIES

The purpose of the last five chapters was to get you started using Quicken's features quickly. The basics you learned in those chapters will help you manage your checking account transactions better. For some individuals, this will be sufficient. Others will want to increase their knowledge of Quicken to take full advantage of its capabilities. Even if you think you learned all the tasks you need in the first few chapters, read the first two sections in this chapter. These sections will teach you about Quicken files and setting up an account separate from the one you used for the practice exercises. Then, if you feel you know enough to meet your needs, stop reading at the end of the section titled "Quicken Files" and enter some of your own transactions.

Even personal finances can be too complex to be handled with a single account. In one household, there may be transactions for both individual and joint checking accounts, credit card accounts, and savings accounts. Quicken allows you to set up these different accounts within one Quicken file, which enables you to include information from multiple accounts in reports.

Accounts alone are not always enough to organize transactions logically. You might find you need to change the categories to assign to your transactions; you might even want to establish main categories with subcategories beneath them. You used categories earlier to identify transactions as utilities expense or salary income. Using subcategories, you might create several groupings under the utilities expense for electricity, gas, and water.

Classes are another way of organizing your transactions to provide a different perspective from categories. You might think of classes as answering the "who," "what," "when," or "where" of a transaction. For example, you could assign a transaction to the clothing category and then set up and assign it to a class for the family member purchasing the clothing.

In this chapter you will also learn how to assign transactions to more than one account—for example, how to transfer funds between accounts.

All of these features are presented here using the assumption that you are recording transactions for your personal finances. If you are interested in using Quicken to record both personal and business transactions, read the chapters in this section first. When you get to Chapter 11, "Setting Up Quicken for Your Business," you learn how to set up Quicken for your business. You can then select a category structure and create accounts that will allow you to manage both business and personal transactions.

The material in these chapters builds on the procedures you have already mastered. You should feel free to adapt the entries provided to match your actual financial transactions. For example, you might want to change the dollar amount of transactions, the categories to which they are assigned, and the transaction dates shown.

Again, be aware of the dates for the transaction entries in these chapters. As you know, the date of the transaction entry, relative to the current date, determines whether a transaction is postdated. The current date triggers the reminder to process groups of transactions you want to enter on a certain date. Using your current date for transaction entries will cause this not to occur. Also, creating reports that match the examples in this book will be difficult unless you use the dates presented for the transaction. The varied dates used permit the creation of more illustrative reports.

Quicken Files

When you first started working in Chapter 2, "Making Register Entries," you created a file called QDATA. Although you only entered one filename, Quicken created several files on your disk to manage your accounts and the information within them. Since all the files have the same filename but different filename extensions, this book will refer to them collectively as a *file*. When you copy a Quicken data file, all four of these files must be copied.

You worked with only one account in QDATA, but you can use multiple accounts within a file. You might use one account for a savings account and a different one for checking. You can also have accounts for credit cards, cash, assets, and liabilities, although most individuals do not have financial situations that warrant more than a few accounts.

You could continue to enter the transactions from this chapter in the 1st U.S. Bank account in the QDATA file, or you could set up a new account in the QDATA file. However, if you adapted the chapter entries to meet your own financial situation, your new data would be intermingled with the practice transactions from the last few chapters. To avoid this, you will need to establish a file for the practice transactions. In this section, you will learn how to set up new transactions that are stored separately from the existing entries. You will also learn how to create a backup copy of a file to safeguard the data you enter.

Adding a New File

You already have the QDATA file for all the transactions entered in the first section of this book. Now you will set up a new file and create accounts within it. Later, if you wish, you can delete the QDATA file to free the space it occupies on your disk.

The file will be called PERSONAL and will initially contain a checking account called Cardinal Bank. This account is similar to the 1st U.S. Bank checking account you created in QDATA. Since it is in a new file, a different name is used. Other appropriate names might be BUSINESS CHECKING and JOINT CHECKING, depending on the type of account. Naturally, if you have more than one account at Cardinal Bank, they cannot all be named Cardinal Bank. In the section "Creating a New Savings Account" later in this chapter, you will add the account Cardinal Saving to the PERSONAL file.

From the Main Menu, follow these steps to set up the new file and to add the first account to it:

1. Select **F**ile Activities.
2. Select **S**elect/Set Up File.

   Quicken displays the window shown in Figure 6-1. Notice the entry for the existing file, QDATA.
3. Move the cursor to Set Up New File > and press Enter.

   Quicken presents a window for entering the filename and the file location categories you wish to use.
4. Type **PERSONAL** as the name for the file and press Enter.
5. Check the directory shown on the line "Location for data files" and make changes to reference a valid directory if a change is required.
6. Press Enter to complete the creation of the new file.
7. Type **1** and press Enter. This will restrict your categories to Home categories when Quicken presents the Default Categories window.

   Quicken creates several files for each filename by adding different filename extensions to the name you provide. This means you must provide a valid filename of no more than eight characters. Do not include spaces or special symbols in your entries for filenames.

   Quicken displays the window for selecting or creating files with the PERSONAL file added, as shown in Figure 6-2.

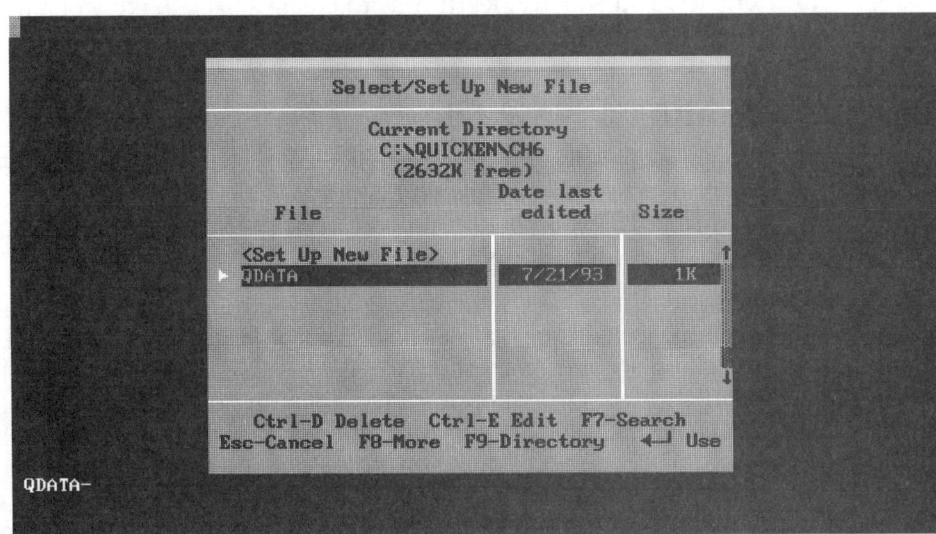

Setting up a new file
Figure 6-1.

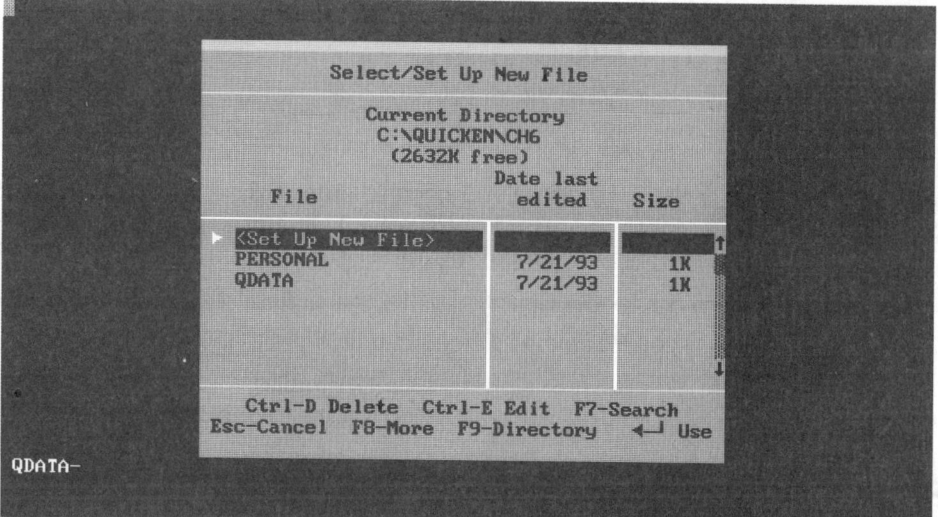

Window showing the new PERSONAL file
Figure 6-2.

8. Move the cursor to PERSONAL.
9. Press Enter, and Quicken displays the Set Up New Account window, shown in Figure 6-3.
10. Type **1** to choose Bank Account for the account type and press Enter.
11. Type **Cardinal Bank** and press Enter.

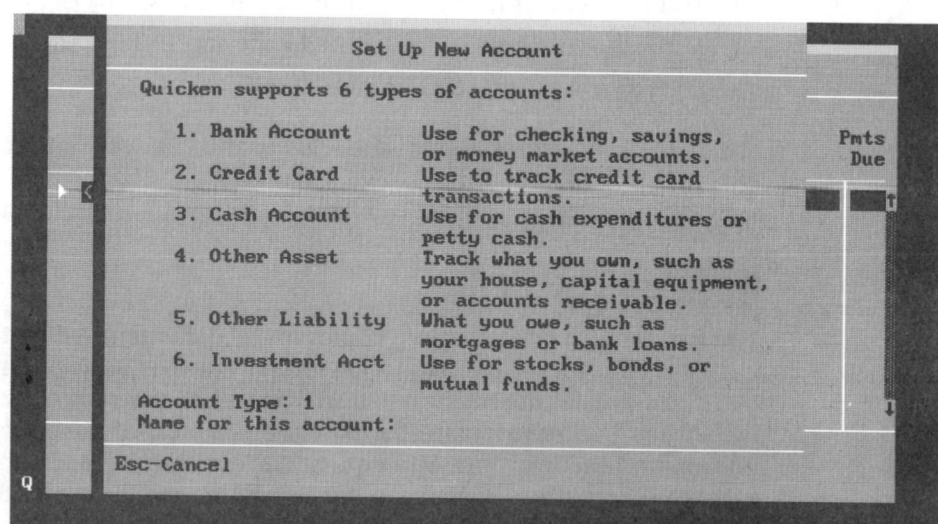

The Set Up New Account window
Figure 6-3.

The Starting Balance and Description Window displays.

12. Type **2500** for the balance and press Enter.
13. Type **7/13/94** and press Enter.

NOTE: Any time you need to enter a date you can use the calendar feature discussed in Chapter 1. Just pop up the calendar with Ctrl-K, highlight the desired date, and paste it into the register with F9.

14. Type **Personal Checking** and press Enter.
15. Type **1**, press Enter to specify the Bank Statement as the source for the 2500 entry, and press Enter again to continue.

    Quicken returns you to the window for selecting an account.
16. Highlight Cardinal Bank and press Enter.

Changing the Active File

The result of the last exercise was the creation of a second file. You can work in either file at any time and select any account within a file. To change from the current file, PERSONAL, to QDATA, follow these steps:

1. Press Esc to return to the Main Menu.
2. Select **F**ile Activities.
3. Select **S**elect/Set Up File.
4. Move the cursor to QDATA in the list and press Enter.
5. Move the cursor to 1st U.S. Bank in the account list and press Enter.
6. Press Esc to return to the Main Menu.

The QDATA file is now active. The register and check writing screen show the 1st U.S. Bank account as active. Change the file back to PERSONAL and activate the account for Cardinal Bank by following the same steps.

Backing Up a File

You will want to create backup copies of the data managed by the Quicken system on a regular basis. This allows you to recover all your entries in the event of a disk failure because you will be able to use your copy to restore all the entries. You need a blank formatted disk to record the backup information the first time. Subsequent backups can be made on this disk without reformatting it. You can create a formatted disk without exiting Quicken.

Formatting a Disk

To format the disk from within Quicken, first open the register from the Main Menu, and then follow these steps:

1. Select **A**ctivities and then select Use **D**OS.

   The DOS prompt displays on your screen; you can enter DOS commands as if Quicken were not in memory.
2. Type **FORMAT A:** and press Enter.

   The system will ask you to insert a new disk for drive A and press Enter when ready.
3. Place a blank disk in drive A, close the drive, and press Enter in response to the DOS prompt to insert a disk.

   The system will format the disk and ask you if you want to format another disk.
4. Type **N** and press Enter.
5. Type **EXIT** and press Enter to return to Quicken.

The disk you just formatted will be used to store a backup copy of the current files. You can also exit Quicken, format the disk, and start Quicken again.

Creating Backup Files

Quicken has a Backup and Restore feature that allows you to safeguard the investment you have made in entering your data. You can back up all your account files from the **P**rint/Acct menu on the register screen. To back up selected files, select the **B**ack Up File option found in the File Activities item in the Set **P**references selections. Follow these steps to back up the current file:

1. Press Esc to return to the Main Menu.
2. Select **F**ile Activities.
3. Select **B**ack Up File.
4. Place your blank, formatted disk in drive A, type **A** as the drive, and press Enter.
5. Select PERSONAL and press Enter.
6. Press Enter to acknowledge the completion of the backup when Quicken displays the successful backup message.
7. Press Esc until the Main Menu appears.

With backups, if you ever lose your hard disk, you can re-create your data directory and then use the Restore option to copy your backup files to the directory. You can also copy Quicken data files from one floppy drive to another as a quick means of backup if you do not have a hard disk.

8. Select Use **R**egister to open the register screen, as shown in Figure 6-4.

Customizing Categories

When you set up the new PERSONAL file, you selected Home categories as the standard categories option. This selection provides access to the more than 50 category choices displayed in Table 6-1. You can see that some categories are listed as expenses and others as income; some of them even have subcategories. Any subcategories that you create later will also be shown in this column. The last column in the table shows which categories are tax related.

Editing the Existing Category List

You can change the name of any existing category; change its classification as income, expense, or subcategory; or change its tax-related status. To modify a category, use the steps listed in the following:

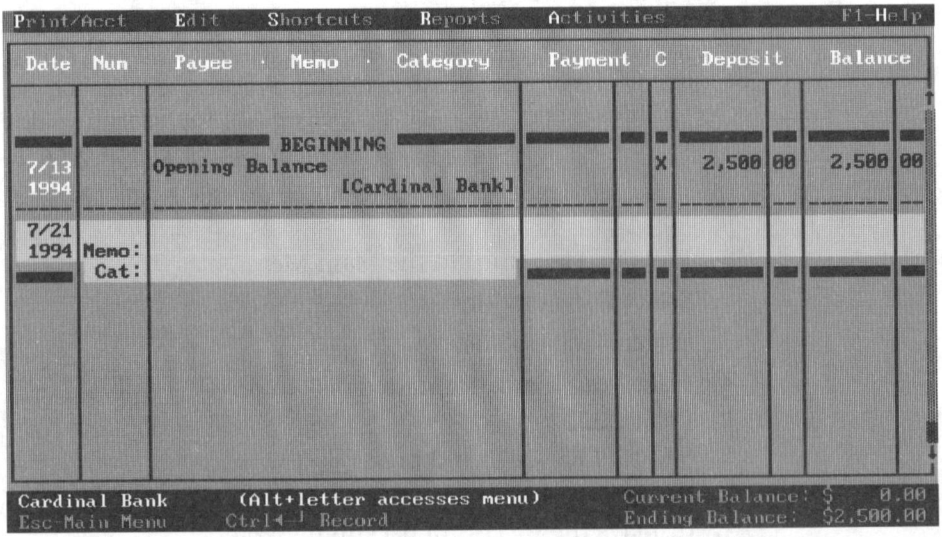

Register for the new account
Figure 6-4.

Category	Type	Tax Related
Bonus	Income	Yes
Canada Pen	Income	Yes
Div Income	Income	Yes
Gift Received	Income	Yes
Int Inc	Income	Yes
Invest Inc	Income	Yes
Old Age Pension	Income	Yes
Other Inc	Income	Yes
Salary	Income	Yes
Auto	Expense	No
Fuel	Subcategory	No
Loan	Subcategory	No
Service	Subcategory	No
Bank Chrg	Expense	No
Charity	Expense	Yes
Cash	Subcategory	Yes
Non-Cash	Subcategory	Yes
Childcare	Expense	Yes/No depending on income bracket
Christmas	Expense	No
Clothing	Expense	No
Dining	Expense	No
Dues	Expense	No
Education	Expense	No
Entertain	Expense	No
Gifts	Expense	No
Groceries	Expense	No
Home Rpair	Expense	No
Household	Expense	No
Housing	Expense	No

Standard Personal Categories
Table 6-1.

Category	Type	Tax Related
Insurance	Expense	No
Int Exp	Expense	Yes
Invest Exp	Expense	Yes
Medical	Expense	Yes
Doctor	Subcategory	Yes
Medicine	Subcategory	Yes
Misc	Expense	No
Mort Int	Expense	Yes
Other Exp	Expense	Yes
Recreation	Expense	No
RRSP	Expense	No
Subscriptions	Expense	No
Supplies	Expense	Yes
Tax	Expense	Yes
Fed	Subcategory	Yes
Medicare	Subcategory	Yes
Other	Subcategory	Yes
Prop	Subcategory	Yes
Soc Sec	Subcategory	Yes
State	Subcategory	Yes
Telephone	Expense	No
Tax Spouse	Expense	Yes
Fed	Subcategory	Yes
Medicare	Subcategory	Yes
Soc Sec	Subcategory	Yes
State	Subcategory	Yes
UIC (Unemploy Ins)	Expense	Yes
Utilities	Expense	No
Gas & Electric	Subcategory	No
Water	Subcategory	No

Standard Personal Categories (*continued*)
Table 6-1.

1. Press Ctrl-C from the register to display the category list.
2. Move the arrow cursor to the category you want to change.
3. Press Ctrl-E to edit the information for the category.
4. Change the entries you wish to alter.
5. Press Ctrl-Enter to complete the changes.

   If you change the name of the category, Quicken will automatically change it in any transactions that have already been assigned to that category.

Adding Categories

You can also add your own categories to provide additional options specific to your needs. For example, if you have just set up housekeeping, buying furniture might be a major budget category. Since you would otherwise have to lump these purchases with others in the Household category, you might want to add Furniture as a category option. Typing **Furniture** in the category field when you enter your first furniture transaction automatically makes it a category option. When Quicken does not find the category in the existing list, it displays a window asking if you want to select a category or add the category to the list. You would choose Add to Category List.

If you have a number of categories to add, it is simpler to add them before starting to enter data. To use this approach for adding the Furniture category, follow these steps:

1. Press Ctrl-C from the register.
2. Press Home to move to the top of the category list.

   <New Category> will appear as the top entry in the list.
3. Press Enter.

   Quicken will allow you to enter a new category by using the window shown in the following, which contains entries for a new Furniture category that you could add to your Category list:

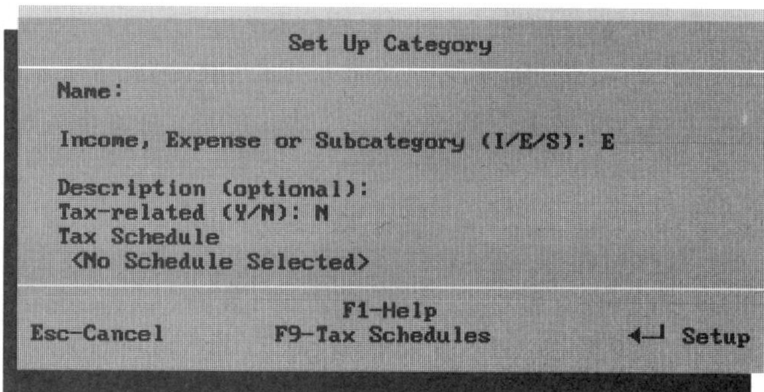

4. Type **Furniture** and press Enter.
5. Type **E** and press Enter.
6. Type **Household Furniture** and press Enter.
7. Type **N** and press Enter to complete the entry.

   Categories that will be added as transactions are entered for the remaining examples in this chapter. You should feel free to customize the categories as you enter them.

NOTE: Available RAM will limit the number of categories you can create in each category list. If you have a 512K system with barely enough memory to run Quicken, you might have a limit of 150 categories, whereas a 640K system might support 1,000 categories. You are also limited to 15 characters for each category entry.

Requiring Categories in All Transactions

Another customization option Quicken offers is a reminder to place a category entry in a transaction before it is recorded. If you attempt to record a transaction without a category, Quicken will not complete the transaction until you confirm that you want to enter it without a category.

To require the entry of categories, choose Set **P**references from the Main Menu and then select **T**ransaction Settings. Press Enter until item 4 is active and type **Y**. Press Ctrl-Enter to finalize the settings change. The next time you attempt to record a transaction without a category, Quicken will stop to confirm your choice before saving.

Using Subcategories

Now that you have set up your file and new account and have customized your categories, you are ready to enter some transactions. Since you are already proficient at basic transaction entry from earlier chapters, you will want to look at some additional ways of modifying accounts as you make entries.

One option is to create categories that are subcategories of an existing category. For instance, rather than continuing to allocate all your utility bills to two Utilities categories, Gas & Electric and Water, you could edit the existing Gas & Electric category to use it for Gas and add a new category for Electric. After the addition and change you can allocate expenses to electricity, water, or gas separately. You could add the Electric subcategory just as you added the new category for furniture, but you can also create it when you are entering transactions and realize that the existing categories do not provide the breakdown you would like.

Entering a New Subcategory

When you enter both a category and a subcategory for a transaction, you type the category name, followed by a colon (:) and then the subcategory name. It is important that the category be specified first and the subcategory second.

You will enter utility bills as the first entries in the new account. Follow these steps to complete the entries for the gas and electric bills, creating a subcategory under Utilities for each:

1. With the next blank transaction in the register highlighted, type **7/25/94** as the date for the first transaction and press Enter. Type **101** and press Enter.
2. Type **Consumer Power** and press Enter. Type **35.45** for the payment amount and press Enter. Type **Electric Bill** and press Enter. Type **Utilities:Electric** and press Enter again.

   Quicken prompts you with the Category Not Found window and allows you to add the category or select one from the category list. Notice that only the Electric entry is highlighted in the Category field, since Utilities is already in the category list.
3. Type **1** to select Add to Category List. Quicken displays the Set Up Category window for you to define the category.
4. Press Enter to accept S for the subcategory.
5. Type **Electric Utilities** and press Enter.

   Although this description is optional, it is a good idea to enter one so your reports will be informative. Your screen now looks like this:

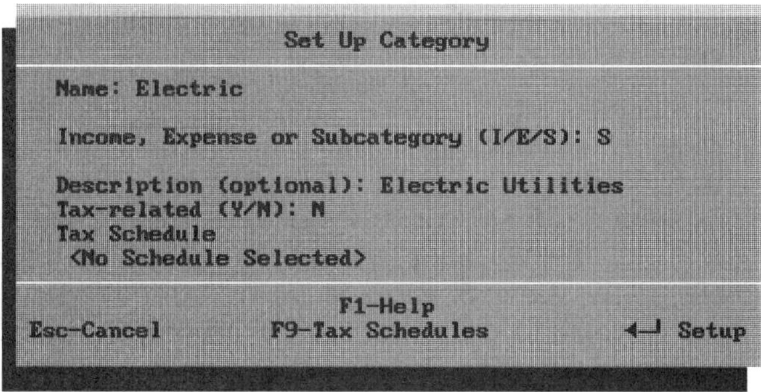

6. Press Enter to select N (for No) for Tax-related. Then press Enter to complete the transaction.
7. Press Ctrl-Enter to record the transaction entry.

Quicken displays a message indicating that this is your first subcategory.

Completing the Utility Subcategories

To create a subcategory for the gas bill, enter the following information in each of the fields shown.

Date:	7/25/94
Num:	102
Payee:	West Michigan Gas
Payment:	17.85
Memo:	Gas Bill

Don't record the transaction. With the cursor in the category field, follow these steps:

1. Press Ctrl-C to display the Category Transfer List window.
2. Use ↓ to move to Utilities Gas & Electric.
3. Press Ctrl-E to edit the current category.
4. Change the name on the Edit Category screen to **Gas** and press Enter twice.
5. Change the description to **Gas Utilities** and press Ctrl-Enter.
6. Press Enter to use the category.
7. Press Ctrl-Enter to finalize the transaction entry.

You still need to enter the telephone bill, but since Quicken already defines Telephone as a Home category, you cannot consider Telephone as a subcategory of Utilities. However, you could edit the Telephone category and change it from an expense to a subcategory. For now, add it as a separate category and put the following entries in the transaction fields.

Date:	7/30/94
Num:	103
Payee:	Alltel
Payment:	86.00
Memo:	Telephone Bill
Category:	Telephone

Splitting Transactions

Split transactions are transactions that affect more than one category. You can decide how the transaction affects each of the categories involved. If you split an expense transaction, you are saying that portions of the transaction should be considered as expenses in two different categories. For example, a check written at a supermarket might cover more than just groceries. You might purchase a $25.00 plant as a gift at the same time you purchase your groceries. Recording the entire amount of the check as groceries would not accurately reflect the purpose of the check. Quicken allows you to record the $25.00 amount as a gift purchase and the remainder for groceries. In fact, after allocating the $25.00 to gifts, it even tells you the remaining balance that needs to be allocated to other categories. You could also enter a transaction in which you cashed a check and use the split transaction capability to account for your spending. With Quicken, you can even split transactions by entering percentages rather than actual dollar amounts. As an example of splitting transactions, enter the following transaction for check number 100.

Date:	7/20/94
Num:	100
Payee:	Cash
Payment:	100.00
Memo:	Groceries & Misc

Don't record the transaction. With the cursor in the Category field, follow these steps:

1. Press Ctrl-S (or select **E**dit and then select **S**plit Transaction).
2. Type **Groceries**, the name of the first category you want to use. You can stop typing as soon as QuickFill provides a match.

3. Press Enter, type **Grocery & Market**, and press Enter again.
4. Type **75%** and press Enter. Quicken records 75 percent of the total entered, or 75.00.
5. Type **Misc** as the next category and press Enter.
6. Type **Drug & Hardware Store** and press Enter.

   Quicken displays 25.00 as the amount for the second category, as shown in Figure 6-5.
7. Press Ctrl-Enter to accept the amount entry.

   The first category entered for the split transaction appears in the register as the category. The word "SPLIT" also appears under the check number.
8. Press Ctrl-Enter to record the transaction.

There are many other times when you might elect to use split transactions. Assigning part of a mortgage payment to interest and the balance to principal is a good example. Credit card purchases can also be handled in this fashion if you elect not to set up a special credit card account. Normally, the split transaction approach is a better alternative if you pay your bill in full each month.

Notice that up to the point when you enter the category, there is no difference between a split transaction entry and any other entry in the register. Complete the entries listed in the following to add another split transaction for a credit card payment:

1. Type **8/3/94** as the date and press Enter.

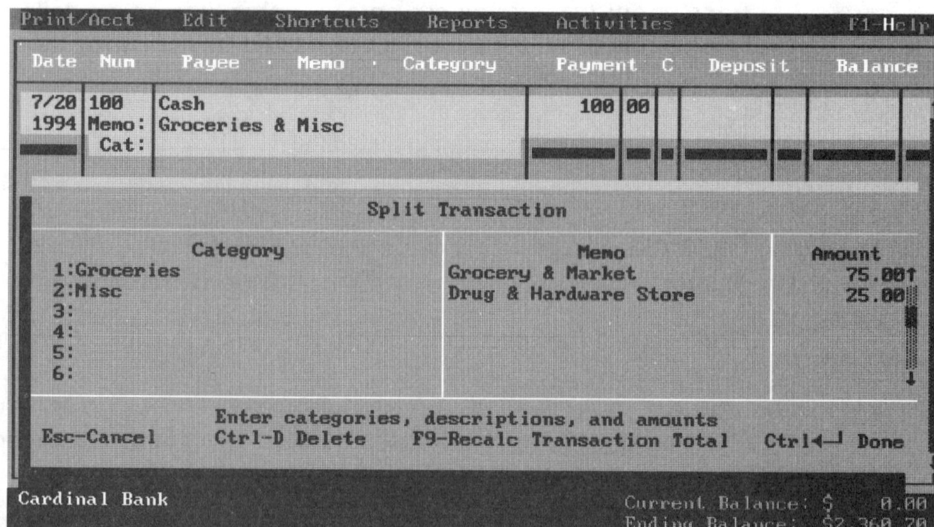

Splitting the cash transaction
Figure 6-5.

2. Type **105** as the check number and press Enter.
3. Type **Easy Credit Card** for the Payee entry and press Enter.
4. Type **450.00** and press Enter to complete the payment amount entry.
5. Type **July 25th Statement** for the Memo field and press Enter.
6. Select **E**dit and select **S**plit Transaction, or press Ctrl-S.

   Quicken displays the Split Transaction screen with up to six category fields displayed. You can assign as many as 30 split categories.
7. Press Ctrl-C with the cursor in the first Category field.
8. Select Clothing and press Enter twice.
9. Type **Blue Blouse** in the Description field and press Enter.
10. Type **50** and press Enter.

    Quicken allocates the first $50.00 of credit card expense to Clothing and shows the $400.00 balance below this entry.
11. Complete the remaining entries shown in Figure 6-6 to detail how the credit card expenses were distributed.

    When you press Ctrl-Enter for final processing, you will see the Number field for this transaction contains the word "SPLIT" under the check number, and "Clothing" is displayed in the Category field.
12. Press Ctrl-Enter to record the transaction.

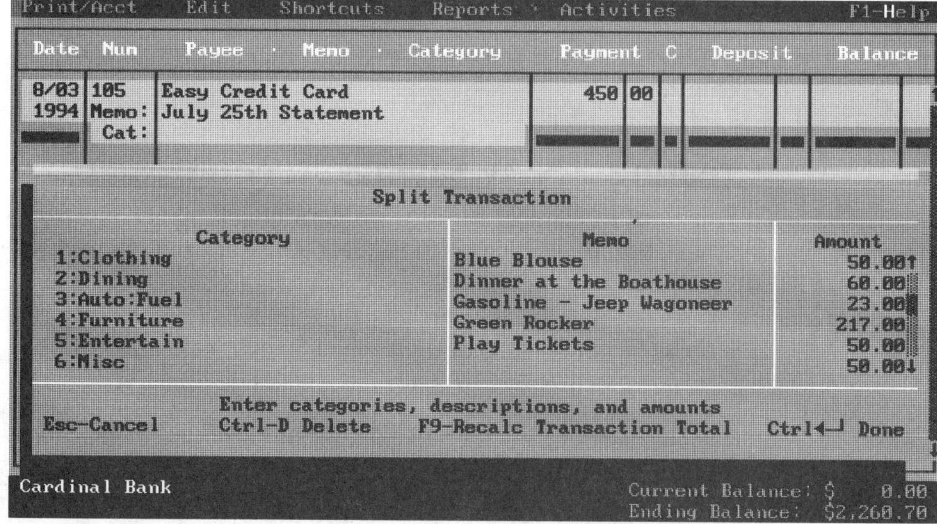

Splitting the credit card transaction
Figure 6-6.

NOTE: Any time you want to go back and look at transactions for a specific date, pop up the calendar with Ctrl-K and use the Ctrl-G Go to Date feature to position on a specific date in the register.

Using Multiple Accounts

Quicken makes it easy to create multiple accounts. Since here all the accounts will be created in the same file, you can choose to have separate reports for each account or one report that shows them all. You will have an account register for each account that you create.

Types of Accounts

Savings accounts, investment accounts, cash accounts, and credit card accounts are all possible additional accounts. Savings accounts and investment accounts should definitely be kept separate from your checking account, since you will want to monitor both the growth and balance in these accounts.

The need for cash and credit card accounts varies by individual. If you pay the majority of your expenses in cash and need a detailed record of your expenditures, a cash account is a good idea. With credit cards, if your purchases are at a reasonable level and you pay the balance in full each month, the extra time required to maintain a separate account might not be warranted. In the initial example in this chapter, neither cash nor credit card accounts are used. If you decide you need them, you can use the same procedures to create them that you used to create the savings account. The section "Using a Separate Credit Card Account" near the end of the chapter provides additional information about maintaining a separate credit card account.

Creating a New Savings Account

If you want to transfer funds from your checking account to a savings account, you must have a savings account set up. Follow these steps to create the new account:

1. Select **P**rint/Acct and then select Select/Set Up **A**ccount.
2. Select <New Account> and press Enter.
3. Type **1** for Bank Account type and press Enter.
4. Type **Cardinal Saving** for the account name and press Enter.
5. Type **500.00** for the balance and press Enter.

6. Type **7/15/94** as the date and press Enter.
7. Type **Savings account** for the description and press Enter.
8. Type **1** as the source of the starting balance and press Enter twice. Quicken will open the Select Account to Use window.
9. Select Cardinal Bank and press Enter.

Transferring Funds to a Different Account

It is easy to transfer funds from one account to another as long as both accounts are established. You might transfer a fixed amount to savings each month to cover long-range savings plans or to cover large, fixed expenses that are due annually or semi-annually. Follow these steps to make a transfer from the checking account to the savings account:

1. Complete these entries for the transaction fields down to Category:

Date:	8/5/94
Payee:	Cardinal Saving
Payment:	200.00
Memo:	Transfer to savings

2. Press Ctrl-C with Category highlighted. Press End to move to the end of the list, select [Cardinal Saving] from the Category and Transfer list, and press Enter.
3. Press Ctrl-Enter to confirm the transaction.

You will notice brackets around the account name in the Category field of the register. Although not visible onscreen, Quicken automatically creates the parallel transaction in the other account. It will also delete both transactions as soon as you specify that one is no longer needed.

Memorized Transactions

Many of your financial transactions are likely to repeat. You pay your rent or mortgage payments each month. Likewise, utility bills and credit card payments are paid at about the same time each month. Cash inflows in the form of paychecks are also regularly scheduled. Other payments such as groceries also repeat, but probably not on the same dates each month.

Quicken can *memorize* transactions that are entered from the register or check-writing screen. Once memorized, these transactions can be used to generate similar transactions. Amounts and dates might change, and you can edit these fields without having to reenter the payee, memo, and category information.

Memorizing a Register Entry

Any transaction in the register can be memorized. Memorized transactions can be recalled for later use, printed, changed, and deleted. To try this, you will need to add a few more transactions to the account register to complete the entries for August. Add these transactions to your register:

Date:	8/1/94
Payee:	Payroll deposit
Deposit	1585.99
Memo:	August 1 paycheck
Category:	Salary

Date:	8/2/94
Num:	104
Payee:	Great Lakes Savings & Loan
Payment:	350.00
Memo:	August Payment
Category:	Mort Pay

NOTE: Mort Pay is a new category you should add, since you do not have the information required to split the transaction between the existing interest and principal categories in the Home category list. Use Entire Mortgage Payment as the description when you add the category.

Date:	8/4/94
Num:	106
Payee:	Maureks
Payment:	60.00
Memo:	Groceries
Category:	Groceries

Date:	8/6/94
Num:	107
Payee:	Orthodontics, Inc.

Payment:	100.00
Memo:	Monthly Orthodontics Payment
Category:	Medical:Doctor
Date:	8/15/94
Num:	108
Payee:	Meijer
Payment:	65.00
Memo:	Groceries
Category:	Groceries

You now have transactions representing an entire month entered in the checking account. You can elect to have Quicken memorize as many as you think will repeat every month. To memorize the transaction for Consumer Power, follow these steps:

1. Highlight the Consumer Power transaction in the register.
2. Select **S**hortcuts and **M**emorize Transaction (or press Ctrl-M to select **M**emorize Transaction without opening the menu).

   Quicken will highlight the transaction and prompt you for a response.
3. Press Enter to confirm and memorize the transaction. You can also memorize transactions that have not been recorded in the register, but you will have to press Ctrl-Enter after memorizing them to update the register.

Using the same procedure, memorize all the remaining transactions except the transactions written to Maureks, Meijer, and the one for Cash.

Quicken will memorize split transactions in the same way as any other transactions. You should review the split transactions carefully for information that changes each month. For example, the entry for the credit card payment is likely to be split across several categories if you are entering the detail in the check register, rather than in a separate credit card account. You will want to edit both the categories and the amounts into which the main transaction is split.

You can use Ctrl-T to display the memorized transactions; your list should match Figure 6-7. If you want to print the list once it is displayed, press Ctrl-P, type a number to select your printer, and press Enter to print. To remove the list from the screen, press Esc. To enter a new transaction, select <New Transaction>.

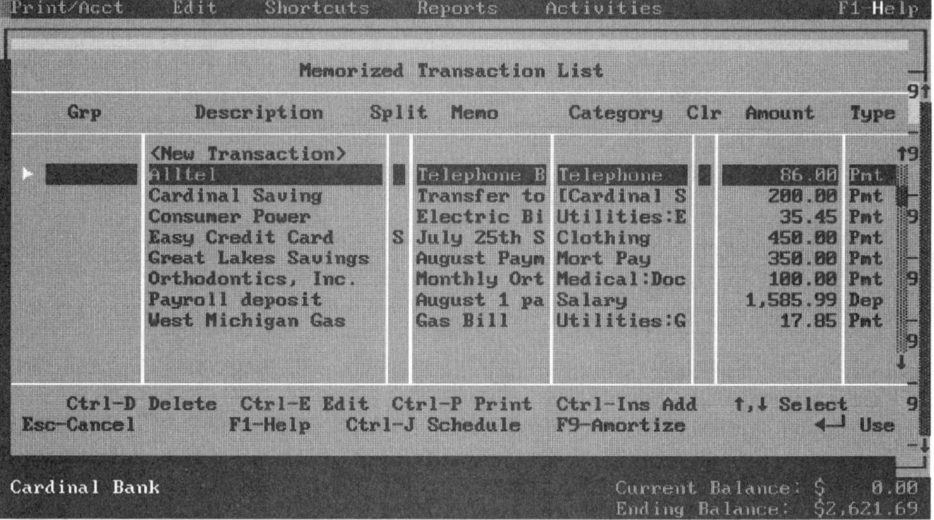

List of memorized transactions
Figure 6-7.

Using Memorized Transactions

To recall a memorized transaction and place it in the register, move to the next blank transaction form (unless you want the recalled transaction to replace a transaction already on the screen). Press Ctrl-T to recall the Memorized Transaction List window. Use the arrow keys to select the transaction you want to add to the register and press Enter. If you type the first few letters of the Payee field after pressing Ctrl-T, Quicken will take you to the correct area of the transaction list, since transactions are displayed in alphabetical order by payee. The selected transaction appears in the register with the date of the last transaction you entered, not that of the date that was stored when you memorized the transaction. You can edit the transaction in the register and press Ctrl-Enter when you are ready to record the entry.

Changing and Deleting Memorized Transactions

Quicken allows you to change a memorized transaction in the Memorized Transaction List by pressing Ctrl-T to activate the list and then pressing Ctrl-E to edit the highlighted transaction.

To delete a memorized transaction, you must first activate the transaction list by pressing Ctrl-T or by selecting **S**hortcuts and then selecting **R**ecall Transaction. Select the transaction you want to delete and press Ctrl-D. A warning message will appear asking you to confirm the deletion. When you press Enter, the transaction is no longer memorized.

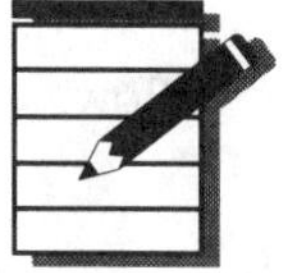

NOTE: If you attempt to memorize a transaction where the payee matches a transaction that has already been memorized, you will be prompted about memorizing the new transaction as a replacement or a second memorized transaction.

Memorizing a Check

The procedure for memorizing transactions while writing checks is identical to the one used for memorizing register transactions, except that you must be in the check-writing window. Memorized check and register transactions for the same account will appear in the same Memorized Transaction List and can be edited, deleted, or recalled from either the check-writing or register window.

Working with Scheduled Transactions and Scheduled Transaction Groups

Although you can recall memorized transactions individually as a way to reenter similar transactions, a better method can be to have Quicken automatically schedule and enter transactions for you. Quicken 7 can schedule individual transactions or groups of transactions. If you want to schedule groups of transactions, they must be memorized first. If you want to schedule individual transactions, they are entered on special transaction windows after telling Quicken which type of transaction you want to schedule.

If you have several memorized transactions that occur at the same time, a scheduled transaction group lets you focus on other tasks while Quicken remembers to enter the transactions you need. Quicken will record the entire group for you without prompting you about its entries, depending on how you define the scheduled transaction.

Defining a Scheduled Transaction Group

Quicken allows you to set up as many as 12 scheduled transaction groups. Defining a group is easy, but it requires several steps after memorizing all the transactions that will be placed in the group. You will need to describe the group. Finally, you will need to assign specific memorized transactions to the group. Although expense transactions are frequently used to create groups, you can also include an entry for a direct deposit payroll check that is deposited at the same time each month.

You will title your scheduled transaction group "Utilities" and will group the gas and electric transactions that occur near the end of each month. Follow these steps to create the group from the Cardinal Bank account register:

1. Select **S**cheduled Transactions from the **S**hortcuts menu.

   Quicken displays the window, shown in Figure 6-8.

2. Be sure the cursor is pointing to <New Transaction or Group> at 1, since this is the first unused transaction group, and press Enter.

   Quicken displays a window to allow you to define the group. Figure 6-9 shows this screen, with the entries you will make in the next steps.

3. Select 4 to tell Quicken that you want to define a scheduled transaction group and press Enter.

   The other transaction type options will result in a special window for the entry of an actual transaction when the New Transaction window is finalized. Other transaction types are payment, deposit, check, and electronic payment.

4. Press Enter to accept Monthly as the frequency for the transaction entry.
5. Press Enter to accept the account listed.
6. Type **8/25/94** as the next scheduled date and press Enter.

   You can choose to be prompted before the transaction is entered automatically. You can also specify how many days before the scheduled date you want to be notified.

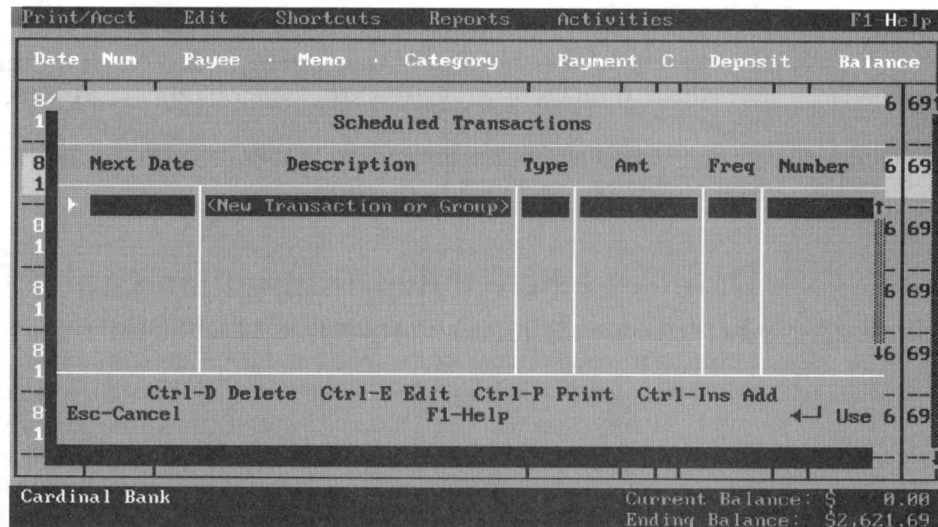

Setting up a scheduled transaction group
Figure 6-8.

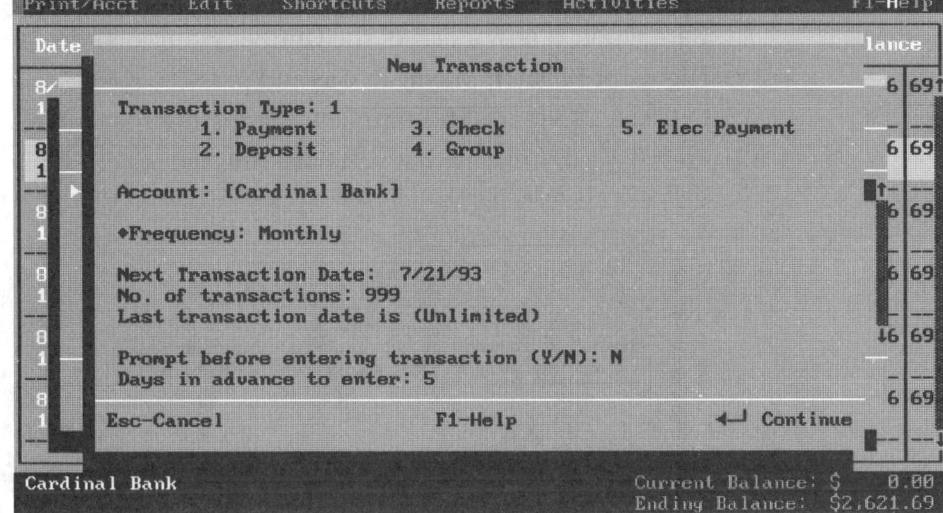

Defining a scheduled transaction group
Figure 6-9.

7. Press Enter to accept 999 as the number of transactions in the future that you want entered.

   This selection allows for unlimited scheduled entries. Quicken uses the next date and the frequency you specified to determine the date of the last transaction.

8. Type **Y** to indicate that you want to be prompted before the group is entered into your register.

9. Press Enter to accept the number of days in advance for the prompt that is currently listed.

   The Group Transaction window shown here is displayed to enter a name for the transaction group:

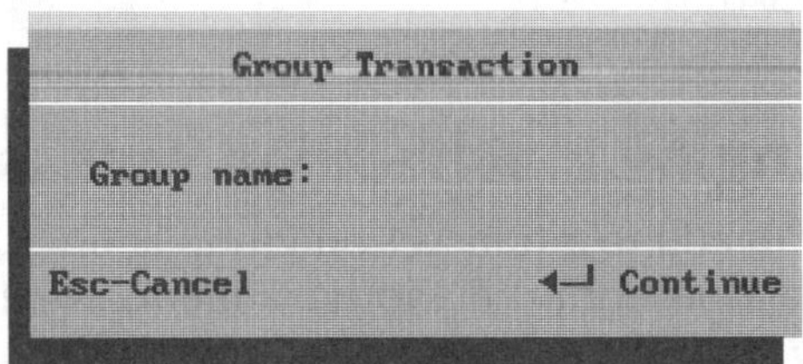

10. Type **Utilities** as the name for the group and press Enter twice until the Assign Transactions to Group window appears.

11. Highlight Consumer Power to select it and press Spacebar to assign the transaction to the Utilities group.

Note Utilities is entered in the group column, which indicates that the transaction is now a part of the Utilities group.

12. Highlight Western Michigan Gas and press Spacebar.

    Quicken also marks this transaction as part of the Utilities group.

13. Press Enter to indicate that you have finished selecting transactions. The message shown here will indicate that the group has been established:

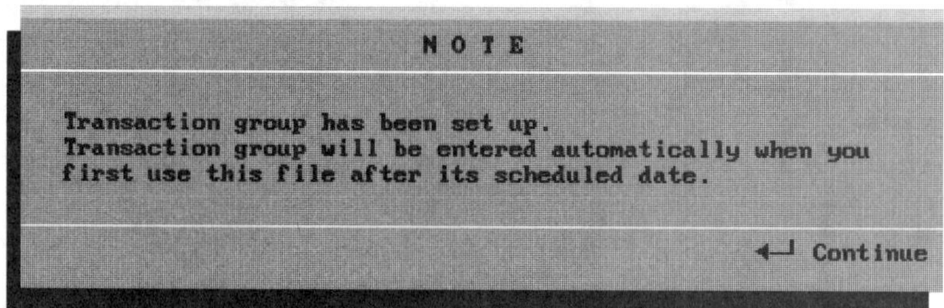

You might want to define other scheduled transaction groups to include mortgage payments and anything else that you might pay at the beginning of the month. You might also want to enter individual scheduled transactions for transactions that occur on a specific date each month. You can either define the transaction as you schedule it or highlight a transaction from the list of the ones memorized and request that it be scheduled. If you choose to use a scheduled transaction, it will display at the top of the screen while you define the scheduled group, as shown in Figure 6-10. You are not required to define additional scheduled groups or transactions in order to complete the remaining exercises in this section.

You can also create transaction groups that generate checks for you. These groups contain transactions that are memorized from the check-writing window. The procedure is the same as that just shown. You can identify these transactions in the Assign Transactions window by the Chk entry in the Type field. Remember that Pmt in the Type field indicates an account register transaction.

Changing a Scheduled Transaction Group

You can add to a transaction group at any time by selecting **S**cheduled Transaction from the **S**hortcuts menu. Next, you need to highlight the group you want to change and press Ctrl-E.

To make a change to the group or the timing of the reminder, use the same procedure and make the necessary changes, pressing Ctrl-Enter when you have finished changing the window. The window for assigning transactions to the group appears next to allow you to select additional transactions for inclusion in the group.

```
Schedule Memorized Transaction

Num    Payee · Memo · Category          Payment   C  Deposit
Paymt  Quick Delivery                    215 00
Memo:  Manuscript Delivery
 Cat:  Del Overngt/B

Account: [ANB Personal]

♦Frequency: Monthly

Next Transaction Date:  7/23/93
No. of transactions: 999
Last transaction date is (Unlimited)

Prompt before entering transaction (Y/N): N
Days in advance to enter: 5

F9 Check              Ctrl-S Split
Esc-Cancel            Shift-Ins Paste            ◄┘ Continue
```

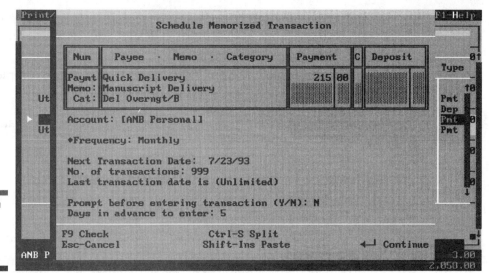

Scheduling an individual transaction
Figure 6-10.

To delete a scheduled transaction group, select **S**cheduled Transactions from the Shortcuts menu. Select the group you want to delete and press Ctrl-D. Quicken eliminates the group, but does not delete the memorized transactions that are part of it. It also does not affect any transactions recorded in the register by earlier executions of the scheduled group.

If you want to alter a transaction that is part of the transaction group, you will need to alter the memorized transaction. This means you have to recall the transaction on the check-writing screen or in the account register, depending on the type of transaction you have. Next, you need to make your changes and memorize the transaction again. Follow the procedures in the "Changing and Deleting Memorized Transactions" section earlier in this chapter.

NOTE: If you want to look at when you have transactions scheduled, pop up the calendar by pressing Ctrl-K. Scheduled transactions are marked with a T on the date, and notes are marked with an N.

Recording a Transaction Group

Once you have defined a scheduled transaction group, you can forget about it. Quicken will handle the entries for you when the time is right. You will receive a prompt about the entries only if you have requested one or if you are using a percentage split and Quicken needs to find out the transaction amount to be allocated. If you want to record the group early for some reason, you do not need to wait for Quicken. You can select the scheduled group and record it yourself.

To execute a transaction group from the account register, complete the following steps:

1. Press Esc to return to the register and select **S**cheduled Transactions from the **S**hortcuts menu.

   Quicken will display a list of transaction groups.
2. Select the Utilities group by moving the highlight to it.
3. Press Enter. Quicken displays the Enter Scheduled Transaction window, which looks like Figure 6-11.
4. Type **1** and press Enter to enter the group of transactions in the account register now.

   The new transactions are entered with a date of 8/25/94.

   Modify the utilities transaction group entries just recorded and add the last transaction for Meijer to complete the August transactions for your account register. (Press Ctrl-Enter to record each transaction after the modifications have been made.) Enter these transactions now:

Num:	109
Payee:	Alltel
Payment:	23.0

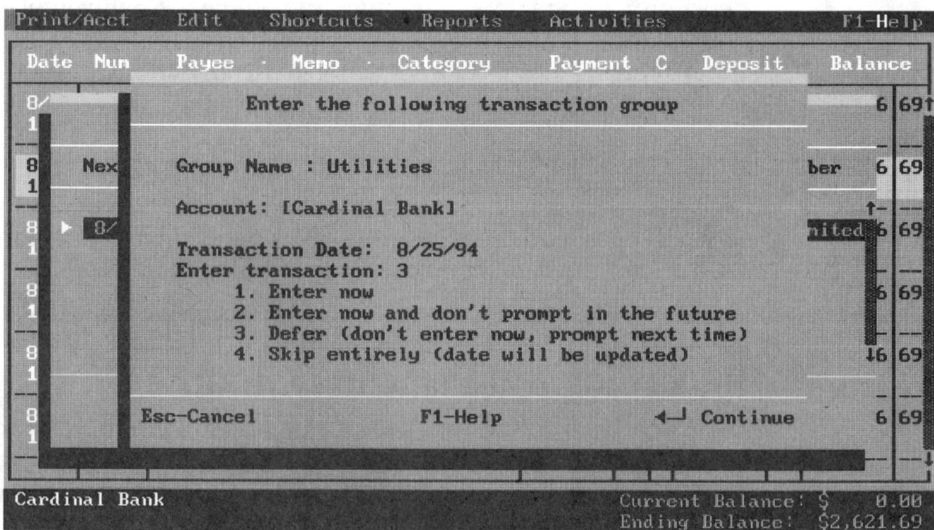

Invoking a scheduled group yourself
Figure 6-11.

Num:	110
Payee:	Consumer Power
Payment:	30.75

Num:	111
Payee:	West Michigan Gas
Payment:	19.25

Record the final transaction for the month of August as follows:

Date:	8/27/93
Num:	112
Payee:	Meijer
Payment:	93.20
Memo:	Food
Category:	Groceries

Notice that Quicken's QuickFill feature completed the entire transaction for you when you typed **Meijer**. You only needed to change the memo and payment amount. The last few transactions entered and modified should now look like this:

Date	Num	Payee / Memo / Category	Payment	Clr	Deposit	Balance
8/25 1994	109	Alltel Telephone Bill Telephone	23 00			2,598 69
8/25 1994	110	Consumer Power Electric Bill Utilities:Elec→	30 75			2,567 94
8/25 1994	111	West Michigan Gas Gas Bill Utilities:Gas	19 25			2,548 69
8/27 1994	112	Meijer Food Groceries	93 20			2,455 49

Responding to Quicken Reminders to Record a Scheduled Group

If you have chosen to be prompted before a scheduled group is recorded, Quicken will begin prompting you the number of days before the scheduled date that you requested. Quicken displays a dialog box that asks you if you want to enter the scheduled group just like the one shown in the previous section, where you requested that the scheduled transaction be entered. The reminder will either occur at the DOS prompt when you boot your system or at the Main Menu when you first load Quicken. Hard disk users who have the default setting for BillMinder still set at Yes will see a message at the DOS prompt reminding them to pay postdated checks or to record transaction groups. If you do not have a hard disk or if you have turned BillMinder off, the prompt will not appear until you start Quicken.

Although recalling a memorized transaction works well for reentering a single transaction, for several transactions that all occur at the same time it is more efficient to define a *transaction group*. When you are ready to pay these transactions, you can have Quicken record the entire group for you automatically, after you make any changes in amounts or other information. You can even have Quicken remind you when it is time to record these transactions again.

Using Classes

You have used categories as one way of distinguishing transactions entered in Quicken. Since categories are either income, expense, or a subcategory, these groupings generally define the transaction to which they are assigned. Also, the status of a category as tax related or not affects the transactions to which it is assigned. Specific category names and descriptions provide more specific information about the transactions to which they are assigned. They explain what kind of income or expense a specific transaction represents. You can tell at a glance which costs are for utilities and which are for entertainment. In summary reports, you might see totals of all the transactions contained in a category.

Classes allow you to "slice the transaction pie" in a different way. Classes recategorize to show where, to whom, or for what time period the transactions apply. It is important not to think of classes as a replacement for categories; they do not affect category assignments. Classes provide a different view or perspective of your data.

For example, you might use classes if you have both a year-round home and a vacation cottage. One set of utility expenses is for the year-round residence and another is for the vacation cottage utility expenses. If you define and then assign classes to the transactions, they will still have categories representing utility expenses, but you will also have class assignments that let you know how much you have spent for utilities in each of your houses.

Since the expenses for a number of family members can be maintained in one checking account, you might want to use classes for those expenses that you would like to review by family member. You can use this approach for clothing expenses and automobile expenses if your family members drive separate cars. Another method for automobile expenses is to assign classes for each of the vehicles you own. You can then look at what you have spent on a specific vehicle at the end of the year and make an informed decision regarding replacement or continued maintenance.

Quicken does not provide a standard list of classes. As with categories, you can set up what you need before you start making entries, or you can add the classes you need as you enter transactions. Once you have assigned a class to a transaction, you enter it in the Category field by placing it after your category name (if one exists) and any subcategories. You always type a slash (/) before entering the class name, as in Utilities: Electric/Cottage.

To create a class before entering a transaction, you can use Ctrl-L to open the Class List window, as shown in Figure 6-12. Then select <New Class> and press Enter to create a new entry. Quicken displays the Set Up Class window, shown here,

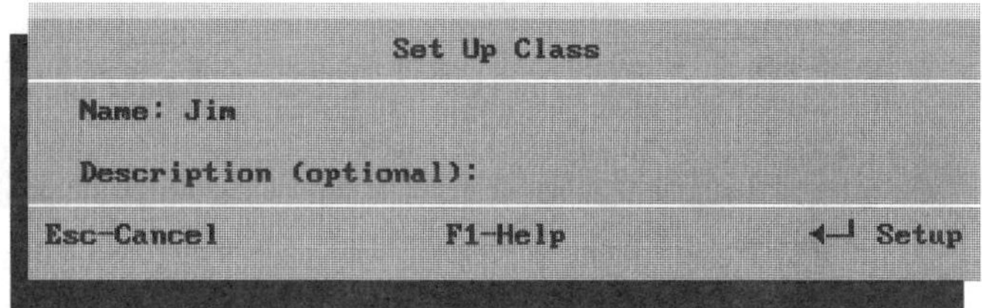

where you can enter the name and description of a class. Each new class is added to the Class List window. To create a class as you enter a transaction, type the category and any subcategories, followed by a slash and the class name you want to use, and press Enter. The following illustration shows an

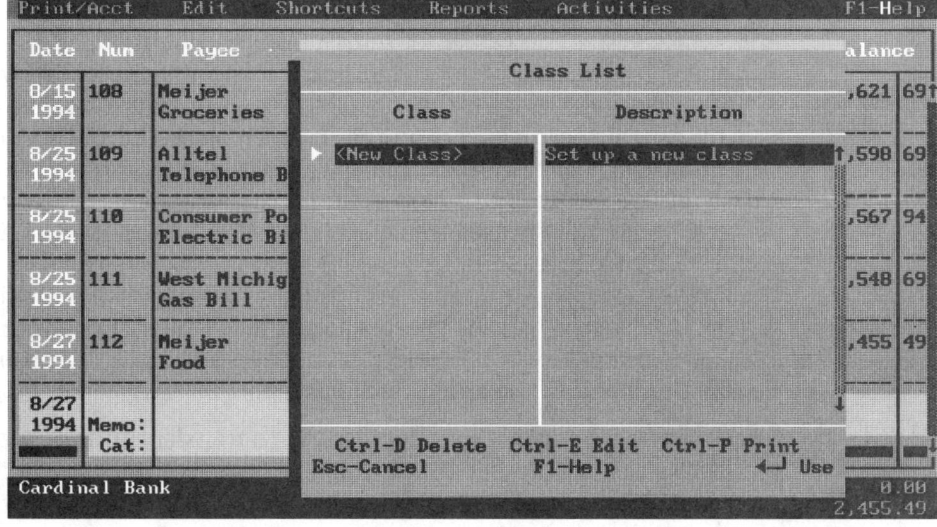

Class List window
Figure 6-12.

example of a class entry for "Jim" that could be used if you wanted to separately categorize personal expenses for each individual in the household:

If Jim were not an existing class, the Class list would appear for your selection, and you could create it. You will find more detailed examples of class entries in later chapters.

Using a Separate Credit Card Account

If you charge a large number of your purchases and do not pay your credit card bill in full each month, a separate account for each of your credit cards is the best approach. It will enable you to better monitor your individual payments throughout the year. Also, your reports will show the full detail for all credit card transactions, just as your checking account register shows the details of each check written.

Setting Up a Credit Card Account and Recording Transactions

You will need to set up accounts for each card by using the procedure followed when you created the account for Cardinal Saving earlier in the chapter. You should select Credit Card as the account type when you create these accounts. You can enter transactions throughout the month as you charge items to each of your credit card accounts, or you can wait until you receive the statements at the end of the month. Figure 6-13 shows how your credit card account appears on the screen. You record transaction information in the same fashion as you record checkbook entries designating the "Payee", "Memo", and "Category" fields for each transaction. The "Charge" field is used to record transaction amounts, and the "Payment" entry is recorded as part of the reconciliation process. You should use a reconciliation procedure similar to the one you used for your checking account to verify that the charges are correct. To reconcile your credit card account and pay your bill, select R**e**concile/Pay Credit Card from the Activities menu of the credit card register.

You can use Quicken's Transfer features to transfer funds between your checking account and credit card. If you have overdraft protection, you can also create a transaction to record the overdraft charges to your credit card and checking accounts.

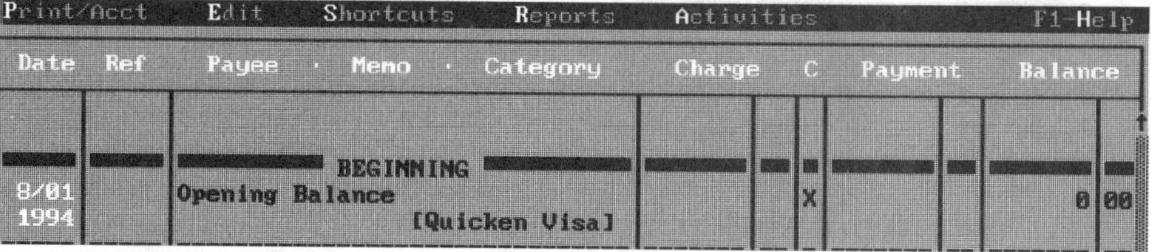

How a credit card account appears on the screen
Figure 6-13.

Recording Credit Card Transactions Automatically with IntelliCharge

Quicken can record all credit card transactions for you if you use IntelliCharge. Intellicharge is your own Quicken Visa card which provides this option. You can receive your IntelliCharge transactions on disk or modem each month. With an IntelliCharge credit card account setup, you can select **G**et IntelliCharge data from the **A**ctivities menu, and your data will be read into your credit card account. Even the categories are completed for you as the data is recorded. You can reconcile your account and decide on the payment amount.

You will use the same procedure described in Chapter 2 when you set up your IntelliCharge account. After selecting Credit Card and completing the balance and date fields on the Starting Balance and Description window, you need to indicate Y for the IntelliCharge option. This changes the optional Description field on the window to a required Account Number field. Your IntelliCharge account number should be in the format of 9999-9999-9999-9999 or 999-999-999-999. After pressing Enter to finalize your entries, you will be presented with the IntelliCharge Account Information window. On this window you must indicate whether or not your statement will be delivered via modem. If you do not select the delivery via modem option, you are telling Quicken that you have arranged for the statement to be delivered on disk. The correct selection is important, as it will determine whether Quicken expects to read a disk or receive data via your modem later when you select **G**et IntelliCharge data. After completing the other fields in this window, you will be ready to utilize the **A**ctivities menu option for IntelliCharge when you need it.

Important Customizing Options as You Set Up Your Accounts

Quicken provides a number of options for customizing the program to meet your needs. These include the addition of passwords for accessing accounts, options already discussed, such as requiring category entries, and other options that affect the display of information on your screen and in reports. Once you know how to access these settings, you will find that most are self-explanatory. All of the changes are made by selecting Set **P**references from the Main Menu.

Adding Passwords

To add passwords, select Pass**w**ord Settings from the Set **P**references menu. Quicken presents the following menu:

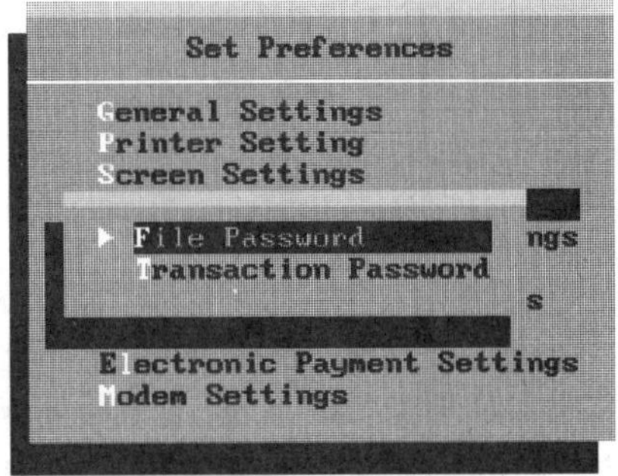

This menu allows you to decide if you want to password-protect a file by using a main password or only existing transactions by using a transaction password. Although you can add protection with a password at both levels, you will need to select each individually.

If you select **F**ile Password, Quicken asks you to enter a password. Once you press Enter, the password will be added to the active file, and anyone wishing to work with that file must supply it. The transaction password is used to prevent changes to existing transactions prior to a specified date without the password. If you choose **T**ransaction Password, you will be presented with a window that requires you to enter both a password and a date.

If you want to change a password or remove it in a subsequent session, you must be able to provide the existing password. Quicken will then provide a Change Password window for the entry of the old and new passwords. After completing the entries and pressing Enter, the new password will be in effect. The window is shown in the following:

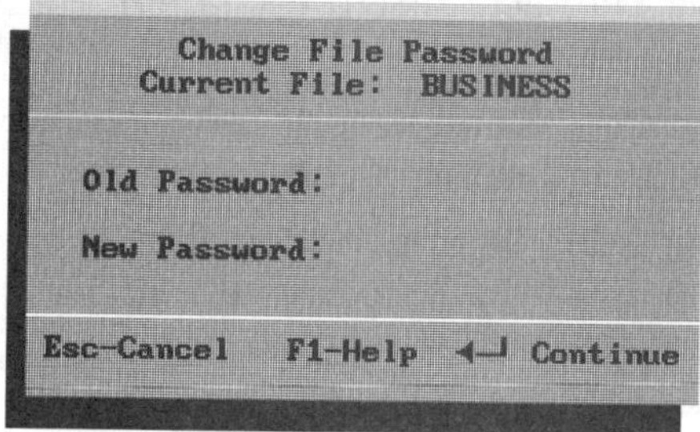

NOTE: If you want to remove the current password, use the same procedure you use for changing the password, except leave the new password blank.

Changing Other Settings

The screen presented when Set **P**references is selected is shown here:

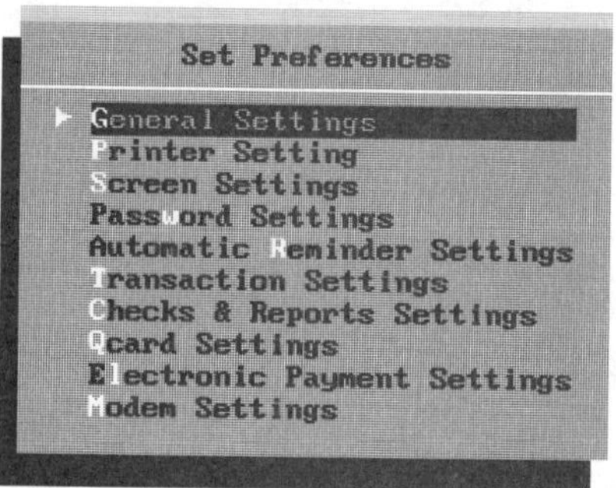

The following is a summary of what each option accomplishes:

- The **G**eneral Settings option allows you to make changes that affect all of your Quicken tasks.
- The **P**rinter Settings option allows you to change the style for the existing printer or choose another printer.
- The **S**creen Settings option allows you to change screen colors and menu display options.
- You looked at adding passwords in this chapter with Pass**w**ord Settings.
- The Automatic **R**eminder Settings option allows you to set the number of days' notice that you want for postdated checks, transaction groups, and investments.

- The **T**ransaction Settings option affects confirmation of entries, categories, dates, and filters.
- The **C**hecks and Reports Settings option affects the numbering of checks and the printing of checks and reports.
- The **Q**card Settings option allows you to control whether or not Qcards pop up with prompting information.
- The E**l**ectronic Payment Settings option affects the account used for electronic payments.
- The **M**odem Settings option allows you to activate electronic payments and set up your modem.

tips finances register expenses DEDUCTIONS
INCOME equity
checks revenue statements bank statements
dividends assets business tips
INCOME
budget reports
cash flow mortgage
net pay taxes revenue
mortgage dividends tips
register investments
taxes
report expenses
equity investments INCOME tips
checks statements assets checks budget finances net pay
$

CHAPTER

investments
banking
FILE
register
expenses
DEDUCTIONS
tips
finances
INCOME
equity
net pay
checks
revenue
bank statements
statements
business tips
dividends
assets
INCOME
cash flow
banking
business tips
FILE
reports
budget
FILE
business tips
checks
DEDUCTIONS
tips
mortgage
statements
cash flow
net pay
taxes
bank
revenue
business tips
mortgage
cash
dividends
tips
business tips
investments
register
statements
taxes
business tips
reports
expenses
tips
equity
investments
INCOME
checks
statements
bank
cash
assets
checks
budget
tips
finances
net pay

7 QUICKEN AS A BUDGETING TOOL

The popular conception of a budget is that it is a constraint on your spending. But that is not what budgets are designed to be. Instead, a budget is a financial plan that shows your projected income and expenses to allow you to plan your expenses within the limits of your income. Although a budget may sometimes necessitate a temporary denial, this denial will supply the funds for expenses you have given greater priority.

Given the same income, five families would prepare five different budget plans. One family might budget to save enough for a down payment on a new house. Another family might construct its budget to afford a new car. A third family might enjoy eating out and traveling and budget accordingly. Within the constraints of your income, the choice is yours.

If a budget is meant to facilitate getting what you want, why do so many people procrastinate in putting together a budget? It may be because budgeting takes time or that it forces decisions, or perhaps it is simply that most people are not sure where to begin. The one thing that is certain is that budgeting is an important component of every successful financial plan. You should create a budget even if you have already successfully built a financial nest-egg. It will allow you to protect your investment and ensure that your spending meets both your short- and long-range goals.

Quicken is ideally suited for maintaining your budget information. The program guides you through the budget development process and requires only simple entries to record budgeted amounts in the categories you specify. After an initial modest investment of time, Quicken generates reports for use in monitoring your progress toward your financial goal, and you do not need to wait until the end of the budget period to record your progress. You can enter your expenses daily and check the status of your actual and budgeted amounts at any time you wish.

In this chapter you will prepare budget entries for several months. Transaction groups from Chapter 6, "Expanding the Scope of Financial Entries," will be used to expedite the entry process while providing a sufficient number of transactions to get a sense of what Quicken can do. After making your entries, you will see how Quicken's standard reports can help you keep expenses in line with your budget and take a quick look at the insight graphs can provide.

Quicken's Budgeting Process

Quicken allows you to enter projected income and expense levels for any category. You can enter the same projection for each month of the year or change the amount allocated by month. Quicken matches your planned expenses with the actual expense entries and displays the results in a budget report. There is one entry point for budget information, but Quicken will combine actual entries from all of your bank, cash, and credit card accounts in the current file. Although Quicken can take much of the work out of entering and managing your budget, it cannot prepare a budget without your projections. If you have never prepared a budget before, you should take a look at a few budget planning considerations, shown in the special

"Budget Planning" section of this chapter. Once you have put together a plan, it is time to record your decisions in Quicken.

You can enter Quicken's budgeting process by selecting the Activities pull-down menu in the account register or the Write/Print Checks options. The process described in the following section assumes you are in the account register for Cardinal Bank that you prepared in Chapter 6. Quicken's budgeting process will be presented in three stages: specifying budget amounts, making modifications, and printing the report.

Setting Up the Budget

The Set Up Budgets window is the starting place for Quicken's budget process. You can access this screen with the Activities menu in any account register. From the Cardinal Bank account register, follow these steps to start the budget procedure:

1. Select **A**ctivities or press Alt-A.

REMEMBER: You can activate any of these menus with the highlighted letter in combination with the Alt key.

2. Select Set Up **B**udgets.

Figure 7-1 shows the top portion of the Set Up Budgets window. The category descriptions are listed down the left side of the screen and the months of the year across the top. The layout of the information is similar to a spreadsheet; if you have ever used a package such as 1-2-3 or Quattro Pro, you will feel instantly familiar with the format.

Only a few of the category descriptions are shown on the screen at any time. Quicken displays the total budget inflows and outflows at the bottom of the screen and updates these totals as you make changes. The instant updating allows you to make changes to a budget amount and immediately assess the effect on budget differences.

3. Select **L**ayout.

You can select budget periods of **M**onths, **Q**uarters, or **Y**ears from the pull-down menu that appears. You can also decide whether to **H**ide Cents or **S**how Cents in the budget window.

4. Select **Q**uarter.

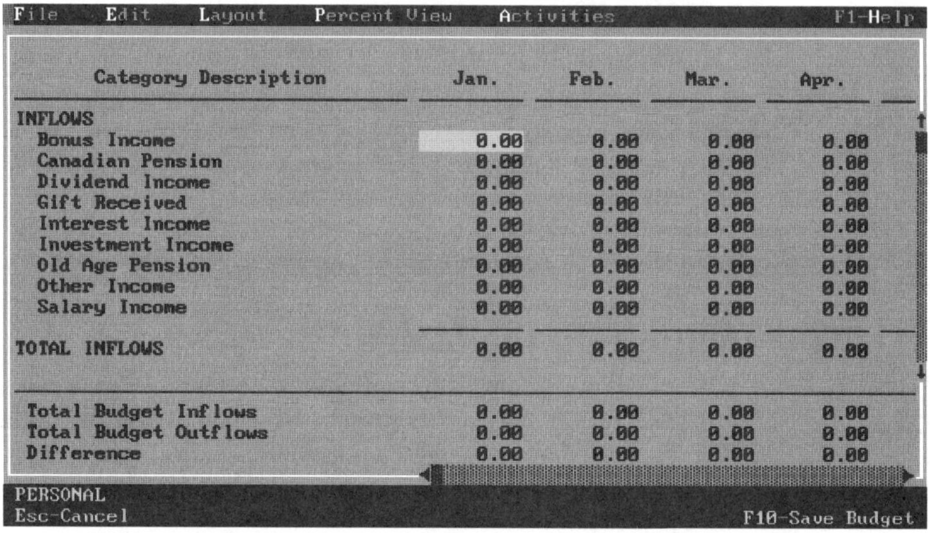

```
File    Edit    Layout    Percent View    Activities                F1-Help

     Category Description          Jan.      Feb.      Mar.      Apr.
INFLOWS
  Bonus Income                     0.00      0.00      0.00      0.00
  Canadian Pension                 0.00      0.00      0.00      0.00
  Dividend Income                  0.00      0.00      0.00      0.00
  Gift Received                    0.00      0.00      0.00      0.00
  Interest Income                  0.00      0.00      0.00      0.00
  Investment Income                0.00      0.00      0.00      0.00
  Old Age Pension                  0.00      0.00      0.00      0.00
  Other Income                     0.00      0.00      0.00      0.00
  Salary Income                    0.00      0.00      0.00      0.00

TOTAL INFLOWS                      0.00      0.00      0.00      0.00

 Total Budget Inflows              0.00      0.00      0.00      0.00
 Total Budget Outflows             0.00      0.00      0.00      0.00
 Difference                        0.00      0.00      0.00      0.00
PERSONAL
Esc-Cancel                                              F10-Save Budget
```

Quicken's Budget window
Figure 7-1.

5. Select **L**ayout again, and then select **M**onth to change the time period back to the original display. (See Figure 7-1.)
6. Select **L**ayout again and then select **H**ide Cents. Quicken presents the budget with the cents deleted from the screen.

Use this format for entering budget values in the remainder of this chapter.

Other Budget Menu Options

You can select options from the menu at the top of your screen with either the mouse or the keyboard in the same way that you can make selections from the menu at the top of the Register window. Although you will look at many of the budget menu options in more detail in the exercises that follow, a quick overview will help you feel comfortable with this new Quicken screen.

You have already seen how you can change the time period for the budget with the **L**ayout selections of **M**onth and **Q**uarter. The other **L**ayout options allow you to look at the budget numbers on an annual basis or to either **H**ide or **S**how Cents in your budget screen.

The **F**ile options allow you to print a copy of the budget as well as to transfer copies of your budget layout to and from disk. You also select this menu to **B**ackup or **R**estore your budget information.

One **E**dit option allows you to create a budget from transactions; it is useful for creating a budget for next year from this year's transactions. Other **E**dit options allow you to enter numbers for two-week intervals, copy a number or a column across the budget layout, control whether subcategories and transfers are shown on the budget layout, and inflate/deflate your budget amounts by fixed percentage amounts.

From the **P**ercent View option you can present your budgets in a **N**ormal View with dollar values (the default setting), or select from three percentage basis presentations: by **I**ncome Total, by **E**xpense Total, and by **R**espective Total. The differences between these options depends on whether you want your budget percentage presentations to be based on the total dollars of income, expenses, or, with the respective method, using both income and expenses.

From the **A**ctivities option, you can return to the Register window, write checks, or use the Calculator.

Entering Budget Projections

Entering budget projections is easy. If you have the same numbers for a category for all of the months of your budget period, you will be able to enter the number for the first month and copy the number across to the other months. You can copy the last number entered across the row or you can copy an entire column across. After completing the copy, you can always customize entries for some of the months by typing a new number.

To set up the budget amounts for this illustration, follow these steps:

1. Press ↓ until the highlight is on the Salary Income category in the Jan column.
2. The regular cursor should be blinking within the highlight. Type **1585.99** and press Enter. Quicken rounds your entry to 1586 and displays it in the Salary Income and Budget Inflow categories at the bottom of your screen.
3. Press ↑ to move back to the Salary Income entry for January. Select **E**dit and then select **F**ill Right to copy the salary across, as shown in Figure 7-2.

It is necessary to move back up to the entry because you finalized the salary entry by pressing Enter, and Quicken moved the highlight down to the next row. You can use **E**dit **F**ill Right immediately after typing an entry without having to move up if you type the entry and do not finalize it with Enter.

4. Using ↓ to scroll down the list, move the highlight to the January entry for the Electric Utilities subcategory under Water, Gas, Electrics.

Budget Planning

The budgeting process must begin before you start making budget entries in Quicken. You must start with an analysis of expected income. If your income flow is irregular, estimate on the low side. Remember to use only the net amount received from each income source. Also, do not include projected salary increases until they are confirmed.

The next step is analyzing projected expenses. The first item considered must be debt repayment and other essentials such as medical insurance premiums. In addition to monthly items such as mortgage and car loan payments, consider irregular expenses that are paid only once or twice a year. Tuition, property tax, insurance premiums, children's and personal allowances, and church pledges are examples. Project expenses such as medical, pharmacy, and dental bills for one year. Compute the required yearly expenses and save toward these major expenses so the entire amount does not need to come from a single month's check.

The next type of expense you should plan into your budget is savings. If you wait until you cover food, entertainment, and all the other day-to-day expenses, it is easy to find that there is nothing left to save. You should plan to write yourself a check for at least five percent of your net pay for savings when you pay your other bills.

The last type of expense you must budget for is the day-to-day expenses such as food, personal care, home repairs, gasoline, car maintenance, furniture, recreation, and gifts.

Naturally, if your totals for expenses exceed income projections, you must reassess before entering projected amounts in Quicken.

During the first few months of budgeting, err on the side of too much detail. At the end of the month you will need to know exactly how your money was spent. You can make realistic adjustments between expense categories to ensure that your budget stays in balance.

Notice as you move down that the bottom part of the screen shows a constant summary of budget inflows and outflows, with the scrolling occurring above this area.

File Edit Layout Percent View Activities F1-Help

Category Description	Jan.	Feb.	Mar.	Apr.
INFLOWS				
Bonus Income	0	0	0	0
Canadian Pension	0	0	0	0
Dividend Income	0	0	0	0
Gift Received	0	0	0	0
Interest Income	0	0	0	0
Investment Income	0	0	0	0
Old Age Pension	0	0	0	0
Other Income	0	0	0	0
Salary Income	1,586	1,586	1,586	1,586
TOTAL INFLOWS	1,586	1,586	1,586	1,586
Total Budget Inflows	1,586	1,586	1,586	1,586
Total Budget Outflows	0	0	0	0
Difference	1,586	1,586	1,586	1,586

PERSONAL
Esc-Cancel F10-Save Budget

Quicken's Budget window after **E**dit **F**ill Right is used for salary
Figure 7-2.

5. Type **25**, but do *not* press Enter.
6. Select **E**dit, and then select **F**ill Right to copy the 25 across for all the months.
7. Move to the Electric Utilities entry for October (use Ctrl-→), type **30**, and press Enter to replace the 25.

Notice that Quicken changed the dollar amount for only one month. If you wanted to change November and December as well, you would need to use **E**dit **F**ill Right again.

8. Press ↑, select **E**dit, and then select **F**ill Right.

Notice that this time, all the values for subsequent months have changed to 30. You might make this type of change because new power rates are expected or because you have installed a number of new outside lights.

9. Using the following information, move to the January column and complete the Budget Amount column for the categories. Remember, the process involves using ↑ or ↓ to move the arrow cursor to a specific category, typing the budget amount shown in the list, and pressing

Enter. You can also enter a budget amount followed by pressing the ↓ or ↑ keys.

Category Description	Budget Amount
Auto Fuel	30
Clothing	70
Dining Out	55
Entertainment	55
Entire Mortgage Payment	350
Groceries	200
Household Furniture	0
Doctor & Dental Visits	120
Miscellaneous	75
Telephone Expense	30
Gas (subcategory under Water, Gas, and Electric)	20

10. To enter a budgeted amount of 200 as a transfer to the Cardinal Saving account each month, select **E**dit and then select Budget **T**ransfers.

Quicken adds the transfer accounts to the categories shown. Budget **T**ransfers is a toggle type selection that allows you to turn these categories on and off each time you select it.

11. Move to the To Cardinal Saving January entry in the Outflow section, type **200**, select **E**dit, and then select Fill **R**ight to copy 200 across for all the months.

In the early stages, it generally takes several months to develop sound estimates for all your expenditure categories. For example, this illustration shows a desired transfer to savings of $200.00 per month. If there are any excess cash inflows at the end of the month, you transfer the excess to savings. On the other hand, if there is an excess of outflow over inflow, you need a transfer from savings. Once you have established your spending patterns and monitored your inflows and outflows, you may find that there are months of excess inflows during parts of the year and excess outflows during others, such as during the holiday season. You can use budgeting to plan for these seasonal needs and anticipate the transfer of funds between savings and checking accounts.

12. Select **E**dit and then select Budget **T**ransfers to toggle the transfer categories off again.
13. Press Home twice and then use **E**dit Fill **C**olumn to copy the values across from January to all the other months, as shown in Figure 7-3.

Notice that this changes the figure for Electric Utilities in Oct-Dec back to 25. When you use Fill **C**olumn, you cannot selectively copy across, you need to customize after using this selection. That is, the Fill **C**olumn feature fills all the budget categories with their January values, while the Fill **R**ight feature only fills the one category you are in when you invoke the command.

14. For the household furniture transaction, enter **185.00** for the month of October and press Ctrl-→ and **250.00** for December and press Ctrl-→. These amounts match your Chapter 6 entries and supply the budget figures for October and December in this chapter's example.

Moving Around the Set Up Budgets Window

Before preparing reports with your budget data, you will want to practice moving around within the budget window. After you complete the entries in the previous section, the highlight should be on the 435 in the Household Furniture total column. Follow these steps from that location:

1. Press Home three times.

File Edit Layout Percent View Activities F1-Help

Category Description	Jan.	Feb.	Mar.	Apr.
Total Automobile Expenses	30	30	30	30
Bank Charge	0	0	0	0
Charitable Donations:				
Cash Contributions	0	0	0	0
Non-Cash Contributions	0	0	0	0
Charitable Donations - Other	0	0	0	0
Total Charitable Donations	0	0	0	0
Childcare Expense	0	0	0	0
Christmas Expenses	0	0	0	0
Clothing	70	70	70	70
Dining Out	55	55	55	55
Dues	0	0	0	0
Total Budget Inflows	1,586	1,586	1,586	1,586
Total Budget Outflows	1,030	1,030	1,030	1,030
Difference	556	556	556	556

PERSONAL
Esc-Cancel F10-Save Budget

Figure 7-3. Some of the budget outflows after **E**dit Fill **C**olumn is used

The highlight appears at the top of your screen.

2. Press End to move to the top cell in the total column.
3. Press End again to move to the bottom of the total column.
4. Press Pg Up to move up one screen and Pg Dn to move down one screen.
5. t moves you to the right one column and Shift-Tab moves you to the left one column.
6. Repeat step 1 to move to the top left of the budget window.

Practice with moving on the budget window will facilitate quick entries for your data.

Creating a Budget Report

Now that you have your initial budget entries complete, you will want to prepare a monthly budget summary to compare budget and actual amounts. To create a budget report like the one shown in Figure 7-4, follow these steps:

1. Select **A**ctivities, then select **R**egister and press Enter.
2. Select **R**eports from the Register menu.
3. Select **H**ome Reports and then select Monthly **B**udget.
4. Press Enter to accept a default title.
5. Type **Custom Date** and press Enter.

Notice that the QuickFill feature will complete this for you as you begin to type. Remember, you could also press Ctrl-L to make your selection from the list of alternative date ranges. You can also change **G**eneral Settings under Set **P**references to have diamond fields pop up a list automatically.

6. Type **8/1/94** and press Enter.
7. Type **8/31/94** and press F8.
8. Press Enter twice, type **N**, and press Ctrl-Enter twice.
9. Press Ctrl-P to open the Print Report window, select your printer, and press Enter to print the report.

If your printer has compressed-print capabilities, you may wish to use that setting when printing reports. That way you will capture more of your report on a page. Some reports will be printed across two pages unless you use the compressed-print feature.

```
                    MONTHLY BUDGET REPORT
                  8/ 1/94 Through 8/31/94
PERSONAL-Bank, Cash, CC Accoun                           Page 1
7/21/94

                                     8/ 1/94      -     8/31/94
       Category Description          Actual     Budget   Diff
---------------------------------- --------------------------
INFLOWS
  Salary Income                       1,586      1,586       0
                                   --------   --------  ------
TOTAL INFLOWS                         1,586      1,586       0

OUTFLOWS
  Automobile Expenses:
    Auto Fuel                            23         30      -7
                                   ---------  --------  ------
  Total Automobile Expenses:             23         30      -7
  Clothing                               50         70     -20
  Dining Out                             60         55       5
  Entertainment                          50         55      -5
  Household Furniture                   217          0     217
  Groceries                             218        200      18
  Medical Expense:
    Doctor & Dental Visits              100        120     -20
                                   ---------  --------  ------
  Total Medical Expense                 100        120     -20
  Miscellaneous                          50         75     -25
  Entire Mortgage Payment               350        350       0
  Telephone Expense                      23         30      -7
  Water, Gas, Electric:
    Electric Utilities                   31         25       6
    Gas Utilities                        19         20      -1
                                   ---------  --------  ------
Total Water, Gas, Electric               50         45       5
                                   ---------  --------  ------
TOTAL OUTFLOWS                        1,191      1,030     161

                                   ---------  --------  ------
OVERALL TOTAL                           395        556    -161
                                   =========  ========  ======
```

Monthly Budget report for all accounts
Figure 7-4.

Modifying the Budget Report

You will notice when you print the budget report that it is dated for the one-month period you defined. Also notice that Quicken automatically combines all the bank, cash, and credit card accounts in the actual and budgeted figures of the Monthly Budget report. This means that as you scroll down the report, you don't see the $200 transfer to Cardinal Saving. Quicken views all of your accounts as a single unit for budget report purposes and considers the transfer to have a net effect of zero since it is within the system. Thus, the $200 is not shown on the report. You will see how you can change this shortly since a transfer of $200 to savings can be a significant event from a budgeting perspective and, consequently, something that you might want to show on a report.

You can see in Figure 7-4 that you were over your budget for the period by $161, represented by a negative value for the overall total difference. When Quicken compares your budgeted versus actual expenditures for each category, if your actual expenditures exceed the budgeted amount, a *positive* number is shown in the Diff column of the report. If the actual expenditure is less than the budgeted amount, a *negative* number appears in that column. In reading the report, you can quickly see whether you met your budget objectives. As already noted, the actual outflows exceed the budgeted outflows (1191 – 1030 = 161).

On closer examination, you can see there was the unexpected expenditure for furniture during the month that was not budgeted. All your budgeted categories appear with the amount you were over or under budget in each. This category-by-category breakdown is the heart of budget analysis and pinpoints areas for further scrutiny.

You may want to modify the report you just printed to cover only the current account, Cardinal Bank. This change will allow you to see the transfer to the savings account as part of your report for the month. This can be accomplished by following these steps:

1. Press Esc until you see the Monthly Budget Report box again.
2. To customize your report, press F7. The Create Budget Report window will open.
3. Press Enter four times, type **5**, and press Enter again. This tells Quicken you want a monthly report prepared.
4. Type **C** and press Enter. The modified report appears. Notice that only the current account was used in preparing this report, and the transfer to savings shows in the outflow section.
5. Press Ctrl-P and the Print Report window will open. Select your printer and press Enter.

Your new budget report for the file PERSONAL and the account Cardinal Bank, shown in Figure 7-5, is displayed on the screen and then printed. Notice that the transfer to Cardinal Saving is shown in your report, but your results haven't changed. The upper-left corner of your report shows that the report is for the Cardinal Bank account only. Reexamine Figure 7-4 and notice that the report included the bank, cash, and credit card accounts. Unless you have chosen otherwise, Quicken lists these three account types, even though such accounts have not been established.

MONTHLY BUDGET REPORT 8/ 1/94 Through 8/31/94 PERSONAL-Cardinal Bank 7/21/94			Page 1
	8/ 1/94	-	8/31/94
Category Description	Actual	Budget	Diff
INFLOWS			
Salary Income	1,586	1,586	0
FROM Cardinal Saving	0	0	0
TOTAL INFLOWS	1,586	1,586	0
OUTFLOWS			
Automobile Expenses:			
Auto Fuel	23	30	-7
Total Automobile Expenses:	23	30	-7
Clothing	50	70	-20
Dining Out	60	55	5
Entertainment	50	55	-5
Household Furniture	217	0	217
Groceries	218	200	18
Medical Expense:			
Doctor & Dental Visits	100	120	-20
Total Medical Expense	100	120	-20
Miscellaneous	50	75	-25
Entire Mortgage Payment	350	350	0
Telephone Expense	23	30	-7
Water, Gas, Electric:			
Electric Utilities	31	25	6
Gas Utilities	19	20	-1
Total Water, Gas, Electric	50	45	5
TO Cardinal Saving	200	200	0
TOTAL OUTFLOWS	1,391	1,230	161
OVERALL TOTAL	195	356	-161

Monthly Budget report for Cardinal Bank account
Figure 7-5.

7

Tying the Budget Report to Other Quicken Reports

You have now completed the basic steps in preparing your budget report. Now let's see how the report relates to the reports prepared in Chapter 3, "Quicken Reports." Figures 7-6 and 7-7 present a Cash Flow report and a portion of an Itemized Categories report for the budget period for the Cardinal Bank account. Since the example is based on only one month, the

Cash Flow report (shown in Figure 7-6) and the Actual column in the Monthly Budget report (in Figure 7-5) contain the same inflows and outflows. Normally, the budget summary would cover information for a longer period of time (such as a quarter or year) and you would prepare a Cash Flow report for each of the months included in the budget report. You should think through your reporting requirements instead of just printing all the reports.

```
                    Cash Flow Report
                 8/ 1/94 Through 8/31/94
PERSONAL-Cardinal Bank                              Page 1
7/21/94

                                          8/ 1/94-
       Category Description               8/31/94
--------------------------------- ------------------
INFLOWS
  Salary Income                                 1,585.99
                                              ----------
TOTAL INFLOWS                                   1,585.99

OUTFLOWS
  Automobile Expenses:
    Auto Fuel                           23.00
                                    ---------
  Total Automobile Expenses:                       23.00
  Clothing                                         50.00
  Dining Out                                       60.00
  Entertainment                                    50.00
  Household Furniture                             217.00
  Groceries                                       218.20
  Medical Expense:
    Doctor & Dental Visits              100.00
                                      --------
  Total Medical Expense                           100.00
  Miscellaneous                                    50.00
  Entire Mortgage Payment                         350.00
  Telephone Expense                                23.00
  Water, Gas, Electric:
    Electric Utilities                   30.75
    Gas Utilities                        19.25
                                      --------
  Total Water, Gas, Electric                       50.00
  TO Cardinal Saving                              200.00
                                               ---------
TOTAL OUTFLOWS                                  1,391.20

                                               ---------
OVERALL TOTAL                                     194.79
                                               =========
```

Cash Flow report for budget period

Figure 7-6.

You may be wondering why the Cash Flow report shows a positive $194.79 net cash inflow, while the budget report indicates that you were over budget by $161. This occurs because the Cash Flow report looks only at actual cash inflows and outflows. On the other hand, the budget examines what you want to spend and what you actually spent. Looking at the budget column of Figure 7-5, you can see that there would have been an additional $356.00 to transfer to savings if you had met your budget objectives.

Figure 7-7 provides selected detailed category information for the budget period. Notice that the Easy Credit Card Split Transaction window provides detail for each of the categories used when recording the credit card payment. Also notice that the Groceries category is printed by check number and provides detail for the groceries amount on the Monthly Budget and Cash Flow reports. When looking at extended budget and cash flow reporting, the details provided from the Itemized Categories report can provide useful insights into your spending patterns by showing where you spent and the frequency of expenditures by category. This information can help in analyzing the changes you might want to make in your spending patterns. (Please note that some of the lines in Figure 7-7 might look slightly different from what appears on your screen. Some adjustments had to be made to fit the material on screen onto the page.)

Budget Report Extension

The reports prepared so far in this chapter give you an overview of the budgeting process by looking at expenditures for one month. You would extend your examination over a longer period to tell if the over-budget situation in August was unusual or part of a trend that should be remedied.

To do this, you will need to add transactions for other months. Fortunately, the transaction groups discussed in Chapter 6, "Expanding the Scope of Financial Entries," can be used to make the task easy. As you add more information to the reports, you will learn how to create wide reports with Quicken.

Additional Transactions

In order to provide a more realistic budget situation, you will extend the actual budget amounts for several months by creating new register transactions. This will also give you an opportunity to practice techniques such as recalling memorized transactions and making changes to split transactions. Remember, you will be using the transactions recorded in Chapter 6. Figure 7-8 presents the check register entries you will make to

```
                     ITEMIZED CATEGORY REPORT
                      8/ 1/94 Through 8/31/94
Personal-All Accounts                                          Page 1
7/21/94

       EXPENSES
         Automobile Expense:
         -------------------

           Auto Fuel
           ---------
8/ 3 Cardinal 105  S Easy Credit Card Gasoline -  Auto:Fuel           -23.00
                                                                    --------
           Total Auto Fuel                                            -23.00
                                                                    --------
         Total Automobile Expenses                                    -23.00

         Clothing
         --------
8/ 3 Cardinal 105  S Easy Credit Card Blue Blouse Clothing            -50.00
                                                                    --------
                                                                      -50.00
         Total Clothing

         Dining Out
         ----------
8/ 3 Cardinal 105  S Easy Credit Card Dinner at t Dining              -60.00
                                                                    --------
         Total Dining Out                                             -60.00

         Entertainment
         -------------
8/ 3 Cardinal 105  S Easy Credit Card Play Ticket Entertain           -50.00
                                                                    --------
         Total Entertainment                                          -50.00

         Household Furniture
         -------------------
8/ 3 Cardinal 105  S Easy Credit Card Green Rocke Furniture          -217.00
                                                                    --------
         Total Household Furniture                                   -217.00

         Groceries
         ---------
8/ 4 Cardinal 106    Maureks          Groceries   Groceries           -60.00
8/15 Cardinal 108    Meijer           Groceries   Groceries           -65.00
8/27 Cardinal 112    Meijer           Food        Groceries           -93.20
                                                                     -------
         Total Groceries                                             -218.20
```

Partial Itemized Categories report for budget period
Figure 7-7.

```
                              Check Register
Cardinal Bank                                                       Page 1
7/21/94

 Date  Num             Transaction               Payment  C  Deposit    Balance
----- ---- -------------------------------- ---------- - ---------- ----------

9/01       Cardinal Saving                      194.79                2,260.70
1994 memo: Transfer to savings
      cat: [Cardinal Saving]

9/02       Payroll deposit                                  1,585.99  3,846.69
1994 memo: September 1 paycheck
      cat: Salary

9/02 113   Great Lakes Savings & Loan           350.00                3,496.69
1994 memo: September Payment
      cat: Mort Pay

9/02 114   Easy Credit Card                     233.00                3,263.69
1994 SPLIT August 25th Statement
              Clothing                           50.00
                Red Blouse
              Dining                             60.00
                Dinner at the Boathouse
              Auto:Fuel                          23.00
                Gasoline - Jeep Wagoneer
              Entertain                          50.00
                Play Tickets
              Misc                               50.00

9/03 115   Maureks                               85.00                3,178.69
1994 memo: Food
      cat: Groceries

9/08       Cardinal Saving                      200.00                2,978.69
1994 memo: Transfer to savings
      cat: [Cardinal Saving]

9/08 116   Orthodontics, Inc.                   170.00                2,808.69
1994 memo: Monthly Orthodontics Payment
      cat: Medical:Doctor

9/20 117   Maureks                               95.00                2,713.69
1994 memo: Food
      cat: Groceries

9/25 118   Alltel                                29.00                2,684.69
1994 memo: Telephone Bill
      cat: Telephone

9/25 119   Consumer Power                        43.56                2,641.13
1994 memo: Electric Bill
      cat: Utilities:Electric
```

Additional account register entries
Figure 7-8.

```
                               Check Register
Cardinal Bank                                                          Page 2
7/21/94

 Date  Num            Transaction                 Payment  C  Deposit    Balance
----- ---- ---------------------------------- ---------- - ---------- ----------

9/25 120   West Michigan Gas                      19.29                2,621.84
1994 memo: Gas Bill
      cat: Utilities:Gas

10/01       Cardinal Saving                      166.35                2,455.49
 1994 memo: Transfer to savings
       cat: [Cardinal Saving]

10/02       Payroll deposit                                 1,585.99   4,041.48
 1994 memo: October 1 paycheck
       cat: Salary

10/02 121   Great Lakes Savings & Loan           350.00                3,691.48
 1994 memo: October Payment
       cat: Mort Pay

10/04 122  Easy Credit Card                      957.00                2,734.48
 1994 SPLIT September 25th Statement
              Clothing                            75.00
                White Dress
              Dining                              45.00
                Dinner at the Boathouse
              Auto:Fuel                           37.00
                Gasoline - Jeep Wagoneer
              Furniture                          550.00
                Table and chairs
              Entertain                          100.00
                Play Tickets
              Misc                               150.00

10/05 123   Maureks                              115.00                2,619.48
 1994 memo: Food
       cat: Groceries

10/05       Cardinal Saving                      200.00                2,419.48
 1994 memo: Transfer to savings
       cat: [Cardinal Saving]

10/08 124   Orthodontics, Inc.                   100.00                2,319.48
 1994 memo: Monthly Orthodontics Payment
       cat: Medical:Doctor

10/19 125   Maureks                              135.00                2,184.48
 1994 memo: Food
       cat: Groceries

10/25 126   Alltel                                27.50                2,156.98
 1994 memo: Telephone Bill
       cat: Telephone
```

Additional account register entries (*continued*)
Figure 7-8.

```
                              Check Register
Cardinal Bank                                                           Page 3
7/21/94

 Date  Num            Transaction              Payment  C  Deposit    Balance
----- ---- ------------------------------- ---------- - ---------- ----------


10/25 127   Consumer Power                      37.34                2,119.64
 1994 memo: Electric Bill
       cat: Utilities:Electric

10/25 128   West Michigan Gas                   16.55                2,103.09
 1994 memo: Gas Bill
       cat: Utilities:Gas
```

Additional account register entries (*continued*)
Figure 7-8.

expand your database for this chapter. Recording the first transaction in the Cardinal Bank account register involves these steps:

1. Press Ctrl-T to display the list of memorized transactions.

You were instructed to memorize most of the transactions in Chapter 6. If you did not, memorize all the transactions from Chapter 6 now, except for the grocery payments to Maureks and Meijer.

2. Move the arrow cursor to the transaction you want to recall, Cardinal Saving, and press Enter.
3. Make any changes in the transaction. In this case, change the date to 9/1 and the amount to 194.79, and press Ctrl-Enter.

As explained earlier, excess cash in any month should be transferred to savings. This helps prevent impulsive buying if you are saving for larger outflows in later months of the year. But remember that when you plan an actual budget, you can build in varying monthly savings rather than use the approach of setting a minimum amount and transferring any excess of inflow or outflow at the beginning of each month.

4. Complete the example by entering all the information in your register exactly as shown in Figure 7-8.

In looking at the transactions shown in Figure 7-8, notice that you will primarily be recalling memorized transactions, scheduled transactions, and split transactions throughout the recording process. The only transactions that are not memorized are the grocery checks; for those you can utilize Quicken's QuickFill feature to minimize typing.

You use the Split Transaction windows to enter the Easy Credit Card transactions for check numbers 114 and 122, respectively. Notice that the Furniture category is not used in check 114 but is part of the credit card transaction for check 122. All the information you need to record these two transactions is included in Figure 7-8.

5. After entering the last transaction in Figure 7-8, select **R**eports, and the Reports menu will open.
6. Select **H**ome Reports and then select Monthly **B**udget.
7. Press Enter to accept Quicken's default report title.
8. Type **Custom Date** and press Enter.
9. Type **8/1/94** and press Enter.
10. Type **10/31/94** and press F7, and the Create Budget Report window will appear.
11. Press Enter, four times.
12. Type **5** to select month for column headings and press Enter.
13. Type **C** and press Enter, and the Monthly Budget report appears.

Wide-Screen Reports

The Monthly Budget report you just generated is spread across more than one screen and may be difficult to comprehend until you realize how it is structured. In this section, you will explore the wide-screen report and become more familiar with Quicken results.

The steps listed here will help you become familiar with the Monthly Budget report generated from the additional data that you entered:

1. Use Tab, Shift-Tab, Pg Up, Pg Dn, Home, and End to become familiar with the appearance of the wide report for the budget.

Notice how easy it is to move around the report. Also notice that the **F**ile/Print option at the top accesses the Print features. Home always returns you to the left side and then the top of the wide-screen report as you press it repeatedly. End always takes you to the right side and then the bottom of the report. Tab moves you right, and Shift-Tab moves you left one screen. Pg Up moves you up one screen, while Pg Dn moves you down one screen. You can move across the report an entire screen at once by pressing the Ctrl-← and Ctrl-→ keys.

2. If you have the compressed print option, it is recommended that you use that setting to produce wide reports. This printer option significantly increases the amount of information you can print on a page.

When you print wide-screen reports, Quicken numbers the pages of the report so you can more easily follow on hard copy.

Report Discussion

The steps for preparing and printing the report will become familiar with a little practice. The real issue is how to use the information. Let's look at the report and discuss some of the findings.

1. Press End twice. Quicken takes you to the lower-right side of the quarterly report. This shows that for the quarter you spent $1,041 more than you had budgeted.
2. Using ↑, move up the report one line at a time.

Notice that a part of the explanation for the actual outflows exceeding the inflows is due to $361 being transferred to savings. Most of us would not view that as poor results. On the other hand, you can see that you have spent $582 more on furniture than you had budgeted. This may be because sale prices justified deviating from the budget. But it could also be compulsive buying that can't be afforded over the long run. If you find yourself over budget, the special section later in this chapter entitled "Dealing with an Over-Budget Situation" provides some suggestions for improving the situation.

Figure 7-9 shows the budget summary for the period 8/1/94 through 10/31/94 for the Cardinal Bank account. It was produced by requesting a Monthly Budget report using Six Months for the column headings. The **L**ayout **H**ide Cents option in the Report window was used to toggle off the display of cents. Remember that the information Quicken uses in the Budget column came from the budgeted amounts you established earlier in this chapter. The information in the Actual column is summarized from the account register entries recorded in your Cardinal Bank checking account. You could also request a Cash Flow report by month for the budget period and examine the monthly outflow patterns. You might want to print out itemized category information for some categories during the period for more detailed analysis of expenditures.

Graph Options

Quicken's graph capabilities provide other budget monitoring tools. Quicken provides different graph options under the View **G**raphs selection on the Main Menu. Both the Income and Expense selection and Budget and the Actual Selections choice that appear on the next menu will provide tools for monitoring your budget.

MONTHLY BUDGET REPORT
8/ 1/94 Through 10/31/94
PERSONAL-Cardinal Bank Page 1
7/21/94

Category Description	8/ 1/94 Actual	- Budget	10/31/94 Diff
INFLOWS			
Salary Income	4,758	4,758	0
FROM Cardinal Saving	0	0	0
TOTAL INFLOWS	4,758	4,758	0
OUTFLOWS			
Automobile Expenses:			
Auto Fuel	83	90	-7
Total Automobile Expenses	83	90	-7
Clothing	175	210	-35
Dining Out	165	165	5
Entertainment	200	165	35
Household Furniture	767	185	582
Groceries	648	600	48
Medical Expense:			
Doctor & Dental Visits	370	360	10
Total Medical Expense	370	360	10
Miscellaneous	250	225	25
Entire Mortgage Payment	1,050	1,050	0
Telephone Expense	80	90	-11
Water, Gas, Electric:			
Electric Utilities	112	75	37
Gas Utilities	55	60	-5
Total Water, Gas, Electric	167	135	32
TO Cardinal Saving	961	600	361
TOTAL OUTFLOWS	4,916	3,875	1,041
OVERALL TOTAL	-158	883	-1,041

Three-month budget report
Figure 7-9.

One interest you may have is taking a look at the composition of your expenditures. This helps you to identify areas of major costs and lets you take a look to see if any of them can be reduced. To display a graph showing expense composition on your screen, follow these steps:

1. From the Main Menu select View **G**raphs to see this menu:

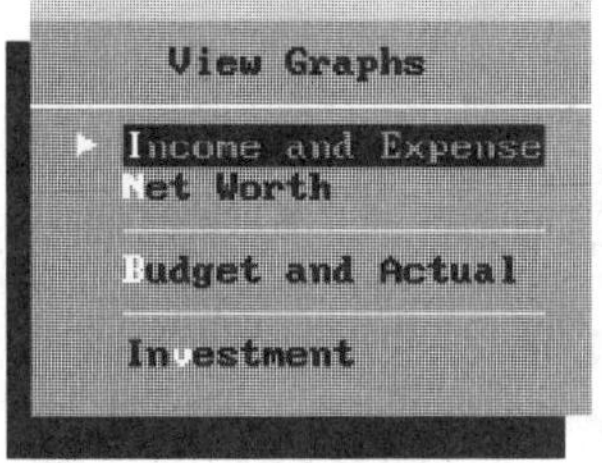

2. Select **I**ncome and Expense.
3. Select **E**xpense Composition.
4. Type **7/94** and press Enter.
5. Type **9/94** and press Enter.
6. If you haven't created a graph before, Quicken will prompt you to establish default graph settings. Press Enter to accept the default graphics driver and Ctrl-Enter to accept the default text and graph size.

Quicken displays the graph shown in Figure 7-10.

7. Select Print to print the graph, otherwise go to the next step.

Quicken will print the graph if your printer is properly set to print graphs. You can also select the Report option and Quicken shows an Expense Composition report that summarizes total expenses in the traditional report format.

6. Press Esc until the Main Menu is displayed.

Quicken allows you to focus in on the detail for budget categories with a graph as well. You might want to look at categories that were either under or over budget. To see a bar chart that displays the actual versus budget for categories under budget follow these steps:

1. Select View **G**raphs from the Main Menu.
2. Select **B**udget and Actual.
3. Select Categories **U**nder Budget.
4. Type **8/94** and press Enter.
5. Type **9/94** and press Enter.
6. Type **E** and press Enter.

Dealing with an Over-Budget Situation

Expenses cannot continue to outpace income indefinitely. The extent of the budget overage and the availability of financial reserves to cover it dictate the seriousness of the problem and how quickly and drastically cuts must be made to reverse the situation. Although the causes of an over-budget situation are numerous, the following strategies can help correct the problem:

- If existing debt is the problem, consider a consolidation loan—especially if the interest rate is lower than existing installment interest charges. Then, don't use your credit until the consolidated loan is paid in full.
- If day-to-day variable expenses are causing the overrun, begin keeping detailed records of all cash expenditures. Look closely at what you are spending for eating out, entertainment, and various impulse purchases such as clothing, gifts, and other nonessential items.
- Locate warehouse, discount, thrift, and used clothing stores in your area and shop for items you *need* at these locations. Garage sales, flea markets, and the classified ads can sometimes provide what you need at a fraction of the retail cost.
- Be certain that you are allocating each family member an allowance for discretionary spending and that each is adhering to the total.
- If you cannot find a way to lower expenses any further, consider a free-lance or part-time job until your financial situation improves. Many creative people supplement their regular income with a small-business venture.
- Plan ahead for major expenses by splitting the cost of car insurance, property taxes, and so on over 12 months and transferring each month's portion to savings until it is time to pay the bill. If you have saved for it, you can then transfer the amount saved to the checking account the month of the anticipated expenditure.

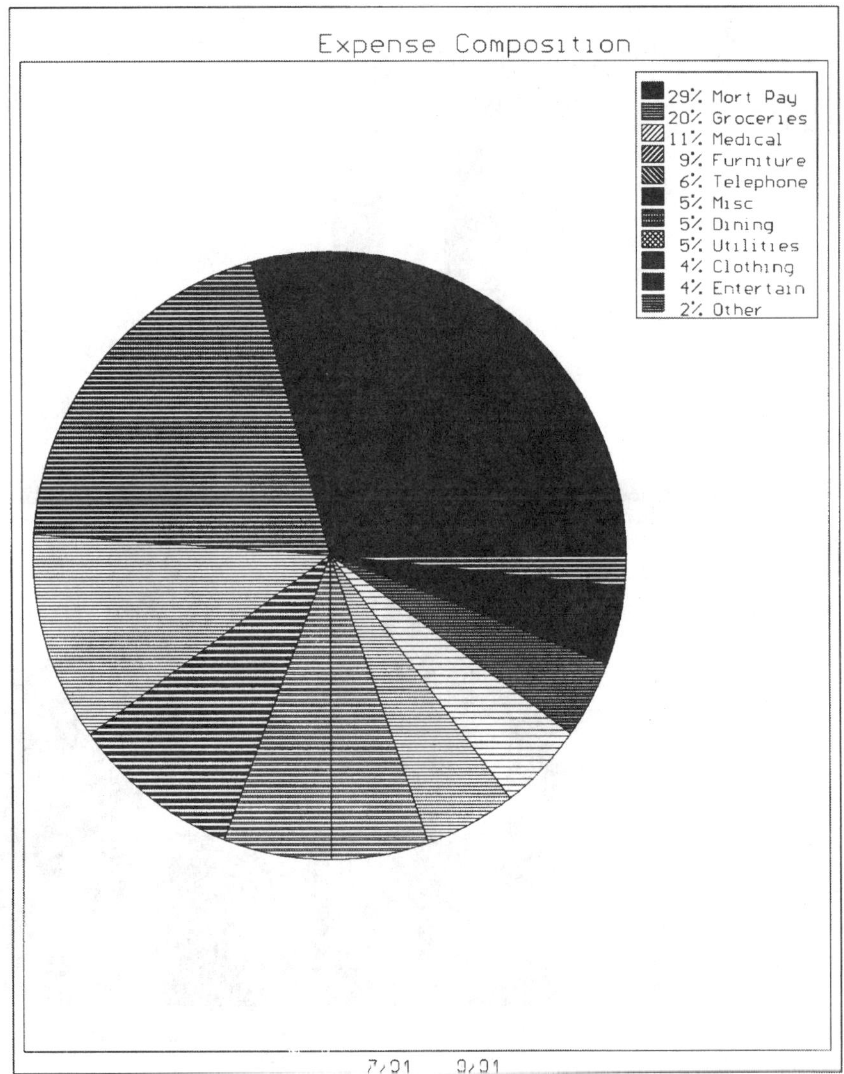

Expense Composition graph
Figure 7-10.

The graph shown in Figure 7-11 displays on your screen.

7. Select Print to print the graph, otherwise go to the next step.
8. Press Esc until the Main Menu displays.

You should feel free to experiment with the other graph types. None of your selections will affect register entries, so you do not have to worry about making mistakes.

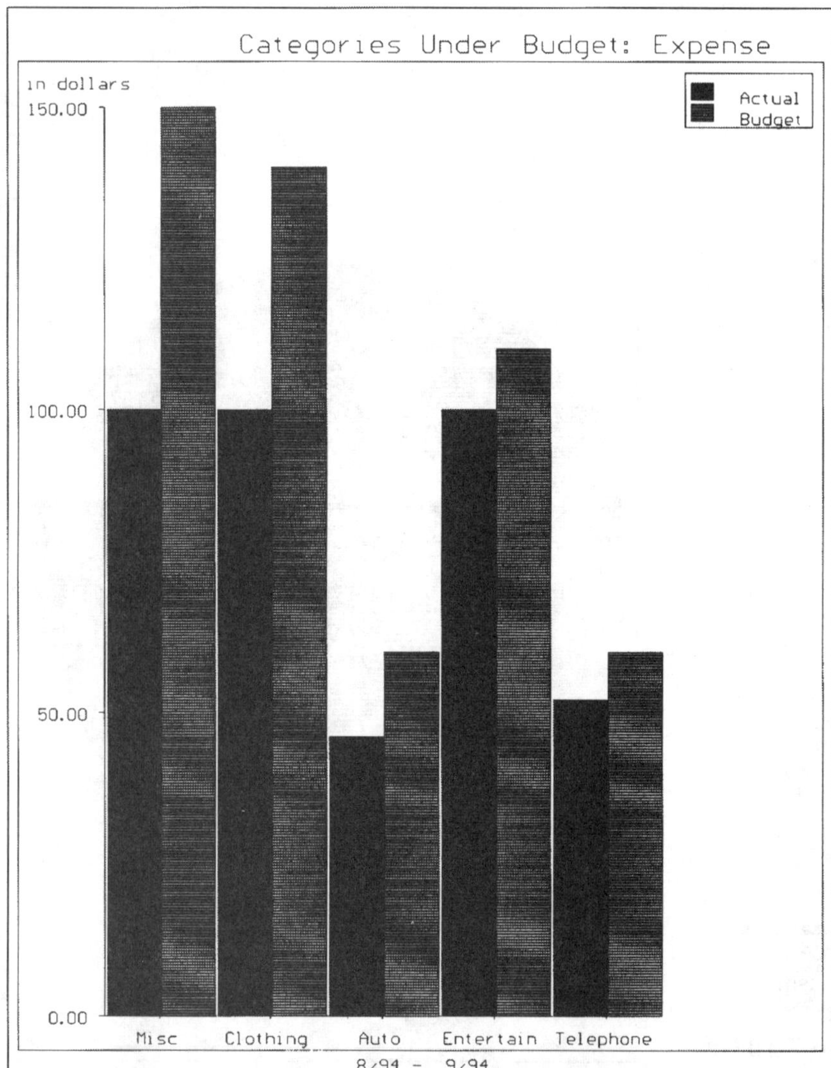

Expense Categories Under Budget graph
Figure 7-11.

Using AutoCreate When Creating Your Own Budgets

Quicken 7's new AutoCreate features make creating a budget easy once you have accumulated some transaction detail. You can use this feature to project a budget for a single category or you can create an entire budget this way. Quicken uses actual transaction data to project the budget and allow you to alter in several different ways the actual numbers as they are recorded in the budget.

If you want to project budget entries based on actual prior year numbers for a single budget category, you will select **E**dit, A**u**toCreate Row. Quicken presents the Automatically Create Budget window. You can use this window to specify which data you want to copy from actual entries to create budget entries, which months you want to use this data for, and whether or not it should be altered before being placed on the budget spreadsheet. A description of each field in the Automatically Create Budget window is provided below:

Copy from	Specifies the month and year of the first actual data you want to use in building your budget
through	Specifies the last month of actual data to use for building a budget
Place budget starting in month	The entry in this field is the month number where you want to begin using the actual data for budget entries. This allows you to select actual data from October and use it to project December's budget figures.
Round values to nearest	You can use this field to round actual data to the nearest $1, $10, or $100 before recording it in the budget. You can also select None to leave the actual data unchanged.
Use average for period	If you enter a Y in this field, Quicken will average the data in the selected period before completing budget entries.
Filter by Class	You can use this field when you want to restrict budget building activities to selected classes.
New budget is ____% of	This entry allows you to increase or decrease actual numbers by any percentage that you like. You can type any percent from 1 to 999. Numbers less than 100 will decrease the actual numbers before recording them; numbers above 100 will increase them.

You are not limited to projecting a category at a time from actual data. You can project your whole budget with this method. Select **E**dit, **A**utoCreate All for this task. You will be presented the same window that you use when specifying a row. You can consult the table of descriptions above for more information on the options available to you.

Once you have some of your financial history recorded, the features just described will enable you to put together flexible budget projections with almost no investment of time.

C H A P T E R

investments banking FILE register expenses DEDUCTIONS
tips finances INCOME equity net pay
checks revenue bank statements
statements
dividends assets business tips
INCOME cash flow
banking business tips
budget FILE FILE reports
DEDUCTIONS business tips checks
statements cash flow tips mortgage
net pay taxes bank revenue
mortgage cash business tips
business tips dividends tips
investments
register statements taxes
reports business tips
expenses tips
equity investments INCOME
checks statements bank cash
assets checks budget tips finances net pay

8 USING QUICKEN TO ORGANIZE TAX INFORMATION

Quicken's contribution to your financial planning and monitoring goes beyond recording transactions. You have already used Quicken to handle your budget entries and reports. Quicken can also help you with your tax preparation. Although using the package probably won't make tax preparation fun, it can reduce the tax-time crunch by organizing your tax information throughout the year. If you plan your categories and classes correctly and you faithfully complete all your entries, the hard part is done. You will then be able to use Quicken's summaries to provide the entries for specific lines on tax forms.

In this chapter, you will see how Quicken can help you at tax time. After looking at a few ideas for organizing needed tax information, you will modify the account register prepared in Chapters 6 and 7 to better show your tax-related information. You will prepare tax summary information from the **H**ome Reports option of the package. You will also look at Quicken's features that allow you to assign categories to lines within tax schedules. This allows Quicken to better organize your tax information.

NOTE: You must remember that Quicken reports will not be considered sufficient documentation of tax-deductible expenses. See the special section later in this chapter, "Essential Tax Documentation," for a list of some of the forms you might need to substantiate expense claims to the IRS in an audit.

Quicken Tax Overview

This chapter focuses on how Quicken can help you prepare your tax returns. You can use Quicken's categories and classes to categorize data for your taxes. Categories are defined as tax related or not and can be assigned to tax schedules. You can change the tax-related status and tax schedule assignment of any of the existing categories by editing the current category in the category list with Ctrl-E. You can also define a tax-related status for any new category as you enter it.

Quicken can be used to collect information for specific line items on tax forms such as Form 1040, Schedule A (itemized deductions), Schedule B (dividends and interest), and Schedule E (royalties and rents). Figures 8-1 and 8-2 show two of these forms. Defining and using classes for your transactions will allow you to collect additional details from your financial transactions. Assigning tax schedules and lines to categories allows Quicken to accumulate the information that you need for a particular line on a tax form.

In fact, once you become familiar with Quicken, you can use the package to accumulate the exact information you need to prepare your taxes. For example, you may decide to tag specific tax information by setting up classes for categories that are tax related and specific to a particular tax form. At the end of the year, you can have Quicken print the transactions that you need for a particular line. In your own Quicken system, you may want to identify

Essential Tax Documentation

The entries in your Quicken register will not convince the IRS that you incurred expenses as indicated. You need documentation of each expense to substantiate your deductions in the event of an audit. Although you may be able to convince the IRS to accept estimates for some categories based on other evidence, the following are some ideas of the optimal proof you will want to be able to present:

Expense Claimed	Proof
Dependents other than minor children	Receipts for individuals' support. Records of the individuals' income and support from others
Interest	Creditor statements of interest paid
Investments	Purchase receipts and brokerage firms' confirmation receipts
Medical and dental care	Canceled check with receipt indicating individual treated
Medical insurance	Pay stubs showing deductions or other paid receipts
Moving expenses	Itemized receipts and proof of employment for 12 months in previous job
Pharmacy/drugs	Itemized receipts and canceled checks
Real estate taxes	Receipt for taxes paid. Settlement papers for real estate transactions in the current year
Unreimbursed business expenses	Itemized receipts, canceled checks, and mileage logs

the specific forms associated with these items. For example, "Tax Fed/1040" indicates a class for transactions affecting Form 1040. Another approach is to create a class that represents a line item on a specific form. For example, "Mort Int/A—9A" is more specific. The class entry "A—9A" indicates Schedule A, line 9A—mortgage interest paid to financial institutions. You could then have Quicken generate the tax-related information by tax form or line item and use these totals to complete your taxes.

The Tax Form Library, 518 W. Main St., Louisville, Ky., 40202, (502) 589-7466

Form **1040** Department of the Treasury—Internal Revenue Service **U.S. Individual Income Tax Return** (T) **1992** IRS Use Only—Do not write or staple in this space.

For the year Jan. 1–Dec. 31, 1992, or other tax year beginning , 1992, ending , 19 OMB No. 1545-0074

Label
(See instructions on page 10.)
Use the IRS label. Otherwise, please print or type.

LABEL HERE

Your first name and initial | Last name | **Your social security number**

If a joint return, spouse's first name and initial | Last name | **Spouse's social security number**

Home address (number and street). If you have a P.O. box, see page 10. | Apt. no.

City, town or post office, state, and ZIP code. If you have a foreign address, see page 10.

For Privacy Act and Paperwork Reduction Act Notice, see page 4.

Presidential Election Campaign (See page 10.)
Do you want $1 to go to this fund? . . . . Yes No
If a joint return, does your spouse want $1 to go to this fund? . Yes No
Note: *Checking "Yes" will not change your tax or reduce your refund.*

Filing Status
(See page 10.)
Check only one box.

1. Single
2. Married filing joint return (even if only one had income)
3. Married filing separate return. Enter spouse's social security no. above and full name here. ▶
4. Head of household (with qualifying person). (See page 11.) If the qualifying person is a child but not your dependent, enter this child's name here. ▶
5. Qualifying widow(er) with dependent child (year spouse died ▶ 19). (See page 11.)

Exemptions
(See page 11.)

6a ☐ **Yourself.** If your parent (or someone else) can claim you as a dependent on his or her tax return, **do not** check box 6a. But be sure to check the box on line 33b on page 2 .
b ☐ **Spouse** . . . . .
c **Dependents:**

(1) Name (first, initial, and last name)	(2) Check if under age 1	(3) If age 1 or older, dependent's social security number	(4) Dependent's relationship to you	(5) No. of months lived in your home in 1992

If more than six dependents, see page 12.

No. of boxes checked on 6a and 6b
No. of your children on 6c who:
• **lived with you**
• **didn't live with you due to divorce or separation (see page 13)**
No. of other dependents on 6c

d If your child didn't live with you but is claimed as your dependent under a pre-1985 agreement, check here ▶ ☐
e Total number of exemptions claimed . . .
Add numbers entered on lines above ▶

Income

Attach Copy B of your Forms W-2, W-2G, and 1099-R here.

If you did not get a W-2, see page 9.

Attach check or money order on top of any Forms W-2, W-2G, or 1099-R.

7	Wages, salaries, tips, etc. Attach Form(s) W-2	7
8a	**Taxable** interest income. Attach Schedule B if over $400	8a
b	**Tax-exempt** interest income (see page 15). DON'T include on line 8a [8b]	
9	Dividend income. Attach Schedule B if over $400	9
10	Taxable refunds, credits, or offsets of state and local income taxes from worksheet on page 16	10
11	Alimony received	11
12	Business income or (loss). Attach Schedule C or C-EZ	12
13	Capital gain or (loss). Attach Schedule D	13
14	Capital gain distributions not reported on line 13 (see page 15)	14
15	Other gains or (losses). Attach Form 4797	15
16a	Total IRA distributions . [16a] b Taxable amount (see page 16)	16b
17a	Total pensions and annuities [17a] b Taxable amount (see page 16)	17b
18	Rents, royalties, partnerships, estates, trusts, etc. Attach Schedule E	18
19	Farm income or (loss). Attach Schedule F	19
20	Unemployment compensation (see page 17)	20
21a	Social security benefits [21a] b Taxable amount (see page 17)	21b
22	Other income. List type and amount—see page 18	22
23	Add the amounts in the far right column for lines 7 through 22. This is your **total income** ▶	23

Adjustments to Income
(See page 18.)

24a	Your IRA deduction from applicable worksheet on page 19 or 20	24a
b	Spouse's IRA deduction from applicable worksheet on page 19 or 20	24b
25	One-half of self-employment tax (see page 20)	25
26	Self-employed health insurance deduction (see page 20)	26
27	Keogh retirement plan and self-employed SEP deduction	27
28	Penalty on early withdrawal of savings	28
29	Alimony paid. Recipient's SSN ▶	29
30	Add lines 24a through 29. These are your **total adjustments** ▶	30

Adjusted Gross Income

31	Subtract line 30 from line 23. This is your **adjusted gross income**. *If this amount is less than $22,370 and a child lived with you, see page EIC-1 to find out if you can claim the "Earned Income Credit" on line 56* ▶	31

Cat. No. 11320B Form **1040** (1992)

Federal Form 1040
Figure 8-1.

SCHEDULES A&B (Form 1040)
Department of the Treasury Internal Revenue Service (L)

Schedule A—Itemized Deductions

(Schedule B is on back)

▶ Attach to Form 1040. ▶ See Instructions for Schedules A and B (Form 1040).

OMB No. 1545-0074
1992
Attachment Sequence No. 07

Name(s) shown on Form 1040 | Your social security number

Medical and Dental Expenses		Caution: *Do not include expenses reimbursed or paid by others.*		
	1	Medical and dental expenses (see page A-1)	1	
	2	Enter amount from Form 1040, line 32. [2]		
	3	Multiply line 2 above by 7.5% (.075)	3	
	4	Subtract line 3 from line 1. If zero or less, enter -0- ▶		4
Taxes You Paid (See page A-1.)	5	State and local income taxes	5	
	6	Real estate taxes (see page A-2)	6	
	7	Other taxes. List—include personal property taxes ▶	7	
	8	Add lines 5 through 7 ▶		8
Interest You Paid (See page A-2.)	9a	Home mortgage interest and points reported to you on Form 1098	9a	
	b	Home mortgage interest not reported to you on Form 1098. If paid to an individual, show that person's name and address. ▶	9b	
Note: Personal interest is not deductible.	10	Points not reported to you on Form 1098. See page A-3 for special rules	10	
	11	Investment interest. If required, attach Form 4952. (See page A-3.)	11	
	12	Add lines 9a through 11 ▶		12
Gifts to Charity (See page A-3.)		Caution: *If you made a charitable contribution and received a benefit in return, see page A-3.*		
	13	Contributions by cash or check	13	
	14	Other than by cash or check. If over $500, you **MUST** attach Form 8283	14	
	15	Carryover from prior year	15	
	16	Add lines 13 through 15 ▶		16
Casualty and Theft Losses	17	Casualty or theft loss(es). Attach Form 4684. (See page A-4.) ▶		17
Moving Expenses	18	Moving expenses. Attach Form 3903 or 3903F. (See page A-4.) ▶		18
Job Expenses and Most Other Miscellaneous Deductions (See page A-5 for expenses to deduct here.)	19	Unreimbursed employee expenses—job travel, union dues, job education, etc. If required, you **MUST** attach Form 2106. (See page A-4.) ▶	19	
	20	Other expenses—investment, tax preparation, safe deposit box, etc. List type and amount ▶	20	
	21	Add lines 19 and 20	21	
	22	Enter amount from Form 1040, line 32. [22]		
	23	Multiply line 22 above by 2% (.02)	23	
	24	Subtract line 23 from line 21. If zero or less, enter -0- ▶		24
Other Miscellaneous Deductions	25	Other—from list on page A-5. List type and amount ▶		25
Total Itemized Deductions	26	Is the amount on Form 1040, line 32, more than $105,250 (more than $52,625 if married filing separately)? • **NO.** Your deduction is not limited. Add lines 4, 8, 12, 16, 17, 18, 24, and 25. • **YES.** Your deduction may be limited. See page A-5 for the amount to enter. ▶ **Caution:** *Be sure to enter on Form 1040, line 34, the **LARGER** of the amount on line 26 above or your standard deduction.*		26

For Paperwork Reduction Act Notice, see Form 1040 instructions. Cat. No. 12614K Schedule A (Form 1040) 1992

Schedule A for itemized deductions
Figure 8-2.

In this chapter a tax-related category for local income tax withholding will be established. You will split entries for mortgage payments into mortgage interest and payments against the principal. Also, you will modify some of the transactions from earlier chapters to provide the additional tax information that you'll need here.

In later chapters, you will combine Quicken's personal tax-related reports with the business reports. In these, you will have a powerful tax-monitoring and planning tool.

Planning to Use Quicken for Taxes

There is no one correct way to record tax information in Quicken. The best method is to tailor your transaction entries to the information that will be required on your tax forms. This is a good approach even if you have an accountant prepare your return. Remember, if you organize your tax information, your accountant will not have to—and you will pay less for tax preparation as a result.

Start the planning process with the forms you filed last year. This may be just the Form 1040 that everyone files or it may include a number of schedules. Although the forms change a little from year to year and your need to file a certain form can be a one-time occurrence, last year's forms make a good starting place. Form 1040, partially shown in Figure 8-1, is the basic tax form used by individuals. Schedule A, shown in Figure 8-2, is used for itemized deductions.

You can choose from three different methods to have Quicken accumulate information for the various tax forms and schedules that you will need to prepare at the end of the year. The first method is to use category assignments to identify tax-related information and to produce a tax summary at the end of the year that contains all of the tax-related category entries. This is the simplest method, but it provides the least detail.

With Quicken you also have the option of assigning each category and subcategory to a tax schedule. You can even assign the category or subcategory to a particular line on this schedule. To make this assignment, you display the category list with Ctrl-C from the Register window, highlight the category for which you want to make a tax schedule assignment, and press Ctrl-E to edit the category. When the Edit Category window appears, you can press F9 (Tax Schedules) to select a tax schedule. After you select a schedule, a second list displays to allow you to select a line entry on the selected schedule. The lines are given names rather than numbers to make your selection easier. If you use these methods, you can produce a tax schedule report that lists all tax-related entries by line within schedules.

The third option for categorizing tax data is to use a class assignment. Class assignments provide a way to further organize categories and subcategories. You can assign multiple classes to your existing categories and subcategories. You make these assignments as you enter transactions by typing a / followed by the class name after a category or subcategory. Although this is more work than using Quicken's tax schedule assignments, it does offer the potential of providing the greatest level of detail within your existing category structure.

If you have unreimbursed business expenses that exceed a certain percentage of your income, you might want to set up a class for Form 2106, which is used exclusively for these expenses, or set up a category for these expenses and assign this category to tax schedule 2106 with Quicken's Tax Schedule feature. If you own and manage rental properties, you must use Schedule E to monitor income and expenses for these properties. With Quicken, you can classify the income and expense transactions for Schedule E.

With Form 2106 expenses, you will not know until the end of the year if you have enough expenses to deduct them. With the class code approach, you would use a class called 2106 for transactions of unreimbursed business expenses and check the total at year-end. If you use the tax schedule assignment method, you would need to set up a new category for unreimbursed business expenses and assign this category to tax schedule Form 2106.

Another thing to watch for is the timing of expense recognition. *Expense recognition* determines which tax year will be affected by expenses incurred at the beginning or end of a year. This is a particular problem for items that are charged on credit cards since the IRS recognizes an expense as occurring the day you charge it rather than the day you pay for it. Unreimbursed air travel charged in December 1993 and paid by check in January 1994 is counted in 1993 totals since you incur the liability for payment the day you charge the tickets. A separate Quicken account for credit purchases makes these necessary year-end adjustments easier than when you just keep track of credit card payments from your checkbook.

If you decide to use classes rather than tax schedule assignments to categorize tax information, you might decide your class codes should indicate more than the number of the tax form where the information is used. As you look at the forms shown in Figures 8-1 and 8-2, you will find that each of the lines where information can be entered is numbered. For example, line 7 of your 1040 is "Wages, salaries, tips, etc.," which you could probably fill in with the total from the Salary category—if you have only one source of income.

But when you set up Quicken categories for income from several sources, you might want to assign a class called "1040—7" to each income transaction, so you could display a total of all the entries for this class. Likewise, you can set up classes for other line items such as "A—6" for real estate tax or "A—13" for cash contributions. You could also set up "1040—21a" for Social Security benefits and "1040—9" for dividend income, but if you do decide to use classes, there is no need to establish a class for every line on every form—only for those lines that you are likely to use.

REMEMBER: When creating a class you must enter the category, a slash (/), and then the class.

Classes are almost a requirement for rental property management since the same types of expenses and incomes will repeat for each property. You might use the street address or apartment number to distinguish the transactions generated by different properties. You can use the Split Transaction feature if one transaction covers expenses or income for more than one property.

Most of your entries will focus on the current tax year, but there is also longer-term tax-related information that is sometimes needed. When you sell assets such as a house or stock holdings, information must be accumulated over the time you own the asset. Maintaining information on these assets in separate accounts is the best approach to use. Separate accounts can make it much easier to calculate the profit on the sale of the asset. For example, if you purchased a house for $100,000 and sold it five years later for $150,000, it might seem as though the profit is $50,000. However, if you have accurately recorded improvements such as a new deck and a fireplace, these amounts can be added to the cost of the asset since they are items that added value. When the $35,000 cost of these improvements is added to the price of the house, the profit is $15,000 for tax purposes. Take a look at the sample transaction in the next section and the tax reports before making your final decisions about classes and categories for your tax information. Depending on the complexity of your tax situation, simple category assignments might be sufficient.

Recording Detailed Tax Information

In Chapter 7, "Quicken as a Budgeting Tool," you recorded detailed transaction information in the account register for your Cardinal Bank checking account. Scroll through those transactions and notice how the monthly paycheck and mortgage payment transactions were treated. For the paycheck, you entered the amount of the check, net of deductions for items such as FICA, federal withholding, medical, and state withholding. For the monthly mortgage payment, you established a tax-related category called Mort Pay and used that for the entire payment. However, Quicken can provide much better tax-related information in both these areas. You will want to make the suggested changes if you want Quicken to accumulate tax schedule information for you. The following sections will show you how.

Gross Earnings and Salary Deductions

Highlight the first payroll transaction you recorded in your Cardinal Bank personal account register in Chapter 6, "Expanding the Scope of Financial Entries." The amount of the net deposit was $1585.99—you didn't record any of the tax-related information for deductions. The entry you made then was adequate for maintaining a correct check register. It is also adequate for budgeting purposes since you only need to match cash inflows and outflows, and the net amount of the payroll check represents the inflow for the period. However, for tax purposes, more information is needed. By completing the following entry, you will be able to monitor the amounts on your pay stub. You will also be able to verify the accuracy of your Form W2 at the end of the year.

To expand the payroll transaction, you need some additional information. The gross earnings for the pay period were $2000.00. The deductions withheld for FICA taxes were $124.00, medicare withholding was $29.00, medical insurance was $42.01, federal taxes were $130.00, state taxes were $80.00, and local taxes were $9.00.

The following steps illustrate how you can use Quicken's Split Transaction feature to capture all the information related to the tax aspects of your paycheck and still show the net deposit of $1585.99 to the checking account.

1. With the first payroll entry highlighted, press Ctrl-S, and the Split Transaction window appears on your screen.
2. Press Enter to leave Salary as the category.
3. Type **Gross Wages Earned** in the Memo field and press Enter.
4. Type **2000.00** in the Amount field and press Enter.

These modifications set your Salary category as your gross earnings for the period. Each time you record your paycheck this way, Quicken accumulates your year-to-date gross earnings. After recording this portion of the transaction, you are left with –414.01 in the Amount field. This is Quicken's way of telling you there is currently a negative difference between the amount of the net deposit and the gross wages recorded. This difference equals the amount of withholding from your paycheck that will be recorded in the remaining steps.

5. Type **Tax:Soc Sec** and press Enter.
6. Type **FICA Withholding** and press Enter.
7. Type **–124.00** and press Enter.

Once again, Quicken records the information in the Split Transaction window and leaves a balance of –290.01 in the Amount field for row 3. This category is predefined as tax related in Quicken, even though FICA withholding is not ordinarily tax deductible on your Form 1040. This is because you should monitor this amount if you change jobs during the year. Since there is a limit on the amount of earnings taxed for FICA, switching jobs can cause you to pay more than you owe; the second employer will not know what was withheld by the first. You can include excess FICA payments on your Form 1040 with other withholding amounts (on line 58). If you earn less than the upper limit, this category will not be used in your tax preparation process.

8. Type **Tax:Medicare** and press Enter.
9. Type **Medicare Withholding** and press Enter.
10. Type **–29.00** and press Enter.
11. Type **Medical** and press Enter.
12. Type **Health Ins** and press Enter.
13. Type **–42.01** and press Enter.
14. Type **Tax:Fed** and press Enter.
15. Type **Federal Income Tax** and press Enter.
16. Type **–130.00** and press Enter to record the amount.
17. Type **Tax:State** and press Enter.
18. Type **State Income Tax** and press Enter.
19. Type **–80.00** and press Enter.
20. Type **Tax:Local** and press Enter.

Quicken will prompt you by stating that this is not a predefined category. Tell Quicken to enter the category with the following steps:

21. Type **1** in response to the Category Not Found window prompt.
22. Type **S** and press Enter.
23. Type **Local Tax Withholding** and press Enter.

24. Type **Y**, press F9 (Tax Schedules), select W-2, then select Local Withholding and press Enter until you return to the Split Transaction window.
25. Move to the Memo field.
26. Type **Local Income Tax**, and press Enter.

You see the screen shown in Figure 8-3. Notice that there is no balance left to explain in the Split Transaction screen.

27. Press Ctrl-Enter and Quicken returns you to the Register window.
28. Press Ctrl-M.

Since you memorized this transaction in Chapter 6, you now need to rememorize it with the split transaction data. You are asked whether you want to memorize the amounts or the percentages.

29. Type **A** and press Enter to memorize the amounts.
30. Press Enter to select Replace with New.

Quicken will erase the old memorized transaction and replace it with the new one.

31. Press Ctrl-Enter again to tell Quicken to accept the changed transaction.

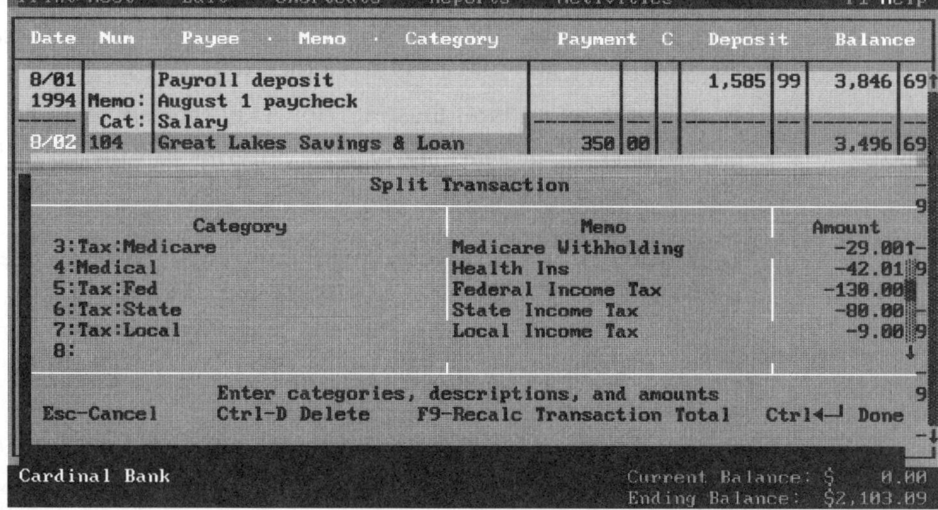

Split Transaction window after recording withholding and other deductions
Figure 8-3.

After you complete this process, all the information in the Split Transaction window is recorded in your accounts. Your reports will show gross earnings for tax purposes at $2000.00, with tax-related deductions for FICA, medicare, medical, and federal, state, and local taxes.

Mortgage Principal and Interest

The mortgage payment transaction recorded in Chapter 6 was fine for recording changes to your checking account balance or monitoring budgeted expenses. However, it didn't capture the tax-related aspects of the transaction. Although you identified the transaction as tax related, the mortgage principal and interest were not isolated. You would not be able to tell how much to list on your tax return as interest expense. But perhaps your bank will provide you a statement with this information at the end of the year. In some cases, the bank even divides your previous month's payment among principal, interest, and escrow on the current month's bill. However, if you purchased from a private individual, you will not receive this information, although you can have Quicken calculate it for you since accurate records are necessary to take the mortgage interest expense as a tax deduction. Quicken will continue to assist you by organizing it in the recording process.

On your screen, highlight the first Great Lakes Savings & Loan mortgage payment of $350.00 on 8/2/94 that you made in Chapter 6. Using Quicken's Split Transaction feature again, you will modify the record of this transaction to distribute the payment between principal and interest. The steps outlined here assume that you know which payment number you are making and that you pay your insurance and taxes directly to the insurer and local taxing unit with checks recorded separately in your register. If the financial institution has established an escrow account for these payments, you could easily add that amount to this transaction.

The following procedures illustrate how Quicken can be used to create a loan amortization schedule and track your mortgage principal and interest payments:

1. With the first mortgage payment entry highlighted on the screen, select **A**ctivities, select **F**inancial Planning, and then select **L**oan Calculator.
2. Type **39999** for the principal and press Enter.
3. Type **9.519** for the annual interest rate and press Enter.
4. Type **25** for the total years and press Enter.
5. Type **12** for the periods per year and press Enter.
6. Press F9 (View Payment Schedule) to view the schedule.

Figure 8-4 shows the top part of this schedule. You can print it out for future reference with Ctrl-P. Since you are about to make your 53rd payment, you would look down the schedule for payment 53 to get the numbers that you need.

7. Press Esc twice to return to the register.
8. Make certain your Great Lakes Savings and Loan transaction for August is highlighted.
9. Press Ctrl-S and the Split Transaction window appears.
10. Type **Mort Prin** and press Enter.

If you do not have this category on your list, add it to your list following the process described in the section "Adding Categories" in Chapter 6. When setting up the category, it is not tax-related.

11. Type **Principal Payment** and press Enter for the memo.
12. Type **49.33** and press Enter to record the portion of the transaction related to principal.
13. Type **Mort Int** and press Enter.
14. Type **Interest Portion of Payment** and press Enter.
15. The amount shown in the last column, 300.67, is correct. You see the screen shown in Figure 8-5.

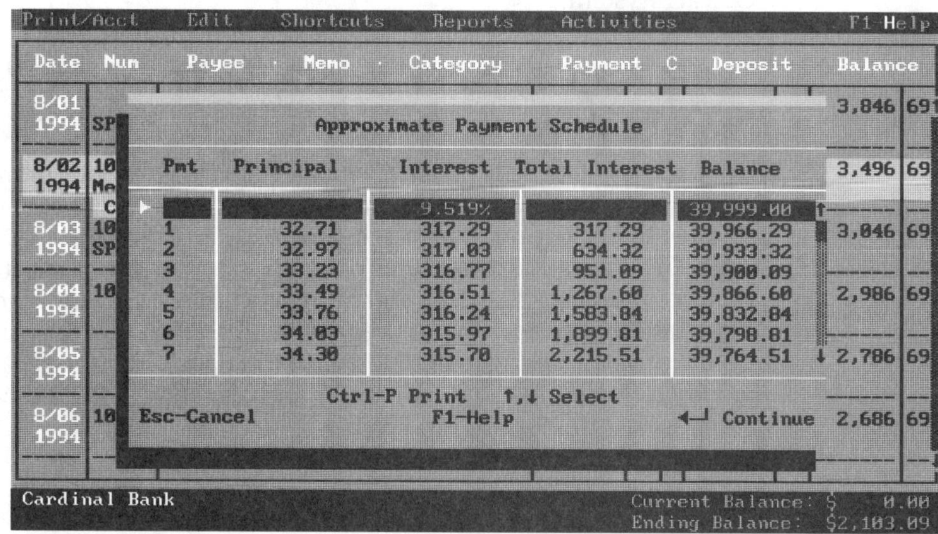

Payment schedule created with Loan Calculator
Figure 8-4.

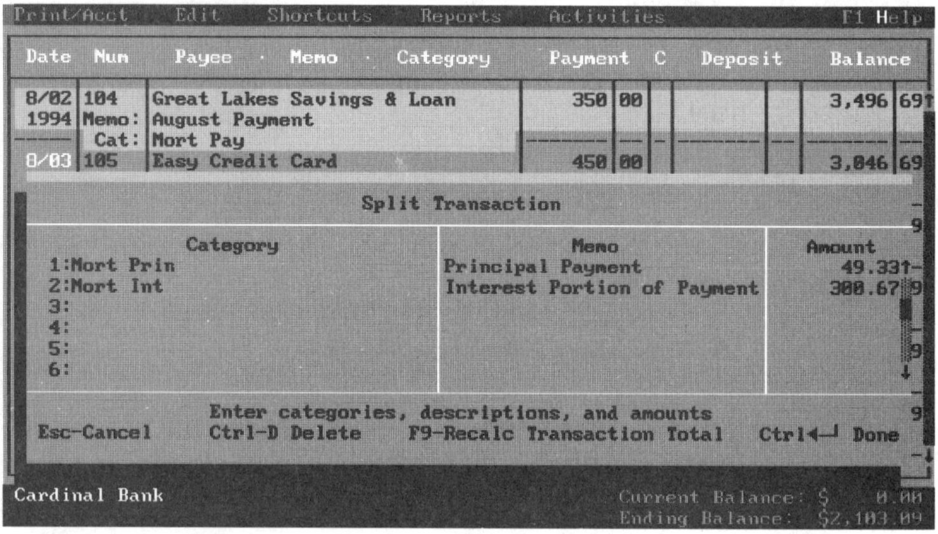

Split Transaction window after distributing principal and interest
Figure 8-5.

16. Press Ctrl-Enter and Quicken returns you to the highlighted transaction for the mortgage payment in your register.
17. Press Ctrl-Enter to record the new split transaction information.

After recording these two transactions, you can see the expanded benefits of the information when it is organized by Quicken. Once again, you want to rememorize this transaction for monthly recording purposes. The next section takes a look at the tax information you have now entered into your Quicken system.

Setting Up a Loan Entry Using Quicken 7's New Feature

Once you use Quicken's Loan Calculator to compute your monthly loan payment, you can use a new loan feature in Quicken 7 to set up a monthly payment. Quicken can create a memorized transaction and later recall it. Quicken automatically allocates the correct amounts to the categories you want for mortgage principal and mortgage interest according to an amortization schedule that it prepares for the loan. This saves you from needing to pull up the loan amortization schedule discussed earlier and modifying your loan payment each month to change the allocations of the amounts to principal and interest.

To set up automatic loan payments, you need to select Set Up Loan from the Activities menu in the register. Quicken presents the Set Amortization Information window shown in Figure 8-6.

You will need to enter specifics on your loan in this window. Quicken needs the regular payment amount, the annual interest rate, the number of periods per year, the total years, and whether you are the borrower or lender. If you need to include escrow fees and insurance, you would include them in the total amount and use the split feature later to specify the amount for each. You may find that the loan amount may be off by a few pennies from the principal in the Loan Calculator if you used this feature to calculate your payment amounts; you can rectify this problem in the amortization schedule entry for the last period of the loan.

You must provide the information needed to create a memorized transaction in the next section of this window. You will enter a payee, a memo, the categories for the principal and interest amount for each period, and whether or not the recorded transaction should be marked as cleared. If you need to account for escrow or insurance, you will want to press Ctrl-S next. The category for the principal must be first in the split window and the interest must be second. Escrow and insurance follow. Quicken ignores split entries beyond line 1 and 3 when amortization is computed. You will press Ctrl-Enter to finalize the split entries. Enter the date of the first payment in the window. If you want to look at the amortization schedule, you can

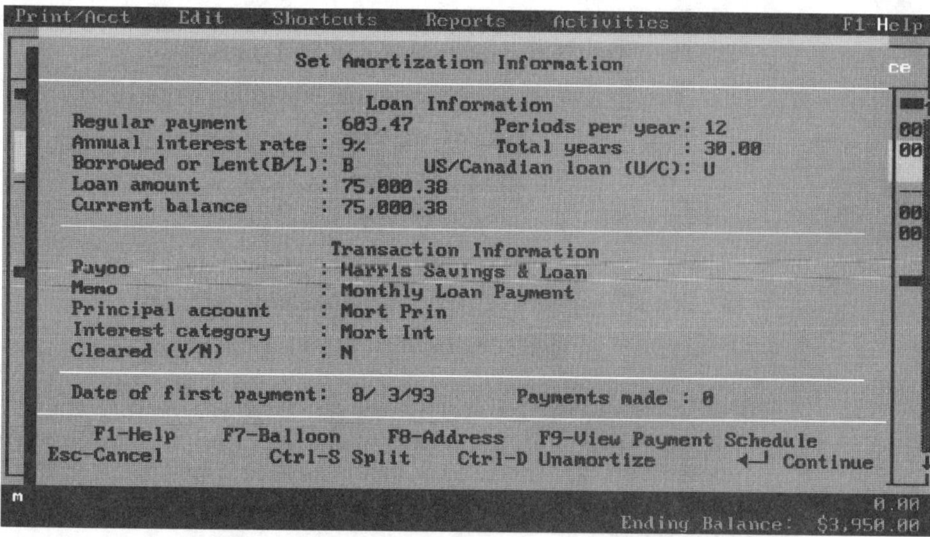

The Set Amortization window

Figure 8-6.

display it with F9, then press Enter when you are finished looking to return to the window where you made your entries. When you press F10, the information is recorded as a memorized transaction that you can recall quickly each month.

NOTE: You can use F7 with this feature to set up a loan with balloon payments.

When you are ready to record loan payment information in the register, you can recall this transaction just like any other memorized transaction.

Printing Quicken's Tax Reports

The summary tax information generated by Quicken can be used to provide detailed information for preparing your taxes. In this section you will examine the reports generated using the information from the Cardinal Bank account register for the first month (8/1/94 through 8/31/94). The following steps generate Quicken's Tax Summary report:

1. From the account register, select **R**eports, select **H**ome Reports, and select **T**ax Summary. Quicken's Tax Summary Report window will appear on your screen.
2. Type **Tax Summary Report** and press Enter.
3. Press F7 and the Create Transaction Report window appears.
4. Press Enter, type **Custom Date**, and press Enter.
5. Type **8/1/94** and press Enter.
6. Type **8/31/94** and press Enter.
7. Press Enter to accept "Subtotal by: Category."
8. Press Enter to accept "Subtotal area by: Account."
9. Type **C** to select the current account and press Enter.

The Tax Summary report will appear on your screen. You can press Alt-L and select Full Column **W**idth to change from half-width to full-width reports. You can also use the arrow keys to move through the report (the directions in which the report extends are shown in the lower-right corner of the screen).

10. Select **F**ile/Print and the **P**rint Report window will appear on the screen.

11. Choose your printer option and press Ctrl-Enter. Quicken will print the tax summary by category, as shown in Figure 8-7.

Tax Summary Report

The report in Figure 8-7 is a half-width version of the report, which is Quicken's default setting. If you printed the same version of the report with the full-width option, the result would be a wider report. Although the same information is included on both reports, the full-width version presents the detail with fewer abbreviations. The additional space between fields also makes it easier to understand. This format would be preferable for presentation to tax consultants and preparers.

Quicken prints the complete detail for each of the tax-related categories as the default report. This format allows you to use the totals generated at the end of the tax year for entry on your tax returns. The totals generated in Figure 8-7 would be used on the following lines of your personal income tax form for 1993:

Income/Expense Category	Tax Return Location
Total Salary Income	Form 1040 line 7
Total Federal Income Tax	Form 1040 line 54
Total Medical & Dental	Schedule A line 1
Total Mortgage Interest Exp	Schedule A line 9a
Total State Income Tax	Schedule A line 5
Total Local Income Tax	Schedule A line 5

This also provides an excellent summary and could prove useful in the event of an IRS tax audit inquiry.

As you will see in Chapter 10, "Creating Custom Reports," all Quicken reports can be customized in many different report formats (months, quarters, half years, and so on). One variation discussed in the previous chapter compared reports prepared for a separate account, Cardinal Bank, and one prepared for all accounts. The report for all accounts used the bank checking accounts, cash, and credit card accounts from the PERSONAL file. Here, while Figure 8-7 was prepared for a single account, Cardinal Bank, Figure 8-8 illustrates a Tax Summary report including all accounts in the PERSONAL file. Note that the second column from the left (Acct) shows the source of the tax-related transaction. In this report, all the sources were from the Cardinal Bank account, but you can see how, in a more complex situation, this would be useful in tracking the source of a tax-related transaction. For year-end tax purposes, a report of all accounts provides an

```
                          Tax Summary Report
                        8/ 1/94 Through 8/31/94
PERSONAL-Cardinal Bank                                              Page 1
7/22/94

  Date    Num       Description          Memo         Category     Clr   Amount
 ----- -------- ----------------- ------------ ---------------- - ----------

        INCOME/EXPENSE
          INCOME
            Salary Income
            -------------
  8/ 1       S Payroll deposit     Gross Wages Salary                  2,000.00
                                                                       ---------
            Total Salary Income                                        2,000.00
                                                                       ---------
          TOTAL INCOME                                                 2,000.00


          EXPENSES
            Medical Expense:
            ----------------

              Doctor & Dental Visits
              ----------------------
  8/ 6 107     Orthodontics, Inc. Monthly Orthod Medical:Doctor          -100.00
                                                                       ---------
              Total Doctor & Dental Visits                               -100.00

              Medical Expense - Other
              -----------------------
  8/ 1        S Payroll deposit    Health Ins     Medical                 -42.01
                                                                       ---------
              Total Medical Expense - Other                               -42.01
                                                                       ---------
            Total Medical Expense                                        -142.01

            Mortgage Interest Exp
            ---------------------
  8/ 2 104  S Great Lakes Savi Interest Po Mort Int                      -300.67
                                                                       ---------
            Total Mortgage Interest Exp                                  -300.67
```

Partial Tax Summary Report for the Cardinal Bank checking account using half-width printing
Figure 8-7.

overview by category that integrates the various accounts. For your tax-reporting needs, you should select the report format best suited to your tax preparation and planning needs.

Another example of modifying Quicken's report features is shown in Figure 8-9. In this case, Quicken was instructed to print only the Medical category.

```
                              Tax Summary Report
                           8/ 1/94 Through 8/31/94
PERSONAL-All Accounts                                                      Page 1
7/22/94

 Date   Acct   Num   Description        Memo          Category       Clr  Amount
 ----- ------ ----- ---------------- ------------- ----------------- - ---------

       INCOME/EXPENSE
         INCOME
           Salary Income
           -------------
  8/ 1 Cardinal   S Payroll deposit  Gross Wages Salary                  2,000.00
                                                                        ---------
           Total Salary Income                                           2,000.00
                                                                        ---------
         TOTAL INCOME                                                    2,000.00


         EXPENSES
           Medical Expense:
           ----------------

             Doctor & Dental Visits
             ----------------------
  8/ 6 Cardinal 107    Orthodontics, In Monthly Ort Medical:Doctor        -100.00
                                                                        ---------
             Total Doctor & Dental Visits                                 -100.00

             Medical Expense - Other
             -----------------------
  8/ 1 Cardinal       S Payroll deposit  Health Ins   Medical              -42.01
                                                                        ---------
             Total Medical Expense - Other                                 -42.01
                                                                        ---------
           Total Medical Expense                                          -142.01

           Mortgage Interest Exp
           ---------------------
  8/ 2 Cardinal 104  S Great Lakes Savi Interest Po Mort Int              -300.67
                                                                        ---------
           Total Mortgage Interest Exp                                    -300.67

           Taxes:
           ------

             Federal Tax
             -----------
  8/ 1 Cardinal       S Payroll deposit Federal Inc Tax:Fed               -130.00
                                                                        ---------
             Total Federal Tax                                            -130.00

             Local Withholding
             -----------------
```

Tax Summary Report for PERSONAL file accounts

Figure 8-8.

```
                     Tax Summary Report
                  8/ 1/94 Through 8/31/94
PERSONAL-All Accounts                                              Page 2
7/22/94

   Date   Acct      Num      Description        Memo        Category     Clr Amount
  ----- -------- ------ ---------------- ----------- --------------- - ---------

8/ 1 Cardinal      S Payroll deposit  Local Incom Tax:Local              -9.00
                                                                     ---------
              Total Local Withholding                                    -9.00

              Medicare Tax
              ------------
   8/ 1 Cardinal      S Payroll deposit  Medicare Wi Tax:Medicare       -29.00


                                                                     ---------
              Total Medicare Tax                                        -29.00

              Soc Sec Tax
              -----------
   8/ 1 Cardinal      S Payroll deposit  FICA Withho Tax:Soc Sec       -124.00
                                                                     ---------
              Total Soc Sec Tax                                        -124.00

              State Tax
              ---------
   8/ 1 Cardinal      S Payroll deposit  State Incom Tax:State          -80.00
                                                                     ---------
              Total State Tax                                           -80.00
                                                                     ---------
            Total Taxes                                                -372.00
                                                                     ---------
          TOTAL EXPENSES                                               -814.68

                                                                     ---------
        TOTAL INCOME/EXPENSE                                          1,185.32
                                                                     =========
```

Tax Summary Report for PERSONAL file accounts (*continued*)
Figure 8-8.

Although this information was included in the report shown in Figure 8-7, you can see the benefits of a filtered report as you increase the number of transactions recorded by Quicken and want details on particular items during the year-end tax planning and reporting process. Quicken's procedures for generating this type of report will be covered in Chapter 10, "Creating Custom Reports."

The final point to note on all Quicken reports is that the date of report preparation is displayed in the upper-left corner of the report. When using Quicken reports, always note the report preparation date to ensure you are using the most recent report when making your financial decisions.

```
                              Tax Summary Report
                           1/ 1/94 Through 12/31/94
PERSONAL-Selected Accounts                                              Page 1
7/22/94

  Date   Acct   Num    Description         Memo          Category     Clr  Amount
  ----- ------ ----- ---------------- ------------ ---------------- - ---------

        INCOME/EXPENSE
          EXPENSES
            Medical Expense:
            ----------------
              Doctor & Dental Visits
              ----------------------
   8/ 6 Cardinal 107    Orthodontics, In Monthly Ort Medical:Doctor      -100.00
   9/ 8 Cardinal 116    Orthodontics. In Monthly Ort Medical:Doctor      -170.00
  10/ 8 Cardinal 124    Orthodontics, In Monthly Ort Medical:Doctor      -100.00
                                                                        ---------
              Total Doctor & Dental Visits                               -370.00

              Medical Expense - Other
              -----------------------
   8/ 1 Cardinal       S Payroll deposit  Health Ins   Medical            -42.01
                                                                        ---------
              Total Medical Expense - Other                               -42.01
                                                                        ---------
            Total Medical Expense                                        -412.01
                                                                        ---------
         TOTAL EXPENSES                                                  -412.01

                                                                        ---------
       TOTAL INCOME/EXPENSES                                             -412.01
                                                                        =========
```

A sample Tax Summary report filtered for a specific category
Figure 8-9.

8

Tax Schedule Report

If you choose to assign categories to tax schedules and lines, you will want to create a Tax Schedule report. This report will provide useful information only if you have edited your categories and assigned them to the schedules and forms where you want the income and expenses that they represent to appear. Figure 8-10 shows a section of a Tax Schedule report that displays the Schedule A home mortgage interest and medical expenses related to health insurance premiums for August 1994. The doctor and dental payments are shown separately on another portion of the report. You saw in Figure 8-9 how you can use a filtered tax summary report to gather information on one account at a time; however, that approach requires you to request many individual reports. In contrast, the Tax Schedule report organizes all your tax information on one easy-to-use report.

To produce the Tax Schedule report, you must have assigned medical expenses and all other tax related categories to the appropriate tax schedules. As you know, Quicken has preassigned many categories to the appropriate tax schedule for you. You must remember as you designate new categories, like

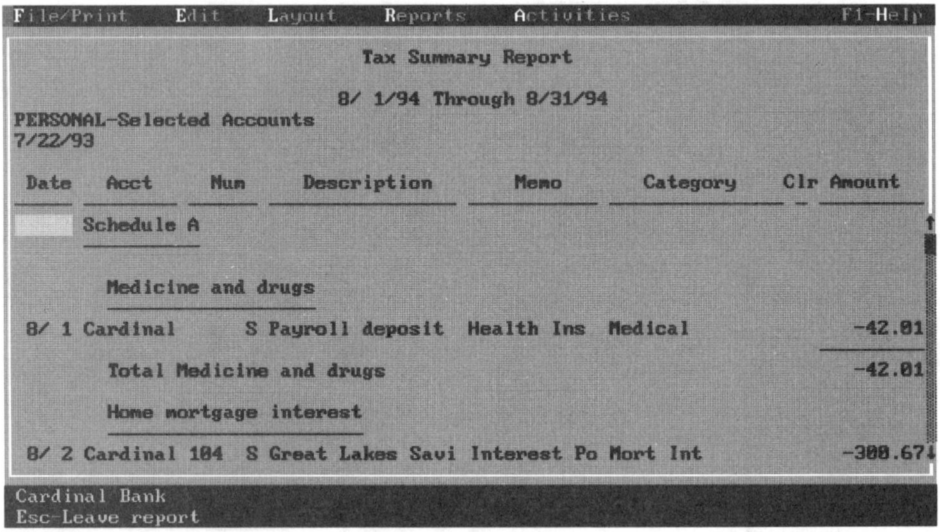

```
File/Print   Edit   Layout   Reports   Activities                          F1-Help
                          Tax Summary Report

                     8/ 1/94 Through 8/31/94
PERSONAL-Selected Accounts
7/22/93

 Date   Acct     Num    Description      Memo       Category     Clr Amount
 ----   ----     ---    -----------      ----       --------     --- ------
        Schedule A

          Medicine and drugs

 8/ 1 Cardinal      S Payroll deposit  Health Ins  Medical            -42.01
                                                                      ------
          Total Medicine and drugs                                    -42.01

          Home mortgage interest

 8/ 2 Cardinal 104  S Great Lakes Savi Interest Po Mort Int          -308.67
Cardinal Bank
Esc-Leave report
```

Portion of Tax Schedule Report showing Medicine and drugs and Home mortgage interest
Figure 8-10.

the Tax:Local category established in this chapter, to assign them to the appropriate tax schedule as part of the setup process. If you have not assigned your tax related categories to a tax schedule, Quicken will not be able to provide you with complete tax information. At year end you may want to review your categories in your Category and Transfer List window to make sure you have properly designated all your tax related categories in the list.

You can prepare the report by selecting **R**eports from the Register window, select **H**ome Reports, and then select **T**ax Schedule. If you press Ctrl-Enter, you can accept the default title and time period for the report.

C H A P T E R

investments banking FILE register expenses DEDUCTIONS
tips equity net pay
checks bank statements
statements
dividends business tips
INCOME cash flow
banking business tips FILE reports
budget FILE business tips checks
DEDUCTIONS
statements cash flow tips mortgage
net revenue
pay taxes bank
business tips
mortgage cash dividends tips
business tips investments
register statements
reports business tips taxes
expenses tips
equity investments INCOME
checks statements bank
cash
assets checks budget tips finances net pay

DETERMINING YOUR NET WORTH

In previous chapters, you used Quicken as a tool for financial planning and monitoring. Many of the activities were simply repetitive steps; you applied the same techniques repeatedly to record transactions. These activities were procedural—they did not require analysis before entry and each transaction followed exactly the same steps.

Although these activities are an important part of managing your finances, they do not provide the total picture.

Basic Concepts of Financial Management

You probably have financial goals you would like to meet, such as buying a new car, purchasing a house, or retiring at age 60. Whatever your goals may be, you will need a certain level of financial resources to meet them. You might attempt to accumulate the necessary resources through savings or the acquisition of investments such as stocks or bonds. In this chapter, you'll learn to measure how successful you have been in your financial management activities.

One important measure of your financial status is your net worth. *Net worth* measures the difference between your total assets and your total liabilities at a given time. By looking at your net financial position at two points in time, you can tell how well you have managed your resources and obligations. The process of preparing a statement of net worth will differ from the procedural activities described in earlier chapters. To determine your net worth, you will need to make judgments estimating the value of items purchased earlier. Some investments, such as stocks, have a clearly defined market value, since they are publicly traded. Other investments, such as land or real estate, require a more subjective evaluation.

You have to look at more than the assets you own to determine your net worth. Although you might live in a $300,000 house, it's likely the bank owns more of it than you do. For net worth purposes, you have to determine what your remaining financial obligation is on the house. If you still have a mortgage of $270,000, your net worth in the property is $30,000. The following equation might give you a better perspective of your financial condition:

Financial Resources – Financial Obligations = Net Worth

As you can see, net worth describes your financial position after considering all your financial holdings and deducting all your financial obligations. In accounting terms, your financial resources are things of value that you hold (*assets*). Your assets can include checking, savings, and money market accounts. These are examples of *liquid assets*—they can be readily converted into cash. Stocks, bonds, real estate holdings, and retirement funds (Individual Retirement Accounts [IRAs] and Keogh plans) are other examples of investments you might hold. These assets are not as liquid as the previous group, since converting them to cash depends on the market at the time you attempt to sell them. Your residence, vacation property, antiques, and other items of this nature would be classified as *personal assets*. These assets are the least liquid, since antique and real estate values can decline, and it might take considerable time to convert these assets to cash.

The other part of the net worth equation is your *financial obligations*. Financial obligations include credit card balances and other short-term loans such as those for automobiles. In addition, you must consider long-term loans for the purchase of a residence, vacation property, or other land.

Net worth is the measure most people focus on when monitoring the success of their financial planning activities. The key point to remember is that net worth increases when your financial resources increase—through savings, compounding, and appreciation, and when you reduce the amount of your financial obligations. Take a look at the "Effects of Compounding Interest" table on the following page to see the effect of compounding on an investment and the rapid rate at which even a small investment can grow. Shown are the results of investing $100 a month at the rates specified.

Remember that financial obligations are not necessarily a sign of poor financial management. If you can borrow money and invest it so that it returns more than you are paying to use it, you have *leveraged* your resources. Of course, there is more risk in this avenue of financial planning. Don't take on more risk than you can handle—either financially or emotionally.

After completing this chapter, you will be able to begin monitoring your financial condition. In accounting terms, you can look at the bottom line. The bottom line in personal financial management is your net worth if you value your assets realistically. How you manage your financial assets and related obligations to increase your personal wealth will determine your net worth.

If you set an annual goal of increasing your net worth by a certain percentage, you can use Quicken to assist in recording your financial activities and monitoring your success in meeting your goal. For example, if you started using Quicken in January and record your assets and obligations throughout the year, you could contrast your financial condition at the beginning and end of the year and compare the results of your financial management with your goals. As a result of this comparison, you might decide to change your strategy in some areas of your financial plan. For instance, you might decide to switch from directly managing your portfolio of stocks to using a mutual fund with its professional managers, or you might decide to shift some assets from real estate to liquid assets that can be converted to cash more quickly.

Effects of Compounding Interest on $100 Invested Monthly for 20 Years

Worth at the End of	6% Return	8% Return	10% Return
1 year	$ 1,234	$ 1,245	$ 1,257
2 years	$ 2,543	$ 2,593	$ 2,645
3 years	$ 3,934	$ 4,054	$ 4,178
4 years	$ 5,410	$ 5,635	$ 5,872
5 years	$ 6,977	$ 7,348	$ 7,744
10 years	$16,388	$18,295	$20,484
15 years	$29,082	$34,604	$41,447
20 years	$46,204	$58,902	$75,973

Establishing Accounts for This Chapter

In earlier chapters, you used bank accounts in a file called PERSONAL to record all your transactions. In this chapter, you'll learn about Quicken's other account types. These accounts are ideally suited for recording information on assets you own, debts you have incurred, and investments. You'll establish a file called INVEST for the examples in this chapter. This will make it easier to obtain the same reporting results shown in this chapter, even if you did not complete the examples in earlier chapters. This new file will be established for illustration purposes only. In fact, for your own financial planning, you will probably record all your activities in a single file. That way, Quicken will have access to all your personal information when preparing your reports and assessing your net worth.

Adding a New File

You have already used the following process in the "Adding a New File" section of Chapter 6, "Expanding the Scope of Financial Entries." In this new file, INVEST, you'll establish six new accounts to use throughout this chapter. From the Main Menu, follow these steps to set up the new file:

1. Select **F**ile Activities.
2. Select **S**elect/Set Up File.

   Your screen will have account groups for QDATA and PERSONAL.

3. Select <Set Up New File> and press Enter.
4. Type **INVEST** as the name of the file and press Enter.

   Quicken creates four files from each filename. This means you must provide a valid filename of no more than eight characters. Do not include spaces or special symbols in your entries for account names.
5. Check the location for your data files and make changes to reference a valid file or directory if a change is required. Press Enter.
6. Type **1** to restrict your categories to home categories and press Enter.

   Quicken displays the screen for selecting or creating files, but this time it also shows INVEST.
7. Select INVEST and press Enter.

Quicken presents a Set Up New Account window, shown in Figure 9-1.

8. Type **6** and press Enter to establish the account type as an Investment account.
9. Type **Investments** and press Enter.

   If you have never used investments before, Quicken displays a warning message indicating the advanced nature of the transactions that will be required. When you continue, Quicken presents an Investment Account Type and Description window, shown in Figure 9-2.


```
                         Set Up New Account

 Quicken supports 6 types of accounts:

    1. Bank Account         Use for checking, savings,
                            or money market accounts.
    2. Credit Card          Use to track credit card
                            transactions.
    3. Cash Account         Use for cash expenditures or
                            petty cash.
    4. Other Asset          Track what you own, such as
                            your house, capital equipment,
                            or accounts receivable.
    5. Other Liability      What you owe, such as
                            mortgages or bank loans.
    6. Investment Acct      Use for stocks, bonds, or
                            mutual funds.
 Account Type: 1
 Name for this account:

Esc-Cancel
```

Set Up New Account window
Figure 9-1.

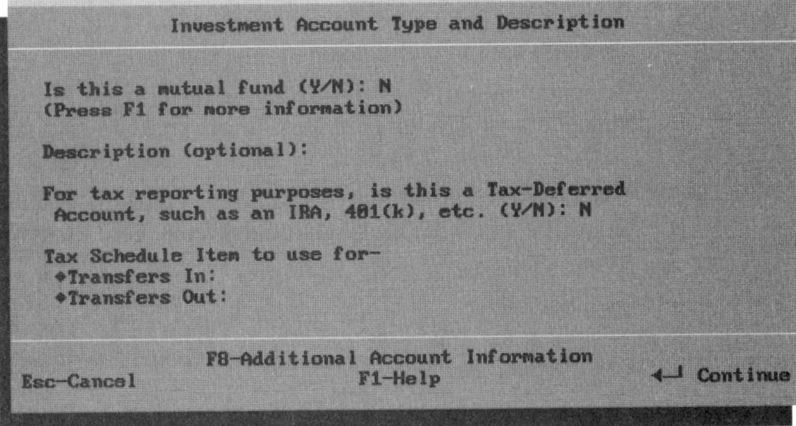

Investment Account Type and Description window
Figure 9-2.

10. Press Enter to accept N for the next entry, since the account will be used to record information on multiple investments. When you wish to establish an account for a single mutual fund, type **Y**.
11. Type **Personal Investments** and press Enter.
12. Press Enter to accept N, since this is not a tax-deferred account.

If this were a tax-deferred account, Quicken would have taken you to the Transfers In field when you entered a Y response in step 12. When you press Ctrl-L, a pop-up window appears that allows you to assign incoming transfers of cash to tax schedules. For example, if this is a Keogh plan, you select "Keogh Deduction" from the Form 1040 list of tax categories. Transfers Out can also be assigned a tax schedule for when you begin to take resources out of your account. In that case you can select "Pension total dist-taxable" from the 1099R list of categories for assignment to this field.

When you complete the Investment Account Type and Description window, Quicken returns you to the Select Account to Use window. Your first account should conform to the Investments account shown at the bottom of the screen in Figure 9-3.

13. Establish the five remaining accounts as shown in Figure 9-3. Be sure to enter the correct account type, **1**, **4**, or **5**, and balance. Use 8/1/94 as the date when entering your beginning balance for each account. When you set up the bank accounts, confirm that your Source Starting Balance is the Bank Statement when completing the Source of Starting Balance window. Also, when you establish your own bank accounts, you might want to press F8 (Additional Account Information). This Quicken window lets you enter additional information such as account numbers,

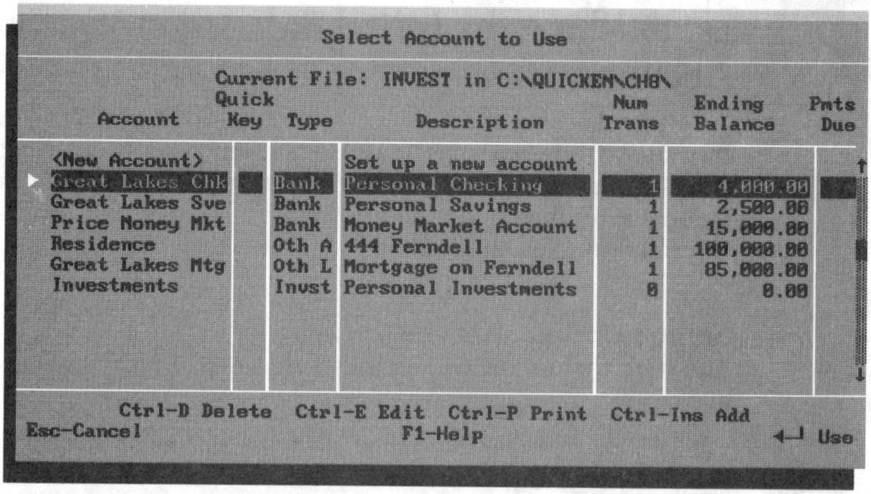

Select Account to Use

Current File: INVEST in C:\QUICKEN\CH8\

Account	Quick Key	Type	Description	Num Trans	Ending Balance	Pmts Due
<New Account>			Set up a new account			
Great Lakes Chk		Bank	Personal Checking	1	4,000.00	
Great Lakes Svg		Bank	Personal Savings	1	2,500.00	
Price Money Mkt		Bank	Money Market Account	1	15,000.00	
Residence		Oth A	444 Ferndell	1	100,000.00	
Great Lakes Mtg		Oth L	Mortgage on Ferndell	1	85,000.00	
Investments		Invst	Personal Investments	0	0.00	

Ctrl-D Delete Ctrl-E Edit Ctrl-P Print Ctrl-Ins Add
Esc-Cancel F1-Help ←┘ Use

Select Account to Use window for the INVEST file
Figure 9-3.

your contact person at the bank, and the bank's phone number. You can also enter brief comments relating to recent discussions with the bank and due dates of CDs or loans.

The new accounts you established in this chapter are used to separately maintain records for different assets and liabilities. A little background on when to use each account type will be helpful in making selections when you start recording your own information. The three new account types and some suggested uses for each follow.

- *Investment accounts* are tailored to investments with fluctuating prices, such as stocks, mutual funds, bonds, 401K plans or Individual Retirement Accounts (IRAs). You can establish an Investment account for each of your investment holdings or establish one account to parallel your transactions with a brokerage firm. In addition to special fields such as shares and investment accounts, these accounts can track a cash balance in an account.
- *Other Asset accounts* are appropriate for investments with a stable price, such as a CD or Treasury bill. They are also the most appropriate selection when there is no share price—for example, a real estate holding.
- *Other Liability accounts* are used to record your debts. A mortgage on a property and a car loan are examples of obligations that decrease your net worth and should be recorded in an Other Liability account.

Establishing the Initial Balance in Your Investments Account

Investment accounts are always established with an initial balance of 0. To transfer existing holdings to an Investment account, you will want to transfer the shares in at cost. You can establish a complete list of securities before beginning or add the information for each security as you enter the information to establish its cost.

Setting Up Your First Security

The steps that follow will establish your first security in your investment account:

1. Press Esc to return to the Main Menu, choose Select **A**ccount, and press Enter.
2. Select Investments and press Enter.

   Quicken displays a first-time setup message telling you to use ShrsIn to establish the cost basis for each security.
3. Press Enter to proceed to the Portfolio Details for Investments window, shown in Figure 9-4.

   As you proceed through these steps, Quicken's pop-up diamond field setting will prompt you with selections for some fields (if you have not changed the default setting).

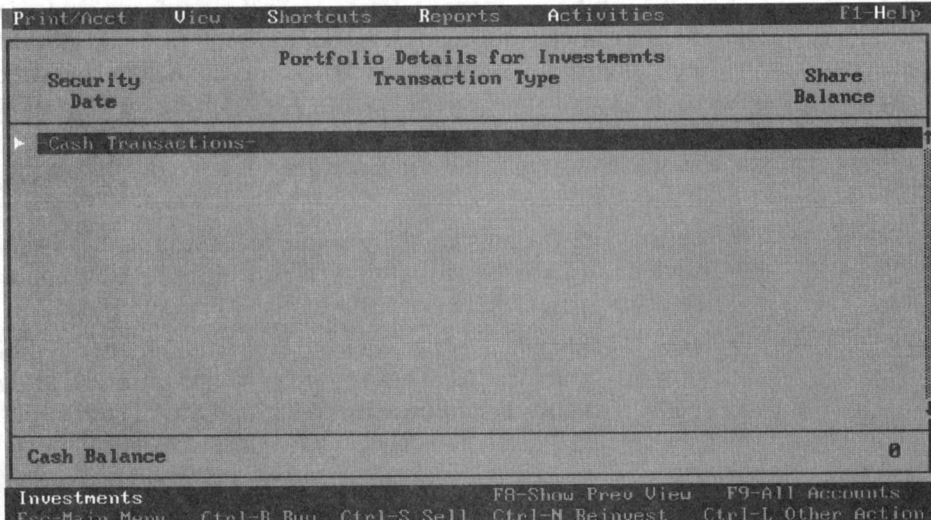

Portfolio Details for Investments window
Figure 9-4.

NOTE: When you follow these steps, if instructed to type an entry in a given field and the pop-up menu has listed the entry as one of your selections, just make the selection from the pop-up window.

4. Press Ctrl-L.

   The arrow cursor is on Add New Security. You must make an investment action selection for each transaction you record in your investment account. Table 9-1 lists all the action options you can encounter during a Quicken session. We will tell you which actions to select here. Later, when you view your Account Register and the Portfolio Details for Investments window, you will see how Quicken attaches the action abbreviations to your transactions.
5. Select ShrsIn and press Enter.

Quicken presents a Set Up Security window.

6. Type **Haven Publishing** and press Enter.
7. Type **HPB** for the symbol and press Enter.
8. Press Ctrl-L to see a list of security types, select Stock, and press Enter.

   The diamond next to this field indicates that this is one of Quicken's automatic pop-up diamond fields. In this case you could select Stock from the pop-up menu Quicken provides. Notice that you could also establish a new Type by selecting <Set Up New Type>. Some suggestions might be international, NYSE or ASE.
9. Press Ctrl-L to see a list of optional investment goals, select Growth, and press Enter.

Once again, this is a diamond field that can utilize the automatic pop-up menu.

10. Press Enter to accept 0.00 in the Estimated annual income field.

    If your security is currently paying dividends, you would enter the dividend per share amount here.

Your screen now looks like the following:

```
                         Set Up Security
  Name: Haven Publishing
  Symbol (optional): HPB

  ♦Type: Stock              ♦Goal (optional): Growth

  Estimated annual income ($ per share): 0.00

  ♦Display Mode: Always

              Ctrl L-List Types, Investment Goals
Esc-Cancel                     F1-Help                    ↵ Continue
```

Alternatively, you can use Ctrl-Y to update the entire security list at once.

11. Press Enter to have Quicken always display this security.
12. Type **10/10/88** in the date field of the Move Shares In window and press Enter.
13. Type **500** for the number of shares and press Enter twice.
14. Type **20** for the per share cost and press Enter.

    You can leave this field blank and enter the total cost in the Total Cost Basis field in the next step. Quicken will compute the cost per share for you and enter it in this field.
15. Press Enter to accept the price computation and move to the Memo field.
16. Type **Initial Cost** in the Memo field; your window now looks like Figure 9-5.
17. Press F10 and then Enter to accept Quicken's prompt requesting that you confirm the transaction and record it.

These steps are only followed for the first security you move into your first Quicken Investment account. For all future selections of the Shares In menu

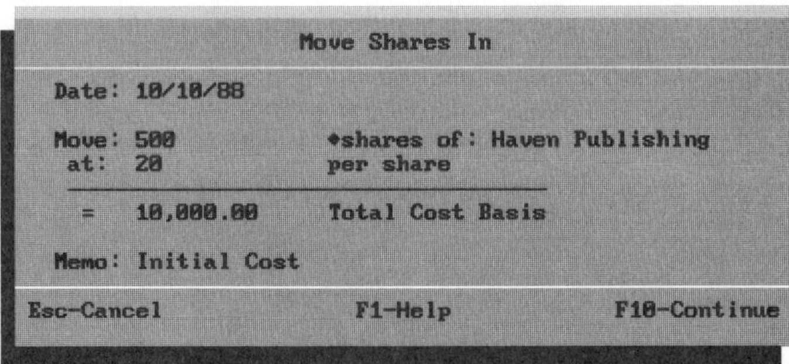

```
                        Move Shares In
  Date: 10/10/88

  Move: 500              ♦shares of: Haven Publishing
   at:  20               per share

    =   10,000.00        Total Cost Basis

  Memo: Initial Cost

Esc-Cancel               F1-Help                 F10-Continue
```

Figure 9-5. Move Shares In window

Action Group	Action	Description
Add/Remove shares	ShrsIn	Used to transfer shares into an investment account
	ShrsOut	Used to transfer shares out of an account
Buy shares	Buy	Used to buy a security with cash in the Investment account
	BuyX	Used to buy a security with cash from another account
Capital gains distr	CGLong	Used to record cash received from long-term capital gains distribution
	CGLongX	Used to transfer cash received from long-term capital gains distribution to another account
	CGShort	Used to record cash received from short-term capital gains distribution
	CGShortX	Used to transfer cash received from short-term capital gains distribution to another account
Dividend	Div	Used to record cash dividends in the Investment account
	DivX	Used to transfer cash dividends to another account
Interest	IntInc	Used to record interest income in the investment account
	MargInt	Used to pay margin loan from cash account
Other transactions	MiscExp	Used to pay miscellaneous expense from cash
	MiscInc	Used to record cash received from miscellaneous income sources
	Reminder	Used with BillMinder feature to notify of pending event
	RtrnCap	Used to recognize cash from return of capital
	StkSplit	Used to change number of shares from a stock split
Reinvest	ReinvDiv	Used to reinvest dividends in additional shares
	ReinvInt	Used to reinvest interest in additional shares

Investment Actions
Table 9-1.

Action Group	Action	Description
	ReinvLg	Used to reinvest long-term capital gains distribution
	ReinvSh	Used to reinvest short-term capital gains distribution
Sell shares	Sell	Used when you sell a security and leave the proceeds in the Investment account
	SellX	Used to transfer the proceeds of a sale to another account
Transfer cash	XIn	Used to transfer cash into the Investment account
	XOut	Used to transfer cash out of the Investment account

Investment Actions *(continued)*
Table 9-1.

item in this and all future investment accounts, you will follow the steps in the next section of the chapter.

Setting Up Additional Securities

Enter the initial cost for the shares of Ganges Mutual Fund and Glenn Packing, using the entries shown in Figure 9-6 and Figure 9-7. Both of these figures show you two views of the same investment transactions. Figure 9-6 shows how your first three transactions will appear in the Portfolio Details for Investments window (detail window), and Figure 9-7 shows the same transactions as they appear in the Investments Account Register (register). Notice how the investment action (Shares In) for Haven Publishing is shown in the Action column of the register as ShrsIn. You can use either the register or the detail window to enter investment transactions. You can move between the register and the detail window view by pressing Ctrl-R. When setting up the new securities use the following information:

	Ganges Mutual Fund	Glenn Packing
Symbol	GMF	GPK
Type	Mutual fund	Stock
Goal	Growth	Income
Est. Inc.	0.00	0.00
Display Mod	Always	Always

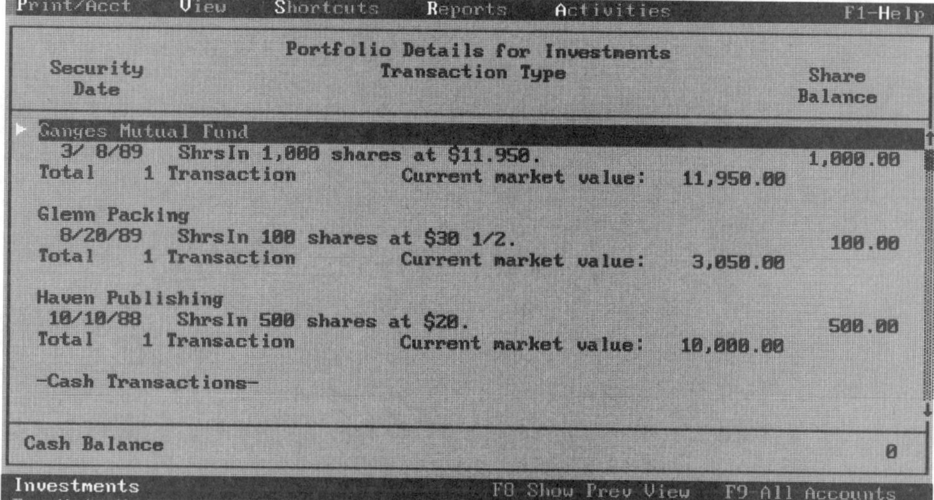

Initial investment transactions in the Portfolio Details for Investments window
Figure 9-6.

Use the following steps to enter the Ganges Mutual Fund initial cost from the detail window:

1. Press Ctrl-L.
2. Select Shares In and press Enter.

Print/Acct Edit Shortcuts Reports Activities F1-Help

Date	Action	Security	Price	Shares	$ Amount	C	Cash Bal
		BEGINNING					
10/10 1988	ShrsIn	Haven Publishing Initial Cost	20	500	10,000 00		0 00
3/08 1989	ShrsIn	Ganges Mutual Fund Initial Cost	11.950	1,000	11,950 00		0 00
8/20 1989	ShrsIn	Glenn Packing Initial Cost	30 1/2	100	3,050 00		0 00
7/23 1994							
		END					

Investments (Alt+letter accesses menu) Ending Cash Bal: $ 0.00
Esc-Main Menu Ctrl↵ Record Market Value: $25,000.00

Initial investment transactions in the Investments Account Register
Figure 9-7.

Quicken presents the Move Shares In window to you.

3. Type **3/8/89** and press Enter.
4. Type **1000** and press Enter.

   If the diamond fields are activated, a list will automatically pop up; if not, press Ctrl-L.
5. Select <New Security> and press Enter.
6. Type **Ganges Mutual Fund** and press Enter.
7. Type **GMF** and press Enter.
8. Press Ctrl-L, select Mutual Fund, and press Enter
9. Press Ctrl-L, select Growth, and press Enter.
10. Press Enter twice to accept Quicken's prompt for Estimated annual income and Display mode fields.

You are returned to the Move Shares In window.

11. Type **11.95** and press Enter.
12. Press Enter to accept the Total Cost Basis computation.
13. Type **Initial Cost**, press F10 and then Enter to complete the transaction.

Follow the same steps to enter the Glenn Packing initial entry.

NOTE: For all new securities added through the Shares In menu selection in any investment account, you will start at the Move In Shares window and complete steps 1–12.

Although you now have your stock holdings entered at cost, you still have an additional step because you want to establish a current market value for your holdings.

Revaluing Your Assets to Market Value

An important point to note when using Quicken is that in order to determine your net worth, you must assign values to your investments, liabilities, and other assets. This means that you need to exercise some judgment in evaluating asset worth. Don't be intimidated; it's not as complex as it might seem. The easiest assets to evaluate are your checking, savings, and money market accounts. In these cases, you know what your cash balance is in each of the accounts, so you can easily determine the value at a specific time. After you complete your monthly reconciliation, you have the current value of your accounts at a given time. If you own stocks and bonds, you can generally determine the valuation at a given time by looking in the financial section of your local newspaper. If you own stock in a closely held corporation, you will have to use other sources for valuation—for example, recent sales of similar companies in your industry or area. In the case of land, you might ask a realtor familiar with the local area the approximate value of your lot or other property holdings, or once again you might be able to use recent sale prices of similar properties in your area.

Your residence presents similar problems. You know what you paid for the property, and with Quicken you can accumulate the additional cost incurred in improving it. The question is what value to place on the property when you prepare your Net Worth report. Once again, watch what properties in your area are selling for, and consider how your house compared in price with neighboring properties when you bought it. This will provide a basis for comparison in the future. However, remember that improvements you made to your house may increase the value of your home relative to others in the area. For example, adding a new bath and renovating the kitchen might significantly enhance the value of your home over time, but adding a swimming pool in a cold climate might not help the value at all.

The amount you owe or the associated liability on your home should be easy to track. You receive annual statements from the financial institutions you have borrowed money from for your residence and any home improvements. These statements indicate the remaining financial obligation you have on the house and should be used for net worth valuation purposes.

Remember to use prudent judgment in determining values for some of your assets when preparing your Net Worth report. A conservative, but not very useful, approach would be to say that any values you cannot determine from external sources should be valued at what you paid for the asset. Accountants call this *historical cost.* For your own planning and monitoring, this is not a realistic approach to determining your net worth. Attempt to determine fair value, or what you think your home could be sold for today, by taking into consideration current national and local economic conditions, and use reasonable values. Those familiar with the local market will certainly have some knowledge of the value of homes in your area. Remember that overinflating the value of your properties does not help in accurately assessing your net worth.

The following steps allow you to enter the current value of your stocks:

1. From the Portfolio Details for Investments window, press Ctrl-U to activate the Portfolio Update Prices for Investments window.

Your next step is to establish 7/31/94 as the date for which you want to make the estimated market values in this example. Normally you will be entering the current market value data on the day for which your machine is currently active. However, if you want to check the market value window for a previous date, you can access that information by activating the Go to Date window.

2. Press Ctrl-G to activate the Go to Date window, type **7/31/94** and press Enter.

You can change the date displayed to the next day with the Ctrl-→, to the previous day with Ctrl-←, to the previous month with Ctrl-Pg Up,and to the next month with Ctrl-Pg Dn. You can also enter new market prices for any security or use the + and - keys to change them by 1/8 in either direction.

3. With the arrow cursor on Ganges Mutual Fund, type **13.210** and press Enter.
4. With the arrow cursor on Glenn Packing, press Ctrl-Backspace, type **30**, and press Enter.
5. With the arrow cursor on Haven Publishing, type **22** and press Ctrl-Enter.

The screen in Figure 9-8 shows the updated prices. Notice that Quicken computes a new market value and shows the last price for each security before this update. Also notice the Cash line that is included in the figure. This line will show the accumulated cash that you may have in your account

```
Print/Acct   View   Shortcuts   Reports   Activities                F1-Help

             Portfolio Update for Investments as of 7/31/94
     Security       Type   Market       Shares      Market      Last       Chg
       Name                 Price                   Value       Price    Mkt Val

 Ganges Mutual Fund Mut  13.210    ↑ 1,000.00   13,210.00  11.950    1,260.00
 Glenn Packing      Sto  30        ↓   100.00    3,000.00  30 1/2      -50.00
 Haven Publishing   Sto  22        ↑   500.00   11,000.00  20        1,000.00
▸ -Cash-

 Total Market Value                              27,210

Investments                                F8-Show Detail     F9-All Accounts
Esc-Main Menu  Ctrl-B Buy  Ctrl-S Sell  Ctrl-N Reinvest  Ctrl-L Other Action
```

Updated prices in the Portfolio Update window
Figure 9-8.

with your broker from transfers from other accounts or sales of stock in this account. If you have a money market account for holding this cash, you probably will want to add the money market account to your list of securities held in this account and accumulate your cash reserves there. In this situation your cash line will not have a balance accumulating. In this example you have not transferred cash into this account. You will see how to handle purchases with cash from other accounts and how to transfer the proceeds of stock sales to other bank accounts.

Viewing Portfolio Information at a Glance

Later you will see how to use Quicken to prepare reports from the Investment Report menu. However, if you are like most investors, you will want to take a quick look at your investments without needing to prepare the formal reports. You can get a quick glance at your investment account from the Portfolio Update window by pressing Alt-V. This pop-up window gives you several opportunities for viewing your investment account data: **H**oldings, **P**erformance, **V**aluation, **S**ummary, and **G**ains.

To access the Portfolio **H**oldings window, you press **H** from the **V**iew pop-up window. This view shows the percentage that each holding in your account represents to your total account balance. You also see the estimated income expected for each security based upon past payouts.

To access the Portfolio **P**erformance window, you press **P** from the **V**iew pop-up window. You will see the return on investment for each of your account holdings with this window.

To access the Portfolio **V**aluation window, you press **V** from the **V**iew pop-up window. This window shows you a comparison of the current market value of each of your holdings with the amount you have invested in each security. The total shows the market value of your holdings at the last date at which you updated your valuations.

To access Portfolio **G**ains window, you press **G** from the **V**iew pop-up window. This window shows the dollar and percentage gains or losses on each security in the account's portfolio.

To access the Portfolio **S**ummary window, shown in Figure 9-9, press **S**ummary from the **V**iew pop-up menu. This window shows the percentage gain or loss you have on each security in your portfolio, as well as your average cost, the number of shares held and the latest market price entered for each security.

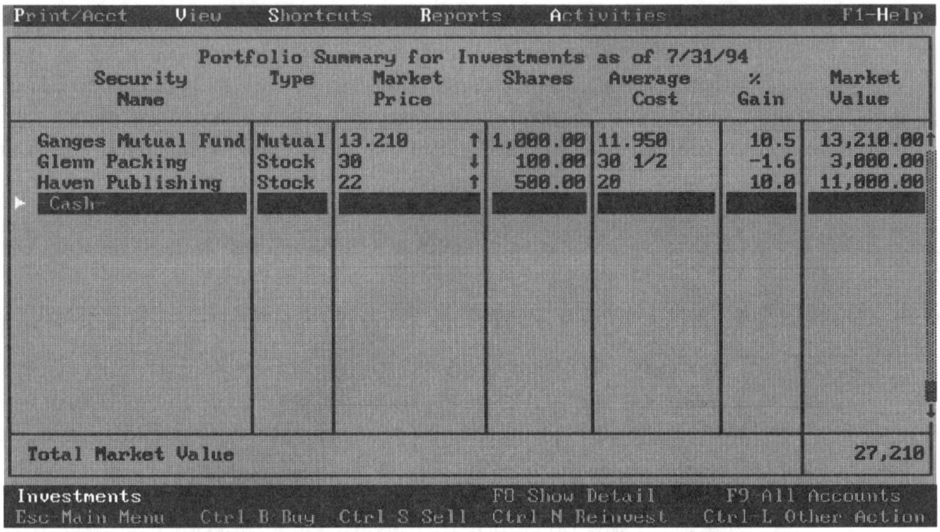

Security Name	Type	Market Price		Shares	Average Cost	% Gain	Market Value
Ganges Mutual Fund	Mutual	13.210	↑	1,000.00	11.950	10.5	13,210.00
Glenn Packing	Stock	30	↓	100.00	30 1/2	-1.6	3,000.00
Haven Publishing	Stock	22	↑	500.00	20	10.0	11,000.00
Cash							
Total Market Value							27,210

Print/Acct View Shortcuts Reports Activities F1-Help

Portfolio Summary for Investments as of 7/31/94

Investments F8 Show Detail F9 All Accounts
Esc Main Menu Ctrl B Buy Ctrl S Sell Ctrl N Reinvest Ctrl-L Other Action

Portfolio Summary view
Figure 9-9.

Using Prodigy Quote Track to Update Security Prices

The manual method of updating security prices works fine when you have only a few stocks. If your portfolio is large, it can take quite a commitment to keep your stock values up to date. Since Quicken will accept stock prices for securities with standard symbols, you might want to download prices from a service such as Prodigy.

If you are a Prodigy member, you might want to download prices for your stocks from the Prodigy system into an ASCII file. There are a few tasks that you need to perform within both Quicken and Prodigy to import this data, but the time savings over manual updates is worth it if you have a number of stocks to track. These are the basic tasks you need to perform.

1. Check your Quicken investment file to ensure that all of your securities you want to import data for have symbols assigned.

   Quicken matches data by symbol.
2. Create a Quote Track list for the securities you want to monitor.
3. Within Prodigy you need to set up a report using a comma-delimited format. You will want to specify closing prices and a comma-delimited file format.
4. Print the results to your file.

5. From the Quicken Portfolio window select **P**rint/Acct, and then select **I**mport Prices.
6. Supply the name of the file you created from within Prodigy and press Enter.
7. Press Enter twice to skip the date entry, and Quicken will import the data for you.

Your First Net Worth Report

In completing the steps in the previous sections, you recorded balances in all the accounts in your INVESTMENTS file and looked at some options for taking a quick view at your portfolio. At this point, you can determine your net worth. Remember, your net worth is determined by this formula:

Financial Resources – Financial Obligations = Net Worth

The following procedure prints your first net worth statement:

1. Press Esc to return to the Main Menu, select **C**reate Reports, and select **H**ome Reports, followed by **N**et Worth.

   The Net Worth Report window appears.
2. Press Enter.
3. Type **8/1/94** and press Enter.

   The Net Worth Report appears on your screen.
4. Press Ctrl-P and the Print Report window appears.
5. Complete the window prompts. When you press Enter to leave the window, your printer prints the report shown in Figure 9-10. (Again, spacing may differ because of adjustments made to fit the material onto these pages.)

Notice that the Net Worth report is presented for a specific date, in this example 8/1/94. The report presents your assets and liabilities at this date and gives you a base point against which to make future comparisons. As you can see, your net worth at 8/1/94 is $63,710.00. At the end of this chapter, you prepare another Net Worth report and compare how your net worth has changed.

```
                         NET WORTH REPORT
                           As of 8/ 1/94
INVEST-All Accounts                                          Page 1
7/24/94
                                                8/ 1/94
                         Acct                   Balance
            -------------------------------- ------------
            ASSETS
              Cash and Bank Accounts
                Great Lakes Chk                   4,000.00
                Great Lakes Sve                   2,500.00
                Price Money Mkt                  15,000.00
                                              ------------
              Total Cash and Bank Accounts       21,500.00

              Other Assets
                Residence                       100,000.00
                                              ------------
              Total Other Assets                100,000.00

              Investments
                Investments                      27,210.00
                                              ------------
              Total Investments                  27,210.00

                                              ------------
            TOTAL ASSETS                        148,710.00

            LIABILITIES
              Other Liabilities
                Great Lakes Mtg                  85,000.00
                                              ------------
              Total Other Liabilities            85,000.00

                                              ------------
            TOTAL LIABILITIES                    85,000.00

                                              ------------
            TOTAL NET WORTH                      63,710.00
                                              ============
```

Net Worth report for 8/1/94
Figure 9-10.

Impact of Investments and Mortgage Payments on Net Worth

In this section, you will record various transactions in the file to demonstrate the effect of certain types of transactions on your net worth. You will see how Quicken can monitor your mortgage balance as part of your monthly record keeping in your checking account. You will also see how you can record a transaction only once and trace the financial impact on both checking and investment account registers.

Additional Stock Transactions

When you printed your Net Worth report, you were in the Investments account. You will now record the acquisition of some additional stock, dividends, dividends reinvested, and the sale of stock. The following steps demonstrate the ease of recording the transaction with Quicken's Investment accounts.

1. You are currently in the Investments account. Press the Esc key until you are in Quicken's Main Menu.
2. Select Use **R**egister, and you are in the Portfolio Details for Investments window. If you are in the Account Register, press Ctrl-R to move to the Portfolio Details for Investments window. If you are returned to the Portfolio Update or Portfolio Summary window, press F8 to return to the Portfolio Details window.
3. Press Ctrl-L, select Buy, and press Enter.

   Quicken presents a Buy window.
4. Type **8/2/94** in the Date field and press Enter.
5. Type **100** and press Enter.
6. Select <New Security> and press Enter.
7. Type **Douglas Marine** and press Enter.
8. Type **DGM** and press Enter.
9. Press Ctrl-L, select Stock, and press Enter.
10. Press Ctrl-L, select Growth, and press Enter.
11. Press Enter twice to accept Quicken's prompt for Estimated annual income and Display mode fields.
12. Type **25** and press Enter.
13. Type **50** for the commission and press Enter.
14. Press Enter to accept the Total purchase price.
15. Type **Buy 100 Douglas Marine** and press Enter.
16. Press Ctrl-C, select Price Money Mkt, and press F10.
17. Press Ctrl-Enter to finalize the entry, then press Enter.

The next transactions record dividends and transfer them to another account or reinvest them in shares of the stock. Rather than transfering funds in and out for each transaction, you can choose to leave a cash balance in your brokerage account. Quicken allows you to mirror almost any investment situation. To record the dividend transaction, follow these steps:

1. Press Ctrl-L, select Record Income, and press Enter.

   Quicken presents a Record Income window.
2. Type **8/10/94** and press Enter.
3. Type **Haven Publishing** and press Enter.

   Remember, if the diamond pop-up setting is activated you need to just select Haven Publishing.
4. Type **200** in the Dividend Amount field and press Enter five times to move to the Category for Miscellaneous field.
5. Press Ctrl-C, select Div Income, and press Enter.
6. Press Ctrl-L, select Great Lakes Sve, and press Enter.
7. Type **Div @ .40 per share** and press F10.
8. Press Ctrl-Enter to finalize the transaction.

   You are returned to the Portfolio Details window.

If you press Ctrl-R, you can see how the dividend income is shown in the account register. Notice that the action column shows DivX, which shows that the dividend check was deposited into your savings account. If you did not designate a transfer account in the Record Income window the amount of the dividend would be shown in the Cash Bal column of the Account Register. Press Ctrl-R to return to the Portfolio Details window.

The next transaction also recognizes a dividend distribution. These dividends are reinvested in shares purchased at the current market price. Follow these steps to record the transaction:

1. Press Ctrl-L, select Reinvest Shares, and press Enter.

   The Reinvest Income window appears.
2. Type **8/15/94** and press Enter.
3. Type **Ganges Mutual Fund** and press Enter.

   If you had typed **G**, Quicken would have completed the name for you using the new QuickFill feature. You have seen QuickFill at work from other entries you made in earlier chapters. Quicken tries to match the characters that you type for the payee, category, security, and action fields to entries in existing lists. If you wanted to use the Glenn Packing security, you would have pressed Ctrl-+ when Ganges Mutual Fund appeared, and Quicken would have displayed that security in the field.
4. Type **100** and press Enter four times.
5. Type **7.531** and press Enter.
6. Press Enter, and Quicken supplies the per share price of 13.2785.

Quicken supplies the number of shares if you enter the price and the amount of the dividend that you are reinvesting.

7. Type **Dividend Reinvestment** and press F10.
8. Press Enter to record the transaction.

To record the sale of stock with the transfer of proceeds to another account, follow these steps:

1. Press Ctrl-L, select Sell, and press Enter.

   Quicken presents a Sell window.
2. Type **8/25/94** and press Enter.
3. Type **100** and press Enter.
4. Type **H** and press Enter.

   Notice that Quicken completes the rest of the typing for you. If you have several securities with names that start with H, you can use the Ctrl-+ or Ctrl-- keypress combinations to select the security you desire in response to Quicken's QuickFill selection. Once again, if your diamond field pop-up window is activated, just select Haven Publishing.
5. Type **23 1/4** and press Enter.
6. Type **25** for the commission and press Enter twice.
7. Type **Sell 100 Haven Publishing** and press Enter.
8. Press Ctrl-C, select Price Money Mkt, and press Enter.

If you had selected the Investments account as the destination of the funds, Quicken would have placed the proceeds in the Cash Bal column of the Account Register.

9. Press F10.
10. Press Enter to record the transaction.
11. Press Ctrl-R to view the Account Register.

Your register entries will look like the ones in Figure 9-11.

Mortgage Payment Transaction

You recorded mortgage payments in earlier chapters, but here you will see how you can monitor your principal balance when you make your payment. In this example, you make your monthly payment from your checking account and monitor the impact of the payment on your principal balance

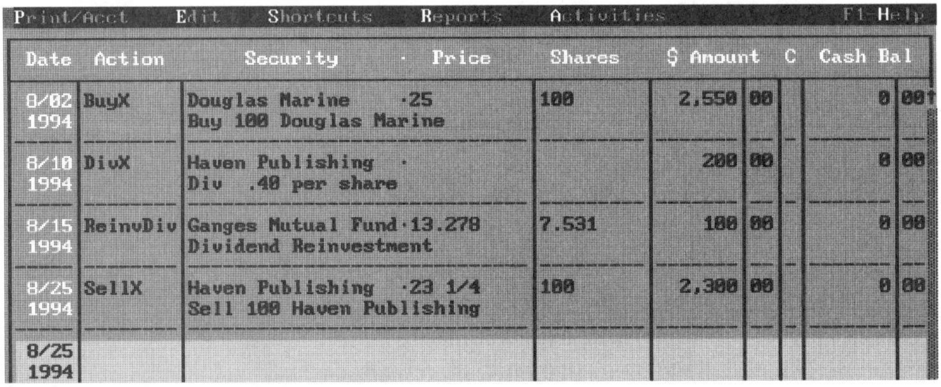

Print/Acct Edit Shortcuts Reports Activities F1-Help

Date	Action	Security	Price	Shares	$ Amount	C	Cash Bal
8/02 1994	BuyX	Douglas Marine Buy 100 Douglas Marine	25	100	2,550 00		0 00
8/10 1994	DivX	Haven Publishing Div .40 per share			200 00		0 00
8/15 1994	ReinvDiv	Ganges Mutual Fund Dividend Reinvestment	13.278	7.531	100 00		0 00
8/25 1994	SellX	Haven Publishing Sell 100 Haven Publishing	23 1/4	100	2,300 00		0 00
8/25 1994							

Investment account register after August transactions
Figure 9-11.

in the Great Lakes Mtg liability account. The following steps record this transaction from the Main Menu:

1. Enter the Great Lakes Chk register and move the cursor to the Date field in the highlighted new transaction form. Type **8/5/94** and press Enter.
2. Type **100** in the Num field and press Enter.
3. Type **Great Lakes Bank** in the Payee field and press Enter.
4. Type **875.00** in the Payment field.
5. Press Enter twice to place your cursor in the Category field.
6. Press Ctrl-S, and the Split Transaction window appears on the screen. When you finish completing this window, your screen will look like the one in Figure 9-12.
7. Press Ctrl-C, and the Category and Transfer List window appears. Select the Great Lakes Mtg account and press Enter.
8. Press Enter, type **Principal Payment**, press Enter, type **25.00** in the Amount field, and press Enter again.

You have recorded the first part of the transaction shown in Figure 9-12.

9. Type **Mort Int** and press Enter. Type **Interest Portion of Payment** and press Enter. Press Ctrl-Enter.

   This step returns you to the account register.
10. Press Ctrl-Enter again and the transaction is recorded in the register.

As you can see, the balance in the account has been reduced by the amount of the payment. At the same time, Quicken has recorded the transaction in

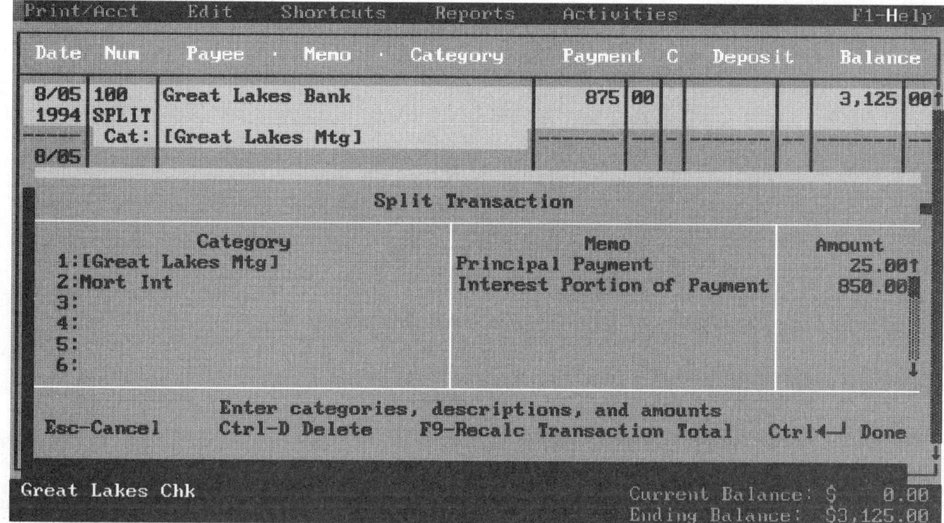

Split Transaction window in checking account
Figure 9-12.

your Great Lakes Mtg account and reduced the obligation by the $25.00 principal portion of the payment.

How Transactions Affect Your Net Worth

Let's take a look at the effect of the previous transactions on net worth. If you compare the report in Figure 9-13 to the previous Net Worth report, you'll see that your net worth has increased by $68, compared to the initial net worth shown in Figure 9-10. This difference is the net effect of the transactions you recorded during the month of August in your investment, cash, and bank accounts.

You can see from this that your net worth can grow if you either increase the value of your financial resources or decrease the amount of your obligations. In the following section, you will see how increases in the value of your investments are recorded and the effect they have on your net worth.

Recording Appreciation in Your Investment Holdings

In this section, you record the increased appreciation in your investments and residence occurring since the Net Worth report prepared on 8/1/94. Although the amounts might seem high, remember that this is an example. Also, remember that what you make in the stock market and housing market this year could be lost next year.

```
                         NET WORTH REPORT
                           As of 8/31/94
INVEST-All Accounts                                              Page 1
7/24/94
                                                        8/31/94
                           Acct                         Balance
             -------------------------------------  ------------
             ASSETS
               Cash and Bank Accounts
                 Great Lakes Chk                        3,125.00
                 Great Lakes Sve                        2,700.00
                 Price Money Mkt                       14,750.00
                                                    ------------
               Total Cash and Bank Accounts            20,575.00

               Other Assets
                 Residence                            100,000.00
                                                    ------------
               Total Other Assets                     100,000.00

               Investments
                 Investments                           28,178.00
                                                    ------------
               Total Investments                       28,178.00

                                                    ------------
             TOTAL ASSETS                             148,753.00

             LIABILITIES
               Other Liabilities
                 Great Lakes Mtg                       84,975.00
                                                    ------------
               Total Other Liabilities                 84,975.00

                                                    ------------
             TOTAL LIABILITIES                         84,975.00

                                                    ------------
             TOTAL NET WORTH                           63,778.00
                                                    ============
```

Net Worth report after stock is acquired and mortgage payment is made
Figure 9-13.

Appreciated Investments

Quicken permits you to record increases and decreases in the value of your holdings. As noted in the net worth formula, changes in the value of your holdings have the potential to significantly affect your net worth over a period of years. Remember the effect of compounding on your investments. The following steps illustrate the changes of your investments for the month of August:

1. Choose Select **A**ccount from the Main Menu to open the Investments account from your INVEST file.
2. From the Portfolio Details for Investments window, press Ctrl-U to access the Portfolio Update window.

Notice that the market value for Ganges Mutual Fund is marked with an asterisk and has been updated since your initial adjustments on July 31, 1994. The asterisk indicates that Quicken has estimated the market value. This estimate is based on the value you entered for the dividend reinvestment transaction on 8/15.

3. Press Ctrl-G, type **8/25/94** and press Enter.

   Notice the asterisks next to the prices. An asterisk tells you that Quicken is using an estimated value for the investment. For example, Quicken valued the Glenn Packing shares at $30 per share. Since there were no shares of this stock bought or sold during August, Quicken will use the 7/31/94 price shown in Figure 9-8 until you revalue the stock. Notice that the Ganges Mutual Fund is shown at its actual value on 8/15/94, since you recorded the dividend reinvestment transaction in your account on that date. The point to note is that Quicken automatically updates your market valuation each time you provide new price information when preparing account transactions throughout the year.
4. Press Ctrl-→ until the date at the top reads 8/31/94.
5. Enter the new market prices for the stocks, as shown in Figure 9-14. Press Enter after recording each new price.
6. Press Ctrl-Enter to record the changes and press Esc to return to the Main Menu.

Print/Acct View Shortcuts Reports Activities F1-Help

Portfolio Update for Investments as of 8/31/94

Security Name	Type	Market Price		Shares	Market Value	Last Price	Chg Mkt Val
Ganges Mutual Fund	Mut	13.400	↑	1,007.53	13,500.92	13.278	122.92
Douglas Marine	Sto	25 1/8	↑	100.00	2,512.50	25	12.50
Glenn Packing	Sto	31	↑	100.00	3,100.00	30	100.00
Haven Publishing	Sto	23 1/2	↑	400.00	9,400.00	23 1/4	100.00
-Cash-							

Total Market Value 28,513

Investments F8-Show Detail F9-All Accounts
Esc-Main Menu Ctrl-B Buy Ctrl-S Sell Ctrl-N Reinvest Ctrl-L Other Action

Portfolio Updated window after recording revaluation
Figure 9-14.

Appreciated Residence

As your home increases in value, you will want to record this change in Quicken, since it will affect your net worth. In this example, as a result of recent sales in your neighborhood, you feel $105,000 would be a conservative estimate of the market value of your home. The following steps illustrate the procedure for valuing your home at $105,000:

1. From the Select Account to Use window select the Residence account and press ENTER.

   Quicken opens the Register window for this account and places the highlighting in the next blank transaction.
2. Select the **A**ctivities (ALT-A) pull-down menu.
3. Select **U**pdate Account Balance.
4. Type **105000** and press ENTER.
5. Press ENTER to move to the Date field in the Update Account Balance window.
6. Type **8/31/94** and press CTRL-ENTER.

Your screen should look like the one in Figure 9-15.

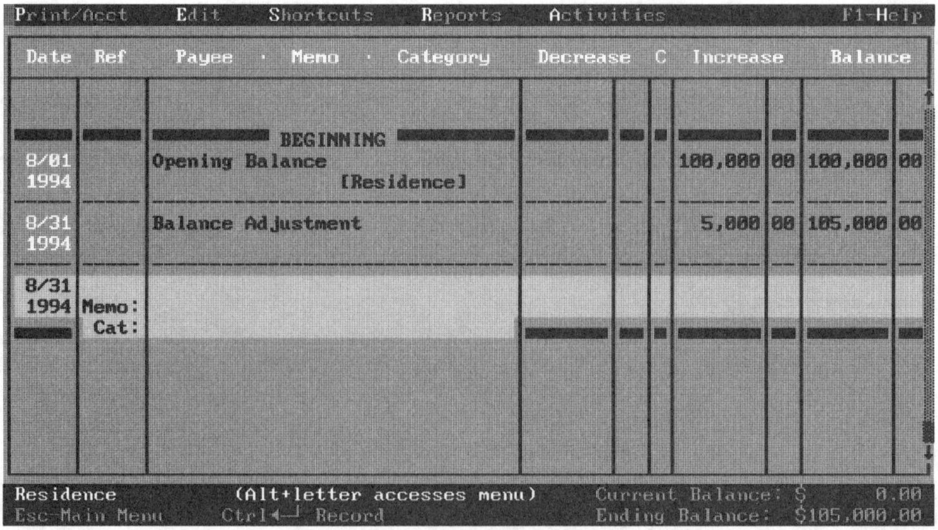

Residence register after adjustment is revalued
Figure 9-15.

Ending Net Worth Determination

Having prepared the adjustments to the various accounts in the INVEST file, you are now prepared to print your Net Worth report for the end of the period.

1. From the Main Menu, select **C**reate Reports, **H**ome Reports, and **N**et Worth. The Net Worth Report window appears.
2. Press Enter, type **8/31/94**, and press Enter.

   The Net Worth report appears on your screen.
3. Press Ctrl-P, and the Print Report window appears.
4. Complete the appropriate selections in the window. When you press Ctrl-Enter to leave the window, your printer prints the report, as shown in Figure 9-16.

An examination of Figures 9-10 and 9-16 reveals that your net worth increased by almost $6000 during the time period. What were the reasons for these changes? For the most part, the increased values of your investments and residence explain the greater net worth.

The importance of monitoring your net worth has been stressed throughout this chapter. The focus of this book is the use of Quicken to assist in your financial planning and monitoring activities. Once you have a good picture of your net worth from the Quicken reports, you can focus on additional planning. You might want to set your net worth goal for a future point or make plans to protect your existing holdings. If you have not taken any actions regarding estate planning, this is another area that must be addressed. Making a will is a most important part of this process and should not be delayed. Although the complexities of planning for the transfer of your estate are significant, the special "The Need for a Will" section near the end of this chapter highlights some problems that can be encountered when estate planning is not combined with financial planning activities. You might also be surprised to learn that a lawyer's fee for a simple will is relatively inexpensive. Another option is writing a will with one of the new software packages specifically designed for that purpose.

Quicken's Investment Reports

Quicken provides five investment reports that provide information on your investments from different perspectives. You can look at detailed investment transactions with these reports or assess your gain or loss in investment value over a period of time. The many options available provide different variations on each of the basic reports.

```
                    NET WORTH REPORT
                     As of 8/31/94
INVEST-All Accounts                                              Page 1
7/24/94
                                                   8/31/94
                          Acct                     Balance
            ---------------------------------- ------------
            ASSETS
              Cash and Bank Accounts
                Great Lakes Chk                    3,125.00
                Great Lakes Sve                    2,700.00
                Price Money Mkt                   14,750.00
                                               ------------
              Total Cash and Bank Accounts        20,575.00

              Other Assets
                Residence                        105,000.00
                                               ------------
              Total Other Assets                 105,000.00

              Investments
                Investments                       28,513.42
                                               ------------
              Total Investments                   28,513.42

                                               ------------
            TOTAL ASSETS                         154,088.42

            LIABILITIES
              Other Liabilities
                Great Lakes Mtg                   84,975.00
                                               ------------
              Total Other Liabilities             84,975.00

                                               ------------
            TOTAL LIABILITIES                     84,975.00

                                               ------------
            TOTAL NET WORTH                       69,113.42
                                               ============
```

Figure 9-16. Net Worth report for 8/31/94 after all transactions affecting the INVEST files are recorded

Portfolio Value Report

A Portfolio Value report values all the investments in your portfolio at a given date based on price information stored in the system. The Portfolio Value report displays the number of shares, the current price, the cost basis of the shares, the gain or loss, and the current value of the shares. Follow these steps to create the report from the Investments account:

1. From the Main Menu select **C**reate Reports.
2. Select **I**nvestment Reports.
3. Choose Portfolio **V**alue.
4. Press Enter to accept the default report title.
5. Type **8/31/94** for the report date and press Enter.

6. Press F8 (Options), type **N**, and press Enter.
7. Press Enter twice to accept the default entries of Don't Subtotal and Current.

The report displays on your screen (a printed copy of the report is shown in Figure 9-17).

Investment Performance Report

The Investment Performance report lets you look at the gain or loss between two points in time. The Investment Performance report indicates your return and projects an average annual return based on results of the period selected. Follow these steps to create such a report:

1. Press Esc until the Investment Reports menu displays, and then select Investment **P**erformance.
2. Press Enter to accept the default report title.
3. Type **Custom Date** and press Enter.
4. Type **8/1/94** and press Enter; then type **8/31/94** and press Enter.
5. Press Enter to accept the default of Don't Subtotal.
6. Type **Y** for Show cash flow detail.
7. Press F8 (Options), type **N**, and press Enter.
8. Press Ctrl-Enter to accept the Current account default calculation of the rate of return with IRR (Internal Rate of Return) and display the report on the screen.

A printed copy of the report showing an annualized return of 64.5% is shown in Figure 9-18. If you had selected R in the Calculate rate of return with IRR/ROI (I/R) field, your rate of return would be shown as 4.2%. This is

PORTFOLIO VALUE REPORT
As of 8/31/94

INVEST-Investments — Page 1
7/24/94

Security	Shares	Curr Price	Cost Basis	Gain/Loss	Balance
Douglas Marine	100.00	25 1/8	2,550	-38	2,513
Ganges Mutual Fund	1,007.53	13.400	12,050	1,451	13,501
Glenn Packing	100.00	31	3,050	50	3,100
Haven Publishing	400.00	23 1/2	7,700	1,700	9,400
Total Investments			25,350	3,163	28,513

Figure 9-17. Portfolio Value report

```
                      INVESTMENT PERFORMANCE REPORT
                         8/ 1/94 Through 8/31/94
INVEST-Investments                                                        Page 1
7/24/94
                                                                       Avg. Annual
 Date Action         Description              Investments   Returns   Tot. Return
----- ------ ---------------------------- ----------- ----------- -----------

       8/ 1/94 -  8/31/94
      -------------------

7/31         Beg Mkt Value                      27,210
8/02 BuyX    100 Douglas Marine                  2,550
8/10 DivX    Haven Publishing                                 200
8/25 SellX   100 Haven Publishing                           2,300
8/31         End Mkt Value                                 28,513
                                            ----------- ----------- -----------
     TOTAL   8/ 1/94 -  8/31/94                 29,760      31,013       64.5%
```

Investment Performance report
Figure 9-18.

the ROI (Rate of Return) for the period 8/1/94 to 8/31/94. As noted, the 64.5% IRR is based on the assumption that the period's ROI is sustainable for the entire year.

Capital Gains Report

The Capital Gains report is useful for tax purposes, since it shows the gain or loss on sales of investments. One example of a Capital Gains report that you can create allows you to look at the difference between short- and long-term capital gains. Follow these steps to create the report:

1. Press Esc until the Investment Reports menu displays.
2. Select **C**apital Gains.
3. Press Enter to accept the default.
4. Type **Custom Date** and press Enter.
5. Type **8/1/94** and press Enter.
6. Type **8/31/94** and press Enter.
7. Press F8 (Options), type **N**, and press Enter.
8. Press Ctrl-Enter to display the Capital Gains report.

Figure 9-19 shows a printout of this report.

Investment Income Report

The Investment Income report shows the total income or expense from your investments. Dividends and both realized and unrealized gains and losses can be shown on this report. Follow these steps to create the report:

Security	Shares	Bought	Sold	Sales Price	Cost Basis	Gain/Loss
	LONG TERM					
Haven Publish	100	10/10/88	8/25/94	2,300	2,000	300
	TOTAL LONG TERM			2,300	2,000	300

CAPITAL GAINS REPORT
8/ 1/94 Through 8/31/94
INVEST-Investments Page 1
7/24/94

Capital Gains report
Figure 9-19.

1. Press Esc until the Investment Reports menu displays.
2. Select Investment **I**ncome.
3. Press Enter to accept the default.
4. Type **Custom Date** and press Enter.
5. Type **8/1/94** and press Enter.
6. Type **8/31/94** and press Enter.
7. Press F8 (Options), press Enter three times, type **N**, and press Enter.
8. Press Ctrl-Enter to display the report on your screen.

Your report will match the printout shown in Figure 9-20.

Investment Transactions Report

The Investment Transactions report is the most detailed of the five, and reports on all investment transactions during the selected period. Use the following steps to create the report:

INVESTMENT INCOME REPORT
8/ 1/94 Through 8/31/94
INVEST-Investments Page 1
7/24/94

Category Description	8/ 1/94- 8/31/94
INCOME/EXPENSE	
INCOME	
Dividend	300
TOTAL INCOME	300
TOTAL INCOME/EXPENSE	300

Investment Income report
Figure 9-20.

1. Press [Esc] until the Investment Reports menu displays.
2. Select Investment **T**ransactions.
3. Press [Enter] to accept the default.
4. Type **Custom Date** and press [Enter].
5. Type **8/1/94** and press [Enter].
6. Type **8/31/94** and press [Enter].
7. Press [F8] (Options) to activate the report options.
8. Press [Enter] twice.
9. Type **Y** to include unrealized gains, and press [Enter].
10. Type **N** to display only whole dollars in the report and press [Enter].
11. Press [Ctrl]-[Enter] to display the report on your screen.

Your report will match the printout shown in Figure 9-21.

INVESTMENT TRANSACTIONS REPORT
8/ 1/94 Through 8/31/94

INVEST-Investments — Page 1
7/24/94

Date	Action	Secur	Categ	Price	Shares	Commssn	Cash	Invest. Value	Cash + Invest.
	BALANCE	7/31/94					0	27,210	27,210
8/02	UnrlzGn	Douglas Marin	Unrealized Gain/	25				-50	-50
8/02	BuyX	Douglas Marin		25	100	50	-2,550	2,550	
			[Price Money				2,550		2,550
8/10	UnrlzGn	Haven Publish	Unrealized G	11.950				-5,025	-5,025
8/10	DivX	Haven Publish	Dividend				200		200
			[Great Lakes				-200		-200
8/15	UnrlzGn	Ganges Mutual	Unrealized G	13.278				68	68
8/15	ReinvDi	Ganges Mutual		13.278	7.531		-100	100	
			Dividend				100		100
8/25	UnrlzGn	Haven Publish	Unrealized G	23 1/4				5,625	5,625
8/25	SellX	Haven Publish		23 1/4	100	25	2,300	-2,300	
			[Price Money				-2,300		-2,300
8/31	UnrlzGn	Haven Publish	Unrealized G	23 1/2				100	100
8/31	UnrlzGn	Ganges Mutual	Unrealized G	13.400				123	123
8/31	UnrlzGn	Glenn Packing	Unrealized Gain/	31				100	100
8/31	UnrlzGn	Douglas Marin	Unrealized G	25 1/8				13	13
	TOTAL	8/ 1/94 - 8/31/94					0	1,303	1,303
	BALANCE	8/31/94					0	28,513	28,513

Investment Transactions report, including unrealized gains/losses
Figure 9-21.

The Need for a Will

A will is important to ensure that your heirs benefit from the net worth that you have accumulated and to make sure your wishes control the distribution of your assets at your death. Without a will, the laws of your state and the rulings of a probate court will decide what happens to your assets and will award the custody of your minor children. The following can also occur

- ✦ A probate court may appoint an administrator for your estate.
- ✦ State laws might distribute your assets differently than you might wish.
- ✦ Fees for probate lawyers will consume from 5 to 25 percent of your estate. The smaller your estate, the higher the percentage will be for the probate lawyer.
- ✦ If your estate is large enough to be affected by federal estate taxes ($600,000 or more), not focusing on a will and neglecting other estate planning tasks can increase the tax obligations on your estate.

Using Quicken's Financial Planning Tools

Quicken has a number of financial planning tools. These tools are designed to perform calculations that can help you with planning and decision making regarding financial goals. You used the financial tool that calculated the split between mortgage principal reductions and interest in Chapter 8. In this section you will see how the Retirement Planning, College Planning, Investment Planning, and the Refinance Calculator are similar; they provide the information you need to make a good decision and allow you to look at different scenarios.

NOTE: All of the financial planning calculators require you to make assumptions about interest rates, yields, and so on. You should continue to monitor your assumptions over time and make corrections as the economy or other factors change.

Using the Refinance Calculator

As interest rates fall, you can use the Refinance Calculator to assess whether to approach your financial institution about refinancing your loan. You can use the information from the Loan Calculator example in Chapter 8 for an example of an actual loan. In the Chapter 8 example, you had a $40,000 loan at 9.519 percent interest for 25 years with payments of $350 a month. If you were reconsidering refinancing after 36 months, you could print out the payment schedule to see that you still had a balance of $38,642.29. You can follow these steps to plug this information into the Refinance Calculator to see how much a lower interest rate will reduce your payments and how long it will take to recover the cost of refinancing:

1. Select **A**ctivities and then **F**inancial Planning and press Enter.
2. Select Re**f**inance Calculator and the Refinance Calculator, shown in Figure 9-22, appears.
3. Press Enter to accept the default currency as US.
4. Type **350.00** and press Enter twice.

   In Chapter 8, the illustration did not provide for an escrow account (insurance, property taxes, and so on) held by the mortgage company. If escrow had been included, you would have entered the monthly escrow account as well. You can obtain your escrow information from the monthly statement that your mortgage company provides.
5. Type **38642.29** and press Enter.

   This is the principal for the remaining mortgage after 36 $350 payments are applied.
6. Type **8.375** and press Enter.

   This is the interest rate quoted by your financial institution.

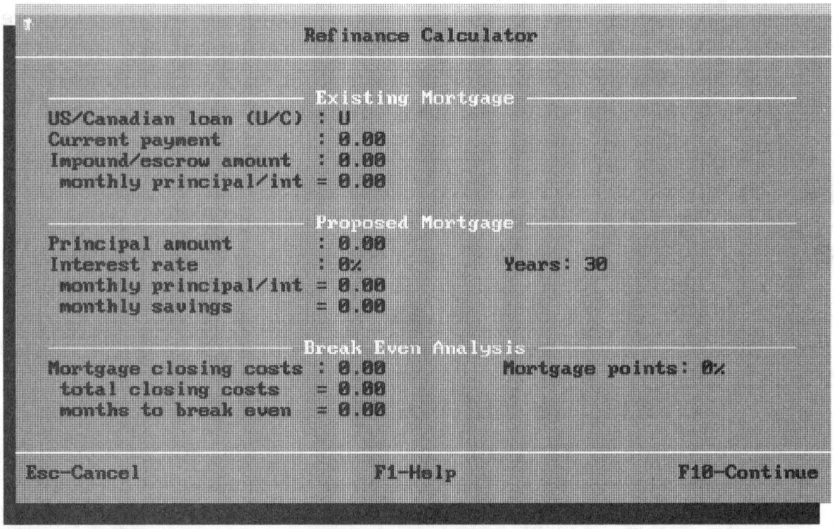

```
                         Refinance Calculator

             ---------- Existing Mortgage ----------
  US/Canadian loan (U/C) : U
  Current payment        : 0.00
  Impound/escrow amount  : 0.00
   monthly principal/int = 0.00

             ---------- Proposed Mortgage ----------
  Principal amount       : 0.00
  Interest rate          : 0%            Years: 30
   monthly principal/int = 0.00
   monthly savings       = 0.00

             ---------- Break Even Analysis ----------
  Mortgage closing costs : 0.00          Mortgage points: 0%
   total closing costs   = 0.00
   months to break even  = 0.00

Esc-Cancel                  F1-Help                  F10-Continue
```

The Refinance Calculator
Figure 9-22.

7. Type **22** and press Enter.

   This number assumes that you want the house paid off within the 25-year goal for the original mortgage. You can negotiate a 15-year or a 30-year loan if you prefer and change the assumption accordingly.

8. Type **900** and press Enter.

   Even when you refinance with your existing loan holder, you can expect to pay closing costs for the new loan. Your lender has provided an estimate of $900.

9. Type **.25** and press Enter, and your screen displays the Refinance Calculator shown in Figure 9-23.

The .25 represents the 1/4 point that your lender will charge to give you the 8.375 percent interest rate on the 22-year loan.

You can see that if you refinance your home under these conditions, your monthly payments will be reduced to $320.85 (principal and interest), saving you $29.15 a month. Since you must pay out $900 in closing costs plus 1/4 point, the last line on the screen tells you that you must stay in the home another 34.18 months before your monthly savings will offset the closing costs and points. You can shop around for better terms with other institutions and use the Refinance Calculator to pick the best deal.

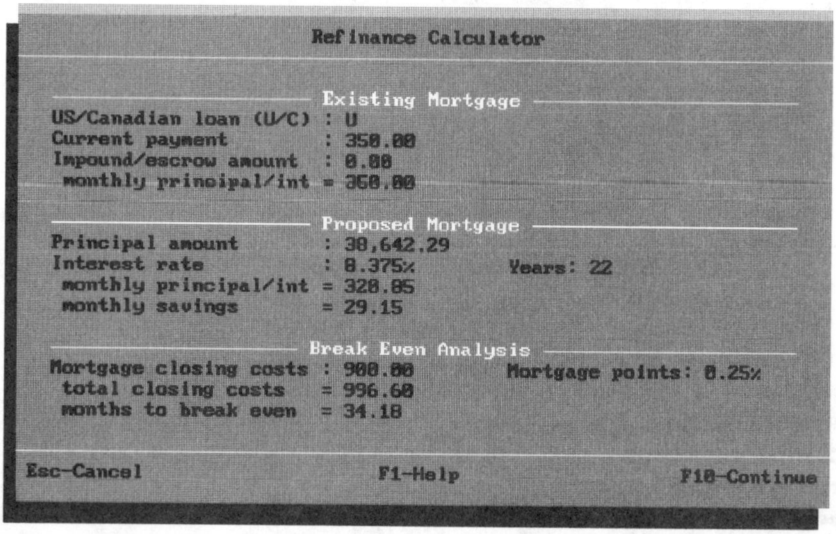

```
                         Refinance Calculator

 ------------------------- Existing Mortgage --------------------------
 US/Canadian loan (U/C) : U
 Current payment        : 350.00
 Impound/escrow amount  : 0.00
  monthly principal/int = 350.00

 ------------------------- Proposed Mortgage --------------------------
 Principal amount       : 30,642.29
 Interest rate          : 8.375%         Years: 22
  monthly principal/int = 320.85
  monthly savings       = 29.15

 ------------------------ Break Even Analysis -------------------------
 Mortgage closing costs : 900.00         Mortgage points: 0.25%
  total closing costs   = 996.60
  months to break even  = 34.18

 Esc-Cancel                   F1-Help                      F10-Continue
```

Sample figures entered into the Refinance Calculator

Figure 9-23.

Investment Planning

Earlier in this chapter you saw a table illustrating the effects of investing $100 a month for 20 years. You can use the Investment Planner in Quicken to see how future value information is generated. The Investment Planner is so flexible that it also allows you to calculate other things such as present value.

In order to complete the entries in the Investment Planning window, shown in Figure 9-24, you must tell Quicken that the present value is 0, since you are starting with no money in the account. The other entries are the $100 monthly payment, a period of 20 years, or 240 months, and the annual expected yield of 8 percent. The expected yield is an educated guess on your part. Quicken displays a future value of $58,902.04, which confirms the value shown in the table earlier in this chapter. Notice that Quicken also tells you that in today's dollars that is the equivalent of $26,501.62 with an expected inflation rate of 4 percent over the 20-year period. This highlights the effect that inflation has on your future purchasing power.

Although it was not used in the example, you can also have Quicken adjust your payments in Figure 9-24 for inflation. You must use the Inflate Payments Monthly option. If you want to have an inflation adjusted value of $58,902 at the end of 20 years, enter **Y** for this option and press F9. Quicken provides a payment schedule that is adjusted for the 4 percent inflation rate. Your first payment would still be $100, but your last payment would be $221.51. Your account would have $81,126.62 to maintain your 8-percent yield and adjust for inflation.

You can see how easy it is to enter a few numbers and get some help from Quicken on your investment decisions. There are many changes that you can make as you select weekly, monthly, quarterly, or annual payment periods by pressing the F7 key. You can adjust annual yield and inflation

```
                    Investment Planning

  Present Value                          : 0.00
  Additions each Month                   : 100.00
  Number of Months                       : 240
  Annual Yield                           : 8%

√ Future Value                           = 58,902.04
    (in today's dollars)                 : 26,501.62

  Predicted Inflation                    : 4%
  Inflate Payments Monthly (Y/N)         : N

F7-Change Periods  Ctrl-D Reset  F8-Select Calculation
Esc-Cancel              F1-Help       F9-Show Payments
```

Investment Planner shows return for investment example

Figure 9-24.

expectations. If you move the checkmark with F8, you can also make present-value computations. For example, if you expect an 8-percent return and wanted to know how much money you need to deposit today to have $58,902 in the future, you can move the checkmark to Present Value. Given a 20-year time period and no new annual payments during the time period, Quicken will compute a $12,637.32 deposit that you might want to make with a finance or insurance company.

Retirement Planning

Quicken can also be used to help project your expected income flows from your various retirement investments (SEP-IRA, Keogh, Individual IRA, 401K, or just your retirement savings account). Figure 9-25 shows the Quicken screen that appears when you select the Retirement Planner by pressing Alt-A and typing typing **F** and **R** when you are in your account register.

To complete the screen, you need to provide your best estimates for some of the information. You should review this information at least annually to see if modifications are needed and what the impact of changes are on your expected retirement income. Let's take a look at the type of information you need to provide.

Present Savings Enter the current balance in your investment account. For example, if your IRA has a balance of $30,000 at the beginning of the year, enter that balance here.

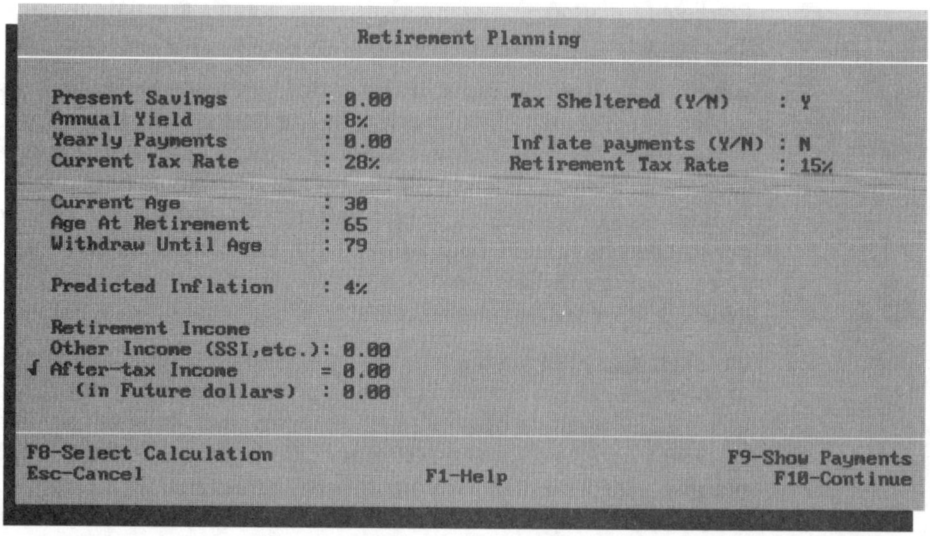

```
                         Retirement Planning

 Present Savings          : 0.00        Tax Sheltered (Y/N)      : Y
 Annual Yield             : 8%
 Yearly Payments          : 0.00        Inflate payments (Y/N) : N
 Current Tax Rate         : 28%         Retirement Tax Rate      : 15%

 Current Age              : 30
 Age At Retirement        : 65
 Withdraw Until Age       : 79

 Predicted Inflation      : 4%

 Retirement Income
 Other Income (SSI,etc.): 0.00
√ After-tax Income        = 0.00
   (in Future dollars)    : 0.00

F8-Select Calculation                                  F9-Show Payments
Esc-Cancel                    F1-Help                   F10-Continue
```

Retirement Planning window
Figure 9-25.

Tax Sheltered Indicate whether the current account is tax sheltered or not. Most retirement investments are tax sheltered; however, personal savings (CDs, mutual fund accounts, and so on) that you plan to use to supplement your retirement plans are taxable.

Annual Yield Enter your estimate of expected annual return on this investment. 8% displays as the default yield. You might use past returns on this investment as a guide, however, you can not rely solely on this source. A word of caution would be to use a conservative, but realistic, estimate of your expected annual yield.

Yearly Payments Enter your best guess of the future annual contributions that will be made to this investment. Remember to include employer matching contributions in addition to your own contributions to the account.

Inflate payments Indicate whether Quicken should adjust your yearly payment schedule to show how much additional money you need to contribute to this investment to protect your investment against inflation. The default setting is for no inflation adjustment to your yearly payments.

Tax rates Enter your current tax rate and your expected retirement tax rate or accept the defaults.

Age information Change Quicken's default ages to match your situation. If you are 48, want to retire at age 62, and want to have income provided from this investment until age 80, just enter that information on your screen.

Predicted Inflation Accept Quicken's default annual rate of 4% or modify it to see what the potential impact of various rates will be.

When you enter the above information, Quicken provides you with retirement planning information in the Retirement Income section of Figure 9-25. The "After Tax Income" amount shows what your expected future income in today's dollars will be. If Quicken shows that this investment will provide $10,000, that is the equivalent to spending in today's dollars. That is, Quicken has taken your future payments and adjusted them for inflation. The "in Future dollars" row shows you what your annual payments will be in actual dollars at the time of receipt.

Quicken also allows you to enter expected payments from Social Security or other sources in order to give you a better picture of your future retirement income. By pressing the F9 key, you can ask Quicken to print out your payment schedule for the retirement. This process provides valuable planning information for your future retirement. As a result of this type of exercise, you might decide that you need to increase your retirement investment contribution in the future, or that you are on track for future financial security. The important point is that this type of review should be an annual planning assessment. With the ease of use and the importance of protecting your retirement quality of living, this Quicken feature can be a valuable tool.

College Planning

The final Quicken financial planning tool is the College Planning calculator, shown in Figure 9-26. The assumptions for this college-planning scenario are

- Your child will attend a nationally known private university with a current tuition of $15,000 a year
- It will be 18 years before your child enrolls in this university
- Your child will pursue a major that requires 5 years of study to complete the degree requirements
- Your annual yield will be 8 percent over the period
- Predicted inflation for tuition is 6 percent

Figure 9-26 shows that you would need to make annual payments of $4977.73 from 1994 to 2016 (note the calculations are based on your continuing payments during the five years your child is in school). By pressing F9, you can see that tuition will rise to $42,815 for your child's freshman year, assuming a 6-percent annual increase. If you change the assumptions to have your child complete a major in an area requiring only four years of study, your annual payments decrease to $4,086.16.


```
                     College Planning

 Current Tuition (annual)          : 15,000.00
 Years Until Enrollment            : 18
 Number of years enrolled          : 5
 Present Savings                   : 0.00
 Annual Yield                      : 8%

√ Yearly Payments                  = 4,977.73
 Predicted Inflation               : 6%
 Inflate Payments Yearly (Y/N)     : N

 All calculations assume saving until student
  graduates from college.

F8-Select Calculation  Ctrl-D Reset  F9-Show Payments
Esc-Cancel             F1-Help            F10-Continue
```

College Planning calculator
Figure 9-26.

Graphing Your Investments

Quicken gives you an opportunity to review visually your investment activities at points in time or for a period of time. Your graphing options include viewing your Portfolio **C**omposition at a point in time, viewing your Portfolio Value **T**rend over time, and viewing Price **H**istory over time. Your graphing activities begin from the Quicken Main Menu.

1. Choose View **G**raphs from the Main Menu.
2. Select In**v**estments, and your screen looks like this:

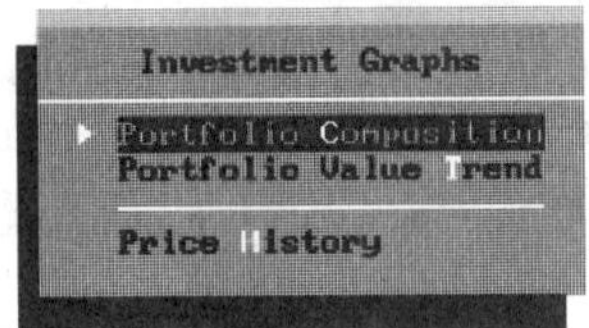

3. Select Portfolio **C**omposition.

   The Portfolio **C**omposition selection prepares a pie chart that shows the composition of your portfolio by individual security.
4. Type **8/31/94** and press Enter.
5. Press Enter to have the graph prepared by security.

   You could have selected to have the graph prepared by type of security or investment goal if you wished. Quicken presents the graph shown in Figure 9-27. From the graph, you can see that Ganges Mutual Fund composes 47 percent of your portfolio's total value, Haven Publishing 33 percent, Glenn Packing 11 percent, and Douglas Marine composes 9 percent of the portfolio's total value.
6. If you want to print the graph, you can select the print button on your screen. If you want a report of the data Quicken used to prepare the graph, you can select Report.

For all the graphs you print with Quicken, the default setting is set to include all your accounts in the graphing option. In Figure 9-27, only the Investments account is included because we have only established one investment account in this illustration. If you have multiple investment accounts, which is highly probable, you can select the F9 (Filter) option and move to the option selection that allows you to select the accounts you want included in the graph. If you have an IRA, 401K, and personal investment account, you can use the filter to select graphing activities for each account. Otherwise Quicken will merge all three accounts into the one graph.

Using the data prepared in the illustration in this chapter, Figure 9-28 and Figure 9-29 show what the Portfolio Value Trend by Security and Price History graphs look like.

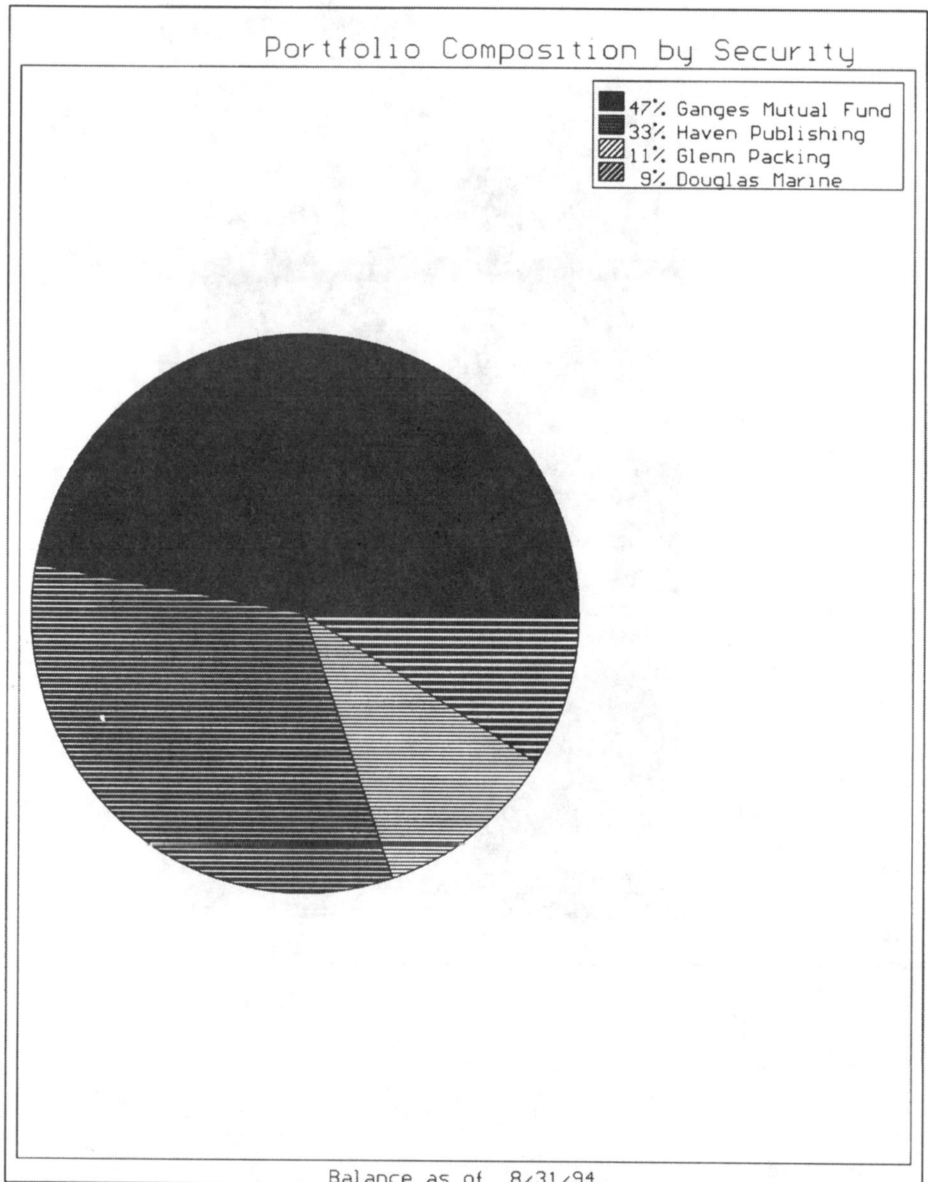

Portfolio Composition by Security graph
Figure 9-27.

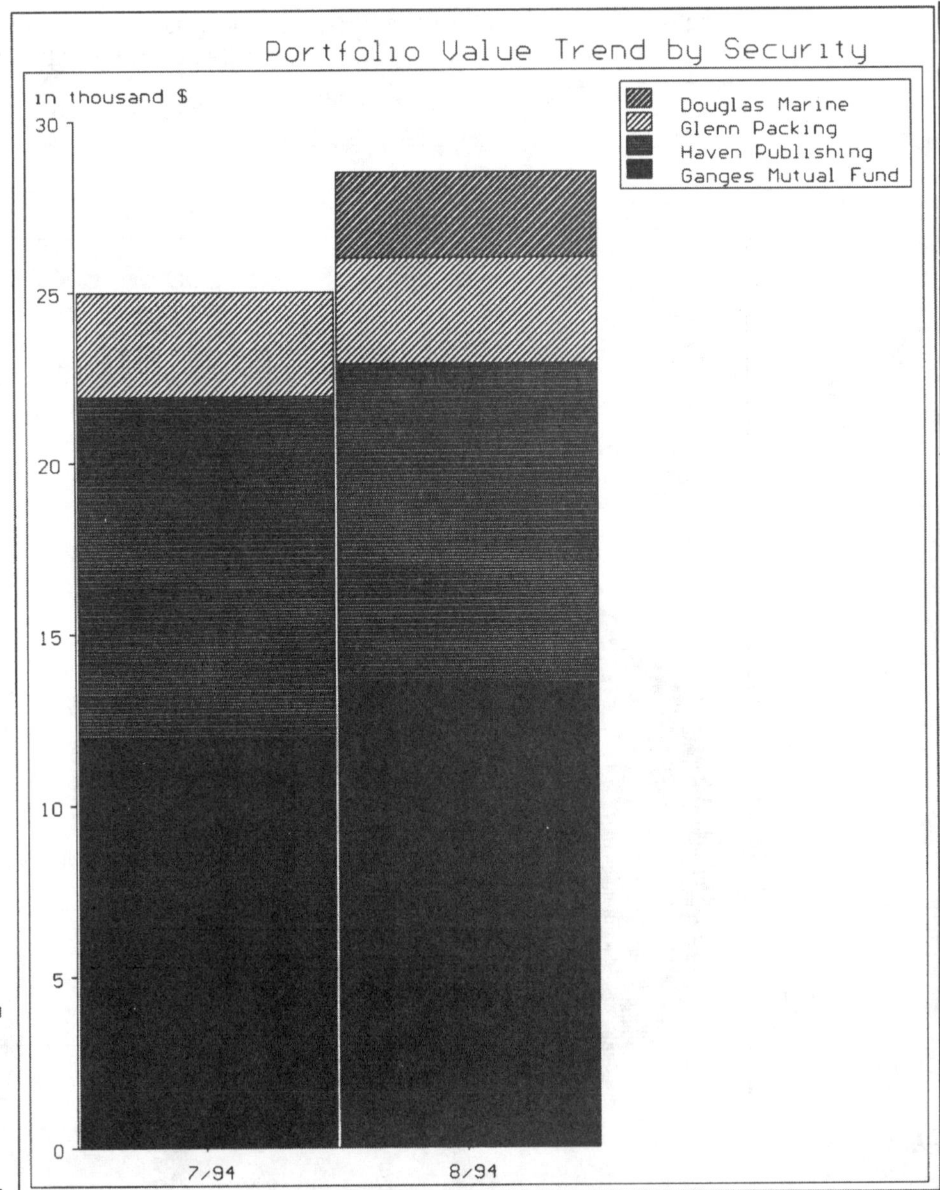

Portfolio Value Trend by Security graph
Figure 9-28.

Price History

in dollars

Douglas Marine
Ganges Mutual Fund
Glenn Packing
Haven Publishing

35.00
30.00
25.00
20.00
15.00
10.00
5.00
0.00

8/ 1/94 8/ 8/94 8/15/94 8/22/94 8/29/94

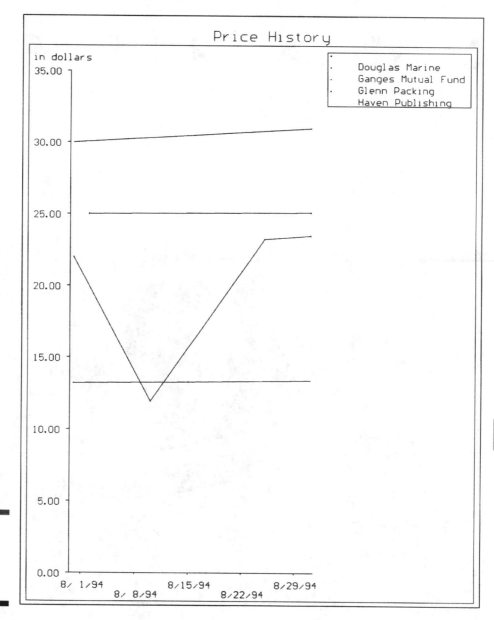

Figure 9-29. Price History graph for Investments Account

C H A P T E R

investments banking FILE register expenses DEDUCTIONS
tips finances INCOME equity net pay
checks revenue bank statements
statements business tips
dividends assets
INCOME cash flow
banking business tips FILE reports
budget FILE business tips checks
DEDUCTIONS tips mortgage
statements cash flow
net pay taxes bank revenue
business tips
mortgage cash dividends tips
business tips investments
register statements taxes
business tips
reports expenses tips
equity investments INCOME
checks statements bank cash
assets checks budget tips finances net pay

10 CREATING CUSTOM REPORTS

Periodically you will want to step back from the detail in your Quicken register and look at the reports and graphs the package can create. Both reports and graphs can be viewed onscreen or printed to share with others.

Quicken can prepare both standard and custom reports. Standard reports have a predefined format most Quicken users will find acceptable for their home, business, and investment reporting needs. However, as you become more familiar with Quicken, you may want to customize your reports to meet your unique needs. Custom reports allow you to alter the report format to meet your specific requirements. You can use the Redo Last Report feature to recapture the last report you prepared during your current Quicken session by accessing the Main Menu or the **R**eports pull-down menu in your register, or by pressing Ctrl-Z at any time. In addition, a new feature of Quicken 7 allows you to recapture any of the last four reports prepared during your current or past Quicken sessions from the **R**eports menu. These report titles are shown in the lower section of the **R**eports menu shown below:

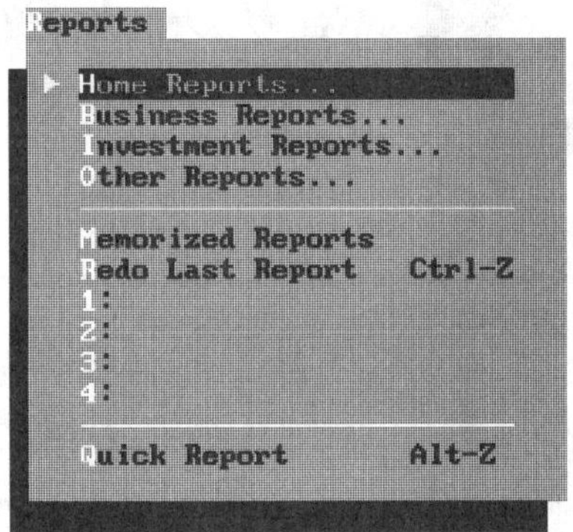

Another new feature in Quicken 7 is the Quick Reports feature. A Quick Report, which can be created from any register except an investment register, presents a simple summary of the register filtered by the value in the current field. This means that if you are on the category field for Medical:Doctor, only those transactions with this entry in the category field will display on the report. Date fields are excluded from the Quick Reports feature, but any other register field can be used. Quick Reports do not have the extras and customization options of other reports but can be created by moving to the field in the register you wish to use to select data for the report and pressing Alt-Z. If you would prefer to use the mouse you can select **Q**uick Report from the **R**eports menu.

Quicken also supports creating different standard reports for personal or home use: Cash Flow, Monthly Budget, Itemized Categories, Tax Summary, Net Worth, Missing Check, and Tax Schedule. You can create any one of these reports by selecting **H**ome Reports from the **R**eports menu.

You have seen several examples of standard reports in earlier chapters. Quicken allows you to customize any of the standard reports while creating them or after the reports are displayed on your screen. The **R**eports menu also shows that Quicken has the ability to access reports that you have memorized. (You will find more on memorized reports at the end of this chapter.)

Quicken also provides five additional report types in a group called **O**ther Reports in the **R**eports menu: Transaction, Summary, Budget, Account Balances, and Comparison. These are all actually customized reports. Selecting any of these items causes a Create Report window to be displayed on the screen, which allows you to create many different report frameworks. Although the exact contents of the window depend on the type of report you are creating, each of these windows allows you to enter information such as the accounts you want to use, directions for totaling and subtotaling the report, the type of cleared status for included transactions, and specific transactions you wish to include. Some of these options are specified with direct entries in the Report window and others require the use of F8 (Options) for additional report options or F9 (Filter) to filter records that will be included.

You already saw one of the reports in the **O**ther Reports option in Chapter 7, "Quicken as a Budgeting Tool," when you selected the current account item to customize the Monthly Budget report for Cardinal Bank, shown in Figure 7-5. In this chapter, you look at additional custom reporting options and report filtering features as you build three new custom reports. After looking at the exercises in this chapter, you will be able to create your own custom reports and memorize them for later use. Be sure to look at the special "Documenting Your Decisions" section to learn how to safeguard your time investment.

In Chapter 7, you had the opportunity to create several graphs to provide a look at your budget performance. These graphs are designed to give you a quick pictorial on your screen to help spot trends and make other analyses without all the detail of reports.

Creating a Custom Net Worth Report

You can create a Net Worth report by selecting the **N**et Worth option from the **H**ome Reports menu. If you choose the standard report item from the list of home reports and don't make any changes, Quicken will prepare the report for assets and liabilities and show the balance of each of your asset and liability accounts. You used this standard option in Chapter 9, "Determining Your Net Worth," to assess your net worth.

Report Intervals

If you want to look at the effect of financial management activities on your net worth over time, the standard report will not provide what you need since it provides your balances at a specific time. The Create Account Balances Report window, which opens when you select F7 (Layout) for the Net Worth report, allows you to specify intervals for the report. Figure 10-1

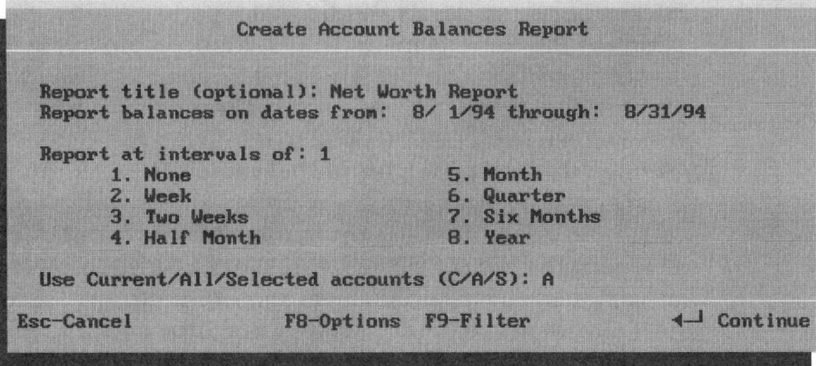

Custom Create Account Balances Report window
Figure 10-1.

shows the Create Account Balances Report window and the many interval options that can be chosen. You can select report intervals ranging from a week to a year. If you don't specify an interval, the default option is the specific time identified as the last date on the line "Report balances on dates through" (see Figure 10-1). In this example, if you request the report interval of Week, Quicken will prepare a Net Worth report at the end of each week for the designated period.

Changing the Accounts Used to Prepare the Report

The standard Net Worth report presents all accounts in the file when preparing the report. If you are concerned with only some of your balances, you can select those accounts you want to appear in the report. Entering **C** in the fifth field of the Create Account Balances Report window produces a report for the current account only. Entering **S** allows you to select from a list of all the accounts in the file.

Displaying Detailed Information on the Net Worth Report

When you created the Net Worth report in Chapter 9, "Determining Your Net Worth," all the detail available on your investments was not displayed. This occurred because Quicken's standard Net Worth report does not show all the detail. Including detailed information would provide a better picture of your investment holdings. To obtain this information, you need to customize the standard report.

Documenting Your Decisions

As you work with Quicken's features, you will probably try a number of custom report options before you decide on the exact set of reports that meets your needs. If you had an accountant prepare these same reports, there might also be some trial and error the first time before the exact format to use would be determined. Once the decisions were made, the accountant would document them to ensure you received the exact reports you requested on a regular basis. You will benefit by following the same procedure and documenting the custom reports and options you select with Quicken. The following are steps to take in putting together your documentation:

- Place all your report documentation in one folder.
- Include a copy of each report you want to produce on a regular basis.
- If you are using a Quicken report to obtain information for another form, include a copy of the form and note on it which field in the Quicken report is used to obtain that number.
- Include the selections you used in the custom report windows. If you have a screen-capture utility, you can capture and print this screen when you create the report the first time.
- Include your entries on the Filter window. You can write them down or use a screen-capture utility.
- If you are creating multiple copies of some reports, write down the information on the extra copies and what must be done with the copies.
- Memorize each custom report to make it instantly available when you need it again.

To include detailed investment information on the Net Worth report, you need to enter **S** for Selected accounts in the last field of the Create Account Balances Report window (Figure 10-1). You will use the Investments account in the INVEST file created in Chapter 9. Since the last example used that file, you may already be there. If not, go to the "Changing Files" section of this chapter for instructions.

Follow these steps from the Main Menu to produce a Net Worth report with investment detail.

1. Select **C**reate Reports.

   Quicken will display the **R**eports menu shown earlier.
2. Select **H**ome Reports.
3. Select **N**et Worth.
4. Press F7 to change the layout of the report.

   Quicken displays the Create Account Balances Report window shown in Figure 10-1.
5. Press Enter to use the default report title.
6. Type **8/1/94** and press Enter.
7. Type **8/31/94** and press Enter.
8. Press Enter to accept None for the Report at intervals of field.

   This selection will show the balances as one total without any breakdown.
9. Type **S** to use selected accounts in the report and press Enter. The Select Accounts To Include window, shown in Figure 10-2, appears on your screen.
10. Press ↓ until the arrow cursor moves to Investments.
11. Press Spacebar until the word "Detail" appears in the Include in Report column.

Pressing Spacebar changes the entry in the Include in Report column from "Include" to "Detail" to blank. "Detail" causes the detailed information, if any exists, to be shown in the report. A blank space means the account will be

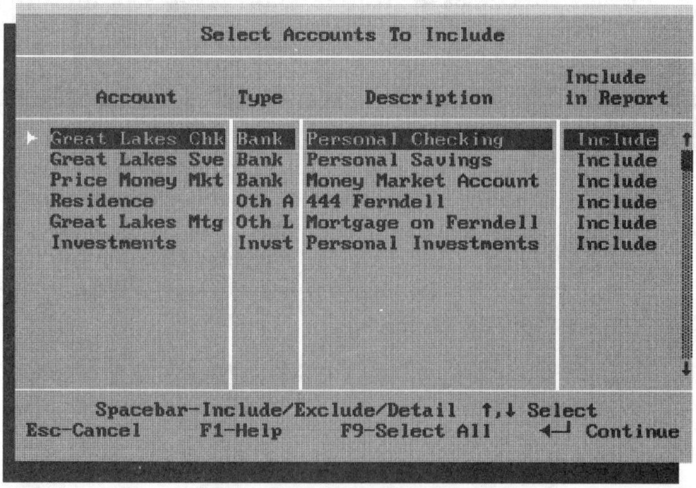

Select Accounts To Include

Account	Type	Description	Include in Report
Great Lakes Chk	Bank	Personal Checking	Include
Great Lakes Sve	Bank	Personal Savings	Include
Price Money Mkt	Bank	Money Market Account	Include
Residence	Oth A	444 Ferndell	Include
Great Lakes Mtg	Oth L	Mortgage on Ferndell	Include
Investments	Invst	Personal Investments	Include

Spacebar-Include/Exclude/Detail ↑,↓ Select
Esc-Cancel F1-Help F9-Select All ↵ Continue

Select Accounts To Include window
Figure 10-2.

excluded from the report. "Include" shows information from the account but does not use all the detail.

12. Press Enter, and the Net Worth report appears on your screen.
13. Select **F**ile/Print, and then select **P**rint Report to display the Print Report window.
14. Select your printer and press Enter.

Quicken will produce the report shown in Figure 10-3. Notice that the report looks the same as the one generated in Chapter 9, except that the Investments section shows detailed stock information.

Creating a Custom Transaction Report

You can print all the transactions in any Quicken account register by opening the Print Register window from the Print/Acct menu. This procedure prints a listing of all the transactions in a given time frame. You can use this approach for printing a complete listing of register activity for backup purposes. However, it does not provide much information for decision making. The custom Transaction report item provides an alternative. By selecting this feature, you can choose to subtotal transaction activity in many different ways, use all or only selected accounts, or show split transaction detail. Thus, you are allowed to select the specific transaction details you need for better decision making. Let's take a look at some examples.

Changing Files

All the remaining examples generated in this chapter are prepared in the PERSONAL file. The following sequence of steps demonstrates how to change from one file to another within Quicken:

1. While in Quicken, press Esc until you return to the Main Menu.
2. Select **F**ile Activities.
3. Choose **S**elect/Set Up File.
4. Move the arrow cursor to the PERSONAL file and press Enter. The Select Account To Use window appears.
5. Move the arrow cursor to the Cardinal Bank account, if necessary, and press Enter. Quicken takes you to the account register for the Cardinal Bank account.
6. Press Esc to go to the Main Menu.

```
                     Net Worth Report
                      As of 8/31/94
INVEST-Selected Accounts                                       Page 1
7/26/94
                                                 8/31/94
                   Acct                          Balance
      ----------------------------------- ------------------------
      ASSETS
        Cash and Bank Accounts
          Great Lakes Chk                                  3,125.00
          Great Lakes Sve                                  2,700.00
          Price Money Mkt                                 14,750.00
                                                       ------------
        Total Cash and Bank Accounts                      20,575.00

        Other Assets
          Residence                                      105,000.00
                                                       ------------
        Total Other Assets                               105,000.00

        Investments
          Investments
            Douglas Marine                    2,512.50
            Ganges Mutual Fund               13,500.92
            Glenn Packing                     3,100.00
            Haven Publishing                  9,400.00
            -Cash-                                0.00
                                          ------------
          Total Investments                               28,513.42
                                                       ------------
        Total Investments                                 28,513.42

                                                       ------------
      TOTAL ASSETS                                       154,088.42

      LIABILITIES
        Other Liabilities
          Great Lakes Mtg                                 84,975.00
                                                       ------------
        Total Other Liabilities                           84,975.00

                                                       ------------
      TOTAL LIABILITIES                                   84,975.00

                                                       ------------
      TOTAL NET WORTH                                     69,113.42
                                                       ============
```

Net Worth report
Figure 10-3.

Showing Split Transaction Detail

If a transaction is split among several categories, the word "SPLIT" will appear in the Category field when the account register is printed. Suppose you want to prepare a customized report that captures all of the detail recorded in each split transaction within a selected time frame.

1. Select **C**reate Reports.

Quicken will display the **R**eports menu showing both standard (**H**ome Reports, **B**usiness Reports, and **I**nvestment Reports) and **O**ther Reports items.

2. Select **O**ther **R**eports from the **R**eports menu and then select **T**ransaction **R**eports.

Quicken displays the Create Transaction Report window.

3. Press Enter to use the default report title.
4. Select Custom Date.
5. Type **8/1/94** and press Enter.
6. Type **8/31/94** and press Enter.
7. Press Enter twice to accept the default options; don't Subtotal and sort within subtotal by account.
8. Type **C** to use the current account in the report.

At this point your screen should match the one in Figure 10-4.

9. Press F8 (Options) and the Report Options window appears.
10. Press Enter to accept option 1, Income and expense, for the Report organization.
11. Press Enter to accept option 1, Include all, in the Transfers field.

This will include in the report all transfers between the Investments account and others in the file.

12. Press Enter to accept N in the Show totals only field.
13. Type **Y** to indicate that you want to show the split transaction detail and press Enter.

Your screen now matches the window shown in Figure 10-5.

14. Press Enter to accept 3 in the next field, indicating that both memo and category data will be displayed.
15. Press Ctrl-Enter to accept the remaining defaults.

The Create Transaction Report window reappears on your screen.

16. Press Enter, and the Transaction report appears on the screen.
17. Select **F**ile/Print and then select **P**rint Report.

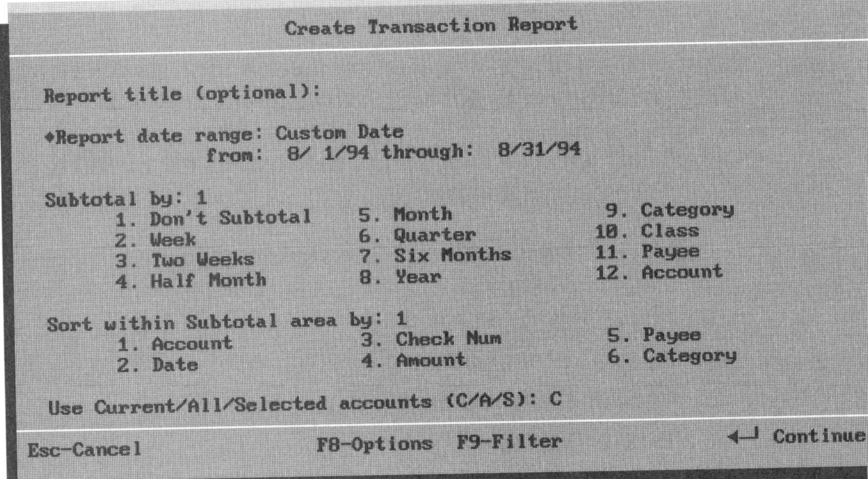

Create Transaction Report window
Figure 10-4.

18. Select Report Printer and press Enter to create the report. Figure 10-6 shows the first few transactions in this report.

Notice that the report shows the details of the split transaction on 8/1, 8/2, and 8/3.

Adding Subtotals to the Transaction Report

When you produce a Transaction report without subtotals, the transactions are simply listed in order by date. If you change the subtotaling option, you

```
                          Report Options

 Report organization: 1
       1. Income and expense            2. Cash flow basis

 Transfers: 1
       1. Include all                   3. External transfers only
       2. Exclude all

 Show totals only (Y/N): N
 Show split transaction detail (Y/N): Y
 Memo/Category display: 3
       1. Memo only          2. Category only     3. Display both

 Show cents when displaying amounts (Y/N): Y
 Normal/Suppressed/Reversed subcategory display (N/S/R): N

Esc-Cancel                  Ctrl-D Reset                  ◄┘ Continue
```

Report Options window for split transaction detail
Figure 10-5.

```
                                TRANSACTION REPORT
                             8/ 1/94 Through 8/31/94
PERSONAL-Cardinal Bank                                                       Page 1
7/26/94

 Date   Num      Description          Memo          Category        Clr Amount
----- ------ ------------------ ------------- ----------------- - ---------

      BALANCE  7/31/94                                                    2,260.70

 8/ 1       S Payroll deposit    Gross Wages Ea Salary                    2,000.00
                                 FICA Withholdi Tax:Soc Sec                -124.00
                                 Medicare Withh Tax:Medicare                -29.00
                                 Health Ins     Medical                     -42.01
                                 Federal Income Tax:Fed                    -130.00
                                 State Income T Tax:State                   -80.00
                                 Local Income T Tax:Local                    -9.00
 8/ 2 104   S Great Lakes Savings Principal Paym Mort Prin                  -49.33
                                 Interest Porti Mort Int                   -300.67
 8/ 3 105   S Easy Credit Card   Blue Blouse    Clothing                    -50.00
                                 Dinner at the  Dining                      -60.00
                                 Gasoline - Jee Auto:Fuel                   -23.00
                                 Green Rocker   Furniture                  -217.00
                                 Play Tickets   Entertain                   -50.00
                                                Misc                        -50.00
```

Transaction report with split transaction detail
Figure 10-6.

can choose from the options Week, Two Weeks, Half Month, Month, Quarter, Half Year, and Year. This still lists the transactions by date but also provides a subtotal of the transactions each time the selected interval occurs; selecting Month results in a subtotal for each month. If you choose one of the options Category, Class, Payee, or Account for the subtotal option, the transactions are ordered by the field selected, and a subtotal is printed whenever the value in the selected field changes. For example, a subtotal by category for 8/1 to 8/31 transactions causes Quicken to list the transactions alphabetically by category and by date within each category, with a subtotal for each category.

Follow these steps from the Main Menu for the Cardinal Bank account (in the PERSONAL file) to create a Transaction report subtotaled by category:

1. Select **C**reate Reports.

Quicken will display the **R**eports menu showing both standard (**H**ome, **B**usiness, and **I**nvestment Reports) and **O**ther Report items.

2. Select **O**ther Reports from the **R**eports menu, then select **T**ransaction **R**eports, and the Create Transaction Report window appears.
3. Press Enter to use the default report title.

4. Select Custom Date.
5. Type **8/1/94** and press Enter.
6. Type **8/31/94** and press Enter.
7. Type **9** and press Enter twice.
8. Type **C** and press Enter to use the current account in the report.

The Transaction Report by Category will display on your screen.

9. Select **F**ile/Print and then select **P**rint Report to display the Print Report window.
10. Select Report Printer and press Enter.

The bottom of the first page of the report will show three transactions for the Groceries category, as shown in this partial report:

```
                          TRANSACTION REPORT BY CATEGORY
                             8/ 1/94 Through 8/31/94
PERSONAL-Cardinal Bank                                                    Page 2
7/26/94

 Date   Num     Description          Memo          Category       Clr Amount
----- ------ ------------------- -------------- ------------------ - ---------

          Groceries
          ---------
 8/ 4 106    Maureks             Groceries      Groceries            -60.00
 8/15 108    Meijer              Groceries      Groceries            -65.00
 8/27 112    Meijer              Food           Groceries            -93.20
                                                                  ---------
          Total Groceries                                           -218.20
```

This report is essentially the same as the Itemized Categories report you saw in Chapter 7, "Quicken as a Budgeting Tool," unless you choose to make additional customization changes, such as selecting accounts or filtering the information presented.

Creating a Summary Report

Summary reports allow you to create reports based on categories, classes, payees, or accounts. You can use them to analyze spending patterns, prepare tax summaries, review major purchases, or look at the total charge card purchases for a given period.

With a Summary report you have more control over the layout of information than in other reports. You can select from a number of options to determine what information to place in rows and columns of the report.

You can combine the summary features with the filtering features to further select the information presented.

Subtotaling a Summary Report by Month

Although you can choose any of the time intervals to control the subtotals for the report, a month is commonly chosen since many users budget expenses by month. This type of report allows you to look at a monthly summary of your financial transactions. Follow these steps from the Main Menu for the Cardinal Bank account (in the PERSONAL file) to create the Summary Report by Month:

1. Select the **C**reate Reports item.

Quicken displays the **R**eports menu showing both standard (**H**ome, **B**usiness, and **I**nvestment Reports) and **O**ther Reports options.

2. Select **O**ther Reports from the **R**eports menu, then select **S**ummary **R**eports, and the Create Summary Report window appears.
3. Press Enter to use the default report title.
4. Select Custom Date.
5. Type **8/1/94** and press Enter.
6. Type **10/31/94** and press Enter.
7. Press Enter to accept the default Row headings item.
8. Type **5** and press Enter to select Month for the Column headings field.
9. Press Enter to not show column percentages.
10. Type **C**, then press F8 (Options). The Report Options window appears.
11. Type **2** and press Enter.

This step instructs Quicken to prepare the report on a cash flow basis. The report will be organized by cash inflows and outflows. This is the same basis as the monthly budget reports prepared in Chapter 7, "Quicken as a Budgeting Tool." It allows you to compare this report with those prepared earlier and provides additional information for assessing your budget results.

12. Type **1** and press Ctrl-Enter. You are returned to the Create Summary Report window.
13. Press Enter, and the Summary Report by Month appears on your screen. Figure 10-7 shows a printout of this report.

SUMMARY REPORT BY MONTH
8/ 1/94 Through 10/31/94

PERSONAL-Cardinal Bank Page 1
7/28/94

Category Description	8/94	9/94	10/94	OVERALL TOTAL
INFLOWS				
Salary Income	2,000.00	1,585.99	1,585.99	5,171.98
TOTAL INFLOWS	2,000.00	1,585.99	1,585.99	5,171.98
OUTFLOWS				
Automobile Expenses:				
Auto Fuel	23.00	23.00	37.00	83.00
Total Automobile Expenses	23.00	23.00	37.00	83.00
Clothing	50.00	50.00	75.00	175.00
Dining Out	60.00	60.00	45.00	165.00
Entertainment	50.00	50.00	100.00	200.00
Household Furniture	217.00	0.00	550.00	767.00
Groceries	218.20	180.00	250.00	648.20
Medical Expense:				
Doctor & Dental Visits	100.00	170.00	100.00	370.00
Medical Expense - Other	42.01	0.00	0.00	42.01
Total Medical Expense	142.01	170.00	100.00	412.01
Miscellaneous	50.00	50.00	150.00	250.00
Mortgage Interest Exp	300.67	0.00	0.00	300.67
Entire Mortgage Payment	0.00	350.00	350.00	700.00
Principal Payment	49.33	0.00	0.00	49.33
Taxes:				
Federal Tax	130.00	0.00	0.00	130.00
Local Withholding	9.00	0.00	0.00	9.00
Medicare Tax	29.00	0.00	0.00	29.00
Soc Sec Tax	124.00	0.00	0.00	124.00
State Tax	80.00	0.00	0.00	80.00
Total Taxes	372.00	0.00	0.00	372.00
Telephone Expense	23.00	29.00	27.50	79.50
Water, Gas, Electric:				
Electric Utilities	30.75	43.56	37.34	111.65
Gas Utilities	19.25	19.29	16.55	55.09
Total Water, Gas, Electric	50.00	62.85	53.89	166.74
TO Cardinal Saving	200.00	394.79	366.35	961.14
TOTAL OUTFLOWS	1,805.21	1,419.64	2,104.74	5,329.59
OVERALL TOTAL	194.79	166.35	-518.75	-157.61

Summary Report by Month
Figure 10-7.

If you adjusted all of your salary and mortgage payment transactions to agree with the August entries discussed in Chapter 8, "Using Quicken to Organize Tax Information," some of your entries will look different. In that situation, your totals would show 6000 for salary, 390 for federal tax, 87 for Medicare, 372 for social security tax, and 240 for state tax.

14. Select **F**ile/Print and then select **P**rint Report to display the Print Report window.

15. Select Report Printer and press Enter.

The report presents a cash inflow and outflow summary by month for the period of August through October. It provides additional cash flow information about the budget reports prepared in Chapter 7. Thus, the Summary Report by Month supplements the previously prepared Monthly Budget reports.

Filtering to See Tax-Related Categories

Filters allow you to selectively present information in a report. In Chapter 3, "Quicken Reports," you used a filter to look for a payee name containing "Small." Other possible selection choices include memo, category, or class matches. You can also choose specific categories or classes for inclusion. Additional options allow you to specify tax-related items or transactions greater or less than a certain amount. You can also choose payments, deposits, unprinted checks, or all transactions. Checking the cleared status is another option; that is, you may wish to prepare a report using only transactions that have cleared the bank as part of your reconciliation process.

In the example that follows, you will create a Summary report for tax-related items. Use the Cardinal Bank account in the PERSONAL file. Starting from the Main Menu, follow these steps:

1. Select **C**reate Reports.

Quicken displays the **R**eports menu showing both standard (**H**ome, **B**usiness, and **I**nvestment Reports) and **O**ther Reports.

2. Select **O**ther Reports from the **R**eports menu, then select **S**ummary **R**eports. The Create Summary Report window appears on your screen.
3. Press Enter to use the default report title.
4. Select Custom Date.
5. Type **8/1/94** and press Enter.
6. Type **10/31/94** and press Enter.
7. Press Enter to accept Category for the row headings.
8. Type **1** and press Enter twice.
9. Type **C** to select the current account.
10. Press F9 (Filter) to display the Filter Transactions window on your screen.

11. Press Enter six times to move to the Tax-related categories only field. Type **Y** and press Enter. The Filter Transactions window will look like the one in Figure 10-8.
12. Press Ctrl-Enter to return to the Create Summary Report window.
13. Press F8 (Options) to open the Report Options window.
14. Type **2** and press Enter.
15. Press Ctrl-Enter to accept the default, option 1, which instructs Quicken to include in the report all transfers between this account and others. You are returned to the Create Summary Report window.
16. Press Enter, and the Summary report appears on your screen.
17. Select **F**ile/Print and then select **P**rint Report to display the Print Report window.
18. Select Report Printer and press Enter.

Don't clear the report from your screen since you will want to use it in the next section.

Figure 10-9 shows the completed report with the information filtered for tax-related transactions only. (The report shown reflects the split salary and mortgage transaction for August only.) This type of report can be used to monitor your tax-related activities for any part of the tax year or for the year-to-date activity. You can use this information for tax planning as well as tax preparation.

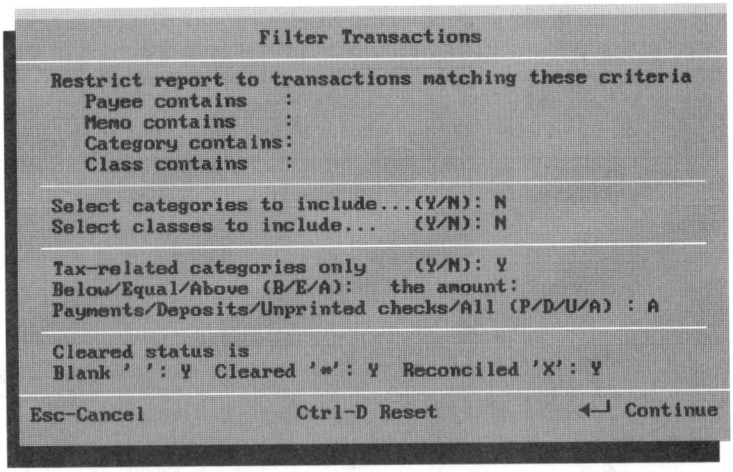

```
                    Filter Transactions

 Restrict report to transactions matching these criteria
    Payee contains    :
    Memo contains     :
    Category contains:
    Class contains    :

 Select categories to include...(Y/N): N
 Select classes to include...    (Y/N): N

 Tax-related categories only     (Y/N): Y
 Below/Equal/Above (B/E/A):   the amount:
 Payments/Deposits/Unprinted checks/All (P/D/U/A) : A

 Cleared status is
 Blank ' ': Y  Cleared '*': Y  Reconciled 'X': Y

Esc-Cancel              Ctrl-D Reset              ↵ Continue
```

Filter Transactions window
Figure 10-8.

```
                         SUMMARY REPORT
                    8/ 1/94 Through 10/31/94
PERSONAL-Cardinal Bank                                          Page 1
7/26/94
                                                8/ 1/94-
             Category Description               10/31/94
             ----------------------------- --------------------
             INFLOWS
               Salary Income                             5,171.98
                                                       ----------
             TOTAL INFLOWS                               5,171.98

             OUTFLOWS
               Medical Expense:
                 Doctor & Dental Visits          370.00
                 Medical Expense - Other          42.01
                                              ----------
               Total Medical Expense                       412.01
               Mortgage Interest Exp                       300.67
               Taxes:
                 Federal Tax                     130.00
                 Local Withholding                 9.00
                 Medicare Tax                     29.00
                 Soc Sec Tax                     124.00
                 State Tax                        80.00
                                              ----------
               Total Taxes                                 372.00
                                                       ----------
             TOTAL OUTFLOWS                              1,084.68

                                                       ----------
             OVERALL TOTAL                               4,087.30
                                                       ==========
```

Filtered Summary report of tax-related transactions
Figure 10-9.

Memorizing Reports

You have already seen the productivity that you can gain with Quicken's memorized transactions. Quicken also allows you to memorize reports. Memorized reports store your custom report definitions and allow you to produce a new report instantly by recalling the memorized report definition. This means you can enter a title or filter once and use it again if you memorize the report.

To memorize a report, you use the same Ctrl-M sequence used to memorize transactions. The only difference is that you must have a report displayed on the screen. Figure 10-10 will display to allow you to enter a name for the report and select whether you want the date of the memorized report to be the current reports date (select 1) or whether you want Quicken to prompt you for a new date each time you select the memorized report (select 2). Depending upon the report you are memorizing, you may have other dating options to select from.

```
                    Memorizing Report

 Title:

 Date(s) to use when running report: 1
       1. Run report using  8/ 1/94 through 10/31/94.
       2. Prompt for date(s) when report is run.

Esc-Cancel               F1-Help              ↵ Continue
```

Memorizing Report window
Figure 10-10.

If you were memorizing the summary report shown in Figure 10-9, you might enter the title as Tax Related Summary Report. Although you can use the entire line for your name, you will want to ensure that the first 27 characters of your entry uniquely define your report since this is the entry that will display in the list of memorized reports. Next you need to tell Quicken the dates to use when running the report. Since the time period is going to be different the next time you want to prepare this report, you should have Quicken prompt you for the reporting period (type **2** in the second field of the window) before preparing the memorized report each time you make the selection.

To create a report from a memorized report definition, select **M**emorized Reports from the **R**eports menu. A list of memorized reports will display in a window like the one shown here,

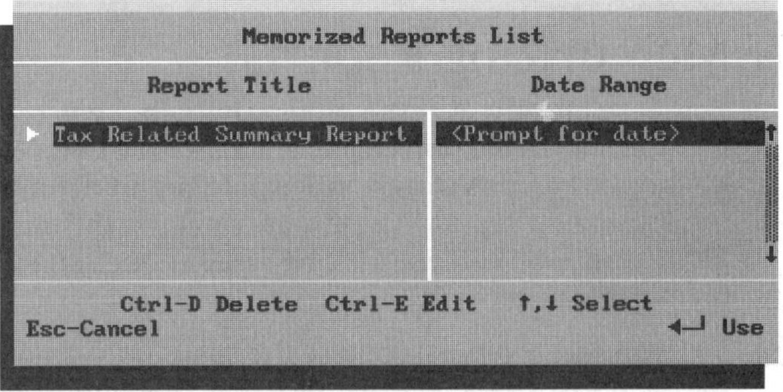

which shows a Tax Related Summary Report. After moving the arrow cursor to the desired report and pressing Enter, you will be asked to select the new report date. When you do this and press Enter the desired report is displayed on the screen.

Redo Last Report

The last report feature shows how you can always recover the previous report that was generated at any point during your current Quicken session. You can press Ctrl-Z at any time in the register to view the last report prepared by Quicken.

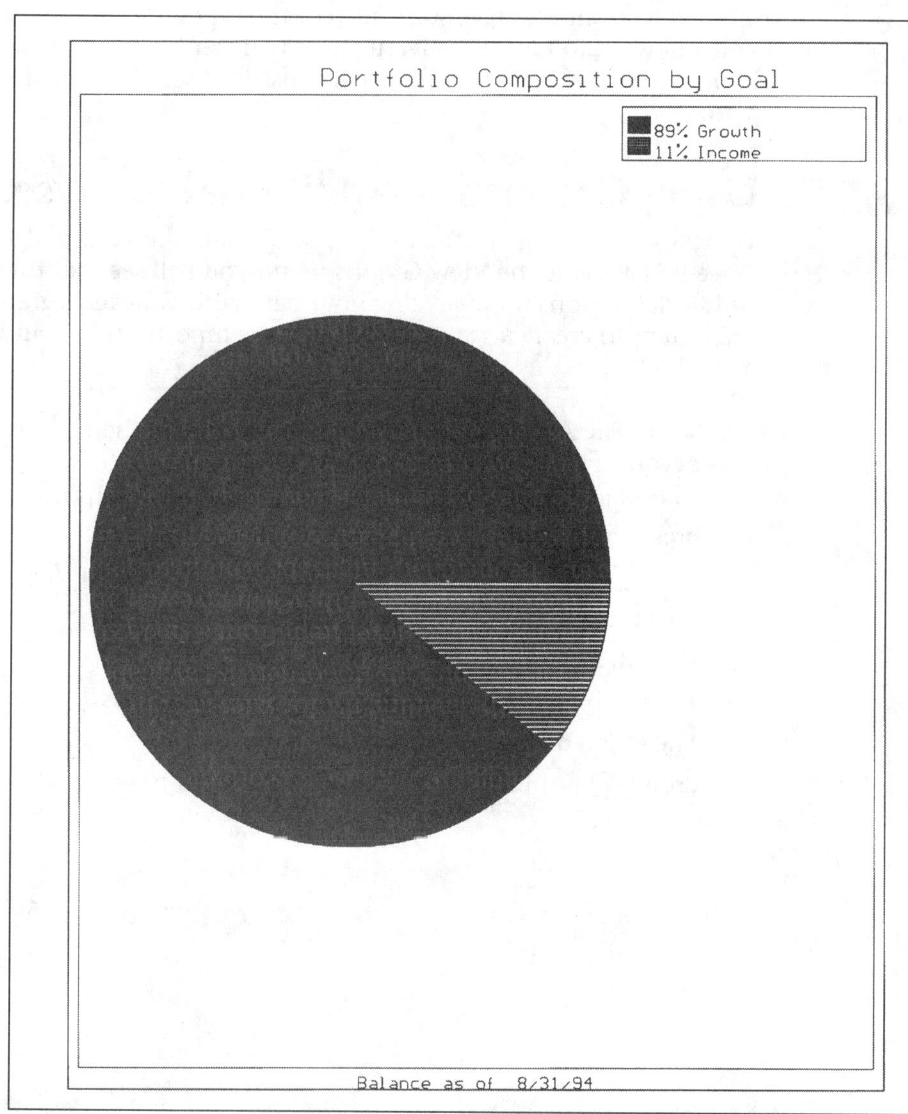

Pie graph showing portfolio composition by goal
Figure 10-11.

Quicken automatically recreates the last report you generated during this session (Figure 10-9). You can also select the **R**edo Last Report option from the **R**eports menu or from the register **R**eports pull-down menu. As discussed earlier in the chapter, another important point to recall is that Quicken can recapture your last four reports generated at any time during the current or previous sessions through the **R**eports menu.

Now that you've had a chance to look at both standard and custom report options, you should have some idea of the types of reports you will need. You will want to take full advantage of Quicken's ability to memorize reports in order to save time and produce a consistent set of reports for each time period.

Using Graphs for Additional Analyses

The graphs that you created in Chapter 7 related to your budget entries. Once you activate the View Graphs menu you will see that there are many additional options for analyzing your data with Quicken's graphs. Follow these steps to create a graph showing the composition of your investment portfolio:

1. Select **F**ile Activities from the Main Menu and then choose **S**elect/Setup Account.
2. Highlight Invest and press Enter, and then highlight Investments and press Enter again.
3. Press Esc to display the Main Menu and then select View **G**raphs.
4. Select In**v**estment and then Portfolio **C**omposition.
5. Type **8/31/94** and press Enter.
6. Type **4** to Display the balances: By Goal and press Enter.

   The graph displays as shown in Figure 10-11.
7. Press Esc until the Main Menu displays again.

T I P S

investments banking FILE register expenses DEDUCTIONS
tips finances INCOME equity net pay
checks revenue bank statements
statements
dividends assets business tips
INCOME cash flow
banking FILE reports
budget FILE business tips checks
DEDUCTIONS tips mortgage
statements cash flow revenue
net pay taxes bank
business tips
mortgage cash dividends tips
business tips investments
regis register statements
reports business tips taxes
expenses tips
equity investments INCOME
bank
checks statements cash
assets checks budget tips finances net pay

101 TIPS FOR SAVING MONEY

It can be difficult to put money into your savings account each month. Even with our suggestion of putting away your savings first, you still need to be able to pay your bills, eat, and have some money for enjoyable activities. The following are a few of the things that we have done over the years to stretch available money to insure that there was enough to do the things we wanted to do. You may find some of these useful and others might seem extreme. After awhile you will develop your own list of cost savers that still let you splurge occasionally on what you find important.

1. Don't buy new when used will do. Garage sales, thrift shops, and newspaper ads offer the opportunity to buy usable merchandise at a fraction of the cost of new.
2. Consider maintenance costs when you purchase clothing. Although you might expect to have your office suits dry-cleaned, avoid leisure clothing that requires dry-cleaning. It can significantly add to the cost of the clothing over its lifetime.
3. Delay purchases until you can afford to pay cash. Although you might like a new car or sofa today, waiting until you can buy it with cash means that you will save the interest charges you would otherwise incur. After paying cash you can make payments to a savings account to have the cash you need for a replacement ready when you need it.
4. Buy ahead. Use the after-Christmas, Easter, and Valentine's Day sales to buy gifts for next year.
5. Be creative with decorating. Fancy sheets can create designer curtains with only a few minutes of work. If designer wallpaper is too expensive, consider using markdown fabric with special fabric glue.
6. A new coat of paint and stenciling can create a decorator look with a 75% savings over wallpaper.
7. Seal exposed wood surfaces with a paint, stain, or sealer to prevent expensive maintenance costs.
8. Patch sidewalk and other cement cracks while small to prevent further damage from rain seepage.
9. Plan your grocery shopping to pick-up the specials at several near-by stores each week. Often these loss leaders are sold at less than cost to bring customers into the store.
10. Check for food co-ops and other buying cooperatives in your area. They often offer bargain prices on spices and bulk foods.
11. Check the local newspaper for farm ads. The whole family might enjoy picking a bushel of apples or corn, a lug of cherries, or cutting down your own Christmas tree.
12. Check to see if your local high school offers any goods or services you might want. Ours offers a beauty salon, a horticulture center, a landscape construction crew, and a trades class that builds sheds. You may find that these goods and services are much lower in cost than retail operations.
13. You can often reduce the cost of expensive dental procedures if you have a dental school nearby. Although the time commitments can be

greater, you can often realize a substantial saving on braces and expensive restorations.

14. If you do much traveling you will find that joining an automobile club can save money. The road and tow services will come in handy if your car ever breaks down. The discounts that our club provides more than pays for the membership as we get discounted hotel rooms, rental cars, and even airport parking. Maps and other travel information are also free once you have a membership.
15. Libraries often loan more than books. Pictures to hang on your wall, books on tape, and videos are all available on a for-loan basis at many libraries at no charge if they are returned on time.
16. Consider spending one evening a month at the local library browsing through their monthly magazines rather than subscribing to as many as you do now.
17. Increase the deductible on your auto, home owners, and health insurance policies if you can afford to self-insure the small mishaps.
18. Cook once to make several meals. You will save energy, preparation time, and be less likely to buy more expensive take-out food.
19. Freeze all left-overs in divided, oven-proof trays. There is no waste and they make a great quick meal.
20. Buy convenience foods only where it really counts. The time you save by buying frozen puff pastry and phyllo dough are probably well worth it. On the other hand, brownie mix, prepared salad dressing, and vegetables with butter can cost double what it would cost if you took a few minutes and made a homemade version.
21. Keep a list of needed items from the store to reduce the number of costly return trips.
22. Change to a programmable thermostat to cut energy costs.
23. Look at alternate transportation if airfares are high. A train or bus ride may be a much cheaper option on certain routes.
24. Turn down your water heater if you will be away for more than a few days.
25. Find out which days your paper includes coupons and grocery sale ads. Plan to study ads closely for the best buys and money-saving coupons.
26. Organize the coupons you clip and keep them where they are easy to find when you need them.
27. If you are going to be staying at a hotel for a few days, ask where the closest grocery store is. If it is in walking distance it may be a great place to pick up some inexpensive meals or snacks at a fraction of what the hotel charges.

28. Some of the items available at gourmet shops are also available at ethnic markets at much lower prices.
29. Try to avoid flashy brand-name clothes. If you are definitely hooked on them, check to see if they have any factory outlet stores near you.
30. Consider buying disks and other computer supplies in bulk to lower your cost.
31. Hire your children to do odd jobs if possible. You will probably give them the money for special things anyway, and it is good training to have them work for it.
32. Fix a big pot of soup once a week. It makes an inexpensive meal and is a great way to use everything from left-over roast to produce scraps.
33. Install water-saving devices on faucets and showers, especially for hot water.
34. If you enjoy eating out check to see if there are any discount books in your area. Many areas sell them as fund-raisers for the local schools. The coupons allow you to sample a variety of restaurants typically under the buy-one-meal-get-one-meal-free plan.
35. Check into annual membership at local tourist haunts. In our area Sea World and other parks offer local residents a significant discount.
36. If you are going to treat a friend to a meal, brunch or lunch may be a much better option if you need to keep the cost down.
37. Have leaky faucets repaired immediately, or better yet, do it yourself.
38. Stick with the special you went to the store to get. Some stores try a bait-and-switch tactic to get you to trade up to full-featured models.
39. Avoid the huge economy size on food items unless you have a large family or have planned how you will use all of it.
40. Check the bulletin board at your store for special manufacturer's rebates on products you use.
41. Check your local paper for entertainment specials. During the past year specials such as the ballet, baseball games, and movies have been available in our local paper for as much as 75% off the regular price. They might require a candy bar wrapper, a coupon available by stopping in a store, a box-top or carton, or a donation for charity.
42. When you are buying a car or a major appliance see if you can get a demonstration model at a discount with a new guarantee.
43. Always check the dates on perishable items you buy to avoid waste or a special trip to return the spoiled item.
44. Recycle old items such as blankets with a new cover.

45. Learn when your grocery store does markdowns. Produce, meat, and bakery items are often reduced at the same time each day or week. If you can be there right after the markdown, the item may cost half or less of its price just ten minutes earlier.
46. See if you can structure your insurance coverage to get it all at the same company for a discount. Inquire about what is needed for home owner's discounts. Often something as simple as a smoke detector and dead-bolt locks can qualify you for a discount.
47. Use every bit of what you buy. Cut open those toothpaste tubes to get out the last bit, swish some water in the sauce can or jar, use produce scraps such as broccoli stems in soup or slaw.
48. Check out generic offerings whether you are looking for paper products or food items. Most are worth a try at least once to see when you may be able to use them in place of the more expensive alternatives.
49. Be willing to wait rather than pay extra for speedy service. Most rush services, whether for film developing or dry cleaning, cost a little more. Spend the extra time rather than the extra dollar.
50. Save greeting cards, colored scrap paper, and advertisements for children's play.
51. Buy greeting cards by the box. Mail order companies such as Currents in Colorado Springs, CO, offer them if you cannot find them in your retail stores.
52. Keep tires properly inflated and rotated to extend their life.
53. Use fireplace ashes and crushed egg shells to fertilize your outdoor flowers.
54. Check for odd-lot wallpaper at wallpaper stores. It makes sturdy wrapping paper, the back is great for finger painting or coloring, and it can even be used to cover accent pieces such as a wastepaper basket for a room in your home.
55. Consider freezing some of summer's bounty for use in the winter. Strawberries, blueberries, and cherries are three of our favorites and take no work to prepare.
56. Write ahead to the local Chamber of Commerce when you are planning a vacation. Once you get to the area, discount deals may be harder to come by. When they are still trying to entice you to their area, they might include some promotional deals from local motels and establishments in the material they send you.
57. Pack a snack when you are taking an outing. It is much cheaper than buying your food at an event such as a ball game.

58. Try your hand at making your own pizza. It's really quite easy. You can get a book at the local library that will tell you how. If you do not want to make the dough, frozen bread dough will work just fine. An Italian deli near our house sells their pizza dough at 3 lbs. for a dollar. Some cheese and a little sauce and you can feed an army for what you would pay for one large take-out pizza.
59. Consider taking an electric skillet and coffee pot with you on your next vacation, along with a supply of paper plates, a can opener, and some utensils. We've bought fresh shrimp in Key West, lobster in Boston, and had many interesting meals in our travels, all from one electric skillet. If you don't want to do the whole meal in the skillet, you can always pick up some deli salads to complement your main course. If you have even a third of your meals this way you can cut your vacation costs enough to stay an extra day or two.
60. Check local barber and beauty schools as an inexpensive way to get a haircut or a perm.
61. Apply caulking and other sealants to leaky doors and windows to prevent heat loss in winter and cooling loss in summer.
62. Install pull shades on the sunny side of the house and pull them down at midday to keep the heat out.
63. Look at the refill packages now available for everything from juice to detergent as a way to lower your cost per ounce.
64. If you are trying to diet, organize a group of friends who are also into dieting as a cheaper alternative than the workshops where you pay to attend.
65. Use different quality paper products for different needs. You might like the premium paper towels in the kitchen but find that generics are just fine for the garage or workshop.
66. Cut the cost of watering plants and shrubs with a trickle system.
67. When traveling by air look at the cost savings possible with a Saturday night stayover. It may more than cover the extra night hotel stay.
68. Consider park-and-ride options where available. You will not have the high cost of parking once you get there and you can relax or read on the way.
69. Work with a travel agent who is willing to find you deals.
70. If you are going to do a movie and a dinner, consider seeing the movie first. Many theatres have a special price before 6 P.M.
71. When you are on vacation eat your main meal at noon. The midday meal tends to be cheaper at most establishments.

72. Buy the local newspaper while you are on vacation. Some meal deals are targeted to local residents and may not be advertised inside the restaurant. You will have to ask in many establishments.
73. Try baking a batch of cookies or loaf of quick bread as an inexpensive gift. When you need a gift and cannot afford to buy one make a few certificates for your services such as a free car wash or an evening of baby-sitting.
74. If the price of flowers does not fit into your gift budget, consider a small planter that you can fill with a live plant.
75. Share cost-saving ideas with others. They will be telling you about their finds before long.
76. Try using household products for cleaners rather than the expensive, purchased options. Vinegar added to water works great for cleaning windows, baking soda is great for cleaning the microwave or refrigerator, and ammonia is cheap and strong and works well for some heavy-duty cleaning jobs.
77. Use lower wattage bulbs in situations where you do not need the extra light.
78. Check activities offered at local parks. They are often free or low cost.
79. Use the flip side of used computer or calculator paper.
80. Ask the grocery store section manger to split a package if you do not need the whole thing. Most stores will make a special smaller package of produce, meat, and bakery items.
81. Catch rain water from the roof in a large trash can and use it for watering your plants.
82. Plant a small herb garden as a cheap way to spruce up meals. Even small pots on a window sill are often large enough for herbs such as parsley, thyme, and rosemary.
83. If you use reading glasses, check the variety available at your local drugstore.
84. Switch to a lower cost energy source where possible. We were able to switch from oil to gas for heat, and electric to gas for hot water. Our conversion investment paid for itself in just a few years as the new hardware was much more energy efficient as well.
85. Check into early bird specials at local restaurants. Some don't advertise it but have it available if you ask.
86. See if local museums in your area have cafes. One of the best *al fresco* dining experiences in Cleveland is at the Art Museum where everything on the menu is less than $5.00.

87. Have extra taxes withheld from your pay if you cannot find any other way to save.
88. Consider buying items such as shades and wallpaper mail order. The prices tend to be at least 30% less than retail.
89. Electronics equipment and cameras are often available at the best prices through mail order. Consider paying COD rather than sending a check to insure that you receive your merchandise.
90. Keep track of the prices you pay for items that you use a lot. If you see a special or a warehouse economy size, you will be able to tell quickly if it is really a good buy for you.
91. Don't buy anything just because it is on sale or because you have a coupon for it.
92. Sign up to be on the mailing list for sales at your favorite stores. Often you receive special coupons not otherwise available.
93. If you are buying a large ticket item from a small shop and plan to charge the merchandise, see if they will give you an extra discount for paying cash. The merchant might be willing to split the fee he would otherwise pay to the credit card company on the charge sale.
94. Talk with the sales personnel as you shop. If they know that you are just looking today, they might tell you about an upcoming sale. Ask for their business card and have them call you when other items you want go on sale.
95. Plan ahead for your next picnic. You can make blocks of ice that will last better than the cubes you buy at the grocery.
96. Do your Christmas shopping and mailing early. You will have a wide selection and there will be no need for extra cost on rush delivery.
97. Use postcards when you just want to send a quick note.
98. Know when the cheapest rates are available with your long distance carrier. If you make many long distance calls check with your carrier to see if there are any special plans that would lower your overall bill.
99. Make your information calls from a pay phone while you are out. At this time there are no charges for these calls made from pay phones, whereas you will be charged for long distance and some local information calls made from home. Also, when you are in a hotel it may be cheaper to make your calls from the pay phone in the lobby rather than from your room.
100. Change the location of furniture exposed to light every few months. Also turn over cushions in sofas once in a while to extend their life.
101. Buy fabric paint to create decorative children's clothes from discount store items at a fraction of the cost of specialty shop items.

register
expenses
INCOME
equity
tips
finances
checks
statements
assets
business tips
budget
cash flow
net
pay
taxes
mortgage
dividends
investments
regis
report
equity
INCOME
statements
assets
checks
budget
finances

C H A P T E R

investments banking FILE register expenses DEDUCTIONS
tips finances INCOME equity net pay
checks revenue bank statements
statements business tips
dividends assets
INCOME cash flow
banking business tips FILE reports
budget FILE business tips checks
DEDUCTIONS
statements cash flow tips mortgage
net pay taxes bank revenue
business tips
mortgage cash dividends tips
business tips investments
register statements taxes
business tips
reports expenses tips
equity investments INCOME tips
checks statements bank cash
assets checks budget tips finances net pay

11

SETTING UP QUICKEN FOR YOUR BUSINESS

Many small businesses will find that the Quicken system of record keeping can improve the quality of financial information used in making business decisions. Quicken can be used to record business transactions in your check register while maintaining cost and depreciation records for assets in other registers. Quicken can also be used to budget cash flow, track the cost of jobs in progress, monitor and record payroll, and generate summary tax information to assist in tax return preparation. If you are a contractor, you can track the cost incurred on various jobs as they progress through construction. If you provide landscaping services, you can track the cost incurred for each job and prepare summary reports to determine the profits generated by job. If you are an author, you can use Quicken to monitor royalties by publisher and record the costs incurred in your writing activities.

Even though Quicken improves your ability to record and monitor your business's financial transactions, it may not eliminate the need for accounting services. There are important tax issues that affect the business transactions you record. In addition, you may want your accountant to establish the hierarchy of categories you use to record transactions. This hierarchy, used to categorize all transactions, is called a *chart of accounts*. Your accountant should help establish the structure for your chart of accounts, which will ensure the information is organized to reduce the time required for other services, such as year-end tax preparation, that the accountant will continue to supply. This is particularly important if you will be recording business expenses in both your personal and business checking accounts.

The first section of this book introduced you to the basic features of Quicken. If you completed the exercises in Chapters 6 through 10, you built on the basic skills with split transactions, such as mortgage payments allocated between principal and interest, and with memorization and scheduled transactions. In those chapters you also used Quicken to prepare and monitor budgets, collect tax-related transactions, and prepare customized reports. In the remaining chapters you will look at some of these concepts again, from a business perspective. If you plan to use Quicken for home and business use, you may find it beneficial to read through the earlier chapters, if you haven't done so, rather than moving directly to business transactions. You will also find many tips in these chapters to help you avoid some of the problems encountered by small businesses. The box, "Ten Common Reasons for Business Failure," will identify some of the pitfalls as well as tell you which ones Quicken can help you avoid.

This chapter is longer than the others since there are many decisions you need to make as you begin. There are also a number of basic skills you need to develop to apply Quicken to all aspects of your business. The first step is to consider some alternatives. The next sections provide an overview of two important decisions that must precede all other activities with the package. If you need additional guidance, consult your accountant to be certain your information will be in the format you need for your entire business year.

Ten Common Reasons For Business Failure

Many of the new businesses that start each year fail. To improve your chances of success, you will want to look at some of the more common reasons for business failures and insure that you are addressing these areas in order to prevent problems in your own business. You will notice that Quicken can help you address some of these common problems.

Insufficient Capital

Many businesses fail because they do not properly plan for the capital they will need to get the business started. Quicken can help you put together a budget and plan your cash flow needs.

Pricing Does Not Cover Costs

Many small-business owners do not properly evaluate their costs and set prices too low to cover all expenses. The need to pay a variety of taxes, cover depreciation expense, and pay for expensive repairs are often overlooked when determining pricing for services. Quicken can help you get a handle on all of your costs so you do not make this mistake.

High Fixed Costs

High fixed costs must be paid even in months where sales are low, placing a strain on a small business. Quicken can help you take a look at your fixed costs for rent, car or truck payments, other loan obligations, telephone and utility expense, and fixed salary costs. With the information Quicken can provide, you are better equipped to make decisions to help you lower fixed costs.

Inadequate Accounting Information and Controls

Shoebox record keeping will not serve you well if you are trying to keep your business afloat. The organizational capabilities that Quicken provides make it easy to see which jobs were profitable ventures. The graph features let you get a quick visual look at this information. Quicken also offers some accounting controls such as password protection.

Employee Theft
Inadequate monitoring of employee activities and lack of controls can cause a business owner to inadvertently overlook theft until it is too late. Quicken provides reports and a framework for you to implement controls to help you protect your business assets.

Poor Location
There has to be a need for your product at the location you select. If buyer traffic is unlikely to visit the area selected, your business can be doomed to failure from the beginning. The Small Business Administration and SCORE can provide some help in overcoming problems with site selection.

Lack of Owner Commitment
Many new business owners do not realize that they will have to put in more time in their own business than they did when working for someone else. If family commitments and other responsibilities do not permit this, the business may be in trouble.

No Demand for Product
If there is no demand for your product or you cannot encourage the needed demand, you will not be able to generate the revenues you need to succeed. Adequate marketing research before starting your business is needed to overcome this potential problem.

Lack of Business Knowledge
Knowing the ropes of any business can be an important first step to success. Although you can succeed without it, your chances for success are enhanced with it. The Small Business Administration provides some low-cost seminars that can help you.

Poor Timing
The best conceived idea with adequate funding, a good location, owner commitment and knowledge can still fail due to bad timing. A strong economic decline just as you start your business can cause significant problems for a new business.

Cash Versus Accrual Accounting

The first decision you need to make is the timing of recording financial transactions. You can record a transaction as soon as you know that it will occur, or you can wait until cash changes hands between the parties in the transaction. The former alternative is accrual basis accounting, and the latter is cash basis accounting. There is a third method, called modified cash basis, that is discussed shortly. If your business is organized as a corporation, the accrual method must be used.

Most small businesses use the cash basis because it corresponds to their tax-reporting needs and because the financial reports prepared provide information summarizing the cash-related activities of the business. With *cash basis* accounting, you report income when you receive cash from customers for services you provide. For example, if you are in the plumbing business, you would recognize income when a customer makes payment for services. You might provide the services in December and not receive the customer's check until January. In this case, you would record the income in January, when you received and deposited the customer's check. Similarly, you recognize your expenses when you write your checks for the costs you incurred. Thus, if you ordered supplies in December but didn't pay the bill until January, you would deduct the cost in January when you wrote a check to the supplier. Briefly, with a purely cash basis accounting system, you recognize the income when you receive cash and recognize expenses when you pay for expenses incurred for business purposes.

With the *accrual basis* approach, you record your revenues and expenses when you provide services to your customer, regardless of when the cash flow occurs. Using the plumbing example from the preceding paragraph, you would recognize the income from the plumbing services in December, when you provided the services to the customer, even though the cash would not be received until the next year. Likewise, if you purchased the supplies in December and paid for them in January, the cost of the supplies would be recorded in December, not in January when they were actually paid for. The same information is recorded under both methods.

The basic difference between the cash and accrual bases of accounting is what accountants call *timing differences*. When a cash basis is used, the receipt of cash determines when the transaction is recorded. When the accrual basis is used, the time the services are provided determines when the revenue and expenses are recorded.

A third method of reporting business revenues and expenses is the *modified cash basis* approach. This method uses the cash basis as described but modifies it to report depreciation on certain assets over a number of years. In this case, you must spread the cost of trucks, computer equipment, office furniture, and similar assets over the estimated number of years they will be used to generate income for your business. The Internal Revenue Service has rules for determining the life of an asset. In addition, the tax laws also allow you to immediately deduct the first $10,000 of the acquisition cost of certain qualified assets each year without worrying about depreciation. Once again, these are areas where your accountant could be of assistance in setting up your Quicken accounts.

Whether you use the cash, accrual, or modified cash basis in recording your transactions is determined by a number of factors. Some of the considerations are listed for you in the special "Cash Versus Accrual Methods" section.

Since many small businesses use the modified cash basis of recording revenues and expenses, this method is illustrated in all the examples in Chapters 11 through 15.

Establishing Your Chart of Accounts

You can use the basic set of categories that Quicken provides to categorize your business transactions, or you can create a whole new set. Each of the existing categories will have a name similar to the category options used in earlier chapters. For example, there is a category name of Ads with the description Advertising. In Quicken, these organizational units are called categories despite the fact that you may have been referring to them as accounts in your manual system.

If you do not have an existing chart of accounts, making a few modifications to Quicken's standard category options is the best approach. The names in Quicken's categories are suitable for most businesses. Later in this chapter, you will learn to add a few accounts of your own.

If you already have an existing set of accounts, you will want to retain this structure for consistency. Many businesses assign a number to each category of income or expense, such as using 4001 as the account number for book sales. They may use the first two digits of the number to group asset, liability, income, and expense accounts together. If you have this structure, you will need to invest a little more time initially to establish your chart of accounts. You can delete the entries in the existing list of categories and then add new categories, or you can edit the existing categories one by one. The category names in your category list (chart of accounts) might be numbers, such as 4001 or 5010, and the corresponding descriptions 4001—Book Sales and 5010—Freight, respectively. When you are finished, each category will contain your account number and each description will contain both the account number and text describing the income or expense recorded in the category. You should work through all the examples in this chapter before setting up your own categories.

A Quick Look at the Business Used in the Examples

An overview of the business used for the examples in Chapters 11 through 15 will be helpful in understanding some of the selections made in the exercises. The business is run by an individual and is organized as a sole proprietorship. The individual running the business is married and must file a Form 1040 showing both business income and W2 income earned by the spouse. Income categories in addition to the standard ones provided with Quicken will be needed for the different types of income generated. Since the company in the example offers services rather than merchandise, the income categories will be appropriate for a service-type business. Quicken can also be used for retail or wholesale businesses that sell goods. You can use Quicken for any organization, including sole proprietorships, partnerships, and small corporate entities. Look at the special "Business Organization Options" section for a definition of these three types of businesses.

The business is home-based, which necessitates splitting some expenses, such as utilities and mortgage interest, between home and business categories. Other expenses, such as the purchase of office equipment, are business expenses. A number of expenses incurred by the business do not have appropriate entries in the category list provided by Quicken; this will require adding categories.

The example selected is a little more complicated than a business run from outside the home that has no transactions split between business and personal expenses. When you have a clear separation, you can simply establish a file for all of your business accounts and another file for personal transactions. The example used here has separate checking accounts for business and personal records but places both accounts within one file. The use of separate accounts should be considered almost mandatory. All business income should be deposited into a separate account and all expenses that are completely business related should be paid from this account. Anyone who has experienced an IRS audit can testify to the necessity of having solid documentation for business transactions. One part of that documentation is the maintenance of a business checking account and supporting receipts for your expenses and revenues. If you maintain a separate business account, your bank statement provides the supporting detail for business transactions in a clear and concise manner that supports your documentation of business activities. If your business is so small that it is not feasible to establish and maintain two checking accounts, you will need to be particularly careful when recording entries in your Quicken register.

Quicken Files

When you first used Quicken, you created a file for your data. You named this file QDATA, and Quicken created several files on your disk to manage all the accounts and information within them. You could use this file to record all your transactions if you decide to handle your business and personal financial transactions through a single file.

In the first five chapters, you worked with only one account in QDATA. If you completed Chapters 6 through 10, you learned that it was possible to create additional accounts such as a separate savings account and an investment account. You can also have accounts for credit cards, cash, assets, and liabilities. A PERSONAL file was created in Chapter 6 to organize all the personal accounts.

You could continue to enter the transactions in this chapter in the QDATA file by setting up a new account. However, since you will want to learn how to set up new transactions that are stored in separate files, you should create a new file. You also learn how to create a backup copy of a file to safeguard your data entry.

Adding a New File

If you completed Chapters 1 through 9, you already have files for QDATA, PERSONAL, and INVEST with all of the transactions entered in the first two sections of this book. If you skipped Chapters 6 through 10, you still have only the QDATA file. In this section, you learn how to create a new file and create accounts within it. You need to decide if you want to delete the other files to free the space on your disk. They can be deleted from the Select/Set Up File window when you are finished creating the new file.

You will use a file called BUSINESS and initially set up a business checking account, a personal checking account, and an asset account. The asset account will be used to record information on equipment. Later in this chapter, you will establish other accounts for this file. From the Main Menu, follow these steps to set up the new file and add the first three accounts to this file:

1. Select **F**ile Activities.
2. Select **S**elect/Set Up File.

   Quicken displays the window for selecting or setting up a file. Notice the existing files. If you skipped Chapters 6 through 10, you will only have one file.
3. Select <Set Up New File> and press Enter.

   Quicken opens the window for creating a new file.
4. Type **BUSINESS** as the name for the file and press Enter.

Cash Versus Accrual Methods

Tax Requirements You must decide what your tax reporting obligations are and whether those requirements alone will dictate the method you select for financial reporting. For most small businesses, this is the overriding factor to consider. For instance, if inventories are part of your business, you must use the accrual method for revenues and purchases. If inventories are not a part of your business, you will probably find it best and easiest to use the cash basis of accounting.

Users of the Financial Reports The people who use your financial reports can have a significant influence on your reporting decisions. For example, do you have external users such as banks and other creditors? If so, you may find they require special reports and other financial information that will influence how you set up your accounting and reporting system.

Size and Type of Business Activity The kind of business you have will influence the type of financial reports you need to prepare and the method of accounting you will adopt. Are you in a service, retail, or manufacturing business? Manufacturing concerns will use the accrual method since they have sales that will be billed and collected over weeks or even months and they carry inventories of goods. Retail stores such as small groceries would also use the accrual method of accounting, at least for sales and purchases, since they have inventories that affect the financial reports they will prepare. On the other hand, a small landscaping business will probably use the cash basis since there are no inventories and the majority of the cost associated with the business is payroll and other costs that are generally paid close to the time the services are performed. In this case, the use of business equipment will call for the modified cash basis to record depreciation on the property.

Quicken creates several DOS files from each filename and adds different filename extensions to the name you provide. This means you must provide a valid filename of no more than eight characters. Do not include spaces or special symbols in your entries for filenames.

5. Check the location for your data files and make changes to reference a valid file or directory if a change is required.

   If you use the default directory, yours will display as C:\QUICKEN.

6. Press Enter to complete the creation of the new file.
7. Type **3** to select the Both Home and Business category list and press Enter.

Business Organization Options

The following are the various options you choose when setting up your business.

Sole Proprietorship A sole proprietorship provides no separation between the owner and the business. The debts of the business are the personal liabilities of the owner. The profits of the business are included on the owner's tax return since the business does not pay taxes on profits directly. This form of business organization is the simplest.

Partnership A partnership is a business defined as a relationship between two or more parties. Each person in the partnership is taxed as an individual for his or her share of the profits. A partnership agreement defines the contributions of each member and the distribution of the profits.

Corporation A corporation is an independent business entity. The owners of the corporation are separate from the corporation and do not personally assume the debt of the corporation. This is referred to as *limited liability*. The corporation is taxed on its profits and can distribute the remaining profits to owners as dividends. The owners are taxed on these dividends, resulting in the so-called "double tax" with the corporate structure. Unlike sole proprietorship and partnership businesses, corporations pay salaries to the owners.

S Corporation An S corporation is a special form of corporation that avoids the double tax problem of a regular corporation. A number of strict rules govern when an S corporation can be set up. Some of the limitations are that only one class of stock is permitted and that there is an upper limit of 35 shareholders.

NOTE: You can see the size of all the files you have created here. You can delete some of them at this time if you need to clear disk space.

Quicken redisplays the window for selecting or creating files but shows the BUSINESS file this time.

8. Move the cursor to BUSINESS and press Enter.

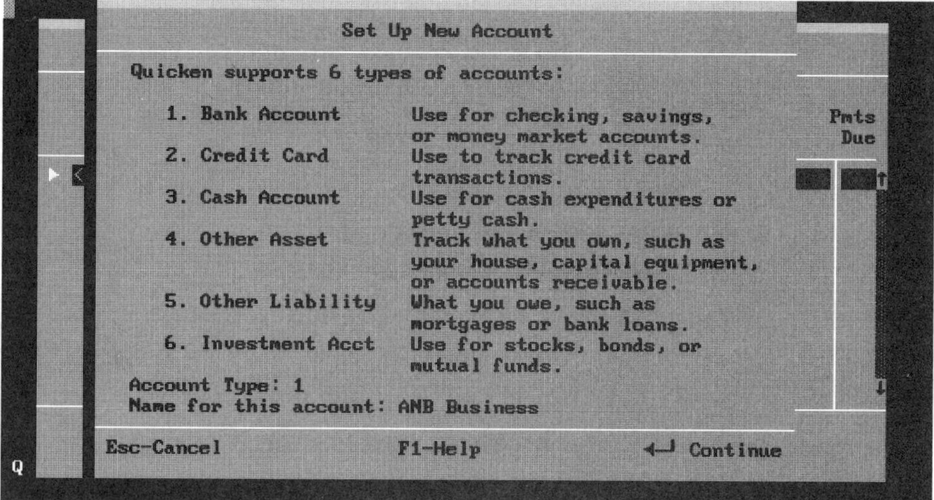

Set Up New Account window
Figure 11-1.

Since this is a new file, Quicken does not have any accounts in the file. The window shown in Figure 11-1 appears to allow you to set up a new account. Leave your screen as it is for a few minutes while you explore some new account options.

Adding Accounts to the New File

Quicken makes it easy to create multiple accounts. All the accounts here will be created in the same file, so you will be able to create one report for all of them as well as print reports for individual accounts. There will be an account register for each account that you create.

Savings accounts, investment accounts, cash accounts, asset accounts, liability accounts, and credit card accounts are all possible additions. Savings accounts and investment accounts should definitely be kept separate from your checking account since you will be interested in monitoring both the growth and balance in these accounts separately. As mentioned earlier, separate business and personal checking accounts are another good idea.

Quicken accounts can be set up to conform to the needs of your business. In this section you will add the first few accounts. In later chapters, additional accounts will be established to monitor other business activities. From the Set Up New Account window, follow these steps to enter the new account:

1. Type **1** to select Bank Account for the account type and press Enter.
2. Type **ANB Business** and press Enter.

ANB represents the bank name and Business indicates that it is the business checking account. Although you could use Cardinal Bank again in this new file, ANB (for American National Bank) will be used to eliminate confusion with the earlier examples.

3. Type **4000** for the balance and press Enter in the Starting Balance and Description window.
4. Type **1/1/94** and press Enter.
5. Type **Business Checking** and press Enter.
6. Select 1 as the source for the starting balance and press Enter twice.
7. Move the arrow cursor to <New Account> and press Enter.
8. Type **1** to select Bank Account and press Enter.
9. Type **ANB Personal** and press Enter.
10. Type **2500** and press Enter.
11. Type **1/1/94** and press Enter.
12. Type **Personal Checking** and press Enter.
13. Select 1 as the source for the starting balance and press Enter twice.
14. Move the arrow cursor to <New Account>, if necessary, and press Enter.
15. Type **4** for Other Asset and press Enter.
16. Type **Equipment** and press Enter twice.

    This account type selection is used to record financial transactions affecting the equipment you use in your business.
17. Type **0** and press Enter.

    You enter the value of these assets later in this chapter.
18. Type **1/1/94** and press Enter.
19. Type **Capital Equipment** and press Enter.

    The Select Account to Use window that looks like Figure 11-2 is displayed.
20. Press Esc twice to return to the Main Menu.

You have now created a new file and three accounts for organizing personal and business transactions.

Changing the Active File

The result of the last exercise was to create another file. You can work in any file at any time and can work with any account within a file. To change from the BUSINESS file to QDATA from the Main Menu, follow these steps:

1. Select **F**ile Activities.
2. Select **S**elect/Set Up File.
3. Select QDATA and press Enter.

   The Select Account to Use window is displayed.
4. Highlight 1st U.S. Bank and press Enter.
5. Press Esc to return to the Main Menu.

The QDATA file is now active. If you went to the register or check writing screen, you would find that the 1st U.S. Bank account was active.

Before continuing, change the file back to BUSINESS and open the account for ANB Business by following the same procedure.

Backing Up a File

You should create backups on a regular basis of the data managed by the Quicken system. This will allow you to recover all your entries in the event of a disk failure since you will be able to use your copy to restore all the entries. You will need a blank formatted disk to record the backup information the first time. Subsequent backups can be made on this disk without reformatting it.

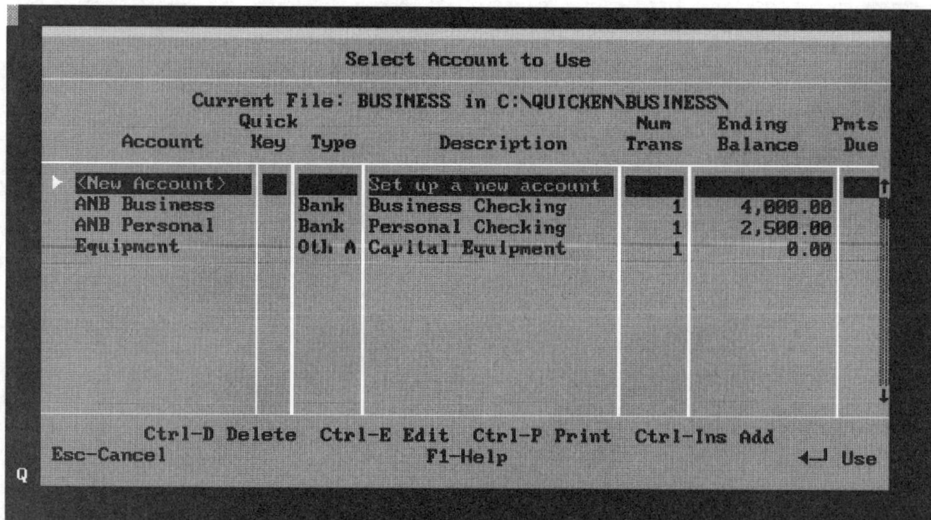

Select Account to Use window
Figure 11-2.

Creating Backup Files

Quicken provides a Backup and Restore feature that allows you to safeguard the investment of time you have made in entering your data. You can back up all your account files from the Print/Acct menu on the register screen. To back up specific files, select the backup option found in the File Activities screen. Follow these steps from the Main Menu to back up the current file:

1. Select **F**ile Activities.
2. Select **B**ack Up File.
3. Place your blank, formatted disk in drive A and then press Enter.
4. Select BUSINESS and press Enter.

   If you use this same name every time you create a backup, the latest copy will always replace the older one as long as you use the same disk.
5. Press Enter to acknowledge the completion of the backup when Quicken displays the successful backup message.
6. Press Esc until the Main Menu displays.
7. Select Use **R**egister to open the register screen, as shown in Figure 11-3, and continue to work in the register.

NOTE: If you ever lose your hard disk, you can re-create your data directory from the File Activities Options by selecting **R**estore File to copy your backup file to the directory. You should schedule backups on a regular basis to minimize the risk of data loss.

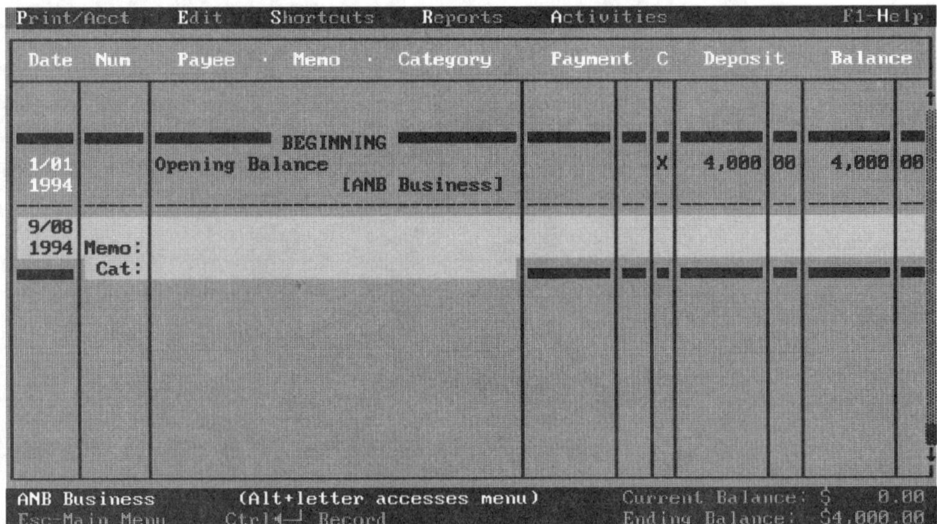

Register for the new account
Figure 11-3.

Customizing Categories

When you set up the new BUSINESS file, you were instructed to select Both Home and Business as the categories option. This selection provides access to the more than 70 category choices shown in Table 11-1. You can see from this table that some categories are listed as expenses and others as income. Notice that some of the expense categories have more detailed subcategories beneath an existing category entry and are labeled Sub in the table. You learn how to create additional subcategories in the "Using Subcategories" section later in this chapter. Note the column in the table that shows you which categories are tax related.

Table 11-1. Category List for a File in the Category Selection of Both

Category	Description	Tax Rel	Type
Bonus	Bonus Income	*	Inc
Canada Pen	Canadian Pension	*	Inc
Div Income	Dividend Income	*	Inc
Gift Received	Gift Received	*	Inc
Gr Sales	Gross Sales	*	Inc
Int Inc	Interest Income	*	Inc
Invest Inc	Investment Income	*	Inc
Old Age Pen	Old Age Pension	*	Inc
Other Inc	Other Income	*	Inc
Rent Income	Rent Income	*	Inc
Salary	Salary Income	*	Inc
Ads	Advertising	*	Expns
Auto	Automobile Expenses		Expns
Fuel	Auto Fuel		Sub
Loan	Auto Loan Payment		Sub
Service	Auto Service		Sub
Bank Chrg	Bank Charge		Expns
Bus. Insurance	Non-health insurance	*	Expns
Bus. Utilities	Water, Gas, Electric	*	Expns
Business Tax	Licences & Taxes	*	Expns
Car	Car & Truck	*	Expns

Category	Description	Tax Rel	Type
Charity	Charitable Donations	*	Expns
Cash	Cash donations	*	Sub
Non-cash	Goods & services donations	*	Sub
Childcare	Childcare Expense		Expns
Christmas	Christmas Expense		Expns
Clothing	Clothing		Expns
Commission	Commissions	*	Expns
Dining	Dining Out		Expns
Dues	Dues		Expns
Education	Education		Expns
Entertain	Entertainment		Expns
Freight	Freight	*	Expns
Gifts	Gift Expenses		Expns
Groceries	Groceries		Expns
Home Rpair	Home Repair & Maint.		Expns
Household	Household Misc. Exp		Expns
Housing	Housing		Expns
Insurance	Insurance		Expns
Int Exp	Interest Expense	*	Expns
Int Paid	Interest Paid	*	Expns
Invest Exp	Investment Expense	*	Expns
L&P Fees	Legal & Prof. Fees	*	Expns
Late Fees	Late Payment Fees	*	Expns
Meals & Entertn	Entertainment & meals	*	Expns
Medical	Medical & Dental	*	Expns
Doctor	Doctor visits	*	Sub
Medicine	Prescription charges	*	Sub
Misc	Miscellaneous		Expns
Mort Int	Mortgage Interst Exp.	*	Expns
Office	Office Expenses	*	Expns

Category List for a File in the Category Selection of Both (*cont.*)
Table 11-1.

Category	Description	Tax Rel	Type
Other Exp	Other Expense	*	Expns
Recreation	Recreation Expense		Expns
Rent on Equip	Equipment rental	*	Expns
Rent Paid	Rent Paid	*	Expns
Repairs	Repairs	*	Expns
Returns	Returns & Allowances	*	Expns
RRSP	Reg. Retirement Sav. Plan		Expns
Subscriptions	Subscriptions		Expns
Supplies	Supplies	*	Expns
Supplies, bus.	Supplies	*	Expns
Tax	Taxes	*	Expns
Fed	Federal Tax	*	Sub
Medicare	Medicare Tax	*	Sub
Other	Misc. Taxes	*	Sub
Prop	Property Tax	*	Sub
Soc Sec	Soc Sec Tax	*	Sub
State	State Tax	*	Sub
Tax Spouse	Taxes for Spouse	*	Expns
Fed	Federal Tax	*	Sub
Medicare	Medicare Tax	*	Sub
Soc Sec	Soc Sec Tax	*	Sub
State	State Tax	*	Sub
Telephone	Telephone Expense		Expns
Travel	Travel Expense	*	Expns
UIC	Unemploy. Ins. Commission	*	Expns
Utilities	Water, Gas, Electricity		Expns
Gas & Electric	Gas and Electricity		Sub
Water	Water		Sub
Wages	Wages & Job Credits	*	Expns

Category List for a File in the Category Selection of Both (*cont.*)
Table 11-1.

Editing the Existing Category List

You can change the name of any existing category, change its classification as income, expense, or a subcategory, or change your assessment of its being tax related. To make a change to a category follow these steps.

1. Press Ctrl-C from the register to display the category list.
2. Move the arrow cursor to the category you want to change.
3. Press Ctrl-E to edit the information for the category.
4. Change the fields you wish to alter.
5. Press Ctrl-Enter to complete the changes.

If you change the name of the category, Quicken will automatically and simultaneously update any transactions that have already been assigned to the category.

If you need to totally restructure the categories, you may find it easier to delete the old categories and add new ones with the instructions in the next section. To delete a category, follow these steps:

1. Press Ctrl-C from the register to display the category list.
2. Move the arrow cursor to the category you want to delete.
3. Press Ctrl-D to delete the information in the category.

   You should not delete categories already assigned to transactions. If you do, you delete that part of the transactions in your register. Make any changes in which you delete categories before you start recording transactions.
4. Press Ctrl-Enter to complete the changes.

Adding Categories

You can add categories to provide additional options specific to your needs. Each type of business will probably have some unique categories of income or expenses. For the example in this chapter, both income and expense category additions are needed.

The business in this example has three sources of business income: consulting fees, royalties, and income earned for writing articles. It would be inappropriate to use the salary category since this should be reserved for income earned from a regular employer (reported on Form W2 at year-end). You could use the Gross Sales category to record the various types of income for the business. Another solution would be to create new categories for each income source. The examples in this chapter use three new income categories.

Many of the existing expense categories are suitable for recording business expenses, but for this example additional expense categories are needed. Equipment maintenance, computer supplies, and overnight mail service categories are needed. Although a category already exists for freight, a more specific postage category is also needed. New categories are not needed to record computer and office equipment and furniture purchases. These will be handled through an "other asset" type account, with the specific purchase listed in the Payee field to the transaction.

You can add a new category by entering it in the Category field when recording a transaction in a register or on a check writing screen. Pressing Enter to record the transaction will cause Quicken to indicate that the category does not exist in the current list. You are then given the choice of selecting another category already in the list or adding the new category to the list. You would choose to add it, just as you did with the category for auto loans in Chapter 4, "Reconciling Your Quicken Register."

If you have a number of categories to add, it is simpler to add them before starting data entry. To use this approach to add the new categories needed for the exercises in this chapter, follow these steps:

1. Press Ctrl-C (or select **S**hortcuts and then select **C**ategorize/Transfer).

   Either one will open the Category and Transfer List window.

2. Press Home to move to the top of the category list.

   <New Category> is the top entry in the list.

3. Select <New Category>.

   Quicken will allow you to enter a new category using the window shown here which already contains the entries for the new royalty income category:

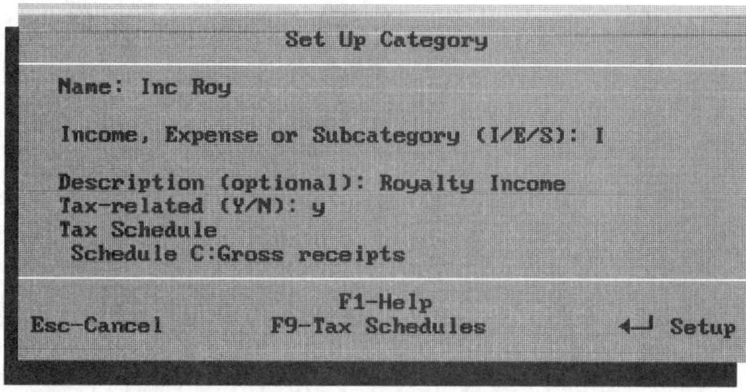

The new royalty income category is called "Inc Roy." Note the use of Inc first in the category name. This allows you to later select all income categories by entering **Inc** in your report filter window (see Chapter 3, "Quicken Reports").

4. Type **Inc Roy** and press Enter.
5. Type **I** and press Enter.
6. Type **Royalty Income** and press Enter.
7. Type **Y** and press F9 (Tax Schedules).

Quicken presents a Tax Schedule window that looks like this:

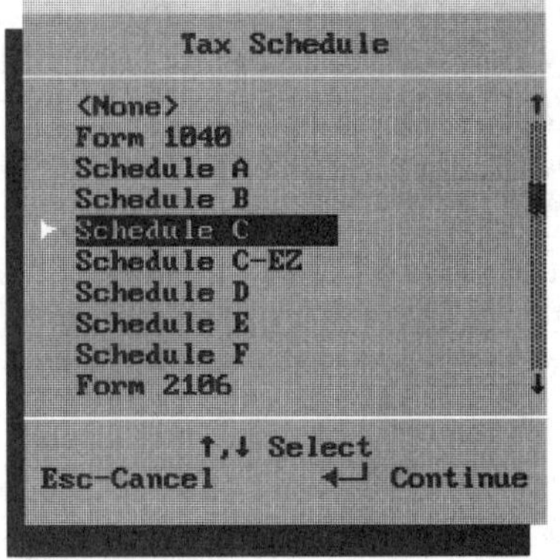

8. Select Schedule C and press Enter.

   A Tax Line window that displays Schedule C lines by name is shown here:

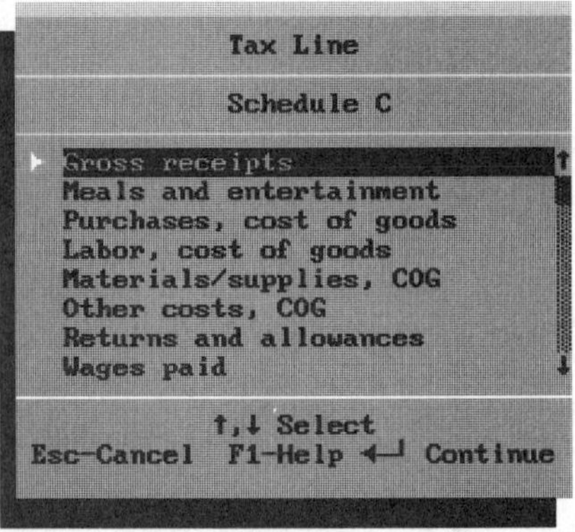

9. Select Gross Receipts and press Enter.

10. Select Copy 1 and press Enter.

    If you prepare multiple copies of a schedule, Quicken allows you to select different copies.

11. Press Enter to have Quicken return you to the Category and Transfer List window.

12. Repeat steps 3 through 11 for each of the categories that follow. Use the abbreviations shown to conform with the length limitations for names. When you are finished, press Esc to return to the Register window.

    Name: Inc Cons
    Income: I
    Description: Consulting Income
    Tax Related: Y
    Tax Schedule: Schedule C: Gross receipts

    Name: Inc Art
    Income: I
    Description: Article Income
    Tax Related: Y
    Tax Schedule: Schedule C: Gross receipts

    Name: Equip Mnt
    Expense: E
    Description: Equipment Maintenance
    Tax Related: Y
    Tax Schedule: Schedule C: Repairs and maintenance

    Name: Supp Comp
    Expense: E
    Description: Computer Supplies
    Tax Related: Y
    Tax Schedule: Schedule C: Supplies

    Name: Postage
    Expense: E
    Description: Postage Expense
    Tax Related: Y
    Tax Schedule: Schedule C: Other business expense

Name:	Del Overngt
Expense:	E
Description:	Overnight Delivery
Tax Related:	Y
Tax Schedule:	Schedule C: Other business expense

You should feel free to customize Quicken by adding any categories you need. However, be aware that available random-access memory limits the number of categories you can create in each category list. With a 512K system, approximately 1000 categories can be created.

Requiring Categories in All Transactions

Another customization option Quicken offers is a reminder that a category should be entered for each transaction before it is recorded. If you attempt to record a transaction without a category, Quicken will not complete the process until you confirm that you want the transaction added without a category.

To utilize Quicken's warning when you attempt to finalize transactions without a category entry, choose Set **P**references from the Main Menu and then select **T**ransaction Settings. Select the fourth item in the Transaction Settings window, "Warn if a transaction has no category," and type **Y**. Press Ctrl-Enter to finalize the settings change. The next time you attempt to record a transaction without a category, Quicken will stop to confirm your choice before saving.

Using Classes

Classes are another way of organizing transactions. They allow you to define the who, when, or why of a transaction. It is important to understand that although they, too, allow you to group data, classes are distinct from categories. You will continue to use categories to provide specific information about the transactions to which they are assigned. Categories tell you what kind of income or expense a specific transaction represents. You can tell at a glance which costs are for utilities and which are for entertainment. In summary reports, you might show transactions totaled by category.

Classes allow you to slice the transaction pie in a different way. They provide a different view or perspective of your data. For example, you can continue to organize data in categories such as Utilities or Snow Removal yet also classify it by the property requiring the service. Classes were not needed in the earlier chapters of this book since categories provide all the organization you need for very basic transactions. But if you want to combine home and business transactions in one file, classes are essential for differentiating between the two types of transactions. Here, every transaction you enter will be classified as either personal or business. Business transactions will have a class entered after the category. By omitting the class entry from personal transactions, you classify them as personal. Class assignments can be used without category assignments, but in this chapter they are used in addition to categories.

Defining Classes

Quicken does not provide a standard list of classes. As with categories, you can set up what you need before you start making entries, or you can add the classes you need as you enter transactions. To assign a class while entering a transaction, you type the class name in the Category field after the category name (if one is used). A slash (/) must be typed before the class name.

NOTE: Even though Quicken 7 has separate Home & Business categories, classes may be used to distinguish utility expense allocated to business versus home use, and to distinguish among different business locations for supplies purchased. Since classes are useful when filtering the data to be shown on a report, you might find it simpler to use the approach shown here and reduce the number of categories needed.

To create a class before entering a transaction, follow these steps from the account register to add a class for business:

1. Press Ctrl-L to open the Class List window.
2. Press Enter with the arrow cursor on <New Class>. Quicken displays the Set Up Class window, shown here:

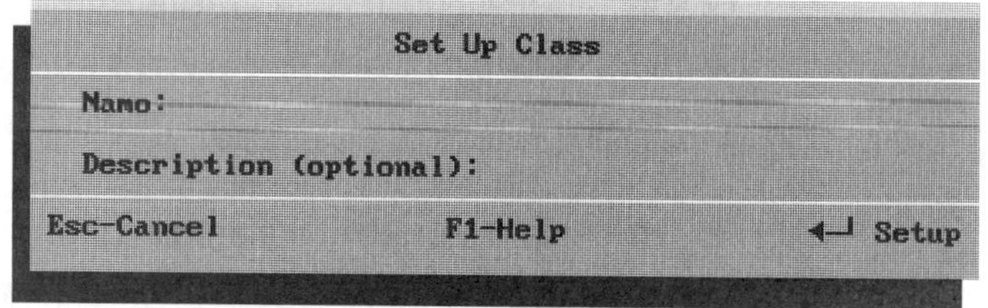

3. Type **B** and press Enter.

   You can use a longer entry, such as Business, but you are limited in the number of characters used to display categories, classes, and other organizational groupings, so you should keep it as short as possible.

11

4. Type **Business** and press Enter.

   Quicken completes the entry for the first class and adds it to the list in the Class List window. You could create a second class for personal transactions, but it is not really necessary. You can consider any transaction without a class of B to be personal.

5. Press Esc to return to the Register window.

Each new class is added to the Class List window.

REMEMBER: To create a class as you enter a transaction, simply type the category followed by a slash (/) and the class you want to use, and then press Enter.

6. Move the highlight to the opening balance transaction.
7. Tab to the Category field; then press the End key.
8. Type **/B**.
9. Press Ctrl-Enter to record the changed entry.

Entering Transactions with Classes

You record the business transaction in the same manner as earlier transactions. It is important that you remember to enter the class in the Category field. Follow these instructions:

1. Press Home twice to move the Date field.
2. Type **1/2/94** and press Enter twice.
3. Type **Arlo, Inc.** and press Enter three times.
4. Type **12500** in the Deposit field and press Enter.
5. Type **Seminars conducted in Nov. 93** and press Enter.
6. Type **Inc Cons/B**.

   The first part of this entry categorizes the transaction as consulting income. The slash (/) and the B classify the transaction as business related.

   When you start to record this category Quicken 7 uses its QuickFill feature to assist you in entering the transaction. In this case Quicken supplies the category Inc Art. You can easily move to the desired category by pressing the Ctrl-+ or Ctrl-- keys to move through the list of categories that match the letter I that you entered since Quicken reveals all the expense and income categories that begin with I. If your category is not on the standard list you need to add it as you did earlier in this chapter. You can always continue to type the entire category entry without using QuickFill's suggestions and complete the transactions.

7. Press Ctrl-Enter to record the transaction. Your screen looks like the one shown here:

```
1/01        Opening Balance                                X   4,000 00    4,000 00
1994                            [ANB Business]→
1/02        Arlo, Inc.                                        12,500 00   16,500 00
1994  Memo: Seminars conducted in Nov. 93
       Cat: Inc Cons/B
```

You can record an expense transaction in the ANB Business account in a similar fashion. Follow these instructions:

1. Type **1/2/94** and press Enter.
2. Type **101** and press Enter.
3. Type **Office All** and press Enter.
4. Type **65** and press Enter.
5. Type **Cartridge for copier** and press Enter.
6. Type **Su** then press Ctrl-+ to highlight Supplies.
7. Type **/B** and press Ctrl-Enter.

The Register window matches the one in Figure 11-4.

The next transaction is for clothing. Since this is a personal expense paid with a personal check, it cannot be added to the current account. You must open the ANB Personal account for your entry. Follow these steps:

1. Press Esc to return to the Main Menu.
2. Choose Select **A**ccount.
3. Select ANB Personal and press Enter.

When you enter the transaction for the clothing, the fact that you are not using a class will indicate that it is a personal expense. Although you could have created another class, called P, for personal entries, the approach used here minimizes typing; only business transactions require the extra entry. Follow these steps to add the transaction:

1. Type **1/3/94** and press Enter.
2. Type **825** and press Enter.

This check number is not sequential with the last business check used since it is in your personal account.

3. Type **Discount Coats** and press Enter.
4. Type **120** and press Enter.
5. Type **New winter coat** and press Enter.
6. Type **Clothing**.

   Notice that no slash (/) is used since a class is not being added for personal expenses.
7. Press Ctrl-Enter to record the transaction. Your entries should match the ones shown here:

1/01 1994		Opening Balance [ANB Personal]			X	2,500	00	2,500	00
1/03 1994	825	Discount Coats New winter coat Clothing	120	00				2,380	00

Splitting Transactions

Split transactions are transactions that affect more than one category or class. You decide how a transaction affects each of the categories or category-class combinations involved. If you split an expense transaction,

```
Print/Acct   Edit   Shortcuts   Reports   Activities                F1-Help
Date  Num   Payee · Memo · Category      Payment  C  Deposit    Balance
                       BEGINNING
1/01        Opening Balance                       X   4,000 00   4,000 00
1994                        [ANB Business]→
1/02        Arlo, Inc.                               12,500 00  16,500 00
1994        Seminars conduc→Inc Cons/B
1/02  101   Office All                   65 00                  16,435 00
1994        Cartridge for c→Supplies/B
1/02
1994  Memo:
       Cat:
ANB Business        (Alt+letter accesses menu)     Current Balance: $      0.00
Esc-Main Menu      Ctrl◄┘ Record                  Ending Balance:  $16,435.00
```

Recording business transactions in the Register window

Figure 11-4.

you are saying that a portion of the transaction should be considered as an expense in two different categories or classes. For example, a purchase at an office products store might include school supplies for your children and products for the office. You need to know exactly how much was spent for personal versus business expenses in this transaction. Many expenses can be part business and part personal, especially if you operate a business from your home. Quicken allows you to allocate the amount of any transaction among different categories or classes with a special Split Transaction window. Before using the Split Transaction feature, you can define categories more precisely with the Subcategory feature, explained in the next section.

Quicken displays a Split Transaction window for entries in the Category field if you press Ctrl-S. You can enter different categories or classes for each part of the transaction with this method. Even though the largest portion of the following expense was for business, it was paid with a personal check and so must be recorded in the ANB Personal account. Follow these steps to complete an entry for the purchase at Campus Stationery, which includes both personal and office supply expenses:

1. Type **1/3/94** and press Enter.
2. Type **826** and press Enter.
3. Type **Campus Stationery** and press Enter.
4. Type **82** and press Enter.
5. Type **New calendar and computer paper** and press Enter.
6. Press Ctrl-S to activate the Split Transaction window.
7. Type **Sup,** to have QuickFill display Supp Comp, then type **/B**. Press Enter.
8. Type **Paper for laser printer** and press Enter.

   Quicken displays the entire amount of the transaction in the Amount field but adjusts it as you make a new entry.
9. Type **75.76** and press Enter.

   Quicken subtracts this amount from $82.00 and displays the amount remaining on the next line.
10. Type **Mi** to have QuickFill display Misc and press Enter.
11. Type **New calendar for kitchen**.

    This completes the entries since $6.24 is the cost of the calendar. Your screen should look like the one in Figure 11-5.
12. Press Ctrl-Enter to close the Split Transaction window.
13. Press Ctrl-Enter to record the transaction.

The register entry looks like this:

```
1/03 826   Campus Stationery                        82 00                  2,298 00
1994 SPLIT New calendar and computer paper
     Cat:  Supp Comp/B
```

NOTE: Quicken 7 offers some new options for splitting transactions. It can add the split details to produce one total, and it can allocate an expense between multiple categories based on percentages that you enter. You will look at these options in the next section.

Using Subcategories and the Percentage Split Option

Since you are quickly becoming proficient at basic transaction entry, you will want to see some other options for recording transactions. One new option is to create subcategories of an existing category. These subcategories further define a category. Unlike classes, which use a different perspective for organizing transactions, subcategories provide a more detailed breakdown of the existing category. For instance, you could continue to allocate all your utility bills to the Utilities category but create subcategories that allow you to allocate expenses to electricity, water, or gas. You will still be able to classify

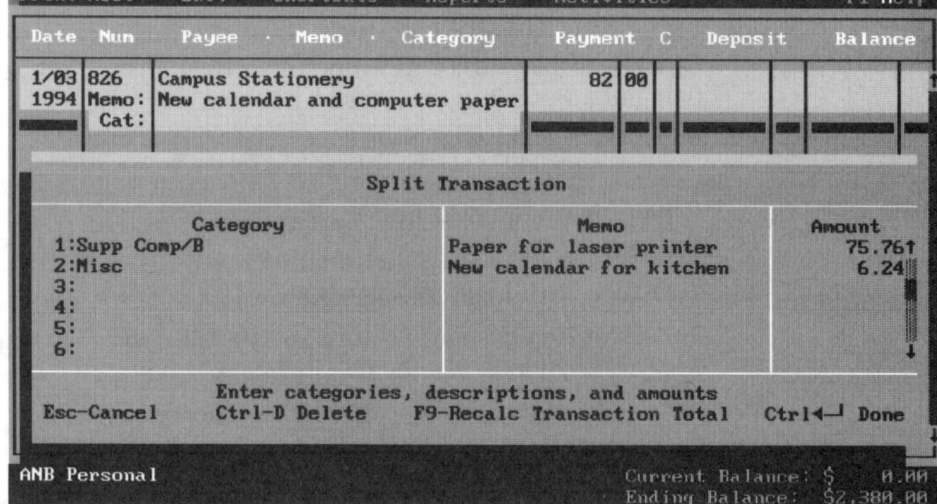

Split Transaction window for Campus Stationery transaction
Figure 11-5.

these transactions as either business or personal expenses using the classes you established.

You can add the subcategories by modifying the category list, as when you add new categories, or you can create them as you enter transactions and realize the existing category entries do not provide the breakdown you want.

Once you establish subcategories, you might want to try some of Quicken 7's new split features that allow you to allocate by percentages.

Entering a New Subcategory

When you enter a subcategory for a transaction, you type the category name, followed by a colon (:), and then the subcategory name. It is important that the category be specified first and the subcategory second. If a transaction has a class assigned, the class name comes third in the sequence, with a slash (/) as the divider.

The business used in this example is run from the home of the owner, which necessitates the splitting of certain expenses between business and personal. As long as other tax requirements are met, tax guidelines state that the percentage of the total square footage in the home that is used exclusively for business can be used to determine the portion of common expenses, such as utilities, allocated to the business. The business in these examples occupies 20 percent of the total square footage in the home. You can use Quicken's Percentage Split feature or Quicken's Calculator to perform these computations and use both subcategories and split transactions to record the first transactions.

Enter the utility bills in the new account. Follow these steps to complete the entries for the gas and electric bills, creating a subcategory under Utilities for each, and allocating 20 percent of each utility bill to business by splitting the transactions between classes:

1. With the next blank transaction in the register highlighted, type **1/3/94** as the date for the transaction.
2. Type **827** and press Enter. You can also press + to have Quicken record the next check for you.
3. Type **Consumer Power** and press Enter.
4. Type **80.00** for the payment amount and press Enter.
5. Type **Electric Bill** and then press Enter.

   The cursor is now in the Category field.
6. Press Ctrl-S to open the Split Transaction window.
7. Type **Ut** to match Utilities then type **:Electric/B** and press Enter.

Quicken prompts you with the Category Not Found window. Quicken has a subcategory for Gas and Electric but not one for just electric. You will set up a new category and later modify the existing one to allow you to track your gas bills separately. Notice that only Electric is highlighted in the Category field since Quicken already has Utilities in the category list and B in the class list.

8. Select Add to Category List. Quicken displays the Set Up Category window for you to define the category.
9. Type **S** to define the entry as a subcategory and then press Enter.

   A note may be displayed by Quicken prompting you to be sure you understand what you are doing since subcategories are considered an advanced technique.
10. Type **Electric Utilities** and press Enter.

    Although this description is optional, it is a good idea to enter one so that your reports will be informative.
11. Type **Y** and press F9 (Tax Schedules).
12. Select Schedule C and press Enter; a Tax Line window appears.
13. Select Utilities and press Enter.
14. Select Copy:1 and press Enter.
15. Press Enter.

    The Set Up Category window shown here should match the one on your screen:

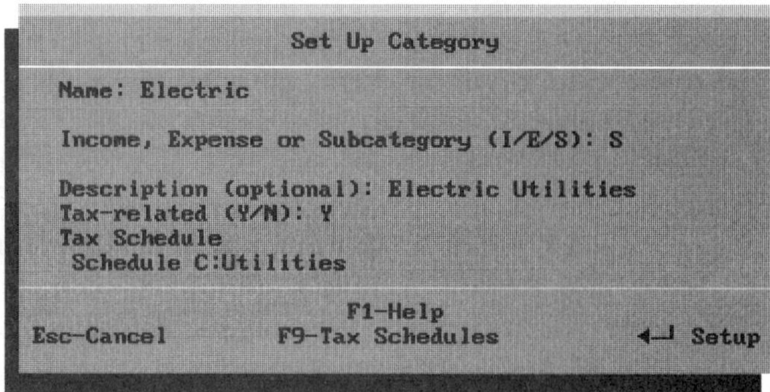

16. Press Enter twice to close the window and move to the Memo field in the Split Transaction window.
17. Type **Business portion of elect** and press Enter.
18. Type **20%** and press Enter to multiply the amount entered earlier by .20.

19. Press Enter to move to the next line.
20. Type **Ut** to display a match with Utilities, then type **:E** to match with Electric and press Enter.

    Note that a class was not added to the entry so Quicken will consider the entry a personal expense.
21. Type **Home portion of electric** and press Enter.

    The Split Transaction window looks like the one in Figure 11-6; Quicken has computed the difference between $80.00 and $16.00 and displayed it in the Amount field.

NOTE: You can use the Percentage Split feature when you are allocating between categories, subcategories, or classes. It works the same way regardless of how you are making the split.

22. Press Ctrl-Enter to close the Split Transaction window.
23. Press Ctrl-Enter to record the transaction entry.

The transaction displays in the Register window, as shown here:

```
1/03 827   Consumer Power                      80 00            2,218 00
1994 SPLIT Electric Bill   Utilities:Elec→
```

Completing the Utility Subcategories

You have one more utility bill to enter. The one for gas utilities requires an edit to the existing Gas & Electric subcategory. Complete the following steps


```
                         Split Transaction
          Category                      Memo                      Amount
 1:Utilities:Electric/B        Business portion of elect          16.00
 2:Utilities:Electric          Home portion of electric           64.00
 3:
 4:
 5:
 6:
               Enter categories, descriptions, and amounts
Esc-Cancel     Ctrl-D Delete     F9-Recalc Transaction Total   Ctrl←┘ Done
```

Split Transaction window for electric utilities
Figure 11-6.

to modify an existing subcategory, use it for the gas bill and complete the transaction entry.

1. Enter the following information in each of the fields shown:

Date:	1/7/94
Check:	828
Payee:	Western Michigan Gas
Payment:	40.00
Memo:	Gas Bill

2. After completing the Memo field entry, press Ctrl-S to request the Split Transaction window.

   Quicken's default categories originally included the subcategories Gas & Electric and Utilities:Water. Since you already have a subcategory established for electric, you will want to modify Gas & Electric for use with Gas Utilities.
3. Press Ctrl-C to display the Category Transfer List window.
4. Highlight Utilities: Gas & Electric.
5. Press Ctrl-E to edit the current category.
6. Change the name on the Edit Category screen to Gas and press Enter.
7. Type **S** to define the entry as a subcategory and then press Enter.
8. Type **Gas Utilities** and press Enter.
9. Type **Y** and press F9 (Tax Schedules).
10. Select Schedule C and press Enter.
11. Select Utilities and press Enter.
12. Select Copy:1 and press Enter.
13. Press Enter.
14. Press Enter, type **/B** and press Enter.
15. Type **Business portion gas bill** and press Enter.
16. Type **20**% and press Enter. Quicken will display 8, the result.
17. Press Enter to move to the next line.
18. Type **Ut** to see QuickFill display Utilities, then type **:G** and press Enter.
19. Type **Home portion gas bill** and press Enter.
20. Press Ctrl-Enter to close the Split Transaction window.
21. Press Ctrl-Enter to record the transaction entry.

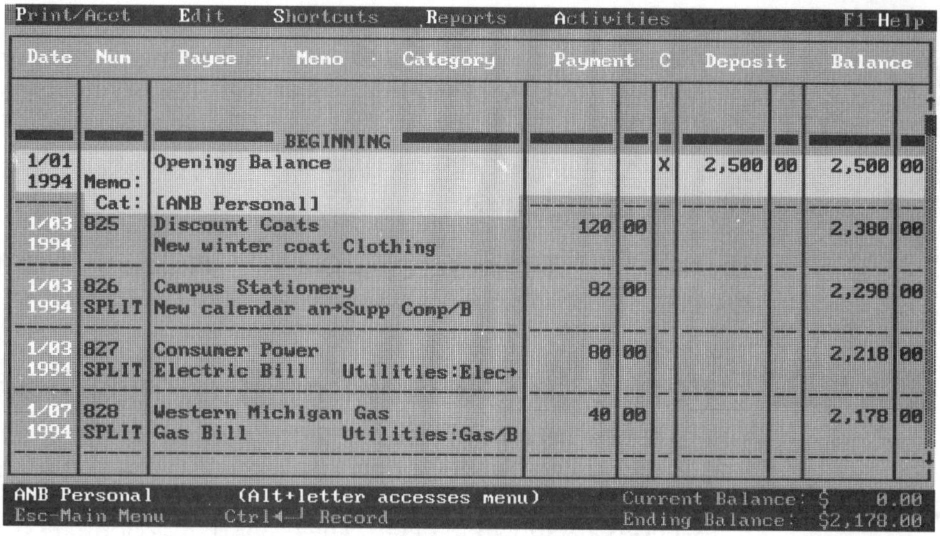

```
Print/Acct   Edit   Shortcuts   Reports   Activities                F1-Help
Date  Num    Payee  · Memo  · Category     Payment  C  Deposit    Balance
                  BEGINNING
1/01         Opening Balance                        X  2,500 00   2,500 00
1994  Memo:
      Cat:   [ANB Personal]
1/03  825    Discount Coats                  120 00               2,380 00
1994         New winter coat Clothing
1/03  826    Campus Stationery                82 00               2,298 00
1994  SPLIT  New calendar an→Supp Comp/B
1/03  827    Consumer Power                   80 00               2,218 00
1994  SPLIT  Electric Bill    Utilities:Elec→
1/07  828    Western Michigan Gas             40 00               2,178 00
1994  SPLIT  Gas Bill         Utilities:Gas/B
ANB Personal        (Alt+letter accesses menu)      Current Balance: $      0.00
Esc-Main Menu      Ctrl←┘ Record                    Ending Balance:  $2,178.00
```

Register entries in ANB Personal account

Figure 11-7.

If you press Ctrl-Home to move to the top of the register, your entries will look like the ones in Figure 11-7.

Letting Quicken Total the Split Detail for You

If you leave the register amount blank when you enter a split transaction Quicken can add the split detail and fill it in for you. Each new entry in the split area will increase the amount displayed in the register Amount field. You can try this with a transaction for three items from the computer outlet.

1. Press Esc to return to the Main Menu.
2. Choose Select **A**ccount.
3. Select ANB Business.
4. Type **1/8/94** and press Enter.
5. Type **102** and press Enter.
6. Type **Computer Outlet** and press Enter four times to move to the Memo field.
7. Type **Cartridges, ribbons, disks** and press Enter.
8. Press Ctrl-S to open the Split Transaction window.

   The same category and class will be used for each transaction entered in this window. The transaction is split to provide additional documentation for purchases.

9. Complete the entries in the Split Transaction window as shown in Figure 11-8. You will need to enter a minus sign (–) in front of each amount to tell Quicken that you are totaling payments rather than deposits.

   You will notice that the Payment field now reads 300.00.
10. Press Ctrl-Enter twice.

The first time you press Ctrl-Enter, Quicken will close the Split Transaction window. The second time, Quicken will record the transaction.

Entering the Remaining Business Transactions

You have now been introduced to all the skills needed to enter transactions that affect either a business or personal account. You should, however, complete the remaining transactions for January. Keystrokes for split transactions are shown in detail. The other transactions are shown in summary form; each field in which you need to enter data is shown with the entry for that field.

1. Enter the following transactions by completing the entries in the fields shown and pressing Ctrl-Enter after each transaction:

Date:	1/15/94
Num:	103
Payee:	Quick Delivery
Payment:	215.00
Memo:	Manuscript Delivery
Category:	Del Overngt/B

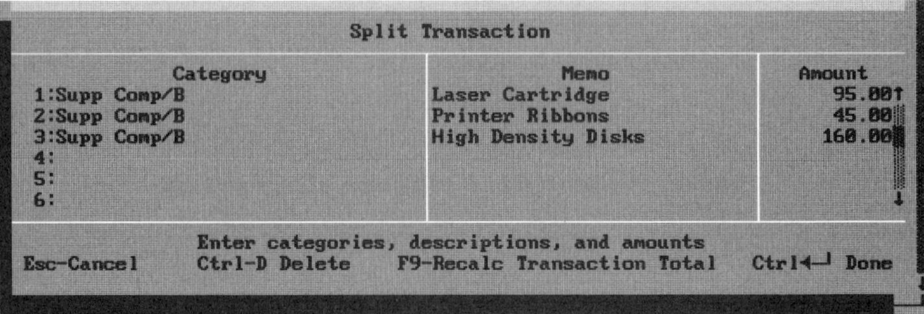

Split Transaction
Category
1:Supp Comp/B
2:Supp Comp/B
3:Supp Comp/B
4:
5:
6:
Memo
Laser Cartridge
Printer Ribbons
High Density Disks
Amount
95.00
45.00
160.00
Enter categories, descriptions, and amounts
Esc-Cancel
Ctrl-D Delete
F9-Recalc Transaction Total
Ctrl↵ Done

Splitting the cash transaction for office supplies
Figure 11-8.

Date:	1/15/94
Num:	104
Payee:	Safety Airlines
Payment:	905.00
Memo:	February Ticket
Category:	Travel/B

Date:	1/20/94
Num:	105
Payee:	Alltel
Payment:	305.00
Memo:	Telephone Bill
Category:	Telephone/B

2. Enter the beginning of this transaction as follows:

Date:	1/20/94
Num:	106
Payee:	Postmaster
Payment:	28.25
Memo:	Postage for Mailing

3. Press Ctrl-S with the cursor in the Category field.
4. Complete the entries shown on the Split Transaction window in Figure 11-9.
5. Press Ctrl-Enter twice.

   If you press ↑ several times you will see that the entries in your register match the ones in Figure 11-10.
6. Complete this transaction to record a maintenance expense for existing equipment:

Date:	1/22/94
Num:	107
Payee:	Fix-It-All
Payment:	1100.00
Memo:	Equipment Contract
Category:	Equip Mnt/B

7. Press Ctrl-Enter to record the transaction.

```
                         Split Transaction
            Category                           Memo                     Amount
 1:Postage/B                    Mail Teach Yourself dBASE               27.96
 2:Postage/B                    Mail Bill                                0.29
 3:
 4:
 5:
 6:
               Enter categories, descriptions, and amounts
 Esc-Cancel    Ctrl-D Delete    F9-Recalc Transaction Total    Ctrl↵ Done
```

Splitting the postage transaction
Figure 11-9.

The only remaining transactions relate to equipment. You will need to use the Equipment account you created earlier to handle these transactions.

Using the Other Asset Account

Earlier in the chapter, you established an other asset type account called Equipment. You will be able to use this account to track total equipment holdings and depreciation expense. Purchase transactions for equipment will be recorded in your business checking account register as a transfer to the Equipment account. Other transactions, such as entering information on equipment purchased before you started using Quicken and a depreciation transaction, will be entered directly in this other asset register. In the next

```
Print/Acct   Edit   Shortcuts   Reports   Activities                    F1-Help
 Date  Num    Payee · Memo · Category          Payment  C  Deposit    Balance
 1/02  101   Office All                          65 00                16,435 00
 1994  Memo: Cartridge for copier
       Cat:  Supplies/B
 1/08  102   Computer Outlet                    300 00                16,135 00
 1994  SPLIT Cartridges, rib→Supp Comp/B
 1/15  103   Quick Delivery                     215 00                15,920 00
 1994        Manuscript Deli→Del Overngt/B
 1/15  104   Safety Airlines                    905 00                15,015 00
 1994        February Ticket Travel/B
 1/20  105   Alltel                             305 00                14,710 00
 1994        Telephone Bill  Telephone/B
 1/20  106   Postmaster                          28 25                14,681 75
 1994  SPLIT Postage for Mai→Postage/B
ANB Business        (Alt+letter accesses menu)      Current Balance: $      0.00
Esc-Main Menu       Ctrl↵ Record                    Ending Balance:  $14,681.75
```

Register entries in ANB Business account
Figure 11-10.

section, you look at recording transactions for existing equipment and a new purchase. In Chapter 14, "Organizing Tax Information and Other Year-End Needs," you learn how to record depreciation expense as the asset ages and declines in value.

Recording Transactions for Existing Equipment Holdings

The existing equipment cannot be recorded as a purchase since you do not want to affect the balance in the business checking account. You need to make the transaction entry directly in the Equipment account. Note that the fields are somewhat different in this type of account compared to previous account registers, as shown in Figure 11-11. Follow these steps to record the equipment:

1. Press Esc to return to the Main Menu.
2. Choose Select **A**ccount.
3. Select the Equipment account.
4. Type **1/1/94** in the Date field and press Enter twice.
5. Type **High Tech Computer** to enter the name of the asset in the Payee field.

   You can record an inventory number as part of this entry if one is assigned.
6. Press Enter three times.
7. Type **3000** and press Enter to record the original purchase price in the Increase field.
8. Type **Original cost of equipment** and press Enter.
9. Type **Equipment/B** and press Ctrl-Enter.

Quicken will display the category as [Equipment] since the category is an account name and will increase the balance of the account. (The brackets are always added when an account name is added in the Category field.)

To change the book value of the asset, another adjusting transaction is required. This transaction reduces the book value by the amount of the depreciation expense recognized last year. It must be recorded against the Equipment account rather than as a depreciation expense, or the amount of the depreciation for last year will appear in this year's expense reports. You do not want to record the depreciation expense in your checking account

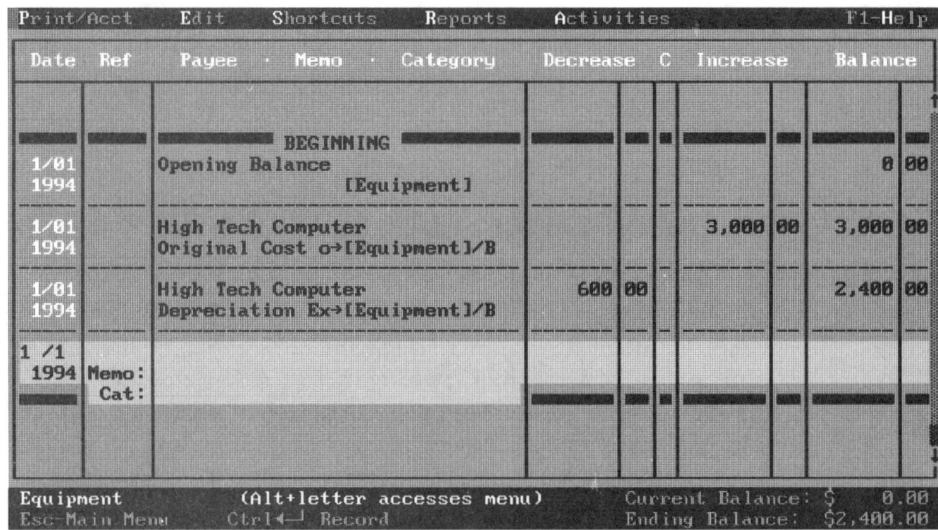

Equipment transactions
Figure 11-11.

register because you are not writing a check for this expense. Follow these steps to complete the second transaction entry:

1. Type **1/1/94** and press Enter twice.
2. Type **High Tech Computer** and press Enter.

NOTE: It is important to use the same name in all transactions relating to a given piece of equipment.

When you typed **H**, Quicken probably used its QuickFill feature to complete the payee field with "High Tech Computer." Quicken reviews all the payees for the past three months and all the payees in the memorized transaction list to make the suggestion for the payee name to use in the transaction. If the QuickFill feature did not work, either the default was changed to turn it off or the dates for the transactions in the example are after the current date. QuickFill never works for the Payee field on postdated transactions, although it is in effect for the Category field.

When QuickFill offers a suggestion, you can use Ctrl-+ and Ctrl-- to review other options beyond QuickFill's first suggestion. When you find the correct payee, press Enter. Quicken records the entire previous transaction for this payee. You must edit the copy of the original transaction if you want to make changes for the new entry. In this case, the following editing steps would be needed:

3. Press Ctrl-Backspace to remove the value in the field.
4. Press Shift-Tab twice.
5. Type **600** in the Decrease field and press Enter.
6. Press Ctrl-Backspace.
7. Type **Depreciation Expense** and press Enter.
8. Press Ctrl-Enter to accept [Equipment]/B for the category.

The register entries should match the ones in Figure 11-11.

Adding a New Equipment Purchase

Purchasing an asset reduces the balance in a checking account. When the asset is equipment, there must also be an entry to the Equipment account. If you list the Equipment account as the Category field in the transaction, Quicken will handle the transfer. The other part of this transaction entry that differs is that you use the name of the asset in the Payee field in the check register. You will have to use the Memo field Equipment account to record the payee's name. Follow these steps to record the purchase of a laser printer:

1. Press Esc to return to the Main Menu.
2. Choose Select **A**ccount.
3. Select ANB Business.
4. Type **1/25/94** and press Enter.
5. Type **108** and press Enter.
6. Type **Laser 1** and press Enter.
7. Type **1500** and press Enter.
8. Type **Printer from Harry's Computers** and press Enter.
9. Type **Equipment/B**.
10. Press Ctrl-Enter to record the transaction.

Your transaction looks like this:

```
1/25|108  |Laser 1                          | 1,500|00| | |  | 12,081|75
1994|Memo:|Printer from Harry's Computers   |
----| Cat:|[Equipment]/B                    |------|--|-|-|--|-------|--
```

11. Press Esc to return to the Main Menu.

11

12. Choose Select **A**ccount and then Equipment.

The screen in Figure 11-12 shows the transactions in the Equipment account after the transfer transaction is recorded.

Memorized and Scheduled Transactions

Many of your financial transactions are likely to repeat; you pay your utility bills each month, for instance. Likewise, overnight delivery charges, phone bills, payroll, and other bills are paid at about the same time each month. Cash inflows for some businesses are daily, weekly, or monthly. Other payments, such as supply purchases, also repeat, but perhaps not on the same dates each month.

As discussed in Chapter 6, "Expanding the Scope of Financial Entries," Quicken can memorize transactions entered in the register or check writing screen. Once memorized, these transactions can be used to generate identical transactions. Although amounts and dates may change, you can edit these fields and not have to reenter payee, memo, and category information. If you want even more automation you can consider grouping memorized transactions in scheduled transaction groups. These groups of transactions can be entered for you automatically with or without a prompt to notify you of their entry. You can also enter an individual transaction as a scheduled transaction after selecting **S**cheduled Transactions from the **S**hortcuts menu.

Memorizing a Register Entry

Any transaction in the account register can be memorized. Memorized transactions can be recalled for later use, printed, changed, and even deleted.

Print/Acct Edit Shortcuts Reports Activities F1-Help

Date	Ref	Payee · Memo · Category	Decrease	C	Increase	Balance
		BEGINNING				
1/01 1994		Opening Balance [Equipment]				0 00
1/03 1994		High Tech Computer Original Cost o→[Equipment]/B			3,000 00	3,000 00
1/03 1994		High Tech Computer Depreciation Ex→[Equipment]/B	600 00			2,400 00
1/25 1994		Laser 1 Printer from Ha→[ANB Business]→			1,500 00	3,900 00

Register entries in Equipment account after printer purchase
Figure 11-12.

You can elect to memorize as many transactions as you feel will repeat in the same relative time frame. To memorize the transaction for Consumer Power, follow these steps:

1. Press Esc to return to the Main Menu.
2. Choose Select **A**ccount.
3. Select ANB Personal.
4. Highlight the Consumer Power transaction in the register.
5. Select **M**emorize Transaction from the **S**hortcuts menu (or press Ctrl-M to select Memorize Transaction without opening the menu).

   Quicken prompts you to memorize split amounts or percentages (A/P). Since you always want to allocate utilities based on a 20%/80% split between business and home usage, percentage will be a better choice.
6. Type a **P** to use Percentage and press Enter to memorize the transaction.

   Using the same procedure, memorize the transaction for Western Michigan Gas. Quicken memorizes split transactions in the same way as any other transactions. You will want to carefully review the split transaction screen transactions for amounts that change each month to reduce errors.
7. Press Ctrl-T to display the memorized transactions; your list should match the one shown in Figure 11-13.

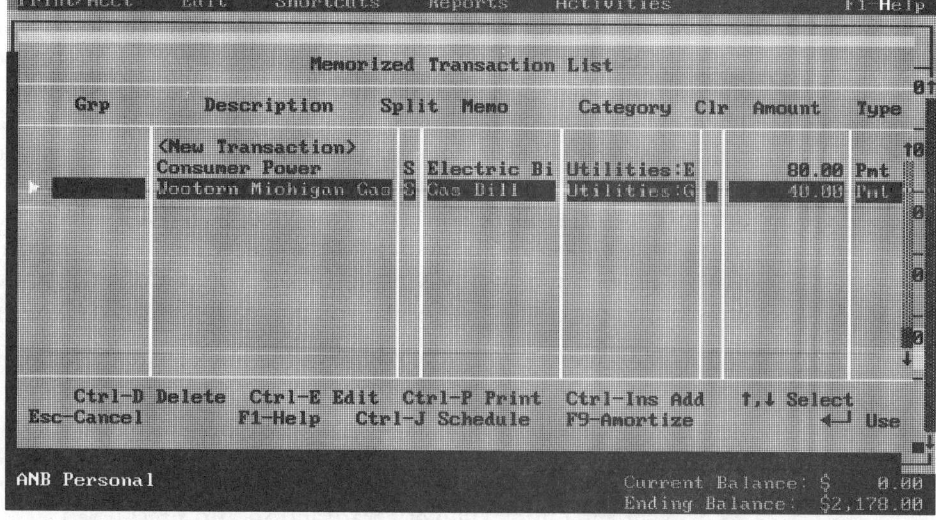

Memorized transactions list
Figure 11-13.

If you want to print the list once it is displayed, press Ctrl-P, type a number to select your printer, and press Enter to print.

Now you can open the ANB Business account and memorize a transaction from that account. Follow the steps listed here:

1. Press Esc twice to return to the Main Menu.
2. Choose Select **A**ccount.
3. Select ANB Business.
4. Highlight the Quick Delivery transaction in the register.
5. Select **M**emorize Transaction from the **S**hortcuts menu (or press Ctrl-M to select Memorize Transaction without opening the menu).

   Quicken will highlight the transaction and prompt you for a response.
6. Press Enter to confirm and memorize the transaction.
7. Press Ctrl-T to display the memorized transactions; your list should include Quick Delivery.

   Quicken maintains only one list of memorized transactions for each file and does not show the filename in the list. Here, each of the memorized transactions has a type of Pmt since it was memorized from the register. Transactions memorized from the check writing window will have a type of Chk.
8. Press Esc to return to the account register.

Using Memorized Transactions To recall a memorized transaction and place it in the register, move to the next blank transaction record. If you recall a memorized transaction while a previously recorded transaction is highlighted, the existing transaction will be replaced by the memorized transaction. Press Ctrl-T to recall the Memorized Transactions List window. The next step is to select the transaction you want to add to the register and then press Enter. If you type the first few letters of the payee name before pressing Ctrl-T, Quicken will take you to the correct area of the transaction list since it is in alphabetical order by payee. When it is added, the selected transaction appears with the date of the preceding transaction in the register, not the date on which it was last recorded. You can edit the transaction in the register and press Ctrl-Enter when you are ready to record the entry.

Follow these steps to record a payment to Quick Delivery for later in the month:

1. Press Ctrl-End to move to the end of the register entries.
2. Press Ctrl-T.
3. Select the Quick Delivery transaction and press Enter.

Quicken adds the transaction to the register.

4. Press Shift-Tab three times, type **1/30/94** in the Date field, and press Enter.
5. Type **109** in the Num field and press Enter twice.
6. Type **55.00** and press Ctrl-Enter to record the transaction.

The transaction looks like this:

```
| 1/30|109   |Quick Delivery                   |    55|00| |        |  |  12,026|75|
| 1994|Memo: |Manuscript Delivery              |      |  | |        |  |        |  |
|-----| Cat: |Del Overngt/B                    |------|--|-|--------|--|--------|--|
```

Changing and Deleting Memorized Transactions

To change a memorized transaction, you must first recall it from the memorized transaction list to a blank transaction in the register. Then make your changes and memorize it again. When you press Ctrl-M to memorize it again, Quicken asks you if you want to replace the transaction memorized earlier or add a new transaction. If you confirm the replacement, Quicken makes the change.

To delete a memorized transaction, you must first open the transaction list by pressing Ctrl-T or by selecting the **S**hortcuts menu and then selecting **R**ecall Transaction. Select the transaction you want to delete and press Ctrl-D. A warning message will appear asking you to confirm the deletion. When you press Enter, the transaction is no longer memorized.

Memorizing a Check

The procedure for memorizing transactions while writing checks is identical to the one used to memorize register transactions. You must be in the check writing window when you begin, but otherwise it is the same. Check and register transactions for the same file will appear in the same memorized transaction list and can be edited, deleted, or recalled from either the check writing or account register window.

Working with Scheduled Transactions

Although you can recall memorized transactions individually as a way to reenter similar transactions, a better method can be to have Quicken automatically schedule and enter transactions for you. Quicken 7 can schedule individual transactions or groups of transactions. If you want to schedule groups of transactions they must be memorized first. If you want to schedule individual transactions, they are entered on special transaction windows after telling Quicken which type of transaction you want to schedule.

If you have several memorized transactions that occur at the same time, a scheduled transaction group lets you focus on other tasks while Quicken remembers to enter the transactions you need. Quicken will record the entire group for you without prompting you about its entries, depending on how you define the scheduled transaction.

Defining a Scheduled Transaction Group

Quicken allows you to set up as many as 12 scheduled transaction groups. Defining a group is easy, but it requires a couple of steps after memorizing all the transactions that will be placed in the group. First, you will need to describe the group. Next, you will need to assign specific memorized transactions to the group. Although expense transactions are frequently used to create groups, you can also include an entry for a direct deposit payroll check that is deposited at the same time each month.

For your first transaction group, which you will title Utilities, you will group the gas and electric transactions that occur near the end of each month. Follow these steps to open the ANB Personal account and create the transaction group:

1. Press Esc to return to the Main Menu and choose Select **A**ccount.
2. Select ANB Personal as the account to use.
3. Select **S**cheduled Transactions from the **S**hortcuts menu.

   Quicken displays the window shown in Figure 11-14.
4. Be sure the cursor is pointing to <New Transaction Group>, since this is the first unused transaction group, and press Enter.

   Quicken displays a window to allow you to define the group. Figure 11-15 shows this screen with the entries you will make in the next steps.
5. Select 4 to tell Quicken that you want to define a scheduled transaction group and press Enter.

   Once the entry in the New Transaction window is finalized, a special window will appear which lists the other transaction type options. These other transaction types are payment, deposit, check, or electronic payment.
6. Press Enter to accept Monthly as the frequency for the transaction entry.
7. Press Enter to accept the account listed.
8. Type **2/3/94** as the next scheduled date and press Enter.

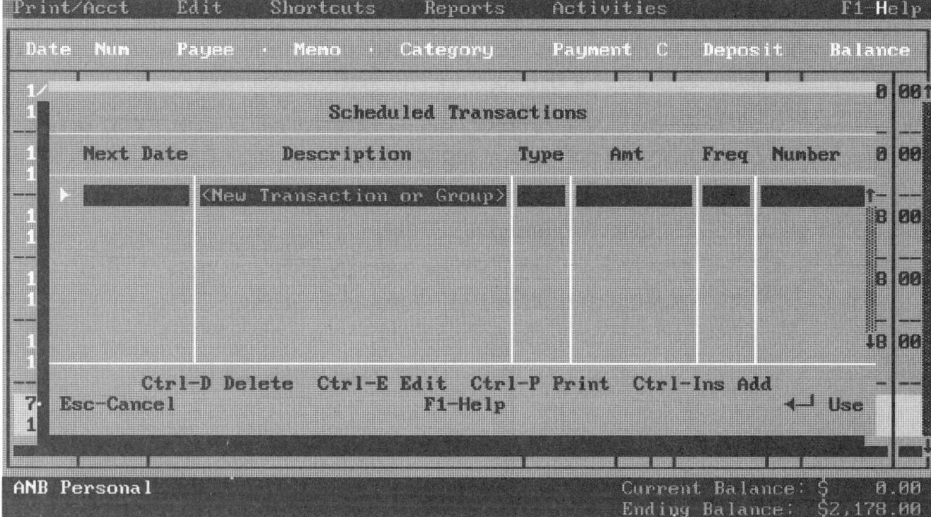

Scheduled Transactions window
Figure 11-14.

You can choose to be prompted before the transaction is entered automatically. You can also specify how many days before the scheduled date you want to be notified.

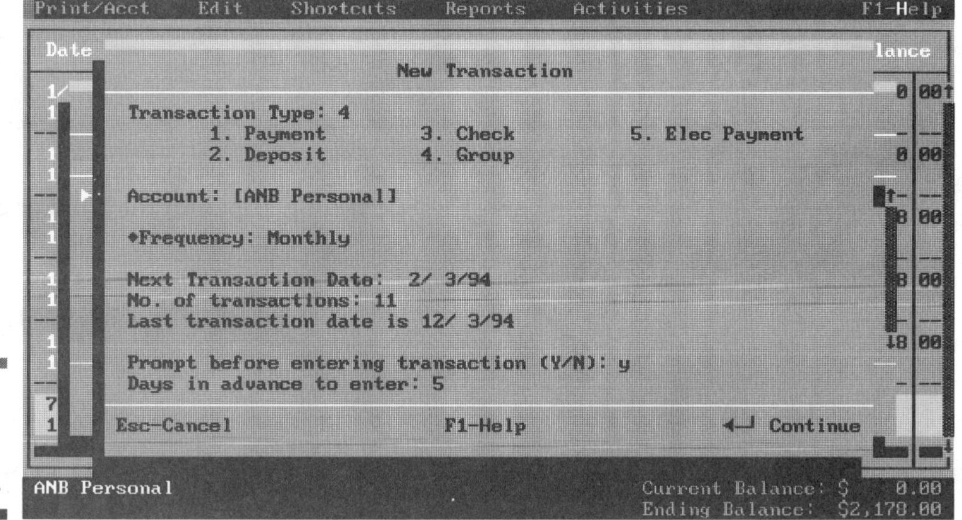

Setting up a Scheduled Transaction
Figure 11-15.

9. Type **11** as the number of transactions in the future that you want entered.

   Quicken uses the next date and the frequency you specified to determine the date of the last transaction.
10. Type **Y** to indicate that you want to be prompted before the group is entered into your register.
11. Press Enter to accept the number of days in advance for the prompt that is currently listed.

   The Group Transaction window shown here is displayed so that you can enter a name for the transaction group:

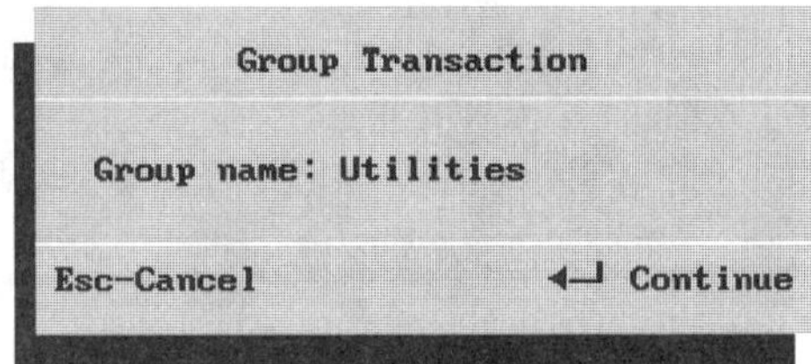

12. Type **Utilities** as the name for the group and press Enter twice until the Assign Transactions to Group window appears.
13. Highlight Consumer Power to select it and press Spacebar to assign the transaction to the Utilities group.

NOTE: Utilities is entered in the group column, which indicates that the transaction is now a part of the Utilities group.

14. Highlight Western Michigan Gas and press Spacebar.

   Quicken also marks this transaction as part of the Utilities group, as shown in Figure 11-16.
15. Press Enter to indicate you are finished selecting transactions. The message shown here will indicate that the group has been established:

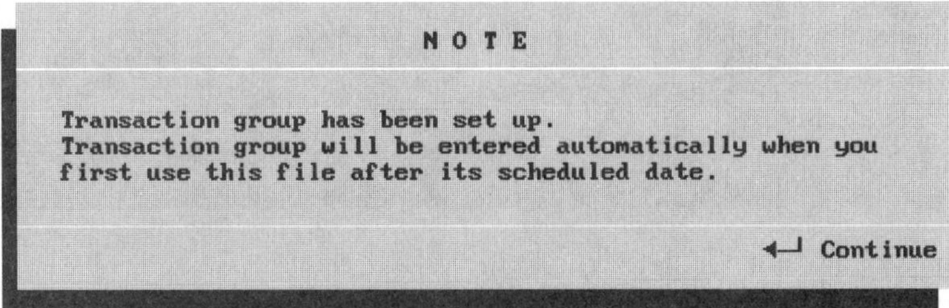

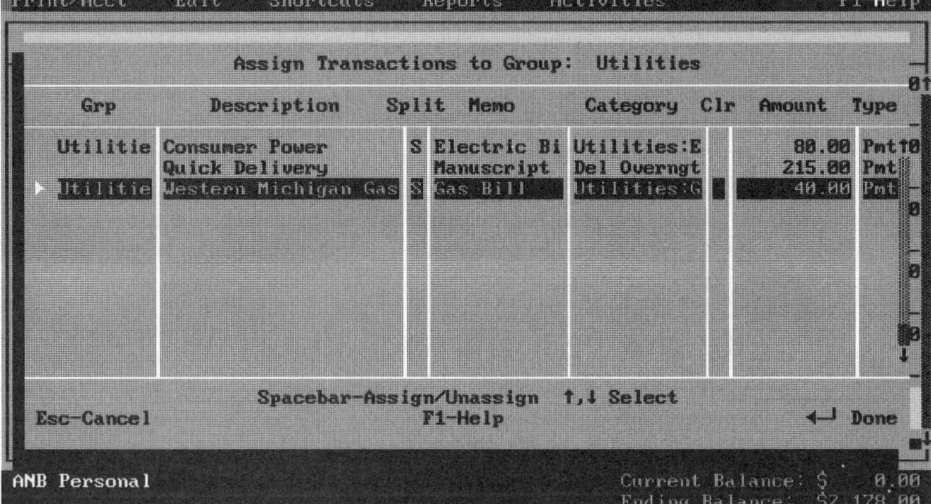

The transaction marked as part of the Utilities group
Figure 11-16.

You may want to define other scheduled transaction groups to include payroll, loan payments, and anything else that you might pay at the beginning of the month. You may also want to enter individual scheduled transactions for transactions that occur on a specific date each month. You are not required to define additional scheduled groups or transactions in order to complete the remaining exercises in this section.

You can also create transaction groups that generate checks for you. These groups contain transactions that are memorized from the check writing window. The procedure is the same as that just shown. You can identify these transactions in the Assign Transactions window by the Chk entry in the Type field.

Changing a Scheduled Transaction Group

You can add to a transaction group at any time by selecting **S**cheduled Transaction from the **S**hortcuts menu. Next, you need to highlight the group you want to change and press Ctrl-E.

To make a change to the group or the timing of the reminder, use the same procedure and make the necessary changes, pressing Ctrl-Enter when you are finished changing the window. The window for assigning transactions to the group appears next to allow you to select additional transactions for inclusion in the group.

To delete a scheduled transaction group, select **S**cheduled Transactions the Shortcuts menu. Select the group you want to delete and press Ctrl-D. Quicken eliminates the group but does not delete the memorized transactions that are part of it. It also does not affect any transactions recorded in the register by earlier executions of the scheduled group.

If you want to alter a transaction that is part of the transaction group, you will need to alter the memorized transaction. This means you have to recall the transaction on the check writing screen or in the account register, depending on the type of transaction you have. Next, you need to make your changes and memorize the transaction again. Follow the procedures in the "Changing and Deleting Memorized Transactions" section earlier in this chapter.

Recording a Transaction Group

Once you have defined a scheduled transaction group, you can forget about it. Quicken will handle the entries for you when the time is right. You will receive a prompt about the entries only if you have requested one or if you are using a percentage split and Quicken needs to find out the transaction amount to be allocated. If you want to record the group early for some reason, you do not need to wait for Quicken. You can select the scheduled group and record it yourself.

To execute a transaction group from the account register, complete the following steps:

1. Press Esc to return to the register, then select **S**cheduled Transactions from the **S**hortcuts menu.

   Quicken will display a list of transaction groups.
2. Select the Utilities group by moving the highlight to it.
3. Press Enter.

   Quicken displays a window that lets you determine whether or not to enter the transaction immediately; it looks like Figure 11-17.
4. Type **1** and press Enter to enter the group of transactions in the account register now.

   Quicken displays the Recall Split Percentage for Consumer Power window as shown here:

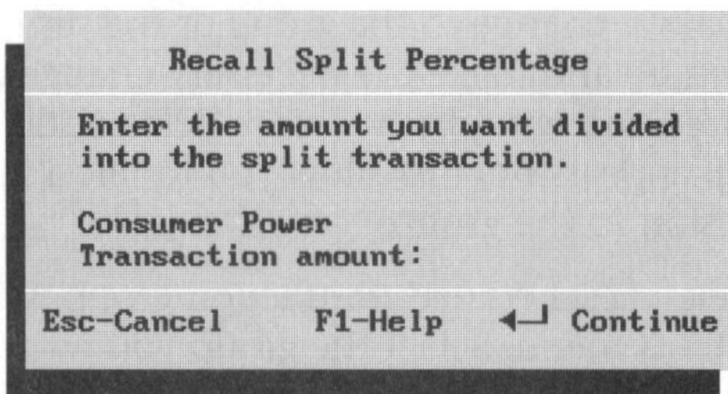

5. Type **72** for the amount of the transaction and press Enter.

   Quicken will allocate it between home and business.

6. Type **45** for the amount to allocate between home and business for West Michigan Gas and press Enter.

   Quicken will allocate the amount based on your percentages for home and business.

The new transactions are entered with a date of 2/3/94, as shown here:

Date	Num	Payee / Memo / Category	Payment	C	Deposit	Balance
2/03 1994	_Pymt SPLIT	Consumer Power Electric Bill	72 00			2,106 00
	Cat:	Utilities:Electric/B				
2/03 1994	_Pymt SPLIT	Western Michigan Gas Gas Bill Utilities:Gas/B	45 00			2,061 00

If you were to examine the split detail you would find that Quicken recorded 14.40 as the business portion of the expense and 57.60 as the home portion of the Consumer Power bill. For the Western Michigan Gas bill the allocation was recorded as 9.00 for the business portion of the expense and 36.00 as the home portion of the bill.

Responding to Quicken Reminders to Record a Scheduled Group

If you have chosen to be prompted before a scheduled group is recorded, Quicken will begin prompting you the number of days before the scheduled

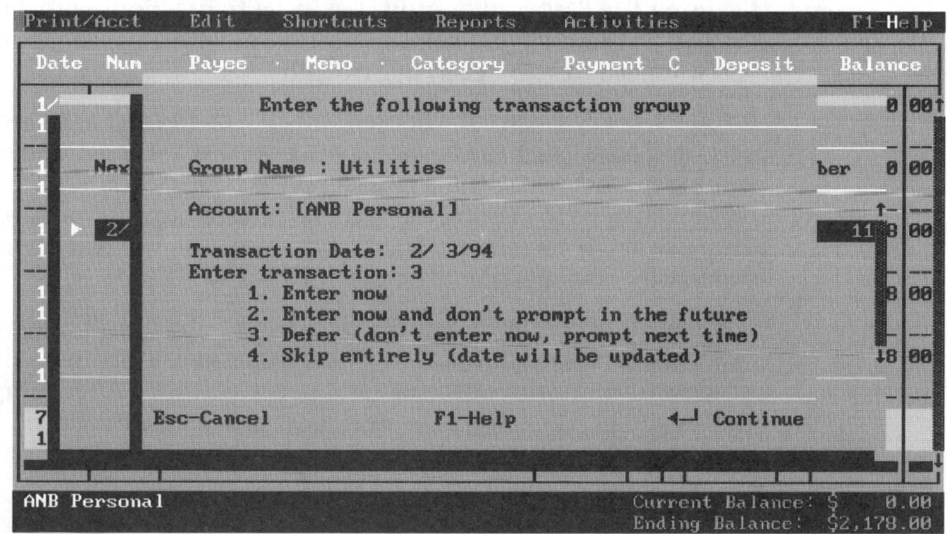

11

Executing the Utilities group
Figure 11-17.

date that you requested. Quicken displays a dialog box that asks you if you want to enter the scheduled group just like the one shown in the previous section where you requested that the scheduled transaction be entered. The reminder will either occur at the DOS prompt when you boot your system or at the Main Menu when you first load Quicken. Hard disk users who have the default setting for Billminder still set at Yes will see a message at the DOS prompt reminding them to pay postdated checks or to record transaction groups. If you do not have a hard disk or if you have turned Billminder off, the prompt will not appear until you start Quicken.

Important Customizing Options as You Set Up Your Files

Quicken provides a number of options for customizing the package to meet your needs. These include the addition of passwords for accessing files, options already discussed such as requiring category entries, and other options that affect the display of information on your screen and in reports. Once you know how to access these settings, you will find that most are self-explanatory. All of the changes are made by selecting Set **P**references from the Main Menu.

Adding Passwords

To add a password, select Pass**w**ord Settings from the Set **P**references menu. Quicken presents a menu that allows you to decide if you want to protect a file using **F**ile Password or protect existing transactions with **T**ransaction Password. Although you can add protection with a password at both levels, you will need to select each individually.

If you select **F**ile Password, Quicken will ask you to enter a password. Once you do so and press Enter, the password will be added to the active file and anyone wishing to work with the file must supply it. **T**ransaction Password is used to prevent changes to existing transactions entered before a specified date without the password. If you choose **T**ransaction Password, you will be presented with a window that requires you to enter both a password and a date.

If you want to change or remove a password, you must be able to provide the existing password. Quicken will then provide a Change Password window for the entry of the old and new passwords. After completing the entries and pressing Enter, the new password will be in effect.

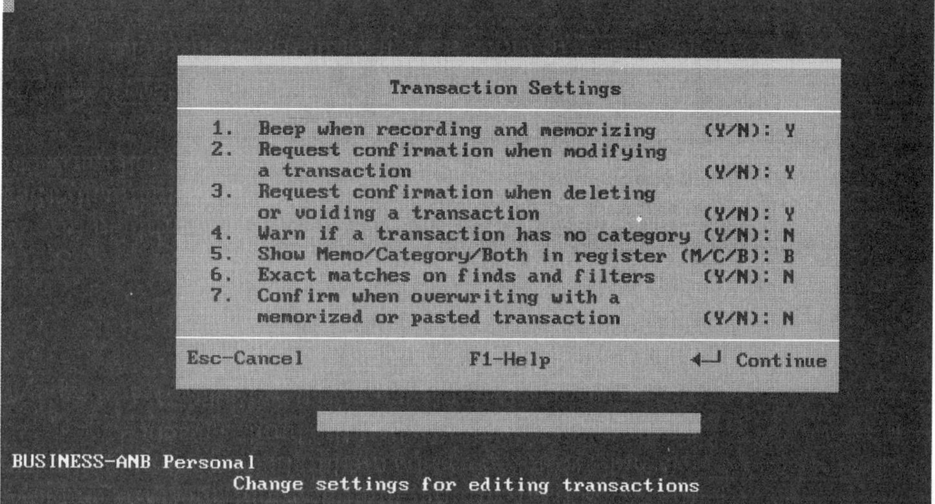

Transaction Settings options
Figure 11-18.

Changing Other Settings

Figure 11-18 shows the window presented when **T**ransaction Settings is selected from the Set **P**references menu. It shows the default choice for each of the options. The first option allows you to turn off the beep you hear when recording and memorizing transactions. The second option controls whether Quicken prompts for confirmation when you make transaction changes.

The third option controls whether Quicken prompts for confirmation when deleting or voiding a transaction. Changing option 4 will require category entries on each transaction.

The information on the second line of a register entry can be changed with option 5. You can use it to display memo information if you change the setting to M. Changing this option to C displays category information only. The default setting of B displays both types of information.

Option 6 controls whether Quicken prompts for exact matches when performing "find" and "filter" commands. For example, if you want to find a payment for J. B. Smith, the default setting allows you to define the payee as J B Smith without the periods, and Quicken searches for a payee that contains your entry with or without the periods. If you change the default setting to Y, Quicken will search for an exact payee match.

Option 7 tells Quicken whether you want a confirmation from prompt if you are about to overwrite an existing transaction with a memorized transaction.

C H A P T E R

investments banking FILE register expenses DEDUCTIONS
tips finances INCOME equity net pay
checks revenue bank statements
statements
dividends assets business tips
INCOME
cash flow
banking business tips
FILE reports
budget FILE
business tips checks
DEDUCTIONS
statements cash flow
tips mortgage
net pay taxes bank
revenue
business tips
mortgage cash
dividends tips
business tips
investments
register statements
taxes
reports
business tips
expenses tips
equity investments
INCOME
checks statements bank cash
assets checks budget tips finances net pay

12 QUICKEN'S PAYROLL ASSISTANCE

For a small-business owner under the day-to-day pressure of running a business, preparing the payroll can be a time-consuming and frustrating task. Besides withholding forms and tables to complete, there are annual earnings limits that affect the amount you withhold in social security taxes from employees. In addition to these weekly considerations, there are monthly, quarterly, and year-end reports that you might need to file for the federal, state, or local government.

In this chapter, you will see how Quicken can help to reduce the effort of preparing your payroll. Although you must still invest some time, you'll find that an early investment will substantially reduce your payroll activities once the system is running. With Quicken, you can easily prepare the payroll entry for each employee and maintain information for the Internal Revenue Service (IRS) about federal income tax withholding, Federal Insurance Contribution Act (FICA) withholding, and employer FICA payments. You can also maintain accounts for any state and local withholding taxes or insurance payments that must be periodically deposited. In addition to this information, you can accumulate data to be used in the preparation of W-2 forms for your employees at the end of the year. See the special "Payroll Forms" section in this chapter for a list of some of the standard payroll-related payment and tax forms that Quicken can assist you in preparing.

Intuit offers a separate program, QuickPay, that can provide additional payroll help with its built-in payroll tables.

The Quicken Payroll System

Payroll entries are processed along with your other business-related payments in your Quicken account register. To set up your system to do this, you will need to establish some new categories and subcategories specifically related to payroll.

Depending upon your state and local tax laws and the benefits you provide your employees, you can use Quicken's payroll support option to create

Category and Transfer List

Category/Transfer	Type	Description	Tax
Payroll	Expns	Payroll transaction	◆
Comp FICA	Sub	Company FICA contribution	◆
Comp FUTA	Sub	Company FUTA contribution	◆
Comp MCARE	Sub	Company Medicare contrib	◆
Comp SDI	Sub	Company SDI contribution	◆
Comp SUI	Sub	Company SUI contribution	◆
Gross	Sub	Compensation to employee	◆
Postage	Expns	Postage Expense	◆
Recreation	Expns	Recreation Expense	
Rent on Equip	Expns	Rent-Vehicle,mach,equip	◆
Rent Paid	Expns	Rent Paid	◆
Repairs	Expns	Repairs	◆
Returns	Expns	Returns & Allowances	◆

Ctrl-D Delete Ctrl-E Edit Ctrl-P Print Ctrl-Ins Add
Esc-Cancel F1-Help F8-Move ↵ Use

Partial category list showing payroll subcategories
Figure 12-1.

some or all of the categories needed to record your payroll transactions:

- Payroll:Gross keeps track of the total wages earned by employees.
- Payroll:Comp FICA keeps track of matching FICA contributions.

The other payroll subcategories shown in Figure 12-1 will be used to record federal unemployment contributions, Medicare contributions, state unemployment contributions, and state disability insurance contributions.

In addition, you need to establish several *liability accounts* to maintain records of taxes withheld and other employee-authorized payroll deductions for medical insurance, charitable contributions, and so on. These are liability accounts since you are holding the withheld funds for payment to a third party. Some examples of these are as follows:

Payroll-FUTA	Federal unemployment taxes
Payroll-FICA	FICA liabilities owed by employer
Payroll-FWH	Federal income tax liabilities for employee withholdings
Payroll-MCARE	Medicare tax liabilities
Payroll-SWHOH	State income tax liabilities for employee withholdings (Ohio in this illustration)
Payroll-SUI	State unemployment tax liabilities
Payroll-SDI	State disability insurance liabilities

Notice that all of these account names begin with "Payroll." This allows Quicken to prepare the payroll report by automatically finding all transactions with a category title beginning with Payroll. All the categories listed in this section start with "Payroll" and have subcategories added, for example Payroll:Gross. When you prepare the payroll report in this chapter, you will see the relationship between the category designation and the preparation of the report.

Another point to note is that although employees must pay federal, state, and local taxes, the employer is responsible for the actual withholding and payment of these funds to the appropriate agencies. In addition, there are certain payroll taxes that the employer must pay, such as unemployment, workers' compensation, and matching FICA. The amount of these taxes is not withheld from the employee's pay, since the responsibility for these payments rests with the employer. With Quicken, you can monitor your liability for these payments. This is important, since you will be assessed penalties and late fees for failing to file these payments on time. Quicken's ability to memorize payment formats and remind you of dates for periodic payments can be most helpful in this situation.

Payroll Forms

If you are thinking of hiring employees, you need to be prepared for your paperwork to increase. You must complete forms at the federal, state, and local levels regarding payroll information.

Federal Payroll Forms

The following list provides an overview of the payroll-related tax forms that employers need to file with the Internal Revenue Service. You can obtain copies of the federal forms you need by calling the IRS toll-free number (800) 829-3676. If this number is not valid in your locale, check your telephone directory for the correct number. You will probably need to file these forms:

- *SS-4, Application for Federal Employer Identification Number* The federal employer identification number is used to identify your business on all business-related tax forms.
- *Form 46-190, Federal Tax Deposit Receipt* This is your record of deposits of withholding and payroll taxes made to a Federal Reserve bank or an authorized commercial bank.
- *Form 940, Employer's Annual Federal Unemployment (FUTA) Tax Return* This is a return filed annually with the IRS summarizing your federal unemployment tax liability and deposits.
- *Form 941, Employer's Quarterly Federal Tax Return* This return summarizes your quarterly FICA taxes and federal income tax withholding liability and the amount of deposits your business has made during the quarter.
- *Form 943, Employer's Annual Tax Return for Agricultural Employees* This is a special form completed annually for FICA taxes and federal income tax withholding liability for agricultural employees.
- *Form 1099-MISC, Statement for Recipients of Miscellaneous Income* This must be filed for all nonemployees paid $600.00 or more in income in the current tax year.
- *Form W-2, Wage and Tax Statement* This is a six-part form (an original and five duplicates) summarizing an employee's gross earnings and tax deductions for the year. The form must be prepared annually for each employee by January 31.

- *Form W-3, Transmittal of Income and Tax Statements* This form summarizes your business's annual payroll, related FICA taxes, and federal income tax withheld during the year. Sent with the Social Security Administration's copy of the W-2 by February 28th of the following year.
- *Form W-4, Employee's Withholding Allowance Certificate* This form is completed annually by employees and is used to declare the number of withholding exemptions they claim.

State and Local Government Payroll Information

These forms vary by state. The following list provides an indication of some of the forms you are likely to need to file:

- Unemployment insurance tax payments
- Workers' compensation tax payments
- State income tax withholding payments
- Local income tax withholding payments
- Form W-2, Wage and Tax Statement (one copy of federal form)

Recording Payroll Activity

You will be using the file BUSINESS, established in Chapter 11, "Setting Up Quicken for Your Business," to record your payroll entries in this chapter. As noted in the previous section, you need to expand your category list and accounts in order to accumulate the payroll information. Once you have completed the example for processing payroll, you will be able to customize your accounts to handle your own payroll needs. For example, you might withhold medical and life insurance premiums from your employees' checks. These amounts can be recorded in another liability account established just for that purpose.

The example used in this chapter assumes your work force consists of salaried workers paid monthly. This means their pay and deductions will be the same month after month. John Smith is paid $2000.00 a month and Mary McFaul is paid $3000.00 a month. If your employees are paid hourly, with a varying number of hours in each pay period, you will need to recompute the pay and deductions for each period. Otherwise, the same procedures shown in this chapter apply. In this example, you draw payroll checks on the last day of the month.

Establishing Payroll Liability Accounts and New Payroll Categories

The first step in recording payroll in the Quicken system is to establish the payroll liability accounts you will use throughout the year. The objective of establishing these accounts is to allow you to accumulate the amounts you withhold from employees so you can make periodic payments when they become due to the various governmental agencies, health insurance companies, and pension plans involved. When a payment is due, you can open the liability account to determine the balance in the account. This tells you the amount of the payment due. Quicken's Use Tutorials/Assistants Main Menu option will be used to establish the payroll liability accounts and new payroll categories used in this chapter's illustration.

Make sure you are in the ANB Business Account in the BUSINESS file. Then, from the Main Menu, follow these steps to establish the payroll liability accounts you will use in this chapter:

1. Select Use **T**utorials and Assistants.
2. Select Create **P**ayroll Support.
3. Press Enter, and your screen appears as follows:

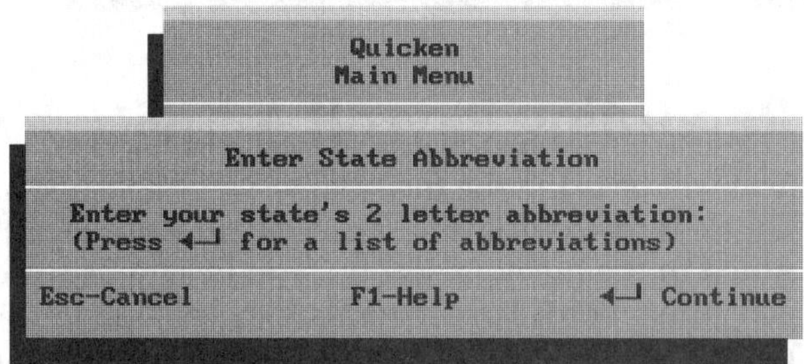

4. Enter your state's abbreviation and press Enter.

   Ohio (OH) is used throughout this book. Quicken automatically creates all the required payroll accounts for your state.
5. Press Enter to acknowledge Quicken's message and return to the Main Menu.
6. Choose Select **A**ccount.

   The screen in Figure 12-2 shows that Quicken has established new payroll liability accounts for FICA, federal unemployment tax, federal income tax, Medicare contributions, State disability insurance, state unemployment tax, and state income taxes.

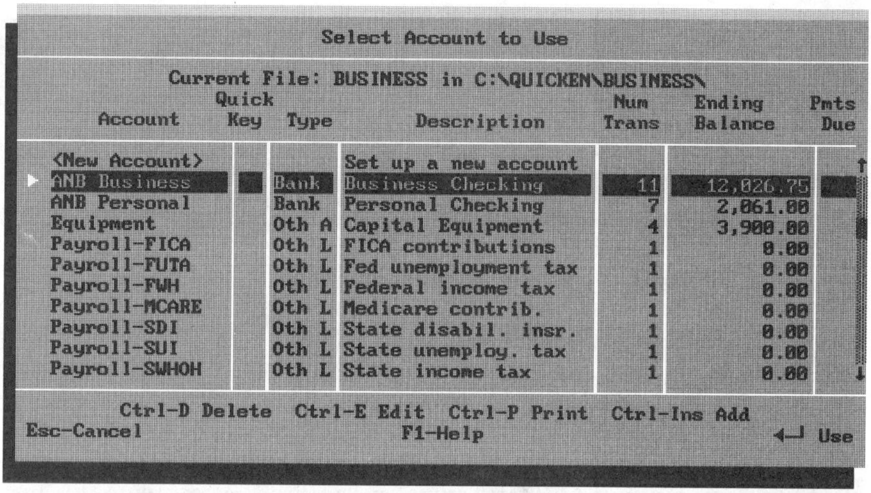

Select Account to Use

Current File: BUSINESS in C:\QUICKEN\BUSINESS\

Account	Quick Key	Type	Description	Num Trans	Ending Balance	Pmts Due
<New Account>			Set up a new account			
ANB Business		Bank	Business Checking	11	12,026.75	
ANB Personal		Bank	Personal Checking	7	2,061.00	
Equipment		Oth A	Capital Equipment	4	3,900.00	
Payroll-FICA		Oth L	FICA contributions	1	0.00	
Payroll-FUTA		Oth L	Fed unemployment tax	1	0.00	
Payroll-FWH		Oth L	Federal income tax	1	0.00	
Payroll-MCARE		Oth L	Medicare contrib.	1	0.00	
Payroll-SDI		Oth L	State disabil. insr.	1	0.00	
Payroll-SUI		Oth L	State unemploy. tax	1	0.00	
Payroll-SWHOH		Oth L	State income tax	1	0.00	

Esc-Cancel Ctrl-D Delete Ctrl-E Edit Ctrl-P Print Ctrl-Ins Add F1-Help ↵ Use

Payroll liability accounts
Figure 12-2.

7. Select the ANB Business account.

   Quicken displays the ANB register.
8. Press Ctrl-C and type **P**.

The Category and Transfer List window, shown in Figure 12-1, appears.

Quicken's Payroll Assistant has created the basic categories, as well as liability accounts you will use in this chapter. If you plan to complete the entries shown in chapter tutorials, there are several editing steps you must complete first.

When you use Quicken's Payroll Assistant feature, the opening balances for the liability accounts show the date in your machine at the time that you used the Assistant. The following steps demonstrate how to edit the account to make the opening balance date 1/1/94. From the Main Menu, follow these steps:

1. Choose Select **A**ccount.
2. Select Payroll-FICA.
3. Highlight the Opening Balance transaction.
4. Type **1/1/94** in the Date field and press Ctrl-Enter.

   Your screen now looks like this:

```
Print/Acct   Edit   Shortcuts   Reports   Activities                    F1-Help
 Date  Ref    Payee  · Memo  · Category    Increase  C  Decrease    Balance

                       BEGINNING
 1/01       Opening Balance                                              0 00
 1994 Memo:
 ----- Cat: [Payroll-FICA]
```

Using the steps just given, edit the Date field in all the other liability accounts established by Quicken's Payroll Assistant. These include FUTA, FWH, MCARE, SDI, SUI and SWHOH.

Monthly Payroll Entries

In this section, you record paycheck entries for John Smith and Mary McFaul on January 31. Many steps are required to complete the entire entry for an individual. After you record basic information, such as check number and employee name, amounts must be determined. You establish each of the withholding amounts and subtract the total from the gross pay to compute net pay. For hourly workers, a computation is needed to determine the gross pay as well. Tax tables are used to determine the correct withholding for federal, state, and local taxes. For figures such as FICA and net pay, you can use Quicken's Calculator when computing the amount.

Once you have determined withholding amounts and net pay, you need to enter this information. Each of the withholding amounts, such as federal

```
Print/Acct   Edit   Shortcuts   Reports   Activities                    F1-Help
 Date  Num    Payee  · Memo  · Category    Payment  C  Deposit     Balance
 1/31 110   John Smith                     1,560 13                10,466 62
 1994 SPLIT 000-00-0001
 ----- Cat: Payroll:Gross/B
 1/31
                          Split Transaction
          Category                        Memo                      Amount
 1:Payroll:Gross/B               Gross Earnings                   2,000.00
 2:[Payroll-FICA]/B              FICA Withholding                  -124.00
 3:[Payroll-FWH]/B               Federal Withholding               -232.00
 4:[Payroll-SWHOH]/B             State Withholding                  -54.87
 5:[Payroll-MCARE]/B             Medicare Withholding               -29.00
 6:Payroll:Comp FICA/B           Payroll Taxes-FICA                 124.00
                  Enter categories, descriptions, and amounts
 Esc-Cancel       Ctrl-D Delete    F9-Recalc Transaction Total    Ctrl↵ Done
ANB Business                                    Current Balance: $      0.00
                                                Ending Balance:  $10,466.62
```

Partial Split Transaction window for Smith payroll entries

Figure 12-3.

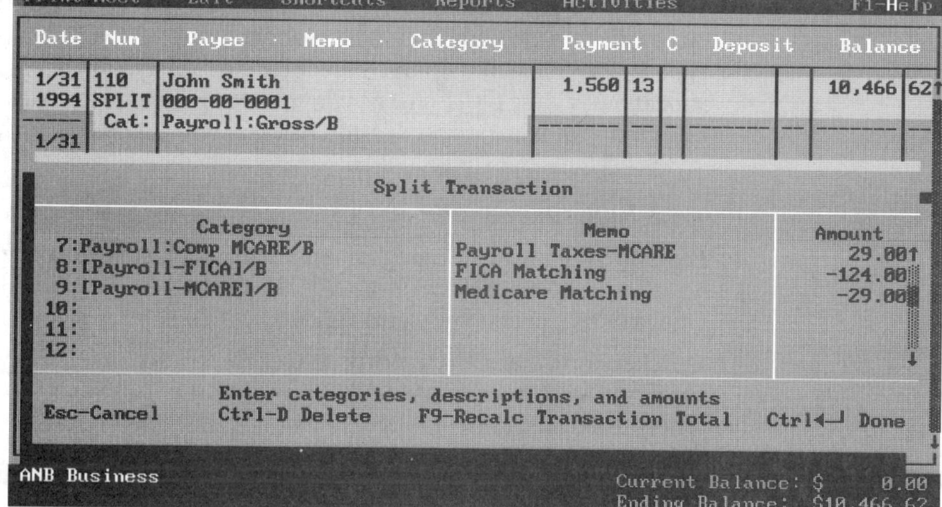

Partial Split Transaction window for remainder of Smith payroll entries
Figure 12-4.

income tax, FICA, and state withholding, is entered on a Split Transaction window. Follow these steps to record the transactions:

1. From the Main Menu, select Select **A**ccount and then select ANB Business.
2. Press Ctrl-End to highlight the next blank transaction in the ANB Business account register.
3. Type **1/31/94** and press Enter.
4. Type **110** and press Enter.
5. Type **John Smith** and press Enter.
6. Type **1560.13** and press Enter.

   This amount is equal to John's gross pay of $2000.00 less federal income tax, state income tax, FICA, and Medicare withholding.
7. Type **000-00-0001** and press Enter.

   This identifies the employee's social security number. You may find this field useful in filtering payroll reports.
8. Press Ctrl-S, and the Split Transaction window appears on your screen.

   The screen in Figure 12-3 shows the top portion of the Split Transaction window you complete in the next series of steps. The final portion of the Split Transaction window is shown in Figure 12-4.
9. Type **Payroll:Gross/B** and press Enter.

You can use the QuickFill capability for the entries throughout this chapter, even though they have subcategories and classes. When you type **P**, Payroll will display. Type **:** to accept Payroll and display the first subcategory. Use Ctrl-+ to advance through the categories to find the one that you want, type /, and Quicken will add the B for you.

10. Type **Gross Earnings** and press Enter.
11. Type **2000.00** and press Enter.
12. Press Ctrl-C, and the Category and Transfer List window appears on your screen. Select [Payroll-FICA], which is near the bottom of the category list, press Enter, and type **/B**.

    Quicken automatically records the brackets around the Payroll-FICA category, as shown in the Split Transaction window in Figure 12-3, when the transaction involves a transfer between two Quicken accounts. Here, Quicken records the other liability account name in the Category field. This indicates that you are keeping track of the amount of your employee withholding in this account until you make your payment to the IRS.
13. Press Enter to move to the Memo field.
14. Type **FICA Withholding** and press Enter.
15. Type **–124.00** and press Enter.

    This is the amount of FICA withheld from John's paycheck. The negative amount indicates that this is a deduction from the $2000.00 gross earnings entered earlier. For 1993, the rate is .062 on the first $57,600.00 of earnings per employee. You can calculate this amount with the Quicken Calculator before starting the transaction. Although the $57,600.00 earnings limit does not affect the employees in this example, Quicken can be used to help monitor employees' gross earnings to determine when the limit is reached.
16. Press Ctrl-C, select [Payroll-FWH], press Enter, and type **/B**.
17. Press Enter to move to the Memo field.
18. Type **Federal Withholding** and press Enter.
19. Type **–232.00** and press Enter.

    This is the amount of federal income tax withheld from John's paycheck. Remember, you must determine manually the amounts from withholding tables before beginning the payroll transaction entry since you need it to compute net pay.
20. Press Ctrl-C, select [Payroll-SWHOH], press Enter, and type **/B**.
21. Press Enter to move the cursor to the Memo field.

22. Type **State Withholding** and press Enter.
23. Type **–54.87** and press Enter.

    Once again, use the appropriate state withholding tables to determine the amount of the deduction from John's paycheck. If you live in an area where local taxes are also withheld, you need to add another liability account to accumulate your liability to that governmental agency. At this point, you have recorded John Smith's gross and net earnings and the related payroll withholding amounts.
24. Press Ctrl-C, select [Payroll-MCARE], press Enter, type **/B**, and press Enter.
25. Type **Medicare Withholding** and press Enter.
26. Type **–29.00** and press Enter.

    For 1993, the rate is .0145 on the first $135,000. The remaining steps record your employer payroll expenses.
27. Type **Payroll:Comp FICA /B** and press Enter.

    As an employer, you have to match your employees' FICA contributions. This is an expense of doing business and must be recorded in your category list.
28. Type **Payroll Taxes-FICA** and press Enter.
29. Type **124.00** and press Enter.

    This records the amount of your matching FICA payroll expense. Notice that this is a positive amount because this is a business expense that Quicken will record in the account register.
30. Type **Payroll:Comp MCARE/B** and press Enter.
31. Type **Payroll Taxes-MCARE** and press Enter.
32. Type **29.00** and press Enter.
33. Press Ctrl-C, select [Payroll-FICA], press Enter, and type **/B**.
34. Press Enter to move the cursor to the Memo field.
35. Typc **FICA Matching** and prcss Enter.
36. Type **–124.00** and press Enter.
37. Press Ctrl-C, select [Payroll-MCARE], press Enter, type **/B**, and press Enter.
38. Type **Medicare Matching** and press Enter.
39. Type **–29.00** and press Ctrl-Enter.
40. Press Ctrl-Enter twice to record the transaction in the current register.

You have now completed the payroll entry for John Smith for the month of January. You must now complete the recording process for Mary McFaul. Follow these steps to record the transaction from the ANB Business account register:

1. Type **1/31/94** and press Enter.
2. Type **111** and press Enter.
3. Type **Mary McFaul** and press Enter.
4. Type **2284.22** and press Enter.
5. Type **000-00-0002** and press Enter.
6. Press Ctrl-S, and the Split Transaction window appears on your screen.
7. Type **Payroll:Gross/B** and press Enter.
8. Type **Gross Earnings** and press Enter.
9. Type **3000.00** and press Enter.
10. Press Ctrl-C, and the Category and Transfer List window appears on your screen. Select [Payroll-FICA], press Enter, and type **/B**.
11. Press Enter to move to the Memo field.
12. Type **FICA Withholding** and press Enter.
13. Type **–186.00** and press Enter.
14. Press Ctrl-C, select [Payroll-FWH], press Enter, and type **/B**.
15. Press Enter to move to the Memo field.
16. Type **Federal Withholding** and press Enter.
17. Type **–382.00** and press Enter.
18. Press Ctrl-C, select [Payroll-SWHOH], press Enter, and type **/B**.
19. Press Enter to move the cursor to the Memo field.
20. Type **State Withholding** and press Enter.
21. Type **–104.28** and press Enter.
22. Press Ctrl-C, select [Payroll-MCARE], press Enter, type **/B**, and press Enter.
23. Type **Medicare Withholding** and press Enter.
24. Type **–43.50** and press Enter.
25. Type **Payroll:Comp FICA/B** and press Enter.
26. Type **Payroll Taxes-FICA** and press Enter.
27. Type **186.00** and press Enter.
28. Type **Payroll:Comp MCARE/B** and press Enter.
29. Type **Payroll Taxes-MCARE** and press Enter.

30. Type **43.50** and press Enter.
31. Press Ctrl-C, select [Payroll-FICA], press Enter, and type **/B**.
32. Press Enter.
33. Type **FICA Matching** and press Enter.
34. Type **–186.00** and press Enter.
35. Press Ctrl-C, select [Payroll-MCARE], press Enter, type **/B**, and press Enter.
36. Type **Medicare Matching** and press Enter.
37. Type **–43.50** and press Ctrl-Enter.
38. Press Ctrl-Enter twice to record the transaction for Mary McFaul in the account register.

The paycheck transactions recorded in this section show the basic payroll expenses and liabilities associated with the payment of wages. Your payroll entries will be more complex if you withhold medical insurance, pension contributions, and other amounts, such as contributions to charity or deposits to savings accounts from employee checks. The basic format of the split transaction remains the same; the number of categories in the split transaction would simply be expanded and additional liability accounts added to cover your obligation to make payment to the parties involved. Regardless of the number of withholding categories, the procedures you just performed can be used to expand your withholding categories and liabilities.

Recording Periodic Deposits for the Internal Revenue Service

You must periodically make deposits to the Internal Revenue Service for the amount of FICA and federal income tax withheld from employees' paychecks, as well as your matching FICA contribution. You make your deposits to authorized banks within the Federal Reserve System. You should check with your bank to be sure they can provide this service; otherwise you must take cash or a bank check, along with the appropriate forms, to an authorized bank and make your deposit. To record the withholding deposit, you will designate the Internal Revenue Service as the payee in your entry.

There are specific guidelines concerning the timing of the payments. At the time of this writing, the fictitious company used in this example would be required to make a withholding deposit for the January paychecks under the IRS's Rule #1 discussed under the new rules in the "IRS Deposit Rules" section of this chapter. The rule states you must make a deposit for social security taxes and withheld federal income tax by the fifteenth of the following month if your total tax liability for last year was $50,000 or less. In this example, your total tax liability for the month is $1379.00. You should consult your accountant or read IRS Form 941 for a full explanation of the other deposit rules. Depending on the size of your payroll, you may have to make periodic payments throughout the month in order to comply with the regulations.

The following entry demonstrates how to record a payment for your business's federal tax liabilities for social security taxes, Medicare, and federal withholding taxes. You record the transaction in the ANB Business account register when you pay the federal government the amount of the liabilities for FICA, Medicare, and federal income tax withholding for the two paycheck entries recorded in the previous section.

From the ANB Business account register, record the following transaction for the required deposit:

1. Press Ctrl-End to highlight the blank new transaction form and move the cursor to the Date field.
2. Type **2/1/94** and press Enter.
3. Type **112** and press Enter.
4. Type **Internal Revenue Service** and press Enter.
5. Type **1379.00** and press Enter.
6. Type **Form 941 Withholding Payment** and press Enter.
7. Press Ctrl-S to open the Split Transaction window.

   The screen in Figure 12-5 shows the entries in the Split Transaction window.
8. Press Ctrl-C, select [Payroll-FICA], press Enter, and type **/B**.

   This account is now recorded in the Category field in the Split Transaction window.
9. Press Enter to move the cursor to the Memo field.
10. Type **FICA Withholding and match** and press Enter.
11. Type **620.00** and press Enter.
12. Press Ctrl-C, select [Payroll-MCARE], press Enter, and type **/B**.
13. Press Enter to move the cursor to the Memo field.
14. Type **Medicare Withhold and match** and press Enter.
15. Type **145.00** and press Enter.
16. Press Ctrl-C, move the arrow cursor to [Payroll-FWH], press Enter, and type **/B**.
17. Press Enter to move the cursor to the Memo field.

18. Type **Federal Withholding** and press Enter.
19. Press Ctrl-Enter.

    This records the split.
20. Press Ctrl-Enter to record the transaction in the account register.

You follow these same steps to record the payment of the state withholding tax liability when the required payment date arrives.

Notice that no expense category was charged in the Split Transaction window shown in Figure 12-5. This is because the deposit reduces the liability account balances that were established when payroll checks were written on 1/31/94. Looking at those transactions in your register, you can see that the gross earnings were charged to the Payroll:Gross category and your matching FICA contribution as an employer was charged to the Payroll:Comp FICA category. Both these categories are classified as expenses and will be shown on your business Profit and Loss statement. On the other hand, the amounts withheld for payroll taxes were charged to liability accounts that will be paid at a future date. Thus, when you pay these liabilities, as you just did, you are meeting your financial obligation to the government, not incurring additional expenses.

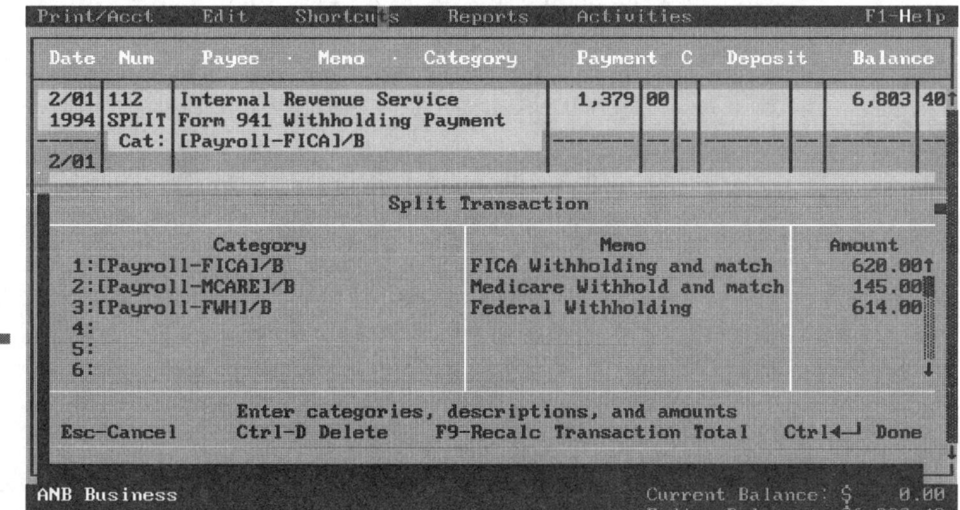

Split Transaction entries for the IRS deposit
Figure 12-5.

IRS Deposit Rules

The frequency with which you must make deposits of social security and federal income taxes is dependent on the amount of your liability. Effective January 1, 1993, the IRS has simplified the rules that affect when you must make these deposits. Each November, the IRS will tell you which rule you should use throughout the upcoming year. If you are not notified, you should use the following rules to make a determination. New employers are to use Rule 1. Since the penalties for noncompliance can be steep, it is important to follow the rules strictly. Notice 931 describes the new rules in detail, but a quick summary is provided here:

New Rules

Rule 1	Tax liability for the previous four quarters was $50,000 or less—Monthly filing
Rule 2	Tax liability for the previous four quarters was greater than $50,000—Semi-weekly filings
Rule 3	Cumulative tax liability of $100,000 or more—Daily deposits.

Through the end of 1993 you can continue to use the old rules, following the instructions that come with Form 941 for the transition. The old rules are summarized as follows:

Old Rules

Rule 1	Tax liability for the quarter less than $500— No deposit required
Rule 2	Tax liability for the month less than $500— Carry forward to the next month
Rule 3	Tax liability for the month between $500 and $3000—Deposit within 15 days from the end of the month
Rule 4	Tax liability at the end of any of the eight monthly periods (the 3rd, 7th, 11th, 15th, 19th, 22nd, 25th, and the last day) greater than $3000 and less than $100,000—Deposit within three banking days
Rule 5	Tax liability at the end of any of the eight monthly periods greater than $100,000—Deposit by the end of the next banking day

Other Liability Accounts

Let's look at the impact of recording the paychecks and the IRS payment on the other liability accounts. Specifically, you will see the effects of these transactions on the [Payroll-FWH] other liability account. Follow these steps to enter the [Payroll-FWH] account from the ANB Business account register:

1. Press Esc to return to the Main Menu.
2. Choose Select **A**ccount, and the Select Account to Use window appears.

   You can quickly view the Select Account to Use window by pressing Ctrl-A when you are in any Quicken account register.
3. Select the Payroll-FWH account and press Enter.

   The screen shown in Figure 12-6 appears.

   Notice that the account accumulated $614.00 as the FWH withholding liability for the January paychecks. Also note that the 2/1/94 entry reduced the balance to 0 when you made your deposit. This will occur each month when you record your deposit to the IRS.
4. Press Esc to return to the Main Menu.
5. Choose Select **A**ccount, select ANB Business, and press Enter.

   You are now back in the ANB Business account register.

Print/Acct Edit Shortcuts Reports Activities F1-Help

Date	Ref	Payee · Memo · Category	Increase	C	Decrease	Balance
		BEGINNING				
1/01 1994		Opening Balance [Payroll-FWH]				0 00
1/31 1994		John Smith 000-00-0001 [ANB Business]→	232 00			232 00
1/31 1994		Mary McFaul 000-00-0002 [ANB Business]→	382 00			614 00
2/01 1994		Internal Revenue Service Form 941 Withho→[ANB Business]→			614 00	0 00
2/01 1994	Memo: Cat:					

Payroll-FWH (Alt+letter accesses menu) Current Balance: $0.00
Esc-Main Menu Ctrl←┘ Record Ending Balance: $0.00

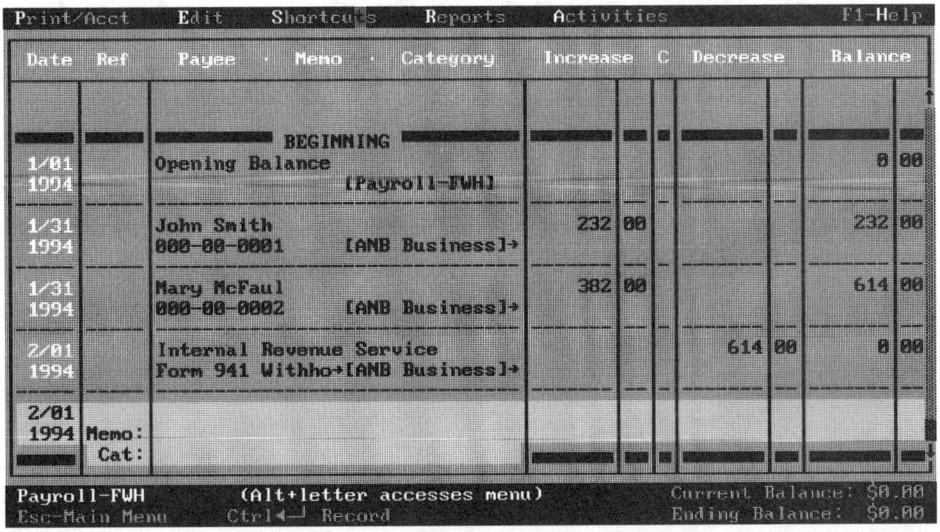

Activating the Payroll-FWH account

Figure 12-6.

Using Memorized and Scheduled Transactions

You can continue to make all of your payroll entries with the techniques you learned earlier in the chapter. Quicken also has features that can make your task a little easier, depending on how much you are willing to automate the process. The first option offered is a memorized transaction capability. Memorized transactions can be saved for later recall and used at your direction. If you want even more automation, you can group memorized transactions into scheduled transaction groups and even have Quicken enter them with no intervention on your part.

Memorized Monthly Paycheck and Withholding Deposit Entries

Since you will be paying your employees on a regular basis and making monthly withholding deposits, you will want to memorize these entries to simplify future recording of the transactions. Since the employees in this example are all salaried, the only changes needed each month are new dates and check numbers on each transaction. All of the split transaction detail will be accurate. For hourly employees or employees making more than the FICA cap amount, some pay periods will require changes to the entries in the split transaction detail. While in the ANB Business account register, complete the following steps to memorize paycheck and withholding deposit transactions:

1. Highlight the John Smith paycheck transaction on January 31, 1994, and press Ctrl-M.
2. Press Enter to memorize the transaction amounts.
3. Highlight the Mary McFaul paycheck transaction on January 31, 1994, and press Ctrl-M.
4. Press Enter to memorize the transaction amounts.
5. Highlight the Internal Revenue Service transaction and press Ctrl-M.
6. Press Enter to memorize the transaction amounts.
7. Press Ctrl-T to display the Memorized Transactions List window.

   Your list should contain entries for Internal Revenue Service, John Smith, and Mary McFaul.
8. Press Esc to return to the account register.

Establishing Scheduled Transaction Groups

In Chapter 11, "Setting Up Quicken for Your Business," you established a transaction group for the utilities payments. The object of transaction grouping is to batch together similar transactions that occur around the same time each month so Quicken can automatically record them for you the next time they need to be made. Remember, only memorized transactions can be batched into transaction groups. From the ANB Business account register, perform the following steps to establish a transaction group for the payroll:

1. Press Ctrl-J, and the Scheduled Transactions window appears.
2. Highlight <New Transaction or Group> and press Enter.

   The New Transaction window appears.
3. Type **4** to select Group for the transaction type and press Enter.
4. Press Enter to select the current account ANB Business.
5. Press Enter to select Monthly for the Frequency field.

   The diamond next to Frequency shows that you can press Ctrl-L to select alternative periods.
6. Type **2/28/94** and press Enter.
7. Press Enter to accept 999.

   This transaction can now be entered monthly for an unlimited time period.
8. Press Enter to accept no prompting.

   Quicken will automatically record the transaction group in the future.
9. Type **2** to have Quicken enter the transactions two days in advance of the payroll payment date.
10. Type **Payroll** and press Enter.
11. Highlight John Smith and press Spacebar to mark the transaction.

    Note the Payroll in the group column, indicating that the transaction is now part of the Payroll group.
12. Highlight Mary McFaul and press Spacebar.

    This transaction also becomes a part of the Payroll group.
13. Press Enter twice to indicate that you have finished selecting transactions.
14. Press Esc.

You are returned to the account register to record further transactions.

Completing the Payroll Entries

In this section, you expand your payroll transactions by adding some entries to the ANB Business account register. These transactions are added so the examples will contain enough pay periods to generate realistic reports later in this chapter. Notice that you will not record check numbers for the remaining example transactions in this chapter. This will not affect the reports prepared in this chapter.

Recording February Transactions

In this section, you add the remaining transactions to the account register to complete the payroll entries for the month of February. You should be in the ANB Business account register to record the following transactions:

1. Press Ctrl-End to highlight the next blank transaction form.
2. Press Ctrl-J.

   Quicken displays a list of scheduled transactions.
3. Select the Payroll Group and press Enter.

   Quicken displays the date of the next scheduled entry of the group, 2/28/94.
4. Press Enter to confirm that this date is valid, type **1** to select enter now. Press Enter to enter and record the scheduled payroll transactions in the account register.

   The following illustration shows that Quicken has entered the scheduled transaction for the monthly payroll for February.

```
 2/28 _Pymt John Smith                          1,560 13          5,243 27
 1994 SPLIT 000-00-0001
       Cat: Payroll:Gross/B
 2/28 _Pymt Mary McFaul                         2,284 22          2,959 05
 1994 SPLIT 000-00-0002      Payroll:Gross/B
```

Notice that Quicken has displayed _Pymt in the Num field. When you write your payroll checks, you can enter the check number in the field then. If you want to search your register to see if there are any _Pymts in the Num field that have not been replaced by check numbers when they were written, you can choose **F**ind from the **E**dit menu. You would place _Pymt in the Num field to locate transactions entered with the scheduled transaction feature.

If the date was not the last date of the month for payroll purposes, you could have typed the correct date in the Scheduled Transactions window and then pressed Enter. In this example, the payroll entries will not be modified, since they are the same from month to month. If you have employees who work on an hourly basis, you would need to select each new transaction, open the

Split Transaction window, and make the necessary modifications to the dollar amounts recorded.

The payroll entries are the only February transactions that are being added to the account register at this time. Figure 12-7 shows a printout of the account register, including the two payroll entries recorded on 2/28/94 and the remaining transactions that will be entered in this chapter.

Recording March Transactions

The March entries can be divided into three groups. The first records a deposit for federal social security, Medicare, and income tax withholding in February. The second and third entries record income earned during the month from consulting and royalties. The last two entries record the payroll transactions for March.

The Entry to Record February Withholding

The entry to record the deposit for taxes withheld during February involves the use of a memorized transaction. From the highlighted blank transaction form in the ANB Business account register, perform the following steps:

1. Press Ctrl-T to recall the Memorized Transaction List window.
2. Select the Internal Revenue Service transaction and press Enter.
3. Move the cursor to the Date field, type **3/1/94**, and press Ctrl-Enter.

Consulting and Royalty Income Entries

In the ANB Business account register, enter the following information for the two deposit entries shown in Figure 12-7:

1. Type **3/1/94** and press Enter twice.
2. Type **Tyler Corp.** and press Enter three times.
3. Type **25000** and press Enter.
4. Type **Seminars conducted Jan. 94** and press Enter.
5. Type **Inc Cons/B** and press Ctrl-Enter. This records the Tyler Corp. revenue transaction.
6. Type **3/31/94** and press Enter twice.
7. Type **Big Books** and press Enter three times.
8. Type **10000** and press Enter.
9. Type **Royalties** and press Enter.
10. Type **Inc Roy/B** and press Ctrl-Enter.

12

```
                           Check Register
ANB Business                                                          Page 1
7/19/94

  Date  Num            Transaction              Payment  C  Deposit    Balance
 ----- ----- ------------------------------- ---------- - ---------- ----------

  2/28 _Pymt John Smith                        1,560.13                5,243.27
  1994 SPLIT 000-00-0001
                Payroll:Gross/B                2,000.00
                  Gross Earnings
                [Payroll-FICA]/B                             124.00
                  FICA Withholding
                [Payroll-FWH]/B                              232.00
                  Federal Withholding
                [Payroll-SWHOH]/B                             54.87
                  State Withholding
                [Payroll-MCARE]/B                             29.00
                  Medicare Withholding
                Payroll:Comp FICA/B              124.00
                  Payroll Taxes-FICA
                Payroll:Comp MCARE/B              29.00
                  Payroll Taxes-MCARE
                [Payroll-FICA]/B                             124.00
                  FICA Matching
                [Payroll-MCARE]/B                             29.00
                  Medicare Matching

  2/28 _Pymt Mary McFaul                       2,284.22                2,959.05
  1994 SPLIT 000-00-0002
                Payroll:Gross/B                3,000.00
                  Gross Earnings
                [Payroll-FICA]/B                             186.00
                  FICA Withholding
                [Payroll-FWH]/B                              382.00
                  Federal Withholding
                [Payroll-SWHOH]/B                            104.28
                  State Withholding
                [Payroll-MCARE]/B                             43.50
                  Medicare Withholding
                Payroll:Comp FICA/B              186.00
                  Payroll Taxes-FICA
                Payroll:Comp MCARE/B              43.50
                  Payroll Taxes-MCARE
                [Payroll-FICA]/B                             186.00
                  FICA Matching
                [Payroll-MCARE]/B                             43.50
                  Medicare Matching

  3/01       Internal Revenue Service          1,379.00                1,580.05
  1994 SPLIT Form 941 Withholding Payment
                [Payroll-FICA]/B                 620.00
                  FICA Withholding and match
                Payroll-MCARE]/B                 145.00
                  Medicare Withhold and match
                [Payroll-FWH]/B                  614.00
                  Federal Withholding
```

Account register showing additional transactions
Figure 12-7.

```
                              Check Register
ANB Business                                                             Page 2
7/19/94

  Date  Num            Transaction                 Payment  C  Deposit    Balance
 ----- ----- -------------------------------- ---------- - ---------- ----------


  3/01       Tyler Corp.                                      25,000.00  26,580.05
  1994 memo: Seminars conducted Jan. 94
        cat: Inc Cons/B

  3/31       Big Books                                        10,000.00  36,580.05
  1994 memo: Royalties
        cat: Inc Roy/B

  3/31 _Pymt John Smith                         1,560.13                 35,019.92
  1994 SPLIT 000-00-0001
                Payroll:Gross/B                 2,000.00
                  Gross Earnings
                [Payroll-FICA]/B                                 124.00
                  FICA Withholding
                [Payroll-FWH]/B                                  232.00
                  Federal Withholding
                [Payroll-SWHOH]/B                                 54.87
                  State Withholding
                [Payroll-MCARE]/B                                 29.00
                  Medicare Withholding
                Payroll:Comp FICA/B               124.00
                  Payroll Taxes-FICA
                Payroll:Comp MCARE/B               29.00
                  Payroll Taxes-MCARE
                [Payroll-FICA]/B                                 124.00
                  FICA Matching
                [Payroll-MCARE]/B                                 29.00
                  Medicare Matching

  3/31 _Pymt Mary McFaul                        2,284.22                 32,735.70
  1994 SPLIT 000-00-0002
                Payroll:Gross/B                 3,000.00
                  Gross Earnings
                [Payroll-FICA]/B                                 186.00
                  FICA Withholding
                [Payroll-FWH]/B                                  382.00
                  Federal Withholding
                [Payroll-SWHOH]/B                                104.28
                  State Withholding
                [Payroll-MCARE]/B                                 43.50
                  Medicare Withholding
                Payroll:Comp FICA/B               186.00
                  Payroll Taxes-FICA
                Payroll:Comp MCARE/B               43.50
                  Payroll Taxes-MCARE
                [Payroll-FICA]/B                                 186.00
                  FICA Matching
                [Payroll-MCARE]/B                                 43.50
                  Medicare Matching
```

Account register showing additional transactions (*continued*)

Figure 12-7.

```
                              Check Register
ANB Business                                                              Page 3
7/19/94

   Date  Num            Transaction              Payment  C  Deposit    Balance
  ----- ----- -------------------------------- ---------- - ---------- ----------

   4/01       Internal Revenue Service           1,379.00              31,356.70
   1994 SPLIT Form 941 Withholding Payment
                 [Payroll-FICA]/B                  620.00
                   FICA Withholding and match
                 [Payroll-MCARE]/B                 145.00
                   Medicare Withhold and match
                 [Payroll-FWH]/B                   614.00
                   Federal Withholding

   4/15       Internal Revenue Service             104.00              31,252.70
   1994 memo: FUTA
         cat: Payroll:Comp FUTA/B

   4/15       Bureau of Employment Services        520.00              30,732.70
   1994 memo: SUTA
         cat: Payroll:Comp SUI/B
```

Figure 12-7. Account register showing additional transactions (*continued*)

After completing these steps, you have recorded both income transactions for March.

March Payroll Entries

In this section, you add the remaining transactions to the account register to complete the payroll entries for the month of March:

1. Press Ctrl-J. Quicken displays a list of Scheduled Transactions.
2. Select Payroll and press Enter. Quicken displays the date of the next scheduled entry of the group, **3/28/94**.
3. Type **3/31/94** and press Enter.
4. Type **1** to select Enter now and press Enter.

Quicken enters the transactions for you in the account register.

Recording April Transactions

The only transactions you will record for April are the Internal Revenue Service deposit for the March payroll and the Federal Unemployment Tax Act (FUTA) and State Unemployment Tax Act (SUTA) payments.

Complete the following steps to record the IRS transaction in the ANB Business account register. (This transaction will help you prepare several reports for the Internal Revenue Service later in this chapter.)

1. Press Ctrl-End to move to the end of the register.
2. Press Ctrl-T to recall the Memorized Transaction List window.
3. Select the Internal Revenue Service transaction and press Enter.
4. Move the cursor to the Date field, type **4/1/94**, and press Ctrl-Enter.

In addition to your withholding tax liabilities, employers must pay unemployment taxes. This program is mandated by the federal government but administered by the individual state governments. Because of this method of administration, you must make payments to both the state and federal government. At the time of this writing, you must contribute .008 percent to the federal government to cover their administrative costs and up to .054 percent to the state agency that administers the program. These percentages apply to the first $7000.00 of earnings for each employee. In some states, the salary cap on earnings may be higher; however, the example in this chapter uses a $7000.00 limit for both federal and state employer payroll tax contributions.

You must make deposits to the federal government whenever your contribution liability reaches $100.00. These deposits are made in the same manner as the FICA, Medicare, and federal income tax withholding payments earlier in this chapter.

Your actual contributions to the state agency will be based on historical rates for your business and industry classification. You may qualify for a percentage rate lower than the maximum rate allowed by law. The contribution rate for the business in this example is assumed to be .04 percent.

Generally, payments to the state agency that administers the program are made quarterly. Each quarter, you are required to complete an Employer's Report of Wages form, summarizing your employees' total earnings during the quarter and the amount of your FUTA and SUTA liabilities.

From the ANB Business account register, make the following payments for federal and state unemployment payroll taxes during the month of April. Follow these steps to record the FUTA and SUTA payments:

1. Press Ctrl-End to make certain you are at the next available form for recording a transaction.
2. Type **4/15/94** and press Enter twice.
3. Type **Internal Revenue Service** and press Enter.

   When you start to type **Internal Revenue Service**, Quicken completes the transaction window with the information from the last IRS transaction recorded on 4/1/94. When you press Enter, that information is actually suggested as the transaction information to record on 4/15/94. While this is a useful feature of Quicken, in this case you will need to edit several of the fields before recording this transaction.

4. Type **104** and press Enter.

   In the "Payroll Reports" section of this chapter, you will see that Smith received $6000.00 and McFaul received $9000.00 in gross pay. McFaul has reached the salary limit for employer unemployment contributions for the year. The amount entered here was determined by multiplying the first $7000.00 of McFaul's salary and all $6000.00 of Smith's by the FUTA rate of .008.

5. Press Ctrl-Backspace to delete Quicken's suggestion for the field, type **FUTA** and press Enter.
6. Press Ctrl-S to open the Split Transaction window.
7. Press Ctrl-D until all the transactions and amounts have been deleted from the Split Transaction window.

   The window will be blank when you complete this step.

8. Press Ctrl-Enter.
9. Type **Payroll:Comp FUTA/B** and press Ctrl-Enter.

   You have now completed the recording of the FUTA payroll tax deposit.

10. Press Enter twice.

    This accepts the 4/15/94 date for the transaction entry and moves the cursor to the Payee field.

11. Type **Bureau of Employment Services** and press Enter.
12. Type **520** and press Enter.
13. Type **SUTA** and press Enter.

    The payment amount of 520 was determined by multiplying 13,000.00 ($7000.00 + $6000.00) by .04.

14. Type **Payroll:Comp SUI/B** and press Ctrl-Enter.

With the recording of these entries, you have completed all the transactions that will be added to the account register in this chapter. These new transactions are shown in Figure 12-7.

Workers' Compensation Payments

As an employer, you will make workers' compensation payments for your employees. The entries are recorded in the way just illustrated for unemployment insurance payments. To record this payroll expense, you need a new category, Payroll:Comp WCOMP.

Payroll Reports

Through the use of filters and customization features, you can obtain a substantial amount of the payroll-related information you need to prepare the various federal, state, and local payroll tax and withholding forms. However, as you will see in the following sections, there are some functions you must perform manually, such as totaling amounts from several Quicken reports to determine the numbers to place in some lines of tax forms.

The objective of this section is to prepare some of the reports you might find useful for your business filing requirements. Although it is impossible to provide illustrations of all the variations, preparing the reports that follow will help you become familiar with the possibilities. You can then begin to explore modifications that best suit your payroll and withholding reporting needs.

From the transactions you entered for January through April, you can gather information that will assist you in preparing your quarterly reports: the FUTA form, SUTA form, workers' compensation report, and federal, state, and local withholding tax reports. Although you have not entered a full year's worth of transactions, you will see that Quicken can also help in the preparation of year-end W-2s, W-3s, 1099s, annual forms for federal, state, and local tax withholding, and other annual tax forms required for unemployment and workers' compensation purposes.

Payroll Report Overview

Quicken's Payroll report summarizes all your payroll activities in any period for which you need information—that is, you can prepare the report for weekly, monthly, quarterly, or yearly payroll summary information. You can gather information for all employees in one report, or you can limit the report to information concerning one employee at a time.

An important point to remember is that Quicken's Payroll report is preset to interface only with the Payroll category. If you recall, it was mentioned early in the chapter that all payroll-related charges would be charged against the main Payroll category. Quicken established subcategories for Payroll:Gross, Payroll:Comp FICA, and so on, to keep track of specific types of payroll charges. If you don't use this format, you need to select **S**ummary Report from the Reports menu and customize your reports to gather the information necessary

Dates for Filing Federal Payroll Tax Returns

Here are some quarterly and annual federal tax return dates for employers:

Form 941, Employer's Quarterly Federal Tax Returns	
First quarter (Jan - Mar)	
If deposit required with filing	April 30
If you deposited all taxes when due	May 10
Second quarter (Apr - June)	
If deposit required with filing	July 31
If you deposited all taxes when due	August 10
Third quarter (July - Sept)	
If deposit required with filing	October 31
If you deposited all taxes when due	November 10
Fourth quarter (Oct - Dec)	
If deposit required with filing	January 31
If you deposited all taxes when due	February 10
Form 943, Employer's Annual Tax Return for Agricultural Employees	
Calendar year filing	
If deposit required with filing	January 31
If you deposited all taxes when due	February 10

for tax-reporting purposes. All the reports prepared in this section are based on the Payroll Report option in the Business Reports menu.

Employer's Quarterly Federal Tax Return

In the previous sections of this chapter, you prepared entries that accumulated FICA and Medicare withholding, the matching employer's contribution, and the federal income tax withheld from each of the employees' paychecks. You also recorded the required payments to the IRS made to a local bank authorized to receive these funds.

Let's now examine how you can use Quicken to assist you in preparing Form 941 (shown in Figure 12-8) to meet your quarterly filing requirements. Consult the special "Dates for Filing Federal Payroll Tax Returns" section for the deadlines for filing quarterly Form 941 and annual Form 943. Starting from the Main Menu of your ANB Business account register, complete the following steps:

1. Select **C**reate Reports.
2. Select the **B**usiness Reports item.
3. Select Pa**y**roll Report, and Quicken displays a Payroll Report window, shown here:

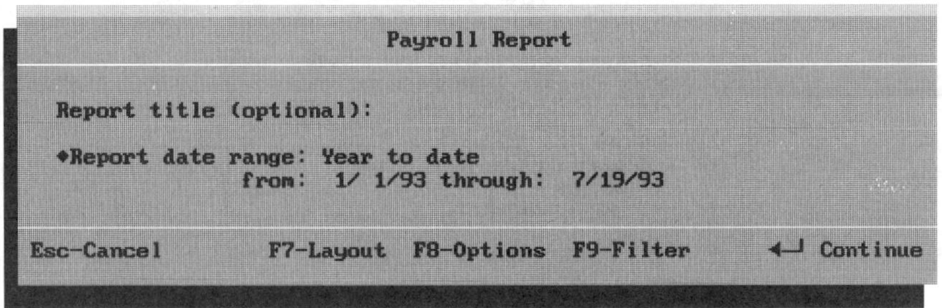

4. Press Enter to accept the default report title of Payroll Report and press F7.

   Quicken presents a Create Summary Report window.
5. Press Enter.
6. Press Ctrl-L and you will see 12 date ranges you can select. Eleven of these are preset, and the last is "Custom Date."
7. Choose Custom Date and press Enter.
8. Type **1/1/94** and press Enter.
9. Type **4/1/94** and press Enter.

   Although the report is for the quarter ending 3/31/94, you need to include the March FICA, Medicare, and income tax withholding payment entered in the register on 4/1/94. You have now set the final date of the reporting period to include the payment date of the last IRS deposit for withholding amounts.
10. Press Ctrl-Enter, and the Payroll report appears on your screen.

    This is a wide-screen report; it will be printed on several pages.
11. Press Ctrl-P to print the report. The Print Report window appears.
12. Select the appropriate printer and press Enter to print the report.

12

Form **941** (Rev. January 1993) Department of the Treasury Internal Revenue Service

4141

Employer's Quarterly Federal Tax Return

▶ **See separate instructions for information on completing this form.**

Please type or print.

Enter state code for state in which deposits made . ▶ (see page 2 of instructions).

Name (as distinguished from trade name) | Date quarter ended

Trade name, if any | Employer identification number

Address (number and street) | City, state, and ZIP code

OMB No. 1545-0029 Expires 1-31-96

T
FF
FD
FP
I
T

If address is different from prior return, check here ▶

IRS Use

If you do not have to file returns in the future, check here . ▶ ☐ Date final wages paid . . . ▶

If you are a seasonal employer, see **Seasonal employers** on page 1 and check here ▶ ☐

1 Number of employees (except household) employed in the pay period that includes March 12th ▶

2 Total wages and tips subject to withholding, plus other compensation	2	
3 Total income tax withheld from wages, tips, pensions, annuities, sick pay, gambling, etc.	3	
4 Adjustment of withheld income tax for preceding quarters of calendar year (see instructions)	4	
5 Adjusted total of income tax withheld (line 3 as adjusted by line 4—see instructions)	5	
6a Taxable social security wages . . . $ × 12.4% (.124) =	6a	
b Taxable social security tips . . . $ × 12.4% (.124) =	6b	
7 Taxable Medicare wages and tips . . . $ × 2.9% (.029) =	7	
8 Total social security and Medicare taxes (add lines 6a, 6b, and 7)	8	
9 Adjustment of social security and Medicare taxes (see instructions for required explanation)	9	
10 Adjusted total of social security and Medicare taxes (line 8 as adjusted by line 9—see instructions)	10	
11 Backup withholding (see instructions)	11	
12 Adjustment of backup withholding tax for preceding quarters of calendar year	12	
13 Adjusted total of backup withholding (line 11 as adjusted by line 12)	13	
14 **Total taxes** (add lines 5, 10, and 13)	14	
15 Advance earned income credit (EIC) payments made to employees, if any	15	
16 Net taxes (subtract line 15 from line 14). **This should equal line 20, col. (d), below or line D of Schedule B** (plus line D of Schedule A if you treated backup withholding as a separate liability)	16	
17 **Total deposits for quarter,** including overpayment applied from a prior quarter, from your records	17	
18 **Balance due** (subtract line 17 from line 16). This should be less than $500. Pay to the Internal Revenue Service	18	

19 **Overpayment,** if line 17 is more than line 16, enter excess here ▶ $ ______ and check if to be: ☐ Applied to next return **OR** ☐ Refunded.

20 **Monthly Summary of Federal Tax Liability. If line 16 is less than $500, you need not complete line 20.** If you are a monthly depositor, summarize your monthly tax liability below. If you are a semiweekly depositor or have accumulated a tax liability of $100,000 or more on any day, attach Schedule B (Form 941) and check here (see instructions) . . . ▶ ☐

	(a) First month	(b) Second month	(c) Third month	(d) Total for quarter
Liability for month				

Sign Here Under penalties of perjury, I declare that I have examined this return, including accompanying schedules and statements, and to the best of my knowledge and belief, it is true, correct, and complete.

Signature ▶ Print Your Name and Title ▶ Date ▶

For Paperwork Reduction Act Notice, see page 1 of separate instructions. Cat. No. 17001Z Form **941** (Rev. 1-93)

☆ U.S. GOVERNMENT PRINTING OFFICE: 1993 339-478

Figure 12-8. IRS Form 941

This is a case where selection of the compressed print option or the landscape option will help you capture more of the report on each page.

Report Discussion

The report prepared is shown in Figure 12-9. (Note that unless you use a wide-carriage printer, the Payroll report will print on several pages instead of just one.) Let's take a look at the information gathered and discuss how you can use it to complete the appropriate lines of the Employer's Quarterly Federal Tax Return form, shown in Figure 12-8.

- *Line 2* This line shows the total wages subject to federal withholding. The Payroll report compensation to employee line shows that a total of $15,000.00 was earned by Smith and McFaul during the quarter.
- *Line 3* This line shows the amount of total income tax withheld from employee wages. The row titled Transfers from Payroll-FWH shows that the total federal income tax withheld from employees was $1842.00. Note that $696.00 was paid by Smith, and $1146.00 was paid by McFaul.
- *Line 6a* The amount of social security taxes accumulated during the quarter totals $1860.00. You obtain the FICA taxes owed from the Transfers from Payroll-FICA row.

To verify this, the gross earnings for the quarter are subject to FICA withholding and matching contributions. This means the total in the Compensation to employee row of the report, $15,000.00, is multiplied by .124 to get the amount on line 6. This should equal the total calculated in the preceding paragraph—$1860.00—which it does.

- *Line 7* The amount of Medicare taxes accumulated during the quarter totals $435.00. You obtain this amount from the Transfers from Payroll-MCARE row of the report. To verify this, the gross earnings for the quarter are subject to Medicare withholding and matching contributions. This means the total in the Compensation to employee row of the report, $15,000, is multiplied by .029 to get the amount on line 7.
- *Line 17* This line shows the total deposits made to the IRS during the quarter. This amount can be obtained from the Internal Revenue Service column in the Payroll report. The Overall Total column shows that $4137.00 was the amount deposited with the Internal Revenue Service during the quarter. Note that this amount includes the 4/1/94 payment. When you complete your IRS deposit slip, you designate the quarter for which the payment applies. In this case, the payment was made for the first quarter and would thus be included in this report.

Notice that the bottom portion of Form 941 requires the calculation of tax liabilities at specified time intervals during the deposit periods. Since you made your payments in a timely fashion during the quarter, you would not

```
                              Payroll Report
                         1/ 1/94 Through 4/ 1/94
BUSINESS-All Accounts                                              Page 1
7/19/94
                                              Internal
           Category Description               Revenue Service
     -------------------------------------- ----------------
     INCOME/EXPENSE
       EXPENSES
         Payroll transaction:
           Company FICA contribution               0.00
           Company Medicare contrib                0.00
           Compensation to employee                0.00
                                             -----------
         Total Payroll transaction                      0.00
                                                 -----------
       TOTAL EXPENSES                                   0.00

                                                 -----------
     TOTAL INCOME/EXPENSE                               0.00

     TRANSFERS
       TO Payroll-FICA                             -1,860.00
       TO Payroll-FWH                              -1,842.00
       TO Payroll-MCARE                              -435.00
       FROM Payroll-FICA                               0.00
       FROM Payroll-FWH                                0.00
       FROM Payroll-MCARE                              0.00
       FROM Payroll-SWHOH                              0.00
                                                 -----------
     TOTAL TRANSFERS                               -4,137.00

     BALANCE FORWARD
       Payroll-FICA                                    0.00
       Payroll-FUTA                                    0.00
       Payroll-FWH                                     0.00
       Payroll-MCARE                                   0.00
       Payroll-SDI                                     0.00
       Payroll-SUI                                     0.00
       Payroll-SWHOH                                   0.00
                                                 -----------
     TOTAL BALANCE FORWARD                             0.00

                                                 -----------
     OVERALL TOTAL                                 -4,137.00
                                                 ===========
```

Payroll report
Figure 12-9.

need to complete this portion. If you did need to complete this portion of the form for the example in this chapter, you can use Quicken to gather the information for you. Figure 12-10 shows the Federal Tax Liability report, which captures the information for the first quarter to help you to complete

```
                                Payroll Report
                           1/ 1/94 Through 4/ 1/94
BUSINESS-All Accounts                                                   Page 2
7/19/94
                                                             OVERALL
John Smith       Mary McFaul     Opening Balance               TOTAL
--------------- --------------- --------------- ---------------



     372.00          558.00            0.00          930.00
      87.00          130.50            0.00          217.50
   6,000.00        9,000.00            0.00       15,000.00
-----------     -----------     -----------     -----------
    6,459.00        9,688.50            0.00       16,147.50
    -----------     -----------     -----------     -----------
    6,459.00        9,688.50            0.00       16,147.50

    -----------     -----------     -----------     -----------
   -6,459.00       -9,688.50            0.00      -16,147.50


        0.00            0.00            0.00       -1,860.00
        0.00            0.00            0.00       -1,842.00
        0.00            0.00            0.00         -435.00
      744.00        1,116.00            0.00        1,860.00
      696.00        1,146.00            0.00        1,842.00
      174.00          261.00            0.00          435.00
      164.61          312.84            0.00          477.45
    -----------     -----------     -----------     -----------
    1,778.61        2,835.84            0.00          477.45


        0.00            0.00            0.00            0.00
        0.00            0.00            0.00            0.00
        0.00            0.00            0.00            0.00
        0.00            0.00            0.00            0.00
        0.00            0.00            0.00            0.00
        0.00            0.00            0.00            0.00
        0.00            0.00            0.00            0.00
    -----------     -----------     -----------     -----------
        0.00            0.00            0.00            0.00

    -----------     -----------     -----------     -----------
   -4,680.39       -6,852.66            0.00      -15,670.05
    ===========     ===========     ===========     ===========
```

Payroll report (*continued*)
Figure 12-9.

Form 941. If you pay your employees weekly, you can produce this same report for weekly periods during the quarter. If you want to reproduce Figure 12-10 with your account register, you can complete the following steps from the ANB Business account register:

1. Press Alt-R to open the Reports window.
2. Select **B**usiness Reports.
3. Select Pa**y**roll Report.
4. Type **Federal Tax Liability By Month** and press F7.
5. Press Enter.
6. Press Ctrl-L, choose Custom Date, and press Enter.
7. Type **1/1/94** and press Enter.
8. Type **3/31/94** and press Enter.
9. Type **3** and press Enter.
10. Type **05** and press F9 (Filter).

    The Filter Transactions window appears. A tilde (~) is used in the Payee matches row to tell Quicken to exclude transactions with this payee from the report.
11. Type **~Internal Revenue Service** and press Enter twice.
12. Type [**Payroll . .** and press Enter twice.

    This command tells Quicken to include only Payroll liability accounts.
13. Type **Y** and press Ctrl-Enter.

    Quicken presents a Select Categories to Include window.
14. Press End and use Spacebar to exclude the following liabilities: [Payroll-SDI], [Payroll-SWHOH], [Payroll-SUI], and [Payroll-FUTA], as shown in Figure 12-11.
15. Press Enter.
16. Press Enter twice, type **C**, and press Enter.
17. Press Ctrl-P, and the Print Report window appears.
18. Select your printer and press Enter to print the Federal Tax Liability report shown in Figure 12-10. Press Esc until the Main Menu appears.

Before leaving this discussion, notice that there are several columns on your Payroll report (Figure 12-9) with 0 balances—the Balance Forward (BAL FWD) columns. These columns represent any unpaid balances in these accounts at the end of the year. In this example, there were no balances in these accounts because the business just hired employees on January 1st. In future years, there would be balances carried forward and shown in this report. However, you still record your first deposit of the year the same way.

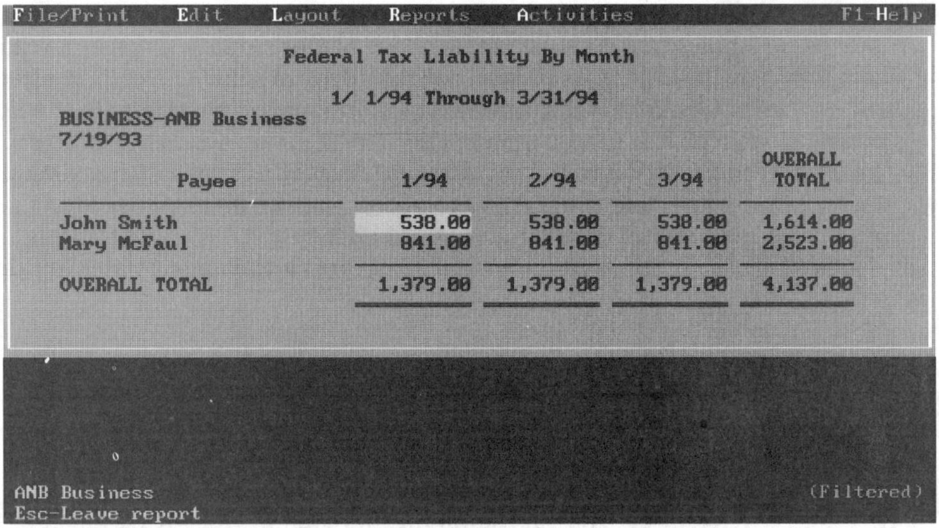

File/Print Edit Layout Reports Activities F1-Help

Federal Tax Liability By Month

1/ 1/94 Through 3/31/94

BUSINESS-ANB Business
7/19/93

Payee	1/94	2/94	3/94	OVERALL TOTAL
John Smith	538.00	538.00	538.00	1,614.00
Mary McFaul	841.00	841.00	841.00	2,523.00
OVERALL TOTAL	1,379.00	1,379.00	1,379.00	4,137.00

ANB Business (Filtered)
Esc-Leave report

Tax report for employee federal tax withholding
Figure 12-10.

Other Quarterly Reports

In addition to the federal quarterly return, you will need to complete several other quarterly tax returns and reports, depending on the state where your business is located. These additional reports and tax forms can include state (SWHOH) and local (LWH) withholding tax reports, state unemployment tax reports (SUTA), and a report for workers' compensation (WCOMP) payments. Figure 12-9 provides the information needed to prepare some of

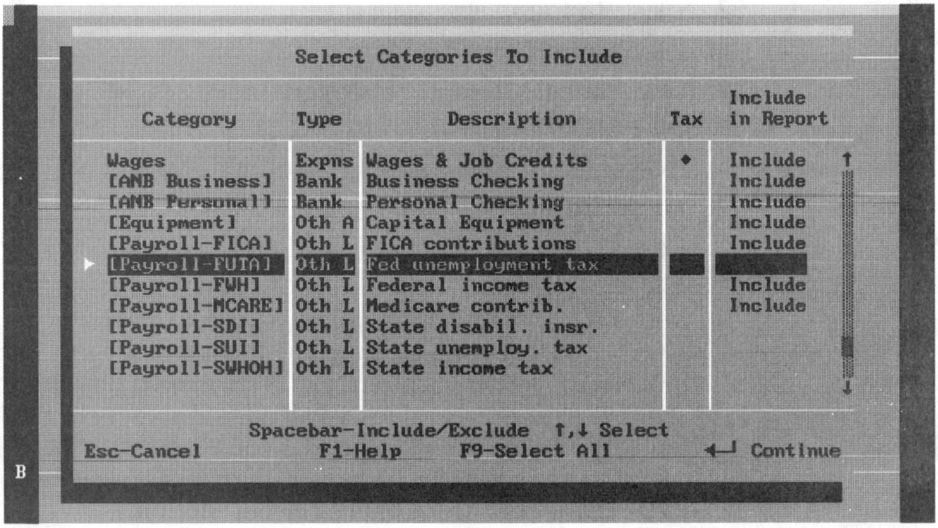

Select Categories To Include

Category	Type	Description	Tax	Include in Report
Wages	Expns	Wages & Job Credits	•	Include
[ANB Business]	Bank	Business Checking		Include
[ANB Personal]	Bank	Personal Checking		Include
[Equipment]	Oth A	Capital Equipment		Include
[Payroll-FICA]	Oth L	FICA contributions		Include
[Payroll-FUTA]	Oth L	Fed unemployment tax		
[Payroll-FWH]	Oth L	Federal income tax		Include
[Payroll-MCARE]	Oth L	Medicare contrib.		Include
[Payroll-SDI]	Oth L	State disabil. insr.		
[Payroll-SUI]	Oth L	State unemploy. tax		
[Payroll-SWHOH]	Oth L	State income tax		

Spacebar-Include/Exclude ↑,↓ Select
Esc-Cancel F1-Help F9-Select All ↵ Continue

Selecting the correct category
Figure 12-11.

12

these reports. For example, the row titled Transfers from Payroll-SWHOH shows that $477.45 was withheld from employee wages for state withholding. You have not recorded this entry in your register; however, it will be handled in the same manner as the payments to the IRS when the check is sent to the state taxing unit. You will also need to monitor individual employees' gross earnings when completing several of the other forms. Determining the total earnings for an employee for a given time period and determining your FUTA and SUTA contributions are discussed in the section "Other Annual Tax Forms and Reports" later in this chapter.

Preparing W-2 Forms

At the end of the year, you must give each employee who worked for you during the year a W-2 form. In the example developed here, assume that John Smith left your business at the end of March and received no further paychecks. The Payroll report prepared in this case is customized for John Smith and uses only the ANB Business account register. You will tell Quicken to limit the report preparation to the business account register, since this is the account from which you write your payroll checks. Thus, all the information concerning John Smith's earnings are included in this account.

Starting from the Main Menu of the ANB Business account register, complete the following steps to gather information to complete John Smith's W-2 form:

1. Select **C**reate Reports.
2. Select **B**usiness Reports.
3. Select Pa**y**roll Report.
4. Type **Payroll Report-John Smith**. Press Spacebar to clear any remaining characters, and press F7.
5. Press Enter, press Ctrl-L, select Custom Date, and press Enter.
6. Type **1/1/94** and press Enter.
7. Type **12/31/94** and press F9 (Filter). The Filter Transactions window appears.

   Notice that Quicken automatically limits all Payroll reports to Payroll category transactions, as shown by the line "Category contains: PAYROLL.." Earlier in the chapter, you learned that this feature of Quicken requires you to record all payroll activity in the Payroll category. Otherwise, Quicken's Payroll report will not gather your payroll transactions in this report. In that case, you need to prepare your reports from the Summary Report option.

8. Type **John Smith**, delete the remaining characters, and press Ctrl-Enter until you are returned to the Payroll Report window. If Quicken returns you to the Select Categories to Include Window, check to see that all are "included". If not, press Spacebar to include all the accounts.

   You have filtered the Quicken report so that it will include only the payroll information for John Smith.

9. Press Enter to move to the Use Current/All/Select accounts field, type **C**, and press Enter. The Payroll report appears on your screen.

   This restricts the report preparation to the ANB Business account, on which all payroll checks were written.

10. Press Ctrl-P, and the Print Report window appears.

11. Select the appropriate setting for your printer and press Enter.

    The Payroll report shown in Figure 12-12 provides the payroll history for John Smith in 1994. Although you have not entered the entire year's payroll transactions for Mary McFaul, the same steps would generate her W-2 information as well.

```
                        Payroll Report-John Smith
                         1/ 1/94 Through 12/31/94
BUSINESS-ANB Business                                               Page 1
7/19/94

                   Category Description        John Smith
              ----------------------------------- --------------------
              INCOME/EXPENSE
                EXPENSES
                  Payroll transaction:
                    Company FICA contribution        372.00
                    Company Medicare contrib          87.00
                    Compensation to employee       6,000.00
                                                 ----------
                  Total Payroll transaction                    6,459.00
                                                             ----------
                TOTAL EXPENSES                                 6,459.00

                                                             ----------
              TOTAL INCOME/EXPENSE                            -6,459.00

              TRANSFERS
                FROM Payroll-FICA                                744.00
                FROM Payroll-FWH                                 696.00
                FROM Payroll-MCARE                               174.00
                FROM Payroll-SWHOH                               164.61
                                                             ----------
              TOTAL TRANSFERS                                  1,778.61

                                                             ----------
              OVERALL TOTAL                                   -4,680.39
```

Annual Payroll report for John Smith
Figure 12-12.

12

Report Discussion

The payroll report can be used to complete John Smith's W-2 Wage and Tax Statement:

- Gross Earnings is the amount ($6000) reported on the Compensation to employee line of the payroll report.
- Federal Withholding is the amount ($696.00) reported on the Transfers from Payroll-FWH line of the payroll report.
- FICA Withholding is one half the amount ($372.00) on the Transfers from Payroll-FICA line. Notice this is equal to the company FICA contribution, since the company matches employee FICA contributions dollar for dollar up to $55,500 of gross earnings.
- Medicare Withholding is one half of the amount ($87.00) shown on the Transfers from Payroll-MCARE line. Notice that this is equal to the company Medicare contributions since the company matches the employee's Medicare contribution dollar for dollar up to the first $135,000 of gross earnings.
- State Withholding is the amount ($164.61) reported on the Transfer from Payroll-SWHOH line of the report.
- Local Withholding shows the local withholding taxes, although there were none in this example. If you do business in an area where local income taxes are withheld, you need to add the appropriate liability accounts to accumulate this information.

Other Annual Tax Forms and Reports

The information provided in the preceding reports can also be used to prepare other year-end tax reports. For example, Payroll reports for the full year, similar to those shown in Figures 12-9 and 12-12, can be used to complete sections of the following reports:

- Form W-3, Transmittal of Income and Tax Statements
- Form 940, Employer's Annual Federal Unemployment (FUTA) Tax Return
- Various state and local withholding and state unemployment tax (SUTA) reports

FUTA and SUTA Contributions

In the "Recording April Transactions" section, you recorded entries on 4/15/94 for your FUTA and SUTA contributions. When you complete your quarterly and annual reports, you can use Quicken's Filter option to prepare a report showing the total FUTA and SUTA contributions paid during the

```
                              FUTA Payments
                        1/ 1/94 Through 4/30/94
BUSINESS-ANB Business                                                Page 1
7/19/94
                                                       1/ 1/94-
                 Category Description                  4/30/94
          ----------------------------------- ----------------
          INCOME/EXPENSE
            EXPENSES
              Payroll transaction:
                Company FUTA contribution       104.00
                                               --------
              Total Payroll transaction                 104.00
                                                       --------
            TOTAL EXPENSES                              104.00

                                                       --------
          TOTAL INCOME/EXPENSE                         -104.00
```

Report showing FUTA payments
Figure 12-13.

quarter or year. This is accomplished by preparing a Summary report and using Quicken's Filter Transactions window to complete the category matches: Payroll:Comp FUTA. Then prepare a second report and complete the category matches: Payroll:Comp SUI. Figures 12-13 and 12-14 show filtered reports prepared from your account register to show FUTA payments of $104.00 and SUTA payments of $520.00.

```
                              SUTA Payments
                        1/ 1/94 Through 4/30/94
BUSINESS-ANB Business                                                Page 1
7/19/94
                                                       1/ 1/94-
                 Category Description                  4/30/94
          ----------------------------------- ----------------
          INCOME/EXPENSE
            EXPENSES
              Payroll transaction:
                Company SUI contribution        520.00
                                               --------
              Total Payroll transaction                 520.00
                                                       --------
            TOTAL EXPENSES                              520.00

                                                       --------
          TOTAL INCOME/EXPENSE                         -520.00
                                                       ========
```

Report showing SUTA payments
Figure 12-14.

12

Reports filtered in this manner can be prepared to determine the total federal and state payments for unemployment withholding during the entire year. That information can then be used in completing Part II, line 4 of federal Form 940 and the corresponding line of your state's SUTA form.

Form 1099

The last payroll-related statement discussed here is Form 1099. You must provide a Form 1099 to all individuals who are not regular employees and to whom you have paid more than $600.00 during the tax year. The easiest way to record transactions for payments of this nature is to type **1099** in the Memo field when you record the transactions in your business account register during the year. You can then prepare a Transaction report for the year filtered by Payee and Memo field matches to gather the information needed to prepare 1099s for each payee. If you are not certain of all the payees to whom you have paid miscellaneous income, you may want to filter the Memo field for 1099 first and print all these transactions. You can then use that information to group your 1099 information by Payee matches. You can also assign all 1099 payments to a category (for example, Consult-1099) and screen a Summary or Transaction report by payee and category to accumulate the necessary 1099 information.

$
banking FILE register expenses DEDUCTIONS
tips finances INCOME equity net pay
checks revenue statements bank statements
dividends INCOME assets business tips
banking business tips cash flow
budget FILE reports
DEDUCTIONS business tips checks
statements cash flow tips mortgage
net pay taxes revenue
mortgage cash business tips dividends tips
business tips investments
register statements taxes
business tips
expenses
equity investments INCOME tips
checks statements cash
assets checks budget tips finances net pay

C H A P T E R

investments banking FILE register expenses DEDUCTIONS
tips equity net pay
checks bank statements
statements business tips
dividends assets
INCOME cash flow
banking business tips FILE reports
budget FILE business tips checks
DEDUCTIONS tips mortgage
statements cash flow revenue
net pay taxes bank business tips
mortgage cash dividends tips
business tips investments
register statements taxes
business tips
expenses tips
equity investments INCOME
checks statements bank cash
assets checks budget tips finances net pay

13

PREPARING BUDGET REPORTS AND CASH FLOW STATEMENTS

Operating a successful business involves more than just having a good product or service to sell to customers or clients; you also need to develop a financial management program that will allow your business to grow and develop. Financial management is more than just being able to prepare the basic reports your banker or other creditors request; it includes a plan of action that will show your creditors you are prepared to manage your business in a changing environment. This means you need to start considering developing a program to manage the finances of your business. Your program would consist of the following:

- A business plan
- The development of strong business relations with your banker or other creditors
- The use of budgets and cash flow statements to help in managing your financial resources

In order to develop a financial management program, you need a sound accounting system that will provide the financial information you need to make better management decisions. Quicken can help you generate this type of information for your business.

Developing a Financial Management Program

If you look closely at the parts of the financial management program just listed, you will notice that two of the three parts do not directly involve the accounting system. Let's take a more in-depth look at the program components.

A business plan is a well-developed concept of where your business has been and where it is going. The special section that follows, entitled "Preparing a Business Plan," highlights the key points that should be covered in a business plan. You can see that nonfinancial considerations play a major role in your business plan—that is, you need to know your product and potential market before you can begin to budget sales and cost for your business. The budget process you follow in this chapter demonstrates how budgeting and cash flow statements are prepared. More important, you will see that the decisions you make in estimating budget income and expenses come from nonfinancial considerations. In short, developing a business plan forces you to think through your business, both financially and operationally, which, in the long run, will make it easier for you to estimate the expected sales and related costs.

The importance of developing strong relations with your banker and creditors cannot be underestimated. However, a word of caution is needed here. Don't expect a bank to finance a new business for you. A good banker is going to expect you to provide a significant part of the capital needed. You might think that you wouldn't need the banker if you had the money to finance your ideas. But from the banker's perspective, it isn't good business to risk the bank's money if you aren't willing to invest your own capital. The special section later in this chapter, entitled "Sources of Funding," shows some alternative ways of obtaining financing for your business if a bank is not a realistic source of cash. An important point to remember is that you need to maintain a strong relationship with your banker over the long term. Although you may not need a loan now, you could in the future. One way of doing this is to obtain a modest bank loan when your business is prospering. This would help strengthen the relationship you have with your bank, and then when you really need a loan, your banker will already be familiar with you and your business activities. This might make the difference between loan approval or rejection.

The final part of the financial management program is the use of budgets and the regular monitoring of your cash flow. A budget is a plan in which you estimate the income and expenses of your business for a period of time: week, month, quarter, year, or longer. Creating a budget report requires some advance work since you enter projected amounts for each category in the budget. Quicken guides you through the budget development process to minimize the work required. Then, you can enter your income and expenses and check the status of your actual and budgeted amounts whenever you wish. You can also use your budget figures to project your business's future cash flow. This type of information is valuable in forecasting loans you may need and demonstrates to your banker that you are anticipating your financial needs. This is a sign of sound business and financial planning.

A cash flow report is related to your budget and allows you to look at the inflow and outflow of cash for your business. This report is valuable since it can enable you to identify problems stemming from a lack of available cash, even though your business may be highly profitable at the current time.

In this chapter, you learn how to use Quicken in the preparation of a business budget. Remember the concepts discussed here as you go through the example; you are learning more than just the procedures involved. Budgeting and cash flow statement analysis can give you and your creditors important information. Quicken provides the necessary ingredients to help you prepare a financial management program that will make you a better business manager.

In the chapter example, you prepare budget entries for several months. Transaction groups from Chapters 11 and 12 are used to expedite the entry process while providing enough transactions to get a sense of what Quicken can do. After making your entries, you will see how Quicken's standard Budget and Cash Flow reports can help you keep expenses in line with your budget.

Preparing a Business Plan

If you have never prepared a business plan before, it can be difficult to determine what to include. Your goal should be to create a concise document that presents a realistic picture of your company, including its needs, assets, and products. Outside lenders will be especially interested in the financial history and resources of the firm and your sales projections. Be sure to include the following as you prepare your plan:

- A brief overview of your firm, its product(s), and its financing requirements. It is important to keep this short and simple.
- A brief history of the firm, including product success(es) and copyrights or patents held. Include a résumé of the firm's owners or partners.
- A short description of your product(s). Include information on the competition, production plans, and prices.
- A description of the market for the product(s) and your distribution plans.
- Sales and cost projections showing current capital and financing requirements.

Sources of Funding

It can be difficult to secure financing for a new business even if you have a good product. Banks are often wary of lending money for a new venture unless you are willing to take the high-risk position of offering your home or other assets as collateral. Some other financing options you might consider are

- A commercial bank loan under the Small Business Administration Loan Guarantee Program.
- Borrowing against your life insurance policy.
- Short-term borrowing through supplier credit extensions.
- Finance companies.
- Venture capitalists; you must normally give up a part of the ownership of your business with this option.
- Small business investment enterprises.
- For economically disadvantaged groups and minority businesses, there may be other options for public or private funding.

Quicken's Budgeting Process

Quicken allows you to enter projected income and expense levels for any category or subcategory. You can enter the same projection for each month of the year or choose to change the amount allocated by month. For the business in this example, it is essential to be able to enter different budget amounts each month, especially for the projected income figures. Royalties are received at the end of each quarter, which causes some months to show a zero income in this category. Also, some other income-generating activities are seasonal and vary widely between months.

Once you have entered the budget amounts, Quicken matches your planned expenses with the actual expense entries and displays the results in a Budget report. Although there is only one entry point for budget information, Quicken can collect the actual entries from all of your bank, cash, and credit card accounts in the current file. Therefore, if you have not paid any business expenses from your personal checking account, you may want to exclude this account from the Budget report. You can do this by selecting the accounts to use with the report. However, since in this example you have paid both personal and business expenses from the ANB Personal account, you cannot exclude it here. Instead, you will use the class code of B to select all business transactions when preparing reports in this chapter. You can also choose whether or not transfers between accounts should be shown in the budget. This is a toggle option; you can change its status with the **E**dit Budget **T**ransfers option in the Budget window.

Although Quicken can take much of the work out of entering and managing your budget, it cannot prepare a budget without your projections. Once you have put together a plan, it is time to record your decisions in Quicken. You can enter Quicken's budgeting process through the Activities menu of an account register. Quicken's budgeting process will be presented in the following stages: retrieving the Set Up Budgets screen, specifying revenue amounts, moving around the Set Up Budgets screen, entering expense projections, printing the report, and creating graphs.

Setting Up the Budget

The Set Up Budgets screen is the starting place for Quicken's budget process. You can access this screen with the Activities menu in any account register. From the ANB Business account register, follow these steps to start the budget procedure:

1. Select **A**ctivities or press Alt-A.
2. Select Set Up **B**udgets.

Figure 13-1 shows the top portion of the Set Up Budgets screen. The category descriptions are listed down the left side of the screen and the months of the year across the top. The layout of the information is similar to a spreadsheet; if you have ever used a package such as 1-2-3 or Quattro Pro, you will feel instantly familiar with the format.

Only a few of the category descriptions are shown on the screen at any time. Quicken displays the total budget inflows and outflows at the bottom of the screen and updates these totals as you make changes. The instant updating allows you to make changes to a budget amount and immediately assess the effect on budget differences.

3. Select **L**ayout.

   You can select budget periods of **M**onths, **Q**uarters, or **Y**ears from the pull-down menu that is displayed.

4. Select **Q**uarter.
5. Select **L**ayout again, and then select **M**onth to change the time period back to the original display (See Figure 13-1).
6. Select **L**ayout again and then select **H**ide Cents. Quicken presents the budget with the cents deleted from the screen.

Use this format for entering budget values in the remainder of this chapter.

Other Budget Menu Options

You can select options from the menu at the top of your screen with either the mouse or the keyboard in the same way that you can make selections

File Edit Layout Percent View Activities F1-Help

Category Description	Jan.	Feb.	Mar.	Apr.
INFLOWS				
Bonus Income	0.00	0.00	0.00	0.00
Canadian Pension	0.00	0.00	0.00	0.00
Dividend Income	0.00	0.00	0.00	0.00
Gift Received	0.00	0.00	0.00	0.00
Gross Sales	0.00	0.00	0.00	0.00
Article Income	0.00	0.00	0.00	0.00
Consulting Income	0.00	0.00	0.00	0.00
Royalty Income	0.00	0.00	0.00	0.00
Interest Income	0.00	0.00	0.00	0.00
Investment Income	0.00	0.00	0.00	0.00
Old Age Pension	0.00	0.00	0.00	0.00
Other Income	0.00	0.00	0.00	0.00
Total Budget Inflows	0.00	0.00	0.00	0.00
Total Budget Outflows	0.00	0.00	0.00	0.00
Difference	0.00	0.00	0.00	0.00

BUSINESS
Esc-Cancel F10-Save Budget

Portion of Set Up Budgets screen
Figure 13-1.

from the menu at the top of the Register window. Although you will look at many of the Budget menu options in more detail in the exercises that follow, a quick overview will help you feel comfortable with this Quicken screen.

You have already seen how you can change the time period for the budget with the **L**ayout selections of **M**onth and **Q**uarter. The other **L**ayout options allow you to look at the budget numbers on an annual basis or to either **H**ide or **S**how Cents in your budget screen.

The **F**ile options allow you to print a copy of the budget as well as to transfer copies of your budget layout to and from disk. You also select this menu to **B**ackup or **R**estore your budget information.

One **E**dit option allows you to create a budget from transactions; it is useful for creating a budget for next year from this year's transactions. Other **E**dit options allow you to enter numbers for two-week intervals, copy a number or a column across the budget layout, control whether subcategories and transfers are shown on the budget layout, and inflate/deflate your budget amounts by fixed percentage amounts.

From the **P**ercent View option you can present your budgets in a **N**ormal View with dollar values (the default setting), or select from three percentage basis presentations: by **I**ncome Total, by **E**xpense Total, and by **R**espective Total. The differences between these options depends on whether you want your budget percentage presentations to be based on the total dollars of income, expenses or, with the respective method, using both income and expenses.

From the **A**ctivities selection, you can return to the Register window, write checks, or use the Calculator.

Entering Revenue Projections

Entering budget projections is easy. If you want the same numbers in January through December, you will be able to enter a number for January and copy the number across to the other months. You can copy the last number entered across the row or you can copy an entire column across. After completing the copy, you can always customize entries for some of the months by typing a new number.

To set up the budget amounts for revenues, follow these steps:

1. Press ↓ until the Jan. column for Article Income contains the highlight.
2. Type **50** and then press Ctrl-→.

   Quicken records 50 as the January amount and then waits for you to enter an amount for February.

3. Repeat step 2 twice to record 50 for February and March, and then position the highlight for an April entry.
4. Type **3575** and press Ctrl-→.
5. Repeat step 4 to enter the same amount for May.
6. Type **2000** and press Ctrl-→.
7. Type **3575** and press Ctrl-→.
8. Type **2000** and select **E**dit.

   You will want to select the Edit menu before finalizing the 2000 entry, or the highlight will move to another row or column.
9. Select **F**ill Right.

   Quicken automatically enters 2000 for the remaining months of the current category.
10. Move the highlight until it is on Consulting Income for January.
11. Type **10000**, select **E**dit, and then select **F**ill Right.
12. Press End twice to move to the far right of the screen; you see the 120,000 total for Consulting Income.
13. Press Home to return to the January column.
14. Press Ctrl-→ until you move to the July column for Consulting Income, type **12000**, and press Enter.
15. Highlight the March column for Royalty Income, type **10000**, and press Ctrl-→.
16. Repeat step 15 for the months of June, September, and December.

Moving Around the Set Up Budgets Window

Before entering additional budget data, you will want to practice moving around within the budget window. After you complete the entries in the previous section, the highlight should be on the 40,000 in the Royalty Income total column. Follow these steps from that location:

1. Press Home three times.

The highlight appears at the top of your screen.

2. Press End to move to the top cell in the total column.
3. Press End again to move to the bottom of the total column.
4. Press Pg Up to move up one screen and Pg Dn to move down one screen.
5. Press Tab to move you to the right one column and press Shift-Tab to move back to the left one column.

6. Repeat step 1 to move to the top left of the budget window.

Practice with moving on the budget window will facilitate quick entries for your data.

Entering Expense Projections

To complete your budget picture, you need to enter projections for your expense categories. Using the information provided, complete the Set Up Budgets screen for the categories. Follow these steps:

1. Enter the following amounts for the categories shown (use the **E**dit **F**ill Right option to enter the amounts for all budget periods):

   Since Quicken displays Category descriptions down the left side of the budget screen, you may want to edit some of the account descriptions you chose when setting up your category list. Notice there are two supply descriptions on your screen, in addition to the computer supplies caption. This occurred because Quicken preset two supply accounts, one for personal and one for business, with the same description of supplies. Use the first supplies row below the computer supplies row when entering budget values below.

Category	Budget Amount
Computer Supplies	210
Dues	25
Equipment Maintenance	100
Freight	20
Insurance	50
Miscellaneous	25
Office Expenses	80
Overnight Delivery	200
Payroll transaction:	
Company FICA contribution	310
Company Medicare contribution	73
Compensation to employees	5,000
Postage Expense	10
Supplies (the first listed)	50
Telephone Expense	120
Travel Expenses	300

Category (*cont.*)	Budget Amount (*cont.*)
Water, Gas, Electric:	
Electric Utilities	30
Gas Utilities	30

2. Press Ctrl-R after completing the last entry and press Enter. You are returned to the ANB Business account register.

Printing the Budget Report

After entering your budget data, you can print your budget report by following these steps:

1. Return to the ANB Business Register window.
2. Select **R**eports, then **O**ther Reports, and then select B**u**dget Reports.

   The Create Budget Report window as you will complete it is shown in Figure 13-2.
3. Type **Johnson & Associates - Budget Report** and press Enter.

   You are limited to 39 characters for a customized title.
4. Press Ctrl-L if the pop-up list for reporting periods is not displayed. Select Custom Date from the pop-up window and press Enter.

NOTE: Other reports expand your list of report options. You can use them for home or business data.

5. Type **1/1/94** and press Enter.

```
                    Create Budget Report

 Report title (optional): Johnson & Associates - Budget Report

 ♦Report date range: Custom Date
              from:  1/ 1/94 through:  3/31/94

 Column headings (across the top): 6
       1. None              4. Half Month        7. Six Months
       2. Week              5. Month             8. Year
       3. Two Weeks         6. Quarter

 Use Current/All/Selected accounts (C/A/S): A

Esc-Cancel      F6-Use Budget  F8-Options  F9-Filter    ↵ Continue
```

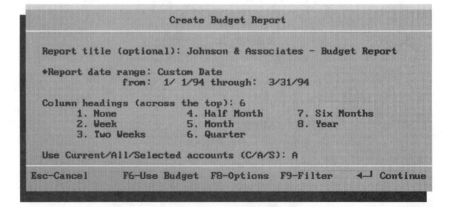

Create Budget Report window
Figure 13-2.

6. Type **3/31/94** and press Enter.
7. Type **6** and press Enter.
8. Press F9 (Filter).
9. Press Enter three times and then type **B**, as shown in Figure 13-3.
10. Press Ctrl-Enter.
11. Press Ctrl-Enter to display the Budget report on your screen.
12. Select **H**ide Cents from the **L**ayout menu.
13. Select Other **O**ptions form the **L**ayout menu, press Enter, type **2** and press Ctrl-Enter.

    Since there were no budget transfers to other Quicken accounts, these steps changed the default setting from including all transfers in the Budget report to excluding them.
14. Press Ctrl-P, select the printer, and press Ctrl-Enter. The report prints as shown in Figure 13-4.

You can also use the Report Options window, by selecting Other **O**ptions from the **L**ayout menu, to tell Quicken which categories you want displayed on your screen. If you designate "All categories" Quicken will show the entire category list even if many of the categories were not used for budgeting purposes (e.g., Canadian Pension). You could also designate "Budgeted or non-zero" or "Budgeted only" categories to be displayed. The default option is "Budgeted or non-zero," where Quicken only displays the accounts for which budget or non-zero information was entered.

If you need to change printer settings, refer to Chapter 3, "Quicken Reports." If your printer has compressed print capabilities, you may want to use a print style that uses a smaller font when printing reports to capture more of

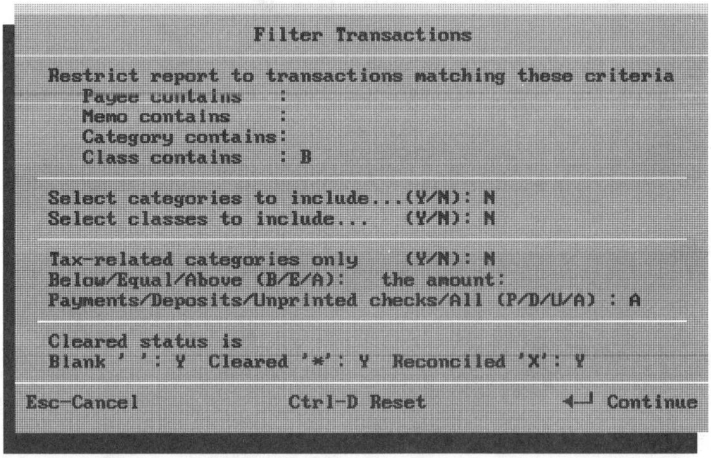

```
                    Filter Transactions

  Restrict report to transactions matching these criteria
     Payee contains    :
     Memo contains     :
     Category contains:
     Class contains    : B

  Select categories to include...(Y/N): N
  Select classes to include...    (Y/N): N

  Tax-related categories only     (Y/N): N
  Below/Equal/Above (B/E/A):   the amount:
  Payments/Deposits/Unprinted checks/All (P/D/U/A) : A

  Cleared status is
  Blank ' ': Y  Cleared '*': Y  Reconciled 'X': Y

Esc-Cancel            Ctrl-D Reset              ↵ Continue
```

Use of a filter to select only business transactions
Figure 13-3.

your report on each page. For example, your monthly report will be printed across two pages unless you use the compressed print feature.

Report Discussion

Let's take a look at the report shown in Figure 13-4. The report compares the actual expenditures made during the quarter with those you budgeted. An analysis of the income section shows you received more income than you

Johnson & Associates - Budget Report
1/ 1/94 Through 3/31/94

BUSINESS-All Accounts — Page 1
7/20/94

Category Description	1/ 1/94 Actual	- Budget	3/31/94 Diff
INCOME/EXPENSE			
INCOME			
Article Income	0	150	-150
Consulting Income	37,500	30,000	7,500
Royalty Income	10,000	10,000	0
TOTAL INCOME	47,500	40,150	7,350
EXPENSES			
Overnight Delivery	270	600	-330
Dues	0	75	-75
Equipment Maintenance	1,100	300	800
Freight	0	60	-60
Insurance	0	150	-150
Miscellaneous	0	75	-75
Office Expenses	0	240	-240
Payroll transaction:			
Company FICA contribution	930	930	0
Company Medicare contrib	218	219	-1
Compensation to employee	15,000	15,000	0
Total Payroll transaction	16,148	16,149	-1
Postage Expense	28	30	-2
Computer Supplies	376	630	-254
Supplies	65	150	-85
Telephone Expense	305	360	-55
Travel Expenses	905	900	5
Water, Gas, Electric:			
Electric Utilities	30	90	-60
Gas	17	90	-73
Total Water, Gas, Electric	47	180	-133
TOTAL EXPENSES	19,244	19,899	-655
TOTAL INCOME/EXPENSE	28,256	20,251	8,005

Budget report for the first quarter of 1994
Figure 13-4.

budgeted during the period. This was due to receiving more in consulting income than anticipated, although you received no income from articles. You would want to examine whether these differences were caused by your failing to project all the consulting activities you were involved in during the quarter or perhaps by a client paying you earlier than you had anticipated.

The expense portion of the report shows the actual and budgeted expenses for the period. An analysis of individual categories is not worthwhile since the data you entered did not include expense entries for all the months in the report. However, you can see that the report compares budgeted with actual expenses during the period and shows the differences in the Diff column. In general, you are concerned with all the differences shown in this report, but you will probably only want to spend your time investigating the large dollar differences between budgeted and actual amounts. For example, you might decide to investigate in detail only those budget differences that exceed $300. For these categories, you might want to examine the underlying transactions in more depth.

The essence of budgeting is to determine where potential problems exist in your business and detect them early. Quicken's budget reporting capabilities can help you in making these business decisions.

Modifying the Budget Report

In the early stages of budgeting, it will generally take several months to develop sound estimates for all your expense categories. You can change your projections at any time by selecting Set Up **B**udgets from the **A**ctivities menu. You can also modify the report you just created to show different time periods or a selected group of accounts. Follow these steps to look at a monthly budget report for the same time period:

1. From the ANB account register, select **R**eports, then **O**ther Reports, and then select B**u**dget Reports.
2. Press Enter four times to accept Johnson & Associates - Budget Report as the title (if the title is not shown, enter it) and 1/1/94 through 3/31/94 as the time period.
3. Type **5** and press Enter again. This tells Quicken you want a monthly report prepared.
4. Press F9 (Filter).
5. Press Enter three times.
6. Type **B** in the Class contains field and press Ctrl-Enter.
7. Type **A** to choose all accounts and press Enter. The modified report appears on your screen.

8. Press Ctrl-P and the Print Report window opens. Select your printer and press Ctrl-Enter, and the report is printed. Since this report is too wide for one page, Figure 13-5 is divided across three pages.

Budget Report Extension

The reports prepared so far in this chapter give you an overview of the budget report preparation process by comparing budget to actual

Johnson & Associates - Budget Report
1/ 1/94 Through 3/31/94

BUSINESS-All Accounts — Page 1
7/20/94

Category Description	1/ 1/94 - Actual	1/31/94 Budget	Diff	2/ 1/94 Actual
INCOME/EXPENSE				
INCOME				
Article Income	0	50	-50	0
Consulting Income	12,500	10,000	2,500	0
Royalty Income	0	0	0	0
TOTAL INCOME	12,500	10,050	2,450	0
EXPENSES				
Overnight Delivery	270	200	70	0
Dues	0	25	-25	0
Equipment Maintenance	1,100	100	1,000	0
Freight	0	20	-20	0
Insurance	0	50	-50	0
Miscellaneous	0	25	-25	0
Office Expenses	0	80	-80	0
Payroll transaction:				
Company FICA contribution	310	310	0	310
Company Medicare contrib	73	73	-1	73
Compensation to employee	5,000	5,000	0	5,000
Total Payroll transaction	5,383	5,383	-1	5,383
Postage Expense	28	10	18	0
Computer Supplies	376	210	166	0
Supplies	65	50	15	0
Telephone Expense	305	120	185	0
Travel Expenses	905	300	605	0
Water, Gas, Electric:				
Electric Utilities	16	30	-14	14
Gas	8	30	-22	9
Total Water, Gas, Electric	24	60	-36	23
TOTAL EXPENSES	8,456	6,633	1,823	5,406
TOTAL INCOME/EXPENSE	4,044	3,417	627	-5,406

Budget Report by Month for the first quarter of 1994
Figure 13-5.

```
                    Johnson & Associates - Budget Report
                         1/ 1/94 Through 3/31/94
BUSINESS-All Accounts                                          Page 2
7/20/94
                                          -      2/28/94    3/ 1/94     -
        Category Description           Budget     Diff      Actual    Budget
------------------------------- ------------------- -------------------

INCOME/EXPENSE
  INCOME
    Article Income                        50       -50          0        50
    Consulting Income                 10,000   -10,000     25,000    10,000
    Royalty Income                         0         0     10,000    10,000
                                    --------  --------   --------  --------
  TOTAL INCOME                        10,050   -10,050     35,000    20,050

  EXPENSES
    Overnight Delivery                   200      -200          0       200
    Dues                                  25       -25          0        25
    Equipment Maintenance                100      -100          0       100
    Freight                               20       -20          0        20
    Insurance                             50       -50          0        50
    Miscellaneous                         25       -25          0        25
    Office Expenses                       80       -80          0        80
    Payroll transaction:
      Company FICA contribution          310         0        310       310
      Company Medicare contrib            73        -1         73        73
      Compensation to employee         5,000         0      5,000     5,000
                                    --------  --------   --------  --------
    Total Payroll transaction          5,383        -1      5,383     5,383
    Postage Expense                       10       -10          0        10
    Computer Supplies                    210      -210          0       210
    Supplies                              50       -50          0        50
    Telephone Expense                    120      -120          0       120
    Travel Expenses                      300      -300          0       300
    Water, Gas, Electric:
      Electric Utilities                  30       -16          0        30
      Gas                                 30       -21          0        30
                                    --------  --------   --------  --------
    Total Water, Gas, Electric            60       -37          0        60
                                    --------  --------   --------  --------
  TOTAL EXPENSES                       6,633    -1,227      5,383     6,633

                                    --------  --------   --------  --------
TOTAL INCOME/EXPENSE                   3,417    -8,823     29,618    13,417
                                    ========  ========   ========  ========
```

Figure 13-5. Budget Report by Month for the first quarter of 1994 (*continued*)

expenditures for the first quarter of 1994. For your own situation, you need to extend the budget over a longer period. It is impractical to enter transactions for all of the included categories at this time, but you can still look at a report for a year, with budget and actual amounts shown monthly. To try working with a larger report, follow these steps from the Main Menu:

1. Select **C**reate Reports, then **O**ther Reports, and then B**u**dget Reports, and the Create Budget Report window opens.

Johnson & Associates - Budget Report 1/ 1/94 Through 3/31/94				
BUSINESS-All Accounts			Page 3	
7/20/94				
	3/31/94	1/ 1/94	-	3/31/94
Category Description	Diff	Actual	Budget	Diff
INCOME/EXPENSE				
INCOME				
Article Income	-50	0	150	-150
Consulting Income	15,000	37,500	30,000	7,500
Royalty Income	0	10,000	10,000	0
TOTAL INCOME	14,950	47,500	40,150	7,350
EXPENSES				
Overnight Delivery	-200	270	600	-330
Dues	-25	0	75	-75
Equipment Maintenance	-100	1,100	300	800
Freight	-20	0	60	-60
Insurance	-50	0	150	-150
Miscellaneous	-25	0	75	-75
Office Expenses	-80	0	240	-240
Payroll transaction:				
Company FICA contribution	0	930	930	0
Company Medicare contrib	-1	218	219	-2
Compensation to employee	0	15,000	15,000	0
Total Payroll transaction	-1	16,148	16,149	-2
Postage Expense	-10	28	30	-2
Computer Supplies	-210	376	630	-254
Supplies	-50	65	150	-85
Telephone Expense	-120	305	360	-55
Travel Expenses	-300	905	900	5
Water, Gas, Electric:				
Electric Utilities	-30	30	90	-60
Gas	-30	17	90	-73
Total Water, Gas, Electric	-60	47	180	-133
TOTAL EXPENSES	-1,251	19,244	19,899	-655
TOTAL INCOME/EXPENSE	16,201	28,256	20,251	8,005

Budget Report by Month for the first quarter of 1994 (*continued*)
Figure 13-5.

2. Press Enter to accept the current report title.
3. If Quicken is not set to pop-up a list for diamond fields, press Ctrl-L to display the pop-up window with the alternative reporting period selections.
4. Select Custom Date and press Enter to move to the "from" field.
5. Type **1/1/94** and press Enter.

6. Type **12/31/94** and press Enter.
7. Type **5** to select Month for column headings and press Enter.
8. Press F9 (Filter).
9. Press Enter three times.
10. Type **B** in the Class matches field and press Ctrl-Enter to have Quicken select only business transactions.
11. Type **A** and press Enter.

The Budget Report by Month appears. Although there are no actual figures beyond the first few months, the instructions in the next section will show you how to look at a wide report like this onscreen.

Wide-Screen Reports

The Monthly Budget report just generated spreads across more than one Quicken screen since it is wider than the screen width of 80 columns. It may be difficult to comprehend until you realize how it is structured. In this section, you explore the wide-screen report and become more familiar with Quicken results. The following discussion will help you become familiar with the Monthly Budget report generated from the additional data you entered.

Use Tab, Shift-Tab, Pg Up, Pg Dn, Home, and End to navigate through the report and become familiar with the appearance of the wide screen for the Budget report. Notice how easy it is to move around the report. Pressing Home twice returns you to the upper-left side of the wide-screen report; pressing End twice takes you to the lower-right side of the report. Tab moves you right one column, and Shift-Tab moves you left one column. Pg Up moves you up, and Pg Dn down, one screen. Note that to open the Print Report window, you only have to press Ctrl-P.

If you have the compressed print option, it is recommended you use that setting to print wide reports. This printer option significantly increases the amount of material you can print on a page. When you print wide-screen reports, Quicken numbers the pages of the report so you can more easily follow on hard copy.

Preparing a Cash Flow Report

Quicken's Cash Flow report organizes your account information by cash inflow and outflow. In this example, the results presented will be the same as the amounts in the budget. In Chapter 14, "Organizing Tax Information and Other Year-End Needs," you are introduced to depreciation expense, which would be shown on the budget report but not on the Cash Flow report. This is because this expense does not require a cash outlay in the current year. Prepare a Cash Flow report for the first quarter by following these steps:

1. From the Main Menu select **C**reate Reports.
2. Select **B**usiness Reports.
3. Select **C**ash Flow.
4. Press F7 (Layout) to open the Create Summary Report window.
5. Press Enter to accept the default report title.
6. Press Ctrl-L to show the pop-up window with alternative reporting periods.
7. Select Custom Date and press Enter.
8. Type **1/1/94** and press Enter.
9. Type **3/31/94**.
10. Press F8 (Options) to open the Report Options window.

    Notice that the Report Organization, option 2, is selected for Cash Flow Basis and that Transfers, option 3, is selected to include only transfers to accounts outside this report. Quicken selected these options by default when you selected the Cash Flow report. Notice that you can also select whether you want to display cents or subcategories and subclasses in your report.
11. Press Ctrl-Enter to accept the current settings.
12. Press F9 (Filter) to open the Filter Transactions window.
13. Press Enter three times.
14. Type **B** in the Class matches field to restrict the report to business transactions.

    This step is essential; you will need to include both ANB Personal and ANB Business in this report because business expenses were paid from both accounts. If you didn't restrict the class to business, all of the personal expenses included in ANB Personal would appear on the report as well.
15. Press Ctrl-Enter.
16. Press Enter four times to move to the Use Current/All/Selected Accounts field.
17. Type **S** and press Enter. The Select Accounts To Include window appears.
18. Move the arrow cursor to Payroll-FICA and press Spacebar until Include appears in the Include in Report field.
19. Repeat step 16 until your screen appears the same as the one in Figure 13-6.

Account	Type	Description	Include in Report
ANB Business	Bank	Business Checking	Include
ANB Personal	Bank	Personal Checking	Include
Equipment	Oth A	Capital Equipment	
Payroll-FICA	Oth L	FICA contributions	Include
Payroll-FUTA	Oth L	Fed unemployment tax	Include
Payroll-FWH	Oth L	Federal income tax	Include
Payroll-MCARE	Oth L	Medicare contrib.	Include
Payroll-SDI	Oth L	State disabil. insr.	Include
Payroll-SUI	Oth L	State unemploy. tax	Include
Payroll-SWHOH	Oth L	State income tax	Include

Select Accounts To Include

Spacebar-Include/Exclude ↑,↓ Select
Esc-Cancel F1-Help F9-Select All ↵ Continue

The Select Accounts To Include window
Figure 13-6.

Equipment is excluded because Quicken does not show transfers between accounts included in the Cash Flow report. However, since the purchase of equipment involved the use of cash funds, that amount should be shown as a cash outflow. Quicken will show this as an outflow to the Equipment account on this report.

20. Press Enter to create the Cash Flow report. Quicken displays the report shown in Figure 13-7.

Remember, you can remove the cents shown on this report by pressing Alt-L and then selecting **H**ide Cents when the report is shown on your screen.

Notice that this report shows the entire amount of payroll ($15,000.00) as a cash outflow, even though you have not paid the entire amount of federal and state withholding to the governmental agencies at the end of the period. This is caused by Quicken's assumption that transfers between accounts included in the report are cash outflows. If you want to eliminate these amounts from the report you can re-create the report with only the ANB Personal and ANB Business accounts included. However, since the liability exists for the withheld amounts, the Cash Flow report shown in Figure 13-7 is a conservative approach to presenting the cash flow.

Graphing Budget Data

Once you have created budget reports, you may find it useful to present some of information in graphic form. You can use Quicken to prepare

```
                           Cash Flow Report
                       1/ 1/94 Through 3/31/94
BUSINESS-Selected Accounts                                    Page 1
7/20/94
                                                  1/ 1/94-
              Category Description                3/31/94
       -------------------------------- ---------------------
       INFLOWS
         Consulting Income                             37,500.00
         Royalty Income                                10,000.00
                                                     -----------
       TOTAL INFLOWS                                   47,500.00

       OUTFLOWS
         Overnight Delivery                               270.00
         Equipment Maintenance                          1,100.00
         Payroll transaction:
           Company FICA contribution         930.00
           Company Medicare contrib          217.50
           Compensation to employee       15,000.00
                                        -----------
         Total Payroll transaction                     16,147.50
         Postage Expense                                   28.25
         Computer Supplies                                375.76
         Supplies                                          65.00
         Telephone Expense                                305.00
         Travel Expenses                                  905.00
         Water, Gas, Electric:
           Electric Utilities                 30.40
           Gas                                17.00
                                         -----------
         Total Water, Gas, Electric                        47.40
         Total Equipment                                1,500.00
                                                     -----------
       TOTAL OUTFLOWS                                  20,743.91

                                                     -----------
       OVERALL TOTAL                                   26,756.09
```

Cash Flow report for the first quarter of 1994
Figure 13-7.

various graphic presentations from your budget data by following these steps from the Main Menu:

1. Select View **G**raphs.
2. Select **B**udget and Actual and Quicken presents this window:

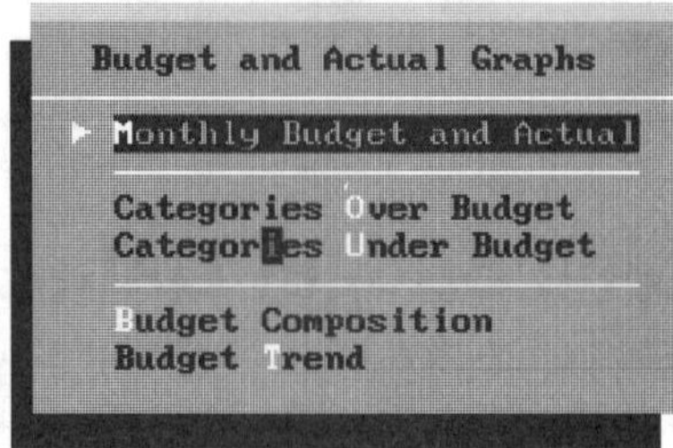

You can make a selection from five graph options. The **M**onthly Budget and Actual option compares budgeted and actual amounts during the budget period in bar chart form. You have options of graphing total income or total expense comparisons separately or combining both

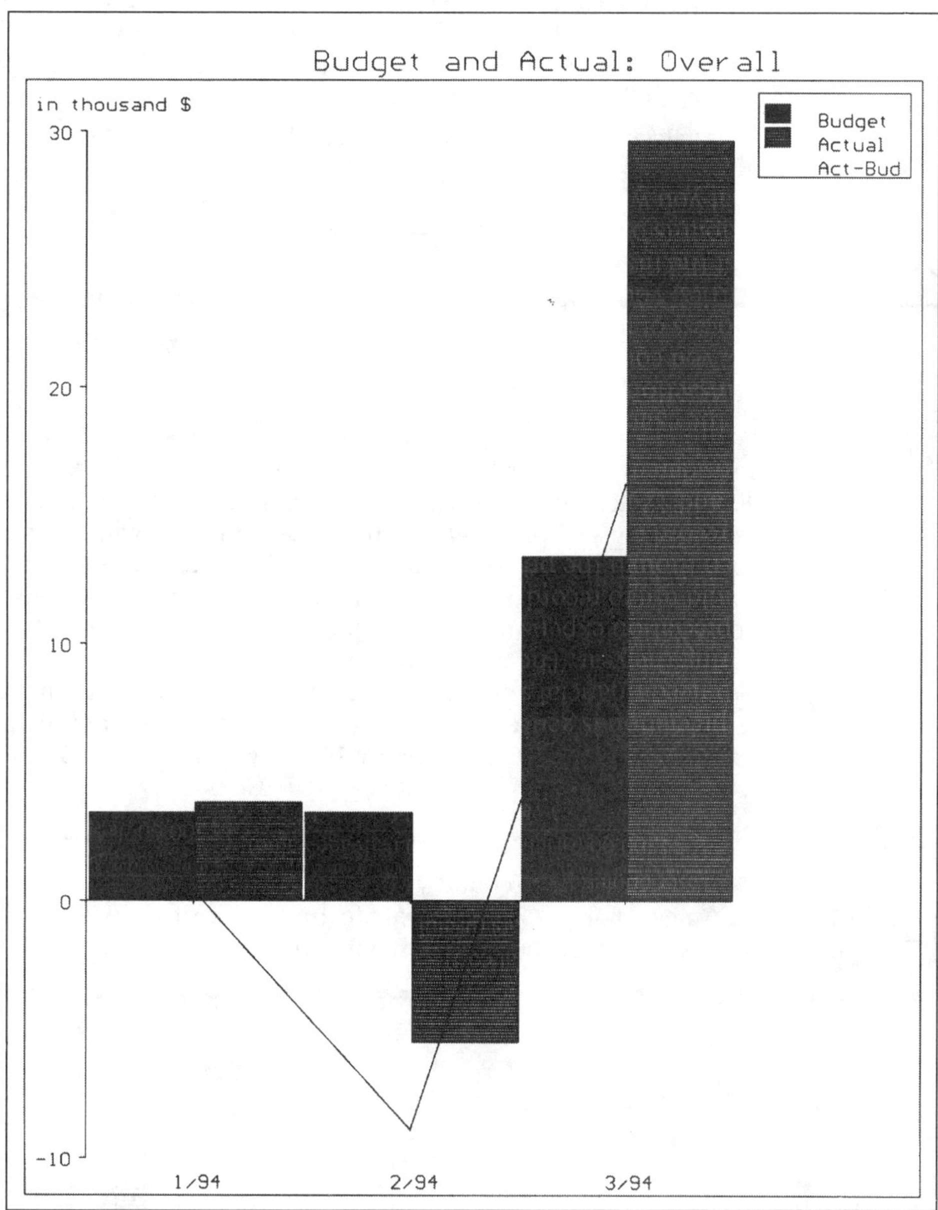

Budget and Actual:Overall graph
Figure 13-8.

income and expense comparisons together as shown in Figure 13-8. The Categories **O**ver Budget option presents a bar chart of actual vs. budgeted comparisons for each category where you were over budget during the budget period. The Categories **U**nder Budget option presents a bar chart for all categories where you were under budget during the period. The **B**udget Composition option presents a pie chart of the percentage of budgeted income or expenses that each category composes of the total income or expense. Finally, the Budget **T**rend option presents a bar chart of the trend in budgeted income or expenses over the budget time period.

3. Select **M**onthly Budget and Actual.
4. Type **1/94** and press Enter.
5. Type **3/94** and press Enter.
6. Type **B** and press Enter.

   Quicken creates Figure 13-8 when you complete these steps.
7. Select Print Graph and Quicken will print the graph if your printer is properly set to print graphs.

A quick review of Figure 13-8 shows a comparison of the overall actual and budget amounts for each of the months of your budget period. For example, during January 1994 your actual budgeted income exceeded expenses by $4,044 dollars, while budget amounts had income exceeding expenses by $3,417. The difference of 627 is the first point in the line graph shown in Figure 13-8. For February you can see that you budgeted for a surplus of income over expenses of $3,417, but you actually had an excess of expenses over income of $5,406 during the month. The total February difference of -8,823 is the second point on your line graph shown in the figure. For the final month your actual surplus of income over expenses exceeded the budget by 16,201 which is the final point on your line graph.

NOTE: Once you build your own transaction history, you can use the new Quicken 7 AutoCreate features to create budget data from actual transactions. This was discussed in Chapter 7.

register expenses DEDUCTIONS
tips finances INCOME equity
checks revenue bank statements
statements
dividends business tips
INCOME assets
cash flow
business tips reports
banking
budget FILE business tips checks
DEDUCTIONS
cash flow tips mortgage
net pay taxes revenue
mortgage dividends tips
business tips investments
register taxes
business tips
expenses
equity investments INCOME tips
checks statements assets checks budget finances net pay

CHAPTER

investments
banking
FILE
register
expenses
DEDUCTIONS
tips
finances
equity
net pay
checks
revenue
statements
dividends
INCOME
assets
business tips
cash flow
banking
budget
FILE
FILE
reports
DEDUCTIONS
business tips
checks
statements
cash flow
tips
mortgage
net pay
taxes
bank
revenue
business tips
mortgage
cash
dividends
tips
business tips
investments
register
statements
taxes
expenses
tips
INCOME
equity
investments
checks
statements
bank
cash
assets
checks
budget
tips
finances
net pay

14

ORGANIZING TAX INFORMATION AND OTHER YEAR-END NEEDS

For the small-business owner, it seems as though tax time is always just around the corner. If it is not time to file one of the payroll tax forms, it is time to file quarterly tax estimates or year-end tax returns. Just as Quicken lent assistance with payroll tax forms in Chapter 12, "Quicken's Payroll Assistance," it can save a significant amount of time and effort when you are preparing income tax returns. You will also want to take a look at the free tax information that you can get from the Federal government. The box, "Free Tax Information," lists some of the information that may be of interest.

In this chapter, you'll see how Quicken can be used to gather information to complete the tax forms for your business-related activities. You are introduced to the concept of depreciation and how it affects business profits. You learn how to use Quicken to prepare your Schedule C, Profit or Loss from Business statements, shown in Figure 14-1. You can also use Quicken features to help you prepare for recording the following year's transactions.

Free Tax Information

Tax regulations can be complex. To help you determine filing options, due dates, payment methods, and estimated tax, the Department of the Treasury provides a number of free tax publications with the information you need to fill out the necessary returns. You can order these publications by calling the IRS toll-free number, (800) 829-3676.

Publication Number	Publication Name
334	Tax Guide for Small Business
463	Travel, Entertainment, and Gift Expenses
510	Excise Taxes
515	Withholding of Tax on Non-Resident Aliens
533	Self-Employment Tax
534	Depreciation
535	Business Expenses
538	Accounting Periods and Methods
541	Tax Information on Partnerships
542	Tax Information on Corporations
544	Sales and Other Dispositions of Assets
551	Basis of Assets
560	Retirement Plans for the Self-Employed
587	Business Use of Your Home
589	Tax Information for S Corporations
686	Certification for Reduced Tax Rates in Tax Treaty Countries
911	Tax Information for Direct Sellers
917	Business Use of a Car
937	Business Reporting
946	How to Begin Depreciating Your Property

SCHEDULE C (Form 1040)

Department of the Treasury Internal Revenue Service (0)

Profit or Loss From Business

(Sole Proprietorship)

▶ **Partnerships, joint ventures, etc., must file Form 1065.**

▶ **Attach to Form 1040 or Form 1041.** ▶ **See Instructions for Schedule C (Form 1040).**

OMB No. 1545-0074

1992

Attachment Sequence No. **09**

Name of proprietor | **Social security number (SSN)**

A Principal business or profession, including product or service (see page C-1) | B Enter principal business code (from page 2) ▶

C Business name | **D Employer ID number (Not SSN)**

E Business address (including suite or room no.) ▶ ....
City, town or post office, state, and ZIP code

F Accounting method: (1) ☐ Cash (2) ☐ Accrual (3) ☐ Other (specify) ▶ ....

G Method(s) used to value closing inventory: (1) ☐ Cost (2) ☐ Lower of cost or market (3) ☐ Other (attach explanation) (4) ☐ Does not apply (if checked, skip line H) — **Yes** | **No**

H Was there any change in determining quantities, costs, or valuations between opening and closing inventory? If "Yes," attach explanation

I Did you "materially participate" in the operation of this business during 1992? If "No," see page C-2 for limitations on losses

J Was this business in operation at the end of 1992?

K How many months was this business in operation during 1992? ▶

L If this is the first Schedule C filed for this business, check here ▶ ☐

Part I Income

1	Gross receipts or sales. **Caution:** *If this income was reported to you on Form W-2 and the "Statutory employee" box on that form was checked, see page C-2 and check here* ▶ ☐	1	47,500 00
2	Returns and allowances	2	
3	Subtract line 2 from line 1	3	47,500 00
4	Cost of goods sold (from line 40 on page 2)	4	
5	**Gross profit.** Subtract line 4 from line 3	5	47,500 00
6	Other income, including Federal and state gasoline or fuel tax credit or refund (see page C-2)	6	
7	**Gross income.** Add lines 5 and 6 ▶	7	47,500 00

Part II Expenses (Caution: *Do not* enter expenses for business use of your home on lines 8–27. Instead, see line 30.)

		Line	Amount			Line	Amount
8	Advertising	8		21	Repairs and maintenance	21	1,100 00
9	Bad debts from sales or services (see page C-3)	9		22	Supplies (not included in Part III)	22	440 76
10	Car and truck expenses (see page C-3—also attach **Form 4562**)	10		23	Taxes and licenses	23	1,147 50
11	Commissions and fees	11		24	Travel, meals, and entertainment:		
12	Depletion	12		a	Travel	24a	905 00
13	Depreciation and section 179 expense deduction (not included in Part III) (see page C-3)	13	275 00	b	Meals and entertainment		
14	Employee benefit programs (other than on line 19)	14		c	Enter 20% of line 24b subject to limitations (see page C-4)		
15	Insurance (other than health)	15		d	Subtract line 24c from line 24b	24d	
16	Interest:			25	Utilities	25	352 40
a	Mortgage (paid to banks, etc.)	16a		26	Wages (less jobs credit)	26	15,000 00
b	Other	16b		27a	Other expenses (**list type and amount**):		
17	Legal and professional services	17			Misc. Expense 298.25		
18	Office expense	18					
19	Pension and profit-sharing plans	19					
20	Rent or lease (see page C-4):						
a	Vehicles, machinery, and equipment	20a					
b	Other business property	20b		27b	Total other expenses	27b	298 25

		Line	Amount
28	**Total expenses** before expenses for business use of home. Add lines 8 through 27b in columns ▶	28	19,518 91
29	Tentative profit (loss). Subtract line 28 from line 7	29	27,981 09
30	Expenses for business use of your home. Attach **Form 8829**	30	
31	**Net profit or (loss).** Subtract line 30 from line 29. If a profit, enter here and on Form 1040, line 12. Also, enter the net profit on Schedule SE, line 2 (statutory employees, see page C-5). If a loss, you MUST go on to line 32 (fiduciaries, see page C-5)	31	27,981 09
32	If you have a loss, you MUST check the box that describes your investment in this activity (see page C-5). If you checked 32a, enter the loss on Form 1040, line 12, and Schedule SE, line 2 (statutory employees, see page C-5). If you checked 32b, you MUST attach **Form 6198.**	32a ☐ All investment is at risk. 32b ☐ Some investment is not at risk.	

For Paperwork Reduction Act Notice, see Form 1040 instructions. Cat. No. 11334P **Schedule C (Form 1040) 1992**

Schedule C
Figure 14-1.

Depreciation

Depreciation is an expense recorded at the end of the tax year (or any accounting period). The concept of depreciation can be confusing, since it does not follow the same rules as other expenses. Depreciation does not require a cash expenditure in the current year; you are recognizing a part of a cash outflow that occurred in a prior year when you record depreciation expense. Tax rules do not allow you to recognize the full cost as an expense in the earlier tax year because the resource is used in business for many tax years. For example, resources such as a truck or piece of machinery are not expensed in the year purchased because they benefit the business over a number of years. Purchases such as paper, on the other hand, are consumed in the year purchased, and their entire cost is recognized in that tax year.

A basic definition of depreciation is that it is a portion of the original cost of an asset charged as an expense to a tax period. For the example developed in this section, suppose you purchased computer hardware that is used in your business. This is an asset of your business that will help generate revenues in the current and future tax years. You might think the cost of the equipment you purchased should be charged to your business in the year you paid for it, just as other cash expenses apply to the year paid. This seems fair, since the purchase involved a significant cash outflow for the year. Unfortunately, from an accounting or tax perspective, the purchase of a piece of equipment is an acquisition that will affect your business operations over a number of years and thus cannot be expensed or deducted from revenues only in the year of purchase. The cost of the asset must be expensed over the years that it is expected to generate business revenues. For this reason, accountants and the Internal Revenue Service require that you apply the concept of depreciation when you prepare your Schedule C, Profit or Loss from Business statements. However, in the section "Section 179 Property" later in this chapter, you will see that there is one important exception to the requirement that you depreciate your long-lived assets.

You can depreciate only assets that lose their productivity as you use them in your business activity. For example, you cannot record depreciation on the land where your building stands. Even though you may feel your land has lost value in recent years, you cannot recognize this decline until you sell the land. Thus, equipment is an example of a *depreciable asset*, while land is not. Throughout this chapter and on income tax forms, you will see the term "depreciable assets" used. This means assets that have a life longer than one year and that will benefit business operations in several accounting periods.

Depreciation Terminology

There are several terms pertaining to depreciation that need to be discussed in more depth. You must always depreciate the original cost of an asset. *Original cost* is the total cost of the asset. For example, if you purchased a piece of machinery and paid shipping charges and sales tax, these additional costs are considered to be associated with getting the asset into an income-producing condition and are therefore part of the original cost. The screen in Figure 14-2 shows the Equipment account register after recording the transactions in Chapter 11, "Setting Up Quicken for Your Business." The first transaction recorded in the register shows the original cost of the High Tech Computer, $3000.00. The printer purchase on 1/25/94 is recorded at its original cost of $1500.00.

In Chapter 9, "Determining Your Net Worth," you learned to revalue personal assets to market value. You cannot do this with business assets. If your asset increases in value, you cannot recognize this increase in your Quicken system. You must always *carry* (show on your business accounting records) your business assets at their original cost.

Another important term is *accumulated depreciation.* This is the amount of depreciation you have recorded for an asset in all previous years. Your assets will always be shown on the balance sheet at original cost minus accumulated depreciation. For example, for the $3000.00 High Tech Computer asset, you recorded depreciation expense of $600.00 in the previous year. You have an accumulated depreciation of $600.00 from the previous year, so your asset carrying value is $2400.00 before recording this year's depreciation.

Establishing Accounts for Assets

You probably will establish another asset account for each major type of depreciable asset used in your business. Follow the same procedures used in Chapter 11, "Setting Up Quicken for Your Business," to set up the Equipment account. If you have equipment, office furniture, and buildings that you use in your business, including the portion of your home used exclusively for

Print/Acct Edit Shortcuts Reports Activities F1-Help

Date	Ref	Payee · Memo · Category	Decrease	C	Increase	Balance
		BEGINNING				
1/01 1994		Opening Balance [Equipment]				0 00
1/01 1994		High Tech Computer Original Cost o→[Equipment]/B			3,000 00	3,000 00
1/01 1994		High Tech Computer Depreciation Ex→[Equipment]/B	600 00			2,400 00
1/25 1994		Laser 1 Printer from Ha→[ANB Business]→			1,500 00	3,900 00
1/25 1994	Memo: Cat:					

Equipment (Alt+letter accesses menu) Current Balance: $ 0.00
Esc-Main Menu Ctrl◄┘ Record Ending Balance: $3,900.00

Equipment Account Register window
Figure 14-2.

business purposes, you will depreciate the original cost of each of the assets. On the other hand, you may decide to establish a separate account for each asset if you have few depreciable assets. Quicken's default limit on the number of accounts in the system is 64, although you can increase this to up to 255 given sufficient memory and disk space. In the example, you learn how to depreciate more than one asset in an account.

NOTE: Quicken provides a shortcut for switching between accounts that you use frequently. Use the Select Account to Use window, and edit the account for which you want a shortcut. Select a number from 1 to 9. Activate the account when you need it by pressing Ctrl in combination with the number that you assigned it.

Depreciation Methods

The straight-line method of depreciation described in the next section is appropriate for income tax purposes. However, for the most part, you will probably use the modified accelerated cost recovery system (MACRS) and the accelerated cost recovery system (ACRS) methods of determining your depreciation amounts. Generally speaking, MACRS covers tangible assets put into business use after December 31, 1986, and ACRS covers tangible assets put into place after December 31, 1980. *Tangible assets* are property that can be felt and touched. All the assets mentioned in our discussion (equipment, office furniture, and buildings) fit this description.

The reason most taxpayers use MACRS is that the method builds in a higher level of depreciation deductions in the early years of an asset's life than would be calculated using the straight-line method of depreciation. Consult IRS Publication 534 before computing your depreciation on tangible assets.

Straight-Line Depreciation Method

In this example, you use the straight-line method to record depreciation on an asset. *Straight-line depreciation* expenses the cost of the asset evenly over the life of the asset. For example, the High Tech Computer has a useful life of five years, and you recorded depreciation expense at $600.00 in 1993. Since this method does not attempt to recognize more depreciation in the early years of an asset's life, it is always acceptable to the IRS. Many other depreciation methods can be used and may be more favorable, since they recognize greater depreciation in the early years of the asset's life. IRS Publication 534 lists the many rules that apply to the selection of a depreciation method. One of the considerations that determines the depreciation method chosen is the year in which you placed the asset in service. A rule that applies to all types of depreciation is that once you select a method of depreciation for an asset, you cannot change to another depreciation method. Table 14-1 lists some of the other depreciation methods. You will need to check with your accountant or check IRS Publication 534 for specific rulings on which methods you can use.

When using the straight-line method of depreciating an asset, use the following formula:

$$\frac{\text{original cost} - \text{salvage value}}{\text{useful life of asset}}$$

The original cost of depreciable assets has already been discussed; however, *salvage value* is a new term. Salvage value is the amount of cash you expect to recover when you dispose of your depreciable asset. This is, obviously, always an estimate and, in the case of a computer, not easily estimated, due to rapid changes in the computer field. For this reason, many accountants assign a salvage value of 0 to this type of asset, stating in effect that it will have no value at the end of its estimated life. This is also the assumption made in the entries recorded here. When you record salvage values for your assets, you can use the history of similar assets when estimating depreciation. If equipment that is five years old typically sells for 20 percent of its original cost, that would be a good estimate for the salvage value of a piece of equipment with an estimated life of five years bought today.

Method	Description
ACRS	The Accelerated Cost Recovery System is an accelerated depreciation method that can be used for assets placed in service after December 31, 1980, and before December 31, 1986.
Declining-balance	This method allows the deduction of depreciation expense at a faster rate than straight-line. There are several different percentages used in computing this type of depreciation. One acceptable option is 150 percent of straight-line depreciation.
MACRS	The Modified Accelerated Cost Recovery System is an accelerated depreciation method used for assets placed in service after December 31, 1986.
Straight-line	This method is the easiest to compute because the cost of the asset is depreciated evenly over the life of the asset. It is also the least advantageous to the business owner because it does not accelerate depreciation expense in the early years of the asset's life.

Depreciation methods
Table 14-1.

Depreciation Calculation

The amounts used in the depreciation entries in this chapter were determined by the calculations shown here:

High Tech Computer:

$$\frac{\$3000.00 \text{ (original cost)} - 0 \text{ (salvage value)}}{5 \text{ years (useful life)}} = \$600.00 \text{ depreciation per year}$$

Laser printer:

$$\frac{\$1500.00 \text{ (original cost)} - 0 \text{ (salvage value)}}{3 \text{ years (useful life)}} = \$500.00 \text{ depreciation per year}$$

Depreciation is generally recorded only once, at the end of the year, unless you need financial statements prepared for a bank or other third party during the year. The amounts calculated in this example are the annual depreciation expenses for the computer and printer—the amounts you would use to record depreciation for the year ending 12/31/94. (Note that even though the printer was acquired at the end of January, it is acceptable to record a full year's depreciation on the asset, since the difference between 11 and 12 months' worth of depreciation is so small that it would not be considered to have a material effect.)

In the examples developed in Chapters 11 and 13, the account register transactions have been limited to the first quarter of the year. (In Chapter 12, you completed several April 1994 entries in order to see the complete process of payroll accounting.) Since there is not a full year of expense entries, you can compute the depreciation on the computer and printer for just the first quarter of 1994. This is accomplished by dividing both annual amounts of depreciation by 4. Thus, the first quarter's depreciation charges that you will record are

High Tech Computer:

$$\frac{\$600.00 \text{ (annual depreciation)}}{4 \text{ (quarters)}} = \$150.00 \text{depreciation for first quarter, 1994}$$

Laser printer:

$$\frac{\$500.00 \text{ (annual depreciation)}}{4 \text{ (quarters)}} = \$125.00 \text{depreciation for first quarter, 1994}$$

Now that you are familiar with the method used to record depreciation in the example and how the amounts you will record were determined, you are ready to begin recording the depreciation entry in your account register.

Establishing Depreciation Categories

Before recording the depreciation entries in this chapter, you establish a Depreciation category with Computer and Printer subcategories in your category list. Select the Equipment account from the BUSINESS file, open the account register, and follow these steps:

1. Press Ctrl-C to open the Category and Transfer List window.
2. Press Home to move to <New Category>.
3. Press Enter to open the Set Up Category window.
4. Type **Depreciation** and press Enter.
5. Press Enter to accept Expense.
6. Type **Depreciation Expense** and press Enter.
7. Type **Y** and press F9 (Tax Schedules).
8. Select Schedule C.
9. Select Other Business expense.
10. Select Copy:1.
11. Press Enter.
12. Highlight the Depreciation category.
13. Press Ctrl-Ins.
14. Type **Computer** and press Enter.
15. Type **S** and press Enter.
16. Type **Depreciation-Computer** and press Enter.
17. Type **Y** and press F9 (Tax Schedules).
18. Select Schedule C.
19. Select Other Business expense.
20. Select Copy:1.
21. Press Enter.
22. Highlight the Depreciation category and press Ctrl-Ins.
23. Type **Printer** and press Enter.
24. Type **S** and press Enter.
25. Type **Depreciation-Printer** and press Enter.
26. Type **Y** and press F9 (Tax Schedules).
27. Select Schedule C.
28. Select Other Business expense.
29. Select Copy:1.

30. Press Enter.
31. Press Esc to return to the register.

You can now begin recording your depreciation expense transactions.

Depreciation Expense Transactions

Let's record the depreciation on the assets in your Quicken account. Starting from the next blank transaction form in the Equipment account register (Figure 14-2) in the BUSINESS file.

You might want to deactivate Quicken's QuickFill option (Set **P**references, **G**eneral Settings and type **N** for the QuickFill setting in option 2, press Ctrl-Enter, and then press Esc until the Main Menu appears) before entering transactions. Otherwise, Quicken will prompt you with proposed transactions for each payee, and you will need to edit these entries. Although QuickFill might actually cause you some extra work if you do not deactivate it, you can still use the information in the steps provided to edit the transactions that QuickFill generates.

1. Type **3/31/94** and press Enter twice.

   Notice that no check numbers are recorded in this register because all checks are written against the business checking account.
2. Type **High Tech Computer** and press Enter.
3. Type **150** and press Enter.
4. Type **Depreciation-1994** and press Enter.
5. Type **Depreciation:Computer/B** and press Ctrl-Enter.

   You have just recorded the depreciation expense on the computer for the months January through March of 1994. The remaining steps record depreciation on the laser printer you acquired in January.
6. Type **3/31/94** in the Date field and press Enter twice.
7. Type **Laser 1** and press Enter.
8. Type **125** and press Enter.
9. Type **Depreciation-1994** and press Enter.
10. Type **Depreciation:Printer/B** and press Ctrl-Enter.

These register entries show how your depreciation transactions will appear after you record both of them:

3/31 1994		High Tech Computer Depreciation-19→Depreciation:C→	150	00				3,750	00
3/31 1994		Laser 1 Depreciation-19→Depreciation:P→	125	00				3,625	00

This completes the depreciation transaction entry for the first quarter of 1994. Remember, depreciation is normally recorded only at year end. However, for purposes of this example, we have prepared the entries at the end of the first quarter.

Customized Equipment Report

After recording the depreciation transactions in the Equipment account, you will want to look at a customized Equipment report. This report, which you will prepare shortly, summarizes all the activity in the account. Figure 14-3 shows the Equipment report for your business since 1/1/94. Notice that the report shows the depreciation expense taken during the first quarter for both the computer and the printer, as well as the total for the category. You can also see that there was a transfer of $1500.00 from business checking for the purchase of the printer in January.

Finally, you can see that the balance forward amount of $2400.00 is the $3000.00 original cost of the asset minus the $600.00 accumulated depreciation taken in the prior year. Thus, when you prepare a balance sheet in Chapter 15, "Monitoring Financial Conditions," the equipment asset will total $3625.00.

If you want to produce the Equipment report, follow these steps, starting from the Equipment account register:

1. Select the **R**eports pull-down menu item.
2. Select **O**ther Reports and **S**ummary Reports, and the Create Summary Report window appears.
3. Type **Equipment Report** and press Enter.
4. Select Custom Date.

   If you do not have the diamond fields set to pop-up automatically, you will need to press Ctrl-L before selecting Custom Date.
5. Type **1/1/94** and press Enter.
6. Type **3/31/94** and press Enter.
7. Press Enter to accept option 1 for the Row Headings field.
8. Type **1** and press Enter twice to select Don't Subtotal for the column headings, and no for Show Percentage Column.

```
                          Equipment Report
                      1/ 1/94 Through 3/31/94
BUSINESS-Equipment                                                     Page 1
7/21/94
                                                        1/ 1/94-
               Category Description                     3/31/94
           ------------------------------------ --------------------
           INCOME/EXPENSE
             EXPENSES
               Depreciation Expense:
                 Depreciation-Computer              150.00
                 Depreciation-Printer               125.00
                                                ----------
               Total Depreciation Expense                     275.00
                                                          ----------
             TOTAL EXPENSES                                   275.00

                                                          ----------
           TOTAL INCOME/EXPENSE                              -275.00

           TRANSFERS
             FROM ANB Business                              1,500.00
                                                          ----------
           TOTAL TRANSFERS                                  1,500.00

           BALANCE FORWARD
             Equipment                                      2,400.00
                                                          ----------
           TOTAL BALANCE FORWARD                            2,400.00

                                                          ----------
           OVERALL TOTAL                                    3,625.00
                                                          ==========
```

Equipment report
Figure 14-3.

9. Type **C** and press Enter.
10. Press Ctrl-P, and the Print Report window appears.
11. Select the printer you are using and press Enter.

Depreciation and the IRS

The transactions in this chapter record depreciation using the straight-line method to determine the amounts for the entries. This method was demonstrated to cover the recording process without going into too much detail about IRS rules for determining depreciation expense for tax purposes. However, we need to discuss briefly one additional aspect of deducting the cost of long-lived assets for IRS purposes, Section 179 property. You should obtain IRS Publication 534 (free upon request) before making decisions concerning the amount of depreciation you will charge against income on your tax return.

Section 179 Property

Many small businesses will be interested in the type of property called *Section 179 property*. Here, certain capital expenditures are treated as deductions in the current year, rather than depreciating the cost of the asset over its life. Buildings, air conditioning units, and structural components of a building do not qualify as Section 179 property. For a complete list of qualified property and the specific rules that apply, consult IRS Publication 534.

At this time, under Section 179 of the Internal Revenue Service code, you can deduct up to $10,000.00 of the cost of property in the current tax year. In this chapter, you would have been able to deduct the entire cost of the laser printer this year against your business income and not depreciate the asset in future years.

Schedule C, Profit or Loss from Business

Schedule C is the tax form sole proprietorships use when reporting business income and expenses during the year. Quicken can be used to provide the information you need to complete your form. If you examine Schedule C (Figure 14-1), you see that it is a business profit and loss statement. This statement can be prepared from the Quicken Reports menu.

Starting from the Main Menu for the ANB Business account register in the BUSINESS account group, complete the following steps:

1. Select **C**reate Reports.
2. Select **B**usiness Reports.
3. Select P & L **S**tatement.
4. Press Enter to accept the default title.
5. Select Custom Date and press Enter.

   If your diamond fields are not set to pop-up a list, you will need to press Ctrl-L first.
6. Type **1/1/94** and press Enter.
7. Type **3/31/94** and press F9 (Filter).
8. Press Tab three times to move the cursor to the Class contains: row.
9. Type **B** and press Ctrl-Enter. You are returned to the Profit and Loss Statement window.
10. Press Enter, and the Profit and Loss statement appears on your screen.
11. Press Ctrl-P, and the Print Report window appears.
12. Select the printer and press Enter.

The Profit and Loss statement is shown in Figure 14-4.

Completing Schedule C

With Quicken's Profit and Loss statement you can now complete the appropriate lines of the federal tax form Schedule C. Because Schedule C is basically just a profit and loss statement, many of the entries can be obtained directly from your Quicken report. The following is a list of line numbers and how you can complete them in Schedule C.

```
                          Profit & Loss Statement
                          1/ 1/94 Through 3/31/94
BUSINESS-All Accounts                                                   Page 1
7/21/94
                                                    1/ 1/94-
          Category Description                      3/31/94
      ------------------------------------ --------------------
      INCOME/EXPENSE
        INCOME
          Consulting Income                              37,500.00
          Royalty Income                                 10,000.00
                                                       -----------
        TOTAL INCOME                                     47,500.00

        EXPENSES
          Overnight Delivery                                270.00
          Depreciation Expense:
            Depreciaton-Computer             150.00
            Depreciation-Printer             125.00
                                        -----------
          Total Depreciation Expense                        275.00
          Equipment Maintenance                           1,100.00
          Payroll transaction:
            Company FICA contribution        930.00
            Company Medicare contrib         217.50
            Compensation to employee      15,000.00
                                        -----------
          Total Payroll transaction                      16,147.50
          Postage Expense                                    28.25
          Computer Supplies                                 375.76
          Supplies                                           65.00
          Telephone Expense                                 305.00
          Travel Expenses                                   905.00
          Water, Gas, Electric:
            Electric Utilities                30.40
            Gas                               17.00
                                        -----------
          Total Water, Gas, Electric                         47.40
                                                        ----------
        TOTAL EXPENSES                                   19,518.91

                                                        ----------
      TOTAL INCOME/EXPENSE                               27,981.09
                                                        ==========
```

Profit and Loss statement
Figure 14-4.

- *Line 1* This line shows gross sales. The total income ($47,500.00) shown on your report would be placed on this line.
- *Line 13* This section shows depreciation and Section 179 deduction from Form 4562, Depreciation and Amortization. The depreciation expense ($275.00) would be entered here.
- *Line 21* This line shows repairs. The amount you show for Equipment Maintenance ($1100.00) would be entered here.
- *Line 22* This line shows the total of all your business supplies. You would add the amounts shown for Computer Supplies ($375.76) and Supplies ($65.00) by using the Calculator and enter the total ($440.76) here.
- *Line 23* This line shows taxes. The amounts shown as Payroll Company FICA and Company Medicare Contributions ($1147.50) would be entered here.
- *Line 24a* This line shows the total amount of your business travel. The amount of Travel Expense ($905.00) would be entered here. This assumes that all these expenses are associated with travel and not meals or entertainment. You can establish separate categories for these items in your Quicken Category and Transfer list.
- *Line 25* The total for utilities and telephone is placed on this line. You would use the calculator to add the amounts shown for Telephone Expense ($305.00) and Water, Gas, and Electric ($47.40) and record the total expense as $352.40.
- *Line 26* This line shows the total wages paid. You would enter the amount shown as Gross Earnings ($15,000.00).
- *Line 27a* This line shows your other business expenses. You would add the amounts shown for Postage Expense ($28.25) and Overnight Delivery ($270.00) and show the total ($298.25) as Misc Exp in this section.
- *Line 28* This line shows your total deductions. This is the amount of Total Expense ($19,518.91).
- *Line 29* This line shows your net profit (or loss). This is the amount of net profit $27,981.09. This amount would also be carried to Line 31 of the return, since there are no expenses for business use of your home in this example.

NOTE: You can round the cents to the nearest dollar when you complete your tax forms.

After you complete this exercise, you can see there are many alternatives for establishing classes to help in gathering your tax information. Remember, one of the constraints faced in this example was that you were recording business expenses in both personal and business checking accounts. However, this example can be modified to use subclasses to designate lines on the different tax forms when recording your entries. This allows you to capture the information by form and line number.

Other Business-Related Tax Forms

When you completed line 13, Depreciation, you used the Total Depreciation Expense amount from your Profit and Loss statement. This information must be included on Form 4562, Depreciation and Amortization. After reading through Publication 534, you would have entered the appropriate amounts for Section 179 property and ACRS or MACRS depreciation, resulting in a total of $275.00, shown on line 20 of Form 4562 and transferred to line 13 on Schedule C.

As a sole proprietor, you also need to complete Schedule SE, Social Security Self-Employment Tax. The net profit from your Schedule C, $27,981.09, would be carried to line 2 of that form, and the rest of the form can be easily completed. See the special "Year-End Business Tax Forms" section for a list of important tax forms for the small-business owner.

Year-End Activities

You are not required to take any special actions at the end of the year to continue to use Quicken. The program allows you to select transactions by date if you want to purge some of the older transactions from your file. Unless you need the disk space or begin to notice sluggish response time from your system, you should plan on keeping at least three years of historical information in your file. You might find it convenient to be able to print historical reports for comparison with this year's results.

To copy accounts, categories, classes, and other information to a new file, you need to use **F**ile Activities **C**opy File from the Main Menu. You can then decide how far back to go in copying transactions to the new file. You can also remove uncleared transactions from an earlier date from this file.

The following steps explain how to copy the BUSINESS file you have been using since Chapter 11. Starting from the Main Menu in the ANB Business account register in the BUSINESS file, complete these steps:

1. From the Main Menu, select **F**ile Activities.
2. Select **C**opy File, and the Copy File window, shown in Figure 14-5, appears.

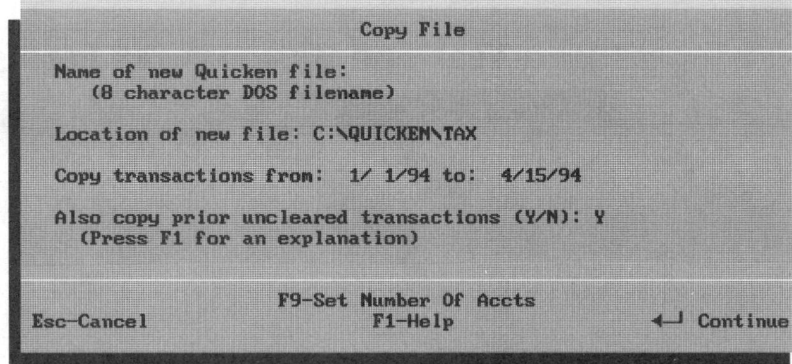

Copy File window
Figure 14-5.

3. Press F9 (Set Number of Accts), and the Set Maximum Accounts in File window appears.

   Quicken will automatically copy up to 64 accounts from the selected file to a backup disk or another location on your hard disk. This number can be increased up to 255 accounts if needed. In this example, the predefined limit is more than enough to cover your needs. If you need to increase the number of accounts to copy, type the desired number and press Enter.
4. Press Esc, and Quicken returns you to the Copy File window.
5. Type **Acct94** and press Enter. This is the name of the new file.
6. Type a new directory location or press Enter to accept the existing location.
7. Type **1/1/94** and press Enter.
8. Type **4/15/94** and press Enter.

   You have now defined all the transactions between 1/1/94 and 4/15/94 as those you want to transfer to the new file.
9. Type **Y** and press Enter.

   This command tells Quicken to copy all uncleared transactions from the period prior to 1/1/94. This means that any checks that clear your bank after the year end will be included in your account register for reconciliation purposes.
10. Type **1** to tell Quicken to use the original file, and you are returned to the Main Menu.

If you were really ready to begin recording transactions in the next accounting period in the ACCT94 file, you would type **2** instead to use the new file.

Year-End Business Tax Forms

Form	Title
Sole Proprietorship	
Schedule C (Form 1040)	Profit or Loss from Business
Form 4562	Depreciation and Amortization
Schedule SE (Form 1040)	Social Security Self-Employment Tax
Form 1040-ES	Estimated Tax for Individuals
Partnership	
Form 1065	U.S. Partnership Return of Income
Schedule D (Form 1065	Capital Gains and Losses
Schedule K-1 (Form 1065)	Partner's Share of Income, Credits, Deduction, etc.
Corporations	
Form 1120-A	U.S. Corporation Short-Form Income Tax Return
Form 1120	U.S. Corporation Income Tax Return
Form 1120S	U.S. Income Tax Return for an S Corporation

banking FILE register expenses DEDUCTIONS
tips finances INCOME equity net pay
checks revenue statements bank statements
dividends assets business tips
INCOME cash flow
budget FILE reports
net pay taxes mortgage revenue
mortgage dividends tips
business tips investments
register taxes
expenses
equity investments INCOME tips
checks statements assets checks budget tips finances net pay

CHAPTER

investments banking FILE register expenses DEDUCTIONS
tips finances INCOME equity net pay
checks revenue bank statements
statements business tips
dividends assets
INCOME cash flow
banking business tips FILE reports
budget FILE business tips checks
DEDUCTIONS tips mortgage
statements cash flow
net pay taxes bank revenue
business tips
mortgage cash dividends tips
business tips investments
register statements taxes
business tips
reports expenses tips
equity investments INCOME
checks statements bank cash
assets checks budget tips finances net pay

15 MONITORING FINANCIAL CONDITIONS

You have already seen that you can prepare financial statements with Quicken's report features. In previous chapters, you created a Profit and Loss statement, a Cash Flow report, and an Equipment report. You can use these reports to monitor the financial condition of your firm and to see how your business has performed over a period of time. These reports not only help you assess the success you've had in managing the business, but they can also be used by outsiders for the same purpose. Bankers and other creditors review your financial statements to determine whether to make loans to your business. Quicken can prove a valuable tool in preparing loan applications or, as you saw in earlier chapters, in providing information to other users of financial statements, such as the Internal Revenue Service.

In this chapter, a final major financial statement, the balance sheet, is presented. The balance sheet provides the reader with a snapshot of the financial resources and obligations of your business. Although the profit and loss statement, the Cash Flow report, and the balance sheet have been introduced separately, they are interrelated. Bankers and other readers will review these statements as a package when assessing the past and projecting the future success of your business.

The Balance Sheet

The balance sheet shows your business assets, liabilities, and equity or investment at a specific date. Remember, assets are things of value that are used in your business to generate revenue. Cash, for example, is an asset that is used to acquire other assets, such as supplies and labor, which are then used to generate revenue.

Liabilities are the obligations incurred as part of your business operations. If you borrow from the bank, this is a financial obligation. This obligation is shown as a liability on your balance sheet.

Owner's equity is the amount of personal resources you have invested in the business. In the example you've been working on in the preceding chapters, you opened your business checking with a $4000.00 deposit and put $2400.00 of equipment in the Equipment account ($3000.00 original cost – $600.00 of accumulated depreciation). This $6400.00 is the amount of your personal assets invested in the business and is your owner's equity at the beginning of the year. Bankers and other creditors are interested in your equity in the business. If you are asking for a loan, they will want to know how much of your own financial resources you are risking. This is measured by your equity in your business, as well as by any other personal assets you may be willing to offer as collateral.

Before you prepare a balance sheet, there are two concepts that need to be covered. First, the balance sheet is prepared at a specific date. Quicken asks you to define the time period you want to use in preparing your balance sheet. For example, you will define the period 1/1/94 to 3/31/94 in this chapter's example; you are telling Quicken to prepare the balance sheet using transactions in that time period. The resulting printed balance sheet will show the balances in your business accounts on 3/31/94.

The second important concept is that the profit and loss statement and the balance sheet are related. While the balance sheet shows your assets, liabilities, and equity at a specific date, the profit and loss statement gives the detail of changes in your assets, liabilities, and equity between two balance sheets. Remember these two concepts as you prepare the balance sheets in this chapter: the balance sheet is prepared at a specific date; the profit and loss statement helps explain how assets, liabilities, and equity changed between two balance sheets. In the examples that follow, you see how the profit and loss statement demonstrates how changes in owner's equity occurred between 1/1/94 and 3/31/94.

Creating a Balance Sheet

In this section, you prepare a Balance Sheet as of 3/31/94 from the transactions you entered in the BUSINESS file in previous chapters. This report will show the assets, liabilities, and owner's equity of the business at the end of the quarter. Starting from the Main Menu of the ANB Business account register in the BUSINESS file, follow these steps:

1. Select **C**reate Reports.
2. Select **B**usiness Reports.
3. Select **B**alance Sheet.
4. Press F7 (Layout) to open the Create Account Balances Report window.
5. Press Enter to accept the default report title.
6. Type **1/1/94** and press Enter.
7. Type **3/31/94** and press Enter.
8. Press Enter to accept the default report interval, None.
9. Press F9 (Filter), and the Filter Transactions window appears.
10. Press Enter three times to move to the Class contains field.
11. Type **B** and press Ctrl-Enter to return to the Create Account Balances Report window.
12. Press Enter to accept A for all in the Current/All/Selected accounts field. The balance sheet appears on your screen.
13. Press Ctrl-P, and the Print Report window appears.
14. Select the desired printer and press Enter. Your balance sheet looks like the one in Figure 15-1.

Balance Sheet Discussion

The total of the Cash and Bank accounts is $32,612.54. This consists of the amount shown in your ANB Business checking account on 3/31/94

```
                         Balance Sheet
                         As of 3/31/94
ACCT94-All Accounts                                        Page 1
7/21/94
                                                     3/31/94
                        Acct                         Balance
         ----------------------------------- -----------
         ASSETS

           Cash and Bank Accounts
             ANB Business                      32,735.70
             ANB Personal                        -123.16
                                             -----------
           Total Cash and Bank Accounts        32,612.54

           Other Assets
             Equipment                          3,625.00
                                             -----------
           Total Other Assets                   3,625.00

                                             -----------
         TOTAL ASSETS                          36,237.54
                                             ===========
         LIABILITIES & EQUITY

           LIABILITIES
             Other Liabilities
               Payroll-FICA                       620.00
               Payroll-FWH                        614.00
               Payroll-MCARE                      145.00
               Payroll-SWHOH                      477.45
                                             -----------
             Total Other Liabilities            1,856.45

                                             -----------
           TOTAL LIABILITIES                    1,856.45

           EQUITY                              34,381.09
                                             -----------
         TOTAL LIABILITIES & EQUITY            36,237.54
                                             ===========
```

Balance Sheet as of 3/31/94
Figure 15-1.

($32,735.70) less $123.16. The deduction is the amount of cash used from your personal checking account to cover business expenses. (Remember that you wrote several personal checks and charged a portion of the cost to business by using the /B class entry.) These amounts were included in the

Profit and Loss statement prepared in the previous chapter and the Cash Flow report in Chapter 13, "Preparing Budget Reports and Cash Flow Statements." Thus, Quicken is adjusting your business cash by the amount of expenses paid from your personal accounts. The importance of this is discussed shortly.

You can also see that the equipment is carried at a balance of $3625.00. The carrying value of depreciable assets was discussed in Chapter 14, "Organizing Tax Information and Other Year-end Needs." The Equipment report produced there shows the underlying transactions that explain the carrying value on this report.

The total assets are the resources available to your business on the date of the report. These resources are used to generate future income.

The liabilities shown are all related to the payroll prepared on 3/31/94. You owe the federal and state governments $1856.45 for withholding and social security tax payments. On 4/1/94, you made a deposit with your bank for all the federal government payroll liabilities. However, this did not affect the balance sheet prepared on 3/31/94. The payroll taxes were liabilities on the date the statement was prepared, even though the deposit on 4/1/94 will reduce your total liabilities by $1379. Likewise, the state withholding liability will remain on the balance sheet until you make a deposit to the state.

The difference between the total assets of the business and the total liabilities is the owner's equity in the business. In this case you have $34,381.09 of your equity invested in the business. Thus, the balance sheet presented shows that most of the assets used in the business were contributed by you, with only $1856.45 outstanding to creditors.

Creating Comparative Balance Sheets

In this section, you will see how Quicken's profit and loss statement helps explain the changes that occur between two balance sheets. First, you will prepare a comparative Balance Sheet; then the relationship with the Profit and Loss statement will be discussed. Starting from the Main Menu of the ANB Business account register in the BUSINESS file, follow these steps:

1. Select **C**reate Reports.
2. Select **B**usiness Reports.
3. Select **B**alance Sheet.
4. Press F7 (Layout) to open the Create Account Balances Report window.
5. Press Enter to accept the default report title.
6. Type **1/1/94** and press Enter.

7. Type **3/31/94** and press Enter.
8. Type **6** to select Quarter for the report interval and press Enter. This entry will cause Quicken to create a comparative balance sheet, with account balances shown at the beginning and the end of the quarter.
9. Press F9 (Filter); the Filter Transactions window appears.
10. Press Enter three times to move to the Class contains field.
11. Type **B** and press Ctrl-Enter to return to the Create Account Balances Report window.
12. Press Enter to accept A for All in the Current/All/Selected accounts field. The Balance Sheet appears on your screen.
13. Press Ctrl-P, and the Print Report window appears.
14. Select your printer and press Enter. Your report will look like that shown in Figure 15-2.

Comparative Balance Sheet Discussion

The comparative Balance Sheet prepared in this section shows the balances of the business on 1/1/94 and 3/31/94 side by side. You can see that the assets of the business on 1/1/94 consisted of the $4000.00 initial deposit made to the business checking account and the $2400.00 carrying value ($3,000.00 – $600.00) of the High Tech computer recorded in the Equipment account on 1/1/94. Thus, the total assets were $6400.00. There were no liabilities at that time, so the owner's equity is the $6400.00 shown as the overall total.

The question you should be asking now is, "What is the cause of the changes in assets, liabilities, and equity between these two balance sheet dates?"

The change in assets is caused by the increase in cash, which is explained in the Cash Flow report. In Chapter 13, you prepared a Cash Flow report (see Figure 13-7) for which you selected all accounts except Equipment in the preparation of the report. Remember that this was a conservative approach to the preparation of the report because federal and state withholding was included as a cash transfer, even though the deposit for these liabilities was not made until 4/1/94. In order for your Cash Flow report to reflect cash transactions for the period 1/1/94 through 3/31/94 accurately, you would need to re-create the report using only the ANB Personal and ANB Business

```
                         Balance Sheet
                         As of 3/31/94
ACCT94-All Accounts                                         Page 1
7/21/94
                                              1/ 1/94      3/31/94
            Acct                              Balance      Balance
 ---------------------------------- ----------- -----------
 ASSETS

  Cash and Bank Accounts
    ANB Business                               4,000.00    32,735.70
    ANB Personal                                   0.00      -123.16
                                             ----------- -----------
  Total Cash and Bank Accounts                 4,000.00    32,612.54

  Other Assets
    Equipment                                  2,400.00     3,625.00
                                             ----------- -----------
  Total Other Assets                           2,400.00     3,625.00

                                             ----------- -----------
TOTAL ASSETS                                   6,400.00    36,237.54
                                             =========== ===========
LIABILITIES & EQUITY

  LIABILITIES
    Other Liabilities
      Payroll-FICA                                 0.00       620.00
      Payroll-FWH                                  0.00       614.00
      Payroll-MCARE                                0.00       145.00
      Payroll-SWHOH                                0.00       477.45
                                             ----------- -----------
    Total Other Liabilities                        0.00     1,856.45
                                             ----------- -----------
  TOTAL LIABILITIES                                0.00     1,856.45

  EQUITY                                       6,400.00    34,381.09
                                             ----------- -----------
TOTAL LIABILITIES & EQUITY                     6,400.00    36,237.54
                                             =========== ===========
```

Comparative Balance Sheet as of 3/31/94
Figure 15-2.

accounts. Figure 15-3 shows how the re-created report would appear. This is important because it shows the connection between the amounts in the Cash and Bank Accounts sections of the comparative Balance Sheet, as shown in Figure 15-2. There is a change of $28,612.54 in the total cash

```
                         Cash Flow Report
                     1/ 1/94 Through 3/31/94
ACCT94-Selected Accounts                                      Page 1
7/21/94
                                                 1/ 1/94-
     Category Description                        3/31/94
  ---------------------------------- ----------------------
  INFLOWS
    Consulting Income                                  37,500.00
    Royalty Income                                     10,000.00
    FROM Payroll-FICA                                   1,860.00
    FROM Payroll-FWH                                    1,842.00
    FROM Payroll-MCARE                                    435.00
    FROM Payroll-SWHOH                                    477.45
                                                     -----------
  TOTAL INFLOWS                                        52,114.45

  OUTFLOWS
    Overnight Delivery                                    270.00
    Equipment Maintenance                               1,100.00
    Payroll transaction:
      Company FICA contribution            930.00
      Company Medicare contrib             217.50
      Compensation to employee          15,000.00
                                       -----------
    Total Payroll transaction                          16,147.50
    Postage Expense                                        28.25
    Computer Supplies                                     375.76
    Supplies                                               65.00
    Telephone Expense                                     305.00
    Travel Expenses                                       905.00
    Water, Gas, Electric:
      Electric Utilities                    30.40
      Gas                                   17.00
                                       -----------
    Total Water, Gas, Electric                             47.40
    TO Equipment                                        1,500.00
    TO Payroll-FICA                                     1,240.00
    TO Payroll-FWH                                      1,228.00
    TO Payroll-MCARE                                      290.00
                                                     -----------
  TOTAL OUTFLOWS                                       23,501.91

                                                     -----------
  OVERALL TOTAL                                        28,612.54
                                                     ===========
```

Cash Flow report
Figure 15-3.

balance between 1/1/94 and 3/31/94, which equals the overall total or the amount of the net cash flow shown in Figure 15-3. If you were presenting financial reports to a banker, you would want to use the Cash Flow report prepared in this chapter. If you were using the report for internal purposes, the one prepared in Chapter 13 would be satisfactory and the more conservative of the two.

The increase in the Equipment account is explained by examining the Equipment report prepared in Chapter 14, and the changes in the liabilities are clearly related to the payroll withholdings you owe on 3/31/94.

The owner's equity (investment) in the business is the difference between the total assets and total liabilities of the business. As just noted, the owner's equity on 1/1/94 was $6400.00, while the owner's equity on 3/31/94 is $34,381.09. Let's look at the $27,981.09 change in the owner's equity. This change can be explained by examining the Profit and Loss statement prepared in Chapter 14, shown in Figure 15-4.

The Profit and Loss statement covers a period of time, in this example the first quarter of 1993. You can see that the net profit (total income – total expenses) is $27,981.09. This is equal to the change in the owner's equity between the two balance sheet dates. Thus, the net profit or loss of a business helps explain changes that occur between balance sheets from the beginning and end of the profit and loss period.

One final point to note is that the number –123.16 shown on the 3/31/94 Balance Sheet appears because you entered business expense transactions in your personal checking account. Although this is not recommended, it is not uncommon for small-business owners to encounter this situation. You must remember that the $123.16 is included in the Profit and Loss statement as a business expense; thus, the reported net profit was reduced by that amount. Since cash was used for the payment, Quicken is telling you that the use of personal funds has reduced the total assets associated with your business activities.

NOTE: Although Quicken can handle the payment of business expenses out of both business and personal checking accounts, it is better to limit business expense payments to your business checking account. If the nature of your business necessitates the payment of expenses in cash rather than from a checking account, you will probably find it useful to establish a Quicken cash account for your business and use it in combination with your business checking account to record payment of business expenses with personal cash.

```
                    PROFIT & LOSS STATEMENT
                    1/ 1/94 Through 3/31/94

ACCT94-All Accounts                                        Page 1

                                                 1/1/94-
      Category Description                       3/31/94
  ----------------------------------  ----------------------
  INCOME/EXPENSE
    INCOME
      Consulting Income                               37,500.00
      Royalty Income                                  10,000.00
                                                   ------------

    TOTAL INCOME                                      47,500.00

    EXPENSES
      Overnight Delivery                                 270.00
      Depreciation Expense:
        Depreciation-Computer            150.00
        Depreciation-Printer             125.00
                                       ---------
      Total Depreciation Expense                         275.00
      Equipment Maintenance                            1,100.00
      Payroll transaction:
        Company FICA contribution        930.00
        Company Medicare contrib         217.50
        Compensation to employee      15,000.00
                                      ----------
      Total Payroll transaction                       16,147.50
      Postage Expense                                     28.25
      Computer Supplies                                  375.76
      Supplies                                            65.00
      Telephone Expense                                  305.00
      Water, Gas, Electric:
        Electric Utilities                30.40
        Gas                               17.00
                                      ----------
      Total Water, Gas, Electric                          47.40
                                                     ----------
    TOTAL EXPENSES                                    19,518.91

                                                     ----------
  TOTAL INCOME/EXPENSE                                27,981.09
                                                     ==========
```

Profit and Loss statement for the period ending 3/31/94

Figure 15-4.

Sole Proprietor Withdrawals from the Business

So far in the example, you have not spent any of the cash generated from your business for personal use. In accounting, it is called a *withdrawal,* or simply *draw,* when sole proprietors take cash or other assets out of the business for personal use. Obviously, these are not business expenses, so the profit and loss statement is not affected. On the other hand, you are reducing the assets of the business when you transfer cash from your business to your personal checking account.

In this section you will see how owner withdrawals affect the balance sheet of the business. Starting from the Main Menu in the ANB Business account register, follow these steps to record your withdrawal of cash from the business checking account:

1. Select Use **R**egister and press Ctrl-End to move to the end of the account register.
2. Press Shift-Tab if you are not in the Date field.
3. Type **3/31/94** and press Enter twice.

   The cash withdrawal is being handled as a transfer between your business and personal checking accounts. Just as it is not good practice to pay business expenses from a personal checking account, neither should you use business checks to pay for personal expenditures.
4. Type **Mr. Johnson** and press Enter.

   The payee name matches the name of the business owner, since it is a withdrawal.
5. Type **5000** and press Enter.
6. Type **Transfer - Withdraw** and press Enter.
7. Press Ctrl-C to open the Category and Transfer List window.
8. Press End to move to the end of the list.
9. Move the arrow cursor up to [ANB Personal] and press Enter.
10. Type **/B** after [ANB Personal] in the Category field and press Ctrl-Enter.

    The class designation indicates to Quicken that this transaction will affect the business checking account balance. This transaction appears in your ANB Business account register after recording the transaction, as shown here:

```
3/31        Mr. Johnson                5,000 00          27,735 70
1994 Memo:  Transfer - Withdraw
      Cat:  [ANB Personal]/B
```

11. Press Ctrl-X to view the transaction in the ANB Personal register after highlighting the transaction you just entered.
12. Press Tab to move to the Memo field.
13. Type **Withdraw from business** and press Ctrl-Enter.

    This is an important step in the recording of the transaction. This memo is used to describe all withdrawals from the business, so it can later be used as a filter in preparing the Balance Sheet. Here is how this transaction appears in your ANB Personal account register after it is recorded:

```
3/31      Mr. Johnson                                     5,000 00    7,061 00
1994 Memo: Withdraw from business
      Cat: [ANB Business]/B
```

14. With the withdrawal transaction highlighted, press Ctrl-X to return to the ANB Business register.
15. Press Esc to return to the Main Menu.

Balance Sheet After an Owner's Withdrawal of Capital

Now that you have recorded your owner's withdrawal, let's take a look at the balance sheet of the business. Follow these steps from the Main Menu of the ANB Business account:

1. Select **C**reate Reports.
2. Select **B**usiness Reports.
3. Select **B**alance Sheet.
4. Press F7 (Layout) to open the Create Account Balances Report window.
5. Press Enter to accept the default report title.
6. Type **1/1/94** and press Enter.
7. Type **3/31/94** and press Enter.
8. Type **6** to select Quarter for the report interval and press Enter. This entry will cause Quicken to create a comparative Balance Sheet with balances shown for the beginning and the end of the quarter.

9. Press F9 (Filter), and the Filter Transactions window appears. Figure 15-5 shows how the window appears when completed.
10. Press Enter to move to the Memo contains field.
11. Type **~Withdraw..** and press Enter twice.
12. Type **B** in the Class contains field and press Ctrl-Enter to return to the Create Account Balances Report window.
13. Press Enter to accept A for all in the Current/All/Selected accounts field. The Balance Sheet appears on your screen.
14. Press Ctrl-P, and the Print Report window appears.
15. Select the printer you will be using and press Enter. Your Balance Sheet looks like the one in Figure 15-6.

Effects of Owner's Withdrawal

As you can see, the Balance Sheet after recording the withdrawal shows your total equity to be $29,381.09. This illustrates how the owner's equity in the business is affected not only by net profits and losses, but also by owner withdrawals of equity. You also know that an investment of additional cash or assets in the business increases the owner's equity. This occurred on 1/1/94 when you invested cash and equipment in setting up the business. Thus, the owner's equity change between the two balance sheets is accounted for by adding the net profits for the period to the beginning owner's equity and then reducing it by withdrawals ($6,400.00 + $27,981.09 – $5,000.00 = $29,381.09).

```
                    Filter Transactions

 Restrict report to transactions matching these criteria
    Payee contains    :
    Memo contains     : ~Withdraw..
    Category contains :
    Class contains    : B

 Select categories to include...(Y/N): N
 Select classes to include...   (Y/N): N

 Tax-related categories only    (Y/N): N
 Below/Equal/Above (B/E/A):   the amount:
 Payments/Deposits/Unprinted checks/All (P/D/U/A) : A

 Cleared status is
 Blank ' ': Y  Cleared '*': Y  Reconciled 'X': Y

Esc-Cancel             Ctrl-D Reset              ◄┘ Continue
```

Filter Transactions window for owner withdrawals
Figure 15-5.

```
                         Balance Sheet
                         As of 3/31/94
ACCT94-All Accounts                                              Page 1
7/21/94
                                                 1/ 1/94      3/31/94
                    Acct                         Balance      Balance
  ----------------------------------- ----------- -----------
  ASSETS

    Cash and Bank Accounts
      ANB Business                              4,000.00    27,735.70
      ANB Personal                                  0.00      -123.16
                                             ----------- -----------
    Total Cash and Bank Accounts                4,000.00    27,612.54

    Other Assets
      Equipment                                 2,400.00     3,625.00
                                             ----------- -----------
    Total Other Assets                          2,400.00     3,625.00

                                             ----------- -----------
  TOTAL ASSETS                                  6,400.00    31,237.54
                                             =========== ===========
  LIABILITIES & EQUITY

    LIABILITIES
      Other Liabilities
        Payroll-FICA                                0.00       620.00
        Payroll-FWH                                 0.00       614.00
        Payroll-MCARE                               0.00       145.00
        Payroll-SWHOH                               0.00       477.45
                                             ----------- -----------
      Total Other Liabilities                       0.00     1,856.45

                                             ----------- -----------
    TOTAL LIABILITIES                               0.00     1,856.45

    EQUITY                                      6,400.00    29,381.09
                                             ----------- -----------
  TOTAL LIABILITIES & EQUITY                    6,400.00    31,237.54
                                             =========== ===========
```

Comparative Balance Sheet after recording owner's withdrawal
Figure 15-6.

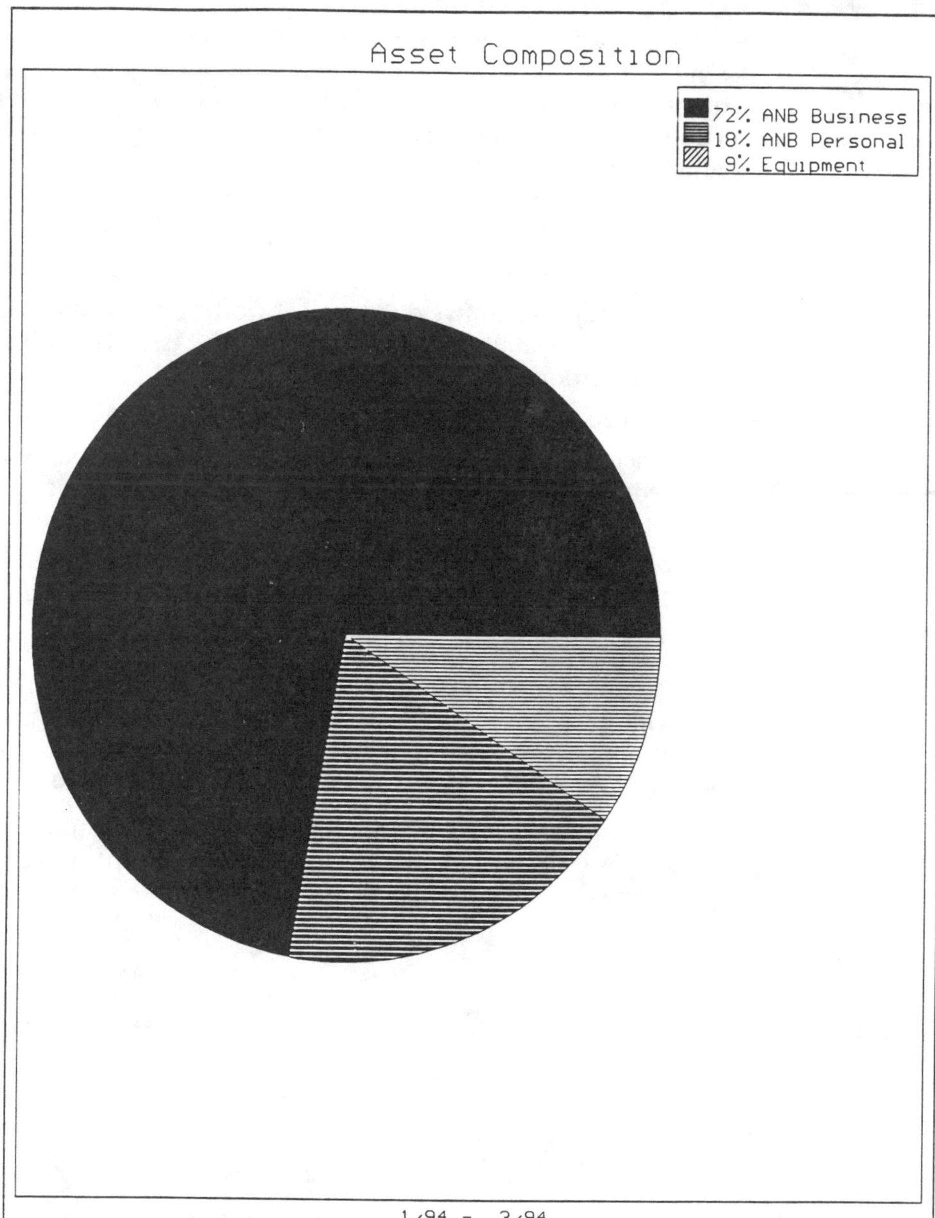

The Asset Composition graph
Figure 15-7.

Quicken Graphs

Now that you have prepared reports for your business data, you will want to learn how to graph this data. Quicken will display graphs of income and expenses, net worth, budget and actual figures, and investments. In this section you will prepare an asset composition pie graph. From the Main Menu follow these steps:

1. Select View **G**raphs.
2. Select **N**et Worth.

   Quicken provides five different net worth graph options: **M**onthly Assets and Liabilities, **A**sset Composition, Asset **T**rend, **L**iability Composition, and L**i**ability Trend.
3. Select **A**sset Composition, type **3/31/94**, press Enter, and type **Y**.

   Notice there is an option for F9 (Filter) to allow you to filter the data used in the graph. Although you will not use it in this example, it works just like the filter option you have used for reports in earlier chapters.
4. Press Enter, and Quicken displays the Asset Composition graph. Select the Print button to create a printout like the one shown in shown in Figure 15-7.

If you have not used the graph feature before, Quicken prompts you with a Select Graphics Driver window and a Graphics Driver Options window. Both have been preset during installation of Quicken for your machine. Unless you need to make changes, just press Enter until the graph appears.

This graph shows that your business bank account constitutes 72 percent of your total assets, your personal bank account 18 percent, and business equipment constitutes 9 percent of your combined business and personal assets.

register
expenses
DEDUCTIONS
tips
finances
INCOME
equity
checks
revenue
statements
bank statements
dividends
INCOME
assets
business tips
budget
reports
cash flow
mortgage
net pay
taxes
revenue
mortgage
dividends
investments
register
taxes
expenses
equity
INCOME
checks
statements
assets
budget
finances
net pay

TIPS

investments banking FILE register expenses DEDUCTIONS
tips finances INCOME equity net PAY
checks statements
dividends assets
INCOME business tips cash flow
banking FILE reports
budget FILE business tips checks
DEDUCTIONS tips mortgage
statements cash flow revenue
net PAY taxes bank business tips
mortgage cash tips
business tips investments
register statements taxes
business tips
expenses tips
equity investments INCOME
checks statements bank cash
assets checks budget tips finances net PAY

101 COST-SAVING IDEAS FOR SMALL BUSINESSES

Whether you are a one-person operation or have a number of employees, you want to spend money on your business where it will count. You will want to be certain not to cut costs too much where customers are concerned or you will lose business. You also want to be certain that you have adequate profit after covering your expenses to reward good employee performance. The list of ideas which follow can get you started with some cost-saving ideas of your own. You will want to ask your employees for their ideas as well. Some of the best ideas in this list were contributed by our employees.

1. If you use a laser printer, look for a reliable source for refilling laser cartridges.
2. Keep a stack of used paper and use the clean side for drafts. Also, test print files that will use preprinted forms before doing the full print run to insure that costly print stock is not wasted.
3. Set your printer to print draft copies lighter to conserve toner. Some programs also have an option that allows you to make the change from your program rather than on the printer.
4. Leave the printer off until the first time you need it each day.
5. Look at cutting printer costs by creating flyers and special brochures with your word processor.
6. Consider self-insurance for equipment rather than maintenance agreements which can add up quickly.
7. See if switching your business and personal insurance to one company will offer a discount.
8. Consider major medical insurance options rather than full coverage plans.
9. Consider HMO coverage for employee health coverage.
10. Ask your insurance agent what you can do to reduce costs—safety training programs, and so on.
11. When funds do not allow for adding costly employee benefits, look for free options such as flex-time or dress-down days.
12. Always close the copier top when copying to avoid wasting toner at the edges of the copy.
13. Consider purchasing used office furniture and equipment.
14. Use a file compression utility to shrink files and therefore extend the useful life of your existing hard disks. It is a good idea to compress files that you will be transmitting via modem to cut transmission time.
15. Consider making some equipment repairs yourself. We have replaced disk drives, changed keyboards, and added memory.
16. Create preprinted forms with your word processor.
17. Consider renting or leasing special equipment rather than purchasing.
18. Buy a switch box to share expensive equipment such as a laser printer.
19. Buy check stock from suppliers such as Currents to save money.
20. Look at buying repossessed or rental company cars for business use.

21. Shop thrift shops and garages sales for items like extra tables, file cabinets, and lamps needed for the office.
22. Sell used equipment before it is totally obsolete.
23. Buy supplies in bulk at warehouse clubs and other outlets.
24. Buy mail order to save money but use COD for your protection. That way you will not pay until you have the merchandise.
25. Look for non-computer products that can substitute for more expensive computer products. A travel case for your notebook computer and disk mailers are two examples where good substitutes might be much cheaper.
26. Arrange to trade current business periodicals with business associates rather than subscribe to all of them yourself.
27. Consider purchasing generic paper towels and other products for office use.
28. Use coupons and other discounts when performing maintenance on company vehicles.
29. Keep a list of office supplies needed to be able to get everything on regularly scheduled trips.
30. Use clear mailing labels rather than typing envelopes. Although the labels are more costly, the time savings will more than offset the cost.
31. Combine fans with air conditioning to achieve a comfortable temperature with lower energy costs.
32. Change temperature settings on nights and weekends to cut heating and cooling costs.
33. Close office blinds when the sun is beating against the windows in summer to cut cooling costs.
34. Turn off most lights at the end of the day to save money.
35. Use cheap labor for some tasks. A high school student might enjoy the opportunity to work in your office several afternoons a week and will probably be willing to work for minimum wage.
36. Consider an intern from one of the local colleges for the summer. They might even work part-time during the school year. Students today are very anxious for experience and if you can offer them a learning experience that they can add to their resume, they may even accept volunteer-type opportunities.
37. Use temps rather than a adding new position until you are sure you will need the position permanently.
38. Contract out for services that you need only occasionally.
39. Consider videotape training or books rather than off-site classes.

40. Look at local training opportunities at community colleges, etc., for reasonably priced employee training.
41. Consider comp time rather than overtime pay for employees if this is an option for your business.
42. Utilize high school business programs where available for envelope stuffing.
43. Consider the retired work pool.
44. Have alcohol-free employee functions.
45. Prohibit smoking in the workplace.
46. Use free services such as SCORE before using paid consultants.
47. Utilize the reference librarians at your local library for business information that you need.
48. Reward employees for cost-saving suggestions.
49. Utilize employees to fill new positions. You can give them a small cash bonus for employees hired who stay at least six months. They are more likely than a head hunter to choose an employee that fits with the corporate culture.
50. Have a policy where employees pay for their own phone calls and copies rather than absorbing these costs yourself.
51. Barter for services with other professionals to cut cash outlays.
52. Be creative about the location for a company outing. A baseball game or community event can offer a new activity at a much lower cost than a dinner dance or other formal affair.
53. Accept all the free help you can get from your children, parents, and spouse. It is often possible to make a fun project out of a repetitive task.
54. Consider overtime or comp time for a period rather than hiring a new employee. This avoids all the overhead costs and allows you to be certain that your business has grown enough to require permanent extra help.
55. Base raises strictly on performance. There is no need to reward mediocre results with even a small raise.
56. Implement profit-sharing plans to allow employees to share in increased profits and cost saving they help to achieve.
57. Retain good employees. It is much less expensive than training new ones.
58. Don't let key employees get so overworked and stressed out that they get sick. If necessary, enroll employees in stress management programs if the work environment is hectic.

59. Don't ignore problem employees. If you do not take action, the morale and productivity of all employees will be affected.
60. Check phone discount options from all of the suppliers.
61. Plan your business calls to utilize rate savings. If you are on EST, wait until evening rates to call the West Coast; they will still have several hours left to work.
62. Fax non-confidential local mailings rather than using postage since there is no charge for the local phone call.
63. Fax non-local mailings after midnight when rates are low.
64. Look at UPS and postal service next-day rates over the other air couriers.
65. Utilize all mailings for multiple purposes. If you are mailing a bill, enclose a flyer on new goods and services, or send a special promotional notice of an upcoming sale.
66. Send mailings bulk rate where information is not time critical.
67. Reuse shipping materials such as styrofoam peanuts.
68. Provide clear instructions to employees as to the types of shipping to use for different priority materials. Many companies routinely send materials overnight or second-day delivery when a slower option would suffice.
69. Check into postal costs for different size mailings to make sure the size you choose will qualify for the type mailing you want to do.
70. Make sure that the packing materials you are using are not adding significantly to the weight of the package. New featherweight options offer protection at reduced mailing costs.
71. Schedule business travel to include a Saturday night stay-over to obtain the lowest possible rate.
72. Establish a per diem for employee meal and miscellaneous expenses when traveling.
73. Ask for the lowest possible hotel rate and inquire about special packages that might include a breakfast. Sometimes there are better rates than corporate rates. Also, sometimes it is better to book two separate reservations to take advantage of special rates on certain days of the week.
74. Plan your travel as far in advance as possible. Lower cost options are normally not available close to the travel date.
75. Look in local papers when traveling for business to take advantage of special meal discounts.
76. On extended business trips try to rent a room with an efficiency kitchen where you can cook meals.

77. Consider services such as MCI Mail as a cheap and convenient way for sales personnel to stay in touch with the office while on the road.
78. Consider buying entertainment books and other discount offers for cities you frequently visit on business.
79. Make sure you take advantage of frequent flyer miles by flying on one airline as much as possible.
80. Look for other promotions that allow you to increase your frequent flyer miles such as car rentals, hotel stays, and so on.
81. Avoid blackout periods when scheduling company travel as airfares will be the highest.
82. If you have a long-term relationship with a bank, speak to the manager about free services such as Traveler's checks, credit or ATM cards, or shop for a better deal.
83. Increase monthly principal payments on business loans where there is no prepayment penalty to cut interest costs.
84. Shop around for a business credit card that charges no fee and offers free points.
85. Watch the dates for payroll deposits closely, as the fees for late payment can be high.
86. Be sure to pay your invoices within the discount period.
87. Look for a bank that bases checking account charges on average monthly balance rather than on minimum monthly balance.
88. If you do not need canceled checks, see if you can get a discount at your bank with a statement-only account.
89. Look at the efficiency of your operation. Since time is money, wasted steps and unnecessary checks are both costly activities.
90. Build a database or merge file for the names and addresses you mail to frequently. You will be able to create labels and letters with in almost no time when you need them a second time.
91. Have employees verify as much output as possible on the screen before printing to avoid the waste of paper and toner or ribbon.
92. Enroll in a time management class or read a good book on time management. Since time is definitely money, you should recoup quickly what you have spent.
93. Utilize books containing sample letters and form templates rather than trying to create everything yourself.
94. Use free government information such as tax publications.
95. Don't spend too much time saving pennies when you can focus on dollar-saving or dollar-making efforts.

96. Join professional organizations in your field. You are bound to learn many tips from individuals faced with problems similar to yours.
97. Have a pot-luck office function when you want to have a party on a low budget.
98. Attend local computer club meetings. You can obtain information for free.
99. Look at renting community facilities for an office function rather than renting a more expensive banquet facility.
100. Keep a record of the discounts available through memberships such as AAA and other associations, and take advantage of them.
101. Be creative when spending your advertising dollars. Sponsoring a local marathon or other community event might get you the same exposure as other more expensive options.

register expenses DEDUCTIONS
tips finances INCOME equity
checks revenue bank statements
statements
dividends assets business tips
INCOME
budget reports
net pay taxes revenue mortgage
mortgage dividends tips
business tips investments
regis register taxes
equity investments expenses tips
checks statements INCOME
assets checks budget finances net pay

PART 4

APPENDIXES

APPENDIX

investments banking FILE register expenses DEDUCTIONS
tips finances INCOME equity net pay
checks revenue bank statements
statements
dividends assets business tips
INCOME
business tips cash flow
banking
budget FILE reports
DEDUCTIONS business tips checks
statements cash flow tips mortgage
net pay taxes bank revenue
business tips
mortgage cash dividends tips
business tips investments
register statements
business tips taxes
reports expenses tips
equity investments INCOME
checks statements bank cash
assets checks budget tips finances net pay

SPECIAL QUICKEN TASKS

Quicken is easy to install with the right equipment. The package handles most of the installation work for you.

Since the package runs on so many different systems, it is likely you have at least the minimum configuration. For the MS-DOS version of the software discussed in this book, you need an IBM PC, XT, AT, PS/2, or a compatible machine. You must have at least 512K of RAM in the machine and an 80-column monitor.

You must have a hard disk with 2.6MB of available disk space. You need MS-DOS version 2.0 or later as your operating system.

Installing Quicken

Quicken is so easy to install that almost all you need to do is put the correct disks in drive A and type **A:INSTALL**. Quicken displays a few prompts during installation and expects you to respond with answers to questions such as whether or not your monitor is color. Quicken's installation program copies all the files to the hard disk.

Quicken will assist you with the installation process. If you want to automate the entire installation process, you can select Express Install from the installation window that Quicken presents. If you want to make changes to the location of the Quicken files or choose a specific printer, you will want to select Custom Install.

Starting Quicken

To start the Quicken program, make the drive containing your Quicken program active. If you are using drive C, you will expect to see the DOS prompt C>. If the wrong drive is active, type the drive letter followed by a colon and press Enter. You also need to make the correct directory active. You can change directories by typing **CD** followed by the directory name. To activate the QUICKEN directory, you type **CD\QUICKEN** and press Enter.

Once you have activated the Quicken drive and directory, type **Q** to start Quicken. Quicken will help you set up your first file and account as descibed in Chapter 2, "Making Register Entries."

Upgrading from an Earlier Release

If you have been using Quicken 5 or 6, Quicken will copy your files to work with Quicken 7. You can use all the new features with your existing data immediately.

If you are upgrading from an earlier release, you will need to consult Chapter 2 for instructions on the conversion process.

register expenses DEDUCTIONS
tips finances INCOME equity net pay
checks revenue bank statements
statements business tips
dividends assets cash flow
INCOME business tips reports
banking budget business tips checks
DEDUCTIONS tips mortgage
statements cash flow revenue
net pay taxes bank business tips
mortgage dividends tips
business tips investments
register taxes
business tips
expenses tips
INCOME
equity investments
checks statements assets checks budget finances net pay

APPENDIX

investments
banking
FILE
register
expenses
DEDUCTIONS
tips
finances
equity
net pay
checks
revenue
statements
dividends
INCOME
assets
business tips
banking
cash flow
budget
FILE
FILE
reports
DEDUCTIONS
business tips
tips
checks
statements
cash flow
tips
mortgage
net pay
taxes
bank
revenue
mortgage
cash
business tips
business tips
tips
investments
statements
taxes
tips
equity
investments
INCOME
checks
statements
bank
cash
assets
checks
budget
tips
finances
net pay

B

GLOSSARY

There are various financial terms that are important to understand how Quicken supports your financial activities. A brief definition of terms used throughout this book is included here for your convenience.

Accelerated Depreciation A method of depreciation in which more expense is recognized in the early years of an asset's life.

Account Quicken document where personal and/or business transactions are recorded that increase or decrease the amount of money in the account. Examples include bank, cash, credit card, other assets, and other liabilities accounts.

Account Balance The amount of money in an account.

Accounts Payable Money owed to suppliers for goods or services.

Accounts Receivable Money owed to you by customers or clients.

Accrual Basis An accounting method in which income is recorded when services are provided rather than when cash is received. Expenses are treated similarly.

Accumulated Depreciation The total amount of depreciation expense taken on an asset since the time it was placed in service.

ASCII (American Standard Code for Information Interchange) This is a standard set of codes used for storing information. When you write information to disk with Quicken, the data is stored in ASCII format. This makes it easy to transfer the data to a word processing package or any other package that reads ASCII data.

Asset Any item of value that a business or individual owns.

Average Annual Total Return The average annual percent return on your investment. Interest, dividends, capital gains distributions, and unrealized gains/losses are used in computing this return on your investment.

Average Cost The total cost of all shares divided by the total number of shares.

Balance Sheet A financial statement that summarizes a business's assets, liabilities, and owner's equity at a specific time.

Book Value The cost of an asset less the amount of depreciation expensed to date.

Brokerage Account An account with a firm that buys and sells shares of stocks and other investments on your behalf.

Budget A plan indicating projected income and expenses. Budget also refers to a comparison between the projections and actual amounts for each income or expense category.

Cash Money or currency.

Cash Basis A method of accounting used for business or tax purposes. Income is recorded when cash is received, and expenses are charged when cash is paid.

Cash Flows The inflow and outflow of cash during a specific time period.

Category Identifies the exact nature of income and expenses, such as salary income, dividend income, interest income, or wage expense. Categories are distinct from classes.

Chart of Accounts A list of the categories used to classify transactions.

Class Allows you to define the time period, location, or type of activity for a transaction. Classes are distinct from categories.

Cleared Item An item that has been processed by the bank.

Control Codes Special codes that can request a specific feature or function from your printer, such as compressed printing. Each manufacturer has its own unique set of codes for each printer model manufactured.

Corporation A form of business organization that limits the liability of the shareholders.

Cost Basis Total cost of stock bought or sold plus commission.

Current Balance The present balance in an account. This does not include postdated items.

Deductions Amounts that reduce the gross pay to cover taxes and other commitments, such as health insurance premiums.

Deposit An amount of funds added to an account. A deposit is sometimes referred to as a "credit" to the account.

Depreciable Base The cost of an asset that will be expensed over its useful life.

Depreciation The portion of the cost of an asset that is expensed each year on a profit and loss statement.

Dividends Cash payments made to the shareholders of a corporation from current or past earnings.

Double Entry System An accounting method that requires two accounts to be used when recording a transaction. For example, when supplies are purchased, both the cash and supplies accounts are affected.

Equity The amount of the owner's investment in the business. For individuals, this is the money invested in a property or other asset.

Expense The cost of an item or service purchased or consumed.

FICA Social security tax paid by employers and employees.

File A group of related accounts, such as a personal checking account, a savings account, and an asset account for your home.

Financial Obligations Commitments to pay cash or other assets in return for receiving something of value—for example, a bank loan for equipment or an automobile.

Financial Resources Objects or property of value owned by a person or business that are expected to increase future earnings.

Financial Statements Periodic reports prepared by businesses to show the financial condition of the firm. Major financial statements include balance sheets, profit and loss statements (income statements), and cash flow reports.

FUTA Federal unemployment tax.

Future value An expected value at some future point, given that today's investments appreciate at the expected rate.

FWH Federal income tax withheld from employees' earnings.

Gross Earnings Total earnings of an employee before deductions are subtracted.

Income The money earned by an individual or business. On a cash basis, it is the amount of cash received for goods or services provided. On an accrual basis, it is the amount of income recognized and recorded during the year for services provided.

Income Statement A summary of the income and expenses of a business.

IRA Individual Retirement Account. Depending upon your income level, you may experience tax benefits from setting up an IRA.

Job/Project Report A method of reporting revenues and expenses on a job or project basis.

Liability The money you owe to a vendor, creditor, or any other party.

Life of an Asset The number of years that the asset is expected to last.

Liquidity A measure of how easy it is to convert an asset to cash.

Memorized Transaction A transaction that you have asked Quicken to remember and recall at a later time.

Menu A related list of commands, called "items," presented for selection. A menu is frequently used in software packages as a means of offering features to choose from.

Money Market Account An account held with a bank or other institution used to preserve capital. Most provide limited checking account privileges.

Mutual Fund An investment vehicle that allows you to purchase shares in the fund; the proceeds are used by the fund to buy shares in a variety of stocks or bonds.

Net Pay The amount of pay received after deductions.

Net Worth An amount determined by subtracting the value of financial obligations from financial resources.

P & L Statement An abbreviation for profit and loss statement; it shows the profit or loss generated during a period.

Partnership A form of business organization where two or more individuals share in the profits and losses of the business.

Payment The amount paid to a vendor, creditor, or other party.

Payroll SDI State disability insurance payments often referred to as Workman's Compensation.

Payroll Taxes The taxes a business pays on employee earnings—for example, matching FICA contributions, federal and state unemployment taxes, and workers' compensation payments.

Point in Time A specific time when some activity is occurring.

Postdated Transaction A check dated after the current date.

Present value A value in today's dollars for a sum that will not be received until a later time.

Reconciliation The process of comparing a copy of the bank's records for your account with your own records. Any differences should be explained in this process.

Revenue The money or income generated.

Salvage The worth of an asset at the end of its useful life.

Security An investment such as a stock, bond, or mutual fund.

Service Charge A fee the bank adds for maintaining your account. This fee can be part of the difference in reconciling a bank statement.

Single Entry System An accounting method in which one account is used to record a transaction. When supplies are purchased, only the cash (or checking) account is affected.

Sole Proprietorship The simplest form of small-business organization. There is no separation between the owner and the company.

Straight-line Depreciation A method of expensing the cost of an asset evenly over its life.

SUTA State unemployment tax.

SWH State income taxes withheld from employee gross earnings.

Transaction Group A group of memorized transactions that can be recalled together whenever you need them.

Transfer A transaction that affects the balance in two accounts at the same time by moving funds between them.

Unrealized Gain/Loss A gain or loss estimated on the basis of current market value.

Valuation The current value of an asset.

APPENDIX

investments banking FILE register expenses DEDUCTIONS
tips finances equity net pay
checks revenue bank statements
statements business tips
dividends assets cash flow
INCOME business tips FILE reports
banking budget FILE business tips checks
DEDUCTIONS statements cash flow tips mortgage
net pay taxes bank revenue
business tips
mortgage cash dividends tips
business tips investments
register statements taxes
business tips
expenses tips
equity investments INCOME
checks statements bank cash
assets checks budget tips finances net pay
$

ADVANCED OPTIONS

You have had enough practice with the examples in this book to feel comfortable with basic transaction entry and report creation. You might want to think about using Quicken for some more sophisticated tasks such as managing your accounts payable and receivable or setting up job order costing. Although these sophisticated tasks can be handled with the same basic Quicken transactions that you have already mastered, the tips in this section will provide the secrets to getting them set up quickly.

Accounts Receivable

You can use Quicken to track invoicing and to record the collection of cash. To set up this accounts receivable monitoring, you will need to create a new account. Name this account to indicate that it contains accounts receivable information and set it up as an other asset account with a zero balance. When you open the account, mark the opening balance as cleared with an asterisk in the Cleared column to prevent its inclusion in reports. You will also want to set up a new category named Sales as an Income category.

As you invoice customers, you will create a transaction for each invoice in the Accounts Receivable account. The Ref field can be used for the invoice number and can be incremented with a + for each new invoice. The amount of the invoice is entered in the Increase field, since it is a credit invoice. The invoice date can be placed in the Memo field.

As customer payments are received, you will want to match them with the invoices that they cover. Highlight the matching invoice transaction and press Ctrl-S. Next, enter your business checking account for the second category, type **a** – and the amount of the payment in the amount field and recalculate the split transaction so it shows a zero total.

You can use the A/R by Customer Business Report to prepare an accounts receivable aging. This report will allow you to track unpaid invoices and attempt collection.

Accounts Payable

Quicken can help you manage your accounts payable by tracking amounts owed and dates due. If you buy from vendors who give a discount for timely payment, you can ensure that you pay within this time period.

You will not need a separate account for accounts payable and can enter the transaction directly into your checking account. You will record these payable when you receive the supplier's invoice but use the due date in the Date field. The other secret is using an * in the Num field and the invoice number in the Memo field.

Since you are recording the payable transaction before the check is written, Quicken handles it as a postdated check. The current balance will not show the effect of the entry although the ending balance will.

Use Quicken Transaction report with headings by week to see which invoices will come due each week. When you make the payment, record the check number in the Num field and finalize the transaction.

Job Order Costing

The objective of a job order costing system is to record the income and costs of jobs over the time period that services are performed. The secret to getting it set up correctly is to create a class for each job that you must track. When you incur expenses that must be allocated to several jobs, use the split transaction to allocate the costs among the jobs and use the classes that you created within the split transaction. Likewise, income is recorded with the classes you created for each job.

You can use Quicken's Job/Project Business report to summarize income and expense by job. The date range for the report should begin with the current date and encompass the due date range that you want to review. You will want to use a filter with ~Opening.. in the Payee field to exclude the opening balance from the report.

APPENDIX

investments banking FILE register expenses DEDUCTIONS
tips finances INCOME equity net pay
checks revenue bank statements
statements
dividends assets
INCOME business tips
cash flow
banking
budget FILE reports
DEDUCTIONS business tips checks
statements cash flow tips mortgage
net pay taxes bank revenue
business tips
mortgage cash dividends tips
business tips investments
statements
taxes
business tips
expenses tips
equity investments INCOME
bank
checks statements cash
assets checks budget tips finances net pay
$

CUSTOMIZING QUICKEN

Throughout the book you have seen some of the changes that you can make to have Quicken function in a way that fits your needs better. You learned how to set up your own categories and classes in Chapters 6 and 12. You also learned how to change some of Quicken's Preference settings to affect options such as your printer settings and whether or not Quicken warns you about missing categories in transactions. There are many more Preference settings. This appendix provides a quick reference to all of the Preference Settings options. You will want to glance through it to see if there are changes you want to make to be able to work more productively with the package.

General Settings

The options in this group of preferences allow you to make changes that affect Quicken regardless of the type of task you are performing. The options presented when you select Set **P**references, then choose **G**eneral Settings are:

- *Enter date as MM/DD/YY or DD/MM/YY* The default setting is M which represents MM/DD/YY. Once you change this setting, all register and reports will use the new default setting.
- *Activate QuickFill* The default setting is Y but you can disable QuickFill by choosing N.
- *Number of months for QuickFill to search for a matching payee* This setting is used when Quickfill is activated. The default is 3 months but any option from 0 to 12 months is accepted.
- *Automatic pop-up diamond field* The default setting is Y but you can disable the automatic pop-up by setting this option to N. Even when set to N, you can still pop-up these lists with Alt-↓.
- *Show To Do List* The default setting is Y but can be set to N. When set to Y when you open a file you will see reminders about electronic payments, IntelliCharge statements, investment reminders, and checks to be printed.

Printer Settings

These options allow you to select a printer and a style. Most popular printer models are supported. Style options might include portrait and landscape (sideways) printings and several type sizes depending on the printer. You can choose the same printer for all four options, or if you have a second printer available, you may want to use one for checks and another for reports. The various selections allow you to set options such as lines per page, printer control codes, and the connecting port for the printer. Even if you select the same printer for all four settings you might want to use a different style for reports than checks. If you select Set **P**references, then choose **P**rinter Settings you will be presented with these options:

- *Settings for Printing Checks* This setting allows you to select the printer and style that you want to use for printing checks.
- *Settings for Printing Reports* This setting configures a report printer for you. If your printer supports both portrait and landscape printers, you might

want to establish one setting as landscape to allow you to print wider reports on one page, and the alternate report printer setting as portrait.

✦ *Alternate Settings for Printing Reports* This provides a second report printer setting that you can switch to easily when printing a report.

✦ *Settings for Printing Graphs* In addition to selecting the printer for graphs you can select the quality of the print for graphs and let Quicken know whether you have a color or black & white printer.

Screen Settings

The screen settings are used to make aesthetic changes in the screen or to change the way menus are activated. You might try changing the color or screen pattern when your eyes are tired. If you normally use a 43- or 50-line display with an EGA or VGA monitor, you might want to return to a 25-line display for the same reason. The changes discussed in this section can be made by choosing Set **P**references, then selecting **S**creen Settings:

✦ *Screen Colors* You can change the Navy/Azure default for color monitors to a number of other settings including monochrome.

✦ *Screen Patterns* The default setting is Modern but you can choose a triangle pattern among other options.

✦ *EGA/VGA 43* If you have a monitor which can support the change, you can use a 43- or 50-line display instead of the default of 25.

✦ *Monitor Speed* This setting is useful on some systems to change the speed at which your screen refreshes to eliminate "snow" on the screen.

✦ *Menu Access* Using the Alt key to activate menus is the default, although you can change this setting to use function keys.

✦ *Screen Graphics* This setting allows you to choose the graphics monitor type you have.

✦ *Register View* This setting lets you choose between the default, 3-line per transaction register display, and a compressed 1-line per transaction view.

Password Settings

Password settings can protect your data from unauthorized access through Quicken. You can set a file password that must be supplied before the file is opened. You can also set a password that will be needed to alter transactions entered before a date you specify. After selecting Set **P**references and choosing Pass**w**ord Settings, you can choose either of these options:

✦ *File Password* Enters a password that will be required before the file is opened.

- *Transaction Password* Lets you specify a date in the past and a password for changing transactions prior to this date. Often used to prevent change to last year's data.

Automatic Reminder Settings

The automatic reminder option lets you set the number of days' notice that you want. Any entry between 0 and 30 days is acceptable. You can also turn off the reminder feature with this option. You can make your change by selecting Set **P**references, then choosing Automatic **R**eminder Settings.

Transaction Settings

These options affect the entry of transactions and their appearance. You can access the list of features that follow after selecting Set **P**references and **T**ransaction Settings:

- *Beep when recording and memorizing* The default setting is Y. If you find the audible noise annoying, change the setting to N.
- *Request a confirmation when modifying a transaction* The default setting is Y to prevent accidental changes.
- *Warn if a transaction has no category* Displays a warning prompt. The default setting is N for no prompt.
- *Show Memo/Category/Both* This setting allows you to control the information displayed for a transaction in the register. The default setting is Both.
- *Exact Match on Find & Filter* This setting allows you to control the level of exactness needed for find and filter matches. The default setting is N.
- *Confirm when overwriting a memorized or pasted transaction* Quicken will automatically overwrite the current transaction unless you change the default setting.

Check and Report Settings

These settings allow you to control the appearance and use of features with reports and checks. They can be accessed by selecting Set **P**references, then choosing Check & Report Settings. The list of available options is:

- *Extra message line on check* This allows you to add a message line to printed checks.

- *Change date of checks to date when printed* Unless you change the default setting of N, checks will be printed with their respective transaction dates.
- *Print Months as Jan Feb* The default setting is N, causing the full month name to print.
- *Print categories on voucher checks* The default setting is Y, allowing category detail to print on voucher checks for the first sixteen entries.
- *Warn if check number reused* The default is N, allowing the reuse of check numbers. You may want to consider changing this option to Y.
- *In reports print category Description/Name/Both* The default setting is D, causing only category descriptions to print.
- *In reports print account Description/Name/Both* The default setting is N to print account names.

Qcard Settings

This setting allows you a one-stop location for changing whether or not Qcards display for different activities. The options you can change are Create Accounts, Registers, Reconcile, Investments, Create Graphs, Create Loans, and Create Reports.

Electronic Payment

This option allows you to set-up an electronic payment account if you use the CheckFree service. You must first activate electronic payments with Modem Settings before you can use this option.

Modem Settings

These settings are used to activate electronic payments. They are also used to specify your communications needs to Quicken with options such as your modem speed, whether you have tone or pulse dialing, and the serial port you are using for the modem.

APPENDIX

investments
banking
FILE
register
expenses
DEDUCTIONS
tips
equity
net pay
checks
statements
business tips
dividends
assets
INCOME
cash flow
banking
business tips
budget
FILE
FILE
reports
DEDUCTIONS
statements
cash flow
business tips
checks
tips
mortgage
net pay
taxes
bank
revenue
business tips
mortgage
cash
tips
business tips
investments
register
statements
taxes
business tips
expenses
tips
equity
investments
INCOME
checks
statements
bank
cash
assets
checks
budget
tips
finances
net pay

E

TRANSFERRING DATA TO AND FROM QUICKEN

Once you enter data into any program, you will want the flexibility to use it wherever you need it. You may want to use your Quicken data with other programs or in a different way with your current program. This is especially true of your Quicken data since it represents a complete personal or business financial history. In Chapter 5 you learned that you could transfer data to and from the CheckFree electronic payment service once you installed the electronic payment option for Quicken. In Chapter 9 you learned how to download stock prices from the Prodigy service to update your portfolio prices in Quicken investments accounts. Quicken 7 provides several additional options that enable you to read data into Quicken files. It also has options for transferring your Quicken data to other programs or between Quicken accounts.

This appendix also includes a short discussion of QuickPay, in the event that you are using Quicken for business and want to use the QuickPay product to save you time with your payroll.

Transferring Data from Quicken to Other Programs

There are two basic formats that you can use for transferring data to other programs. There is an ASCII format that can be used to write any Quicken report to a disk file exactly as you see it on a printed page. You can also use this ASCII format when you have the category, class list, or securities list displayed to write it to a disk rather than print it on your printer. There is also a special ASCII format for transactions, category lists, class lists, and memorized transactions, that is recorded in a special .QIF proprietary format developed by Intuit. This format is primarily used for transferring data between Quicken files since Quicken's import feature will accept this format. The details of the .QIF format are in the Quicken manual, and if you are programming-oriented you might decide to write data stored elsewhere into this format so you can import it into Quicken. Both ASCII options are useful under different circumstances. Let's first take a look at the options for using the ASCII data provided by a report. A special option in the Tutorials and Assistants menu allows you to write ASCII data to a .TXF file if you want to transfer data to Turbo Tax.

Printing Reports or Lists to an ASCII File

Any report that you create from Quicken can be printed to an ASCII file on disk rather than sent to a printer. If you are not familiar with the term ASCII, there is really no cause for concern. An *ASCII file* is nothing more than the text that appears on your reports without any of the printer codes that tell your printer how to display the data on the printed page. The ASCII format is accepted by almost all programs, making this data format almost universally acceptable as a way to transfer Quicken data to other programs. You can transfer ASCII data to a word processor, then enhance it with additional formatting options such as font changes or type style options such as boldface or underlining. You can even add your own logo or other graphic images to these reports, then print them from your word processor with the enhancements added. You may also want to transfer ASCII data to a spreadsheet package such 1-2-3 or Quattro Pro to conduct additional data analysis. Since these other packages all support macros, once you work out the procedure for bringing Quicken data in, you can save it as a macro and run the macro whenever you want.

Creating an ASCII File from Reports and Lists

To create an ASCII file from any report, you must first create the report that you want with any customizing changes such as filters. Next, you will select the **F**ile/Print option then select **P**rint Report. You can also press Ctrl-P. After selecting option 4 to print the report to an ASCII file, you will need to specify the name of the file. If the report is wider than 80 characters you will want to increase the width so the ASCII data is maintained on one line. You can also decide whether pages beyond page 1 should repeat the row heading.

Lists such as categories, classes, and securities have a Ctrl-P option shown at the bottom of the display. This means that you can print these reports on your printer or to a disk file. You can use them as a reference to the entries you have in your custom Quicken lists or to transfer them to another program.

E

Using the ASCII File with a Word Processing Program

Most of the latest word processing programs have a variety of desktop publishing features built into them. Depending on your word processing program and printer, you can use many options to dress up one of the financial reports or lists created with Quicken to a quality that could be used in any annual report. Figure E-1 shows a report that appeared in Chapter 9. In the earlier version a simple net worth report was created without changes. A few simple changes were made to this report with WordPerfect 6 for DOS by altering the font (character style) and adding other enhancements such as the Money Bags graphic image as a watermark behind the text. Most popular word processors have graphic images included when you buy them. You can also buy other images in clip art collections. The image shown was obtained from a clip art library marketed by Presentation Task Force.

WARNING: Data in these ASCII files have spaces separating them. You might want to stay with a monospace font rather than a proportional font when you take your data into a word processor. If you use a proportional font you will need to remove spaces and insert tabs to get the numbers in columns to line up properly.

The exact method for bringing an ASCII file into a word processing program varies from product to product. Your word processing package might require you to take a special action to retrieve an ASCII file, or it might use the same

NET WORTH REPORT

As of 8/31/94

INVEST-All Accounts
8/31/94

Page 1

Acct	8/31/94 Balance
ASSETS	
Cash and Bank Accounts	
Great Lakes Chk	3,125.00
Great Lakes Sve	2,700.00
Price Money Mkt	14,750.00
Total Cash and Bank Accounts	20,575.00
Assets	
Residence	105,000.00
Total Assets	105,000.00
Investments	
Investments	28,513.42
Total Investments	28,513.42
TOTAL ASSETS	154,088.42
LIABILITIES	
Liabilities	
Great Lakes Mtg	84,975.00
Total Liabilities	84,975.00
TOTAL LIABILITIES	84,975.00
TOTAL NET WORTH	**69,113.42**

Net Worth report with enhancements
Figure E-1.

procedure that works with a regular document file in the package. In WordPerfect 6 for DOS all you need to do is open the file and verify that it contains an ASCII format. The file must then be saved as a word processing file to retain all of its enhancements.

Using an ASCII File with a Spreadsheet Program

You might want to bring Quicken data into a spreadsheet package in order to perform additional computations such as ratio analysis. Computations such as current ratio and other common financial ratios can be made if you are using Quicken with your business data. Another reason for using a spreadsheet can be to spruce up a report if you are more familiar with the desktop publishing features in your spreadsheet than you are with your word processing package.

All of the popular spreadsheet programs like Quattro Pro and 1-2-3 can accept ASCII data. With most of these programs ASCII data is accepted into the package with each line of the file placed in a single spreadsheet cell. You would need to use the parsing features of the package to split the one long label entry into component parts so that each field in the line is placed in a cell. You will need to start the parsing at the first line of data or the parsing will follow the pattern established for the report or row headings and record the numbers as labels.

Transferring Quicken Data to TurboTax

TurboTax is one of the leading tax programs available. Although the version that will support the preparation of your 1993 returns was not available at the time this book was printed, Quicken 7 has an option that will automate the preparation of the needed file for you. Before you create this file it is important that you have the appropriate categories (that you want Quicken to use when preparing the file) assigned as tax related with tax schedules specified. This is due to the fact that Quicken uses its Tax Schedule reports when it prepares the TurboTax .TXG file for you. To create the file all you really need to do is select Use **T**utorials and Assistants from Quicken's Main Menu, then select **E**xport Tax Information. You will need to specify the year of the tax schedule report and the beginning date for capital gains information. You are also asked to specify a filename which should be provided without a filename extension since a .TXF extension is automatically added. As with other filenames, you are limited to any one-to-eight character filename acceptable to DOS.

Bringing Data from Other Programs into Quicken

Quicken will only accept data in an ASCII .QIF format file. The *.QIF format* was developed by Intuit and stores less data in each line of the file than when a report is printed to an ASCII file. Since Quicken can only read a .QIF format, other programs must write their data in Quicken's .QIF format or Quicken must have a special menu option for converting the data. Quicken is specifically designed to handle IntelliCharge and Prodigy data through menu selections. The procedure for using data from these sources is discussed in the chapters where these features are covered.

The .QIF format is also well documented in the Quicken manual. The format adds a unique letter at the beginning of the data for each field to tell Quicken what data the field is for. Special headers are used in places to indicate the account for the transactions that follow, as well as other identifying information.

NOTE: Quicken does not support importing and exporting securities data, except for the prices that you can update through Prodigy.

Transferring Quicken Data from One Quicken File or Account to Another

There may be times when you accidentally enter Quicken data in the wrong account. You may want to transfer data to another Quicken file so that you can reuse your category and class list with new data. You may also want to change the account type after entering data and find that there is no menu option to do this. Whatever your reason for wanting to transfer data from one Quicken location to another, you will want to use the **P**rint/Acct option in the register or check writing window. You will need to choose **E**xport from the menu presented to write the source data out to a file. You will need to use **I**mport to bring the data into a Quicken file. Quicken uses the ASCII .QIF format when exporting or importing data. The only data that you cannot use in this way is your securities data. If you are working from the budget window, you can save budget numbers and reload them into the same file or to a different file. You cannot save anything other than the budget amounts, as the budget categories cannot be changed in this way.

Export and Import Options

You have quite a bit of control over the type and amount of data that Quicken exports when you select **P**rint/Acct and **E**xport. After selecting the command and specifying the filename, you need to decide the dates for the transactions to be exported. Next, you can decide whether or not to export transactions at all since in some instances you might just be trying to transfer categories from one file to another. You can select whether or not to export categories and classes. The next option is whether or not the account list for making transfers should be included. When you choose whether or not to export memorized transactions, the determination as to whether investment or non-investment transactions are exported is dictated by the account that is currently open.

When you are ready to import your data into a different account or file, that account or file should be open. If you are just trying to change the type of account, you would create a new account of the desired type and import the data from the other account which you already exported. Again, the first step will be to specify the filename. This can be the name of a directory if you are attempting to import CheckFree data. You need to specify whether or not to import transactions. You must also indicate whether or not duplicate transactions should be ignored. You need to specify Y if you are importing data from several accounts to prevent problems with transfers. You would also need to specify Y if you are using CheckFree 3.0. Your next decisions are whether or not to import categories and classes, accounts, and memorized transactions. If you select Y, the imported entries will be merged with entries that already exist in the current file.

Budget Save and Reload

If you have created a budget that you want to save for use with another file, or would like to save your work in order to explore what-if options and then be able to restore your current projections, you can use the **F**ile, **S**ave Budget As option. Only the amounts are saved, so if you want to use the budget in another file you would need to use the same categories. When you are ready to restore numbers from a saved file, you will need to select **F**ile, **L**oad Budget.

Using Quicken With QuickPay

QuickPay is another program marketed by Intuit that can provide just the solution you are looking for if you are doing payroll with Quicken. The program integrates seamlessly with Quicken, making data transfer unnecessary. Also, the needed tax information is automatically provided for you for the federal, state, and local taxes, as well as other deductions and contributions such as Medicare and FICA. QuickPay has many additional features that provide a full range of options for payroll deductions.

NOTE: If you have been using Quicken to do your payroll without QuickPay, you will want to check to be certain that you are using the correct account names for all of the payroll accounts.

INDEX

B

C

D

E

F

G

H

I

J

K

L

N

O

S

T

U

V

W

X

Y

Z